GUPPY
TRADING

GUPPY TRADING

Essential Methods for Modern Trading

DARYL GUPPY

WILEY

John Wiley & Sons Australia, Ltd

Also by Daryl Guppy:

The 36 Strategies of the Chinese for Financial Traders
Trend Trading
Share Trading, 10th anniversary edition
Snapshot Trading
Better Trading
Chart Trading
Trading Tactics
Bear Trading, second edition

Published under the editorial direction of Daryl Guppy:

Options Strategies
Day Trader's Advantage
Trading Rules

International editions by Daryl Guppy:

Market Trading Tactics
Better Stock Trading
Trading Asian Shares
Trend Trading Master (Chinese)
Market Investment 36 Strategies (Chinese)
Chart Trading (Chinese)
Market Trading Methods (Chinese)
Lo specialista del Trading (Italian)

'Daryl Guppy is a technical analyst who sits in Australia looking both to the east and to the west for his ideas. I can't think of a better perspective for a book on using technical analysis in today's global markets.'

John Bollinger, CFA, CMT
www.BollingerBands.com

'*Guppy Trading* is a "best of Daryl Guppy" that summarises the most enduring and important chapters of all his previous books. In addition to his time-tested ideas Daryl has introduced new methods he has developed in recent years to take advantage of the increase in market volatility. Having been actively involved with traders and markets in 17 countries over the last 22 years Daryl occupies a unique position in the world of active trading—a unique position that has not only benefited himself but also his many followers who have enjoyed reading and learning his ideas. Once again this accomplished wordsmith has written another easy to read, thoughtful and enjoyable trading book that takes a fresh look at the changing financial landscape. A trading book I'm sure will enjoy great success. If you haven't read Daryl Guppy you haven't read an intelligent trading book.'

Brent Penfold, trader and author of *The Universal Principles of Successful Trading*

First published 2011 by John Wiley & Sons Australia, Ltd
42 McDougall Street, Milton Qld 4064

Office also in Melbourne

Typeset in 11/12 pt Berkeley LT

© Daryl Guppy 2011

The moral rights of the author have been asserted

National Library of Australia Cataloguing-in-Publication data:

Author:	Guppy, Daryl, 1954–
Title:	Guppy trading: essential methods for modern trading / Daryl Guppy.
ISBN:	9781742468709 (pbk.)
Notes:	Includes index.
Subjects:	Investments Stocks.
Dewey number:	332.6322

Cover design by Rob Cowpe

Cover image © iStockphoto/Eyeidea®

Printed in China by Printplus Limited

10 9 8 7 6 5 4 3 2 1

Disclaimer
The material in this publication is of the nature of general comment only, and does not represent professional advice. It is not intended to provide specific guidance for particular circumstances and it should not be relied on as the basis for any decision to take action or not take action on any matter which it covers. Readers should obtain professional advice where appropriate, before making any such decision. To the maximum extent permitted by law, the author and publisher disclaim all responsibility and liability to any person, arising directly or indirectly from any person taking or not taking action based upon the information in this publication.

Contents

Introduction   ix

Part I: Modern trading world
1   Different sea—same sharks   3
2   Behavioural finance for crowds   17
3   Self-inflicted injuries   29
4   Modern market education   38
5   Rules to stand by   42

Part II: Analysis
6   Easy to learn, hard to master   57
7   Building stock pools   68
8   Divergence in a smile   83
9   Market trend foundations   92
10 Trading with the GMMA   108
11 Trend Volatility Line analysis   116
12 Dark side trading analysis   136
13 Past into future tense   153
14 Out of the box   160
15 Go straight to profit   175
16 Patterns of opportunity   197

Part III: Managing risk
17 Breaking down risk   219
18 Frightened money   229
19 Risk airbags   237
20 Trade shy   255

Part IV: Trading methods
21 Counting back the profit   267
22 Traders ATR   278
23 Getting ahead of the curves   293
24 Modern tape reading   311
25 Testing shorts   326
26 Patterns of informed trading   335
27 Takeover arbitrage   348
28 Indexing the news   354
29 Derivative gold   362

Part V: Beating the world
30 International investor protection   371
31 Capturing the world   382
32 Global trading and analysis   406
33 The A380 approach to Red Cliff   429

Acknowledgements   433
Publisher's note   435
Index   437

Introduction

What does it take to get you excited in the market? There was a time when an overnight 2% fall in the Dow Jones Index was enough to make people check the windows were locked in tall buildings. In modern markets this level of volatility is considered normal and the windows remain open. Now a 4% overnight plunge is unusual but not unnerving. Modern markets have changed and they cannot be analysed and managed with techniques and understandings developed in the middle section of the last century. Traders use many of the same fundamentals of trading, but the design and application must be different if success is desired in the modern market. The primitive wheel is no substitute for the advanced low-profile, high-performance automobile wheel, but the purpose remains the same. In this book we discuss some of the upgrades necessary to move indicator analysis into the 21st century after the 2008 Global Financial Crisis.

I have been trading markets since 1989 and have been an invited speaker in more than 17 countries. I actively trade and follow multiple markets, providing regular analysis for CNBC SquawkBox in Asia, Europe, India and for Chinese media. This experience has confirmed my fundamental belief about markets—they are driven by human behaviour. The trading methods we develop and use are focused on understanding human behaviour and the way this interacts with price and creates price behaviour. The price goes up not because the company is fundamentally good, but because traders *believe* the company has a good future. Tracking and understanding the behaviour of market participants is the foundation philosophy of my approach to the market.

The analysis foundations of the Guppy trading method are:

- Guppy Multiple Moving Average (GMMA) and enhancements, for market behaviour and trend volatility using the GMMA Trend Volatility Line

- count back line (CBL), for understanding price volatility, combined with traders Average True Range (ATR)

- chart pattern recognition based on trend lines and support and carefully defined chart patterns

- Darvas boxes.

These are the core analysis foundations, and they are teamed with a collection of specialist trading techniques, including:

- a genuine understanding and application of risk management suitable for your trading size

- Guppy parabolic trends for momentum

- modern tape reading of order line activity

- early warning system strategies for identifying informed and insider trading

- news event trading methods.

These foundations rest on analysis of markets and market behaviour. One of the lessons from the 2008 Global Financial Crisis was the increase in the interdependence of global markets. This is no longer an esoteric area. The ripples from China send a tsunami to Australia. The jitters in New York crash on the shores of Europe and reverberate throughout Asia. Impacts that once took days to be felt now land in our markets within minutes thanks to the internet, CNBC, derivatives that provide instant access to world markets, and the tight web of international credit markets. We are frightened, or excited, in real time, and our reactions are transmitted to markets in a fraction of a second. Ignorance is not an affliction. It is a choice you make when you choose to turn off the news or CNBC and switch to Korean or American soap.

Here are essential Guppy trading methods in 23 completely revised and updated chapters and 10 entirely new chapters, with analysis methods and trading techniques we find essential for survival in modern markets. We selected these chapters based on feedback from our newsletter readers, training-class students and seminar participants. These are answers to the questions most frequently asked about trading in the training classes and workshops I present internationally. The questions come from novices, from experienced traders and from professional traders. My son Ryan has joined Guppytraders and he also identified some of the chapters from my previous books he found most useful in learning to trade. The revised chapters include extract summaries from the original chapter mixed with new charts and updates. Readers who want to explore these concepts in more detail can browse the original chapters.

This book is written for independent traders. You have the most significant advantages in the market but most people squander them. In this book I want to show you some of the methods we use to maximise the advantages we have as independent traders. These advantages allow independent traders with small amounts of capital to outperform the market and many institutional traders and fund managers. After the terrible year of 2008 we completed a 14-month exercise with real trades showing newsletter readers how traders can still grow $6000 into $21 000, as discussed in my first book *Share Trading*. In the 21st century the millionaire next door with cash in the bank—not a mortgage—has very often accumulated his wealth by trading the market.

Shortcuts

The new trader wants to jump straight into the 'guts' of the book. He looks for new systems, new indicators, exact buy and sell steps, and trawls the pages for the search formula that will bring up opportunities in the market week after week.

The market doesn't work like this. The savage market collapse of 2008 shows there are no shortcuts to market survival. Trading success depends on a collection of soft skills that continue to defy computer programming, flash trading and algorithms. Trading success starts with the individual and his honest assessment of his location in the financial markets, and his personal strength and weaknesses in terms of personality. The new trader thinks this is psycho-babble. The experienced trader and the veteran know this is where the real market battle begins and ends. The bit in the middle—the trade—is just part of the process.

It has taken me a lifetime to develop my habits and I am unlikely to change these habits quickly. Our attitudes to risk, to greed, to having money or losing money are formed by countless individual experiences. This means we can all take the same system, use the same information and start with the same amount of money and end up with very different results. A handful will have success, but most will lose because they are stuck with habits of thinking and action that effectively allow others to take money from them. It's not a nice thought, so most of us move on to less confronting analysis—and continue to lose money.

Trading is more often than not an exercise in harm minimisation. I cannot easily change my habits, so I want to develop strategies to help minimise the harm they do to my trading. The first chapters examine these psychological factors that stand in the way of trading success. New traders should feel free to skip over them now. Save them for reading later when you have more experience of losing money in the market. Veterans will skim these chapters, using them as a ready reminder of lessons learnt and lessons which continue to need reinforcement every trading day.

The first of the five parts contains an overview of the market changes following the 2008 Global Financial Crisis. From this foundation we look at changes in analysis methods and the impact on managing risk. Then we move on to a collection of detailed trading methods, and conclude with a final section examining the way globalisation of markets provides a wider range of opportunities that are readily understood using the information in the first four parts of the book.

Modern trading world

The world has changed too quickly for our thinking and our regulators to be able to catch up. Investment theories based on work done in the 1930s and updated in the 1970s are still applied to modern markets, which are vastly different in character and behaviour. Modern Portfolio Theory taught in universities is built on work dating from the decades after the 1950s. The 2008 Global Financial Crisis suggested this required a more substantial updating than just an incremental tweaking around the edges. The first part of the book examines what has changed and what has remained unchanged. It's a guide to the new world, and suggests which attitudes and approaches remain appropriate. It offers a quick revision of the timeless losing behaviours that every trader must overcome on the pathway to success. The section ends with the essential rules traders live by in the market.

Analysis

Do you want to be a mechanic or a driver? One set of skills does not automatically transfer to the other. Yet many traders believe they can take the mechanics of analysis and turn these into successful trades. Mastery of analysis is essential for trading, but mastery of analysis does not turn you into a successful trader.

This section brings together the analysis toolkit underpinning our understanding of the market. We use this to develop a stock pool of potential trading opportunities. This is the application of strategic thinking and it reflects our beliefs about the market and its driving forces. Some of these lead naturally to trading, and we discuss the details of the methods in this section.

One of the foundations of our understanding of the market is observed in the Guppy Multiple Moving Average, and this section shows how it is integrated in analysis and trading. This includes updates on the application in fast-moving index, currency and derivative markets where trading evolves from intraday to end-of-day trade management.

Traders must have analysis skills, and these are more than just knowing how to program a market search in your favourite software. Analysis skill includes knowing which type of analysis tools to use and being able to interpret the results. Trading skills are different again. They start, not with identifying opportunity, but by managing risk.

Managing risk

Despite all the wailing to the contrary, the world of risk has not changed. True, markets have become more volatile, both in terms of daily price ranges and in terms of the speed of trend development and collapse. This has created more risk for those whose risk management techniques were always suspect. Snails cannot survive on a race track, and some of the major financial institutions have been very slow to realise this. The methods for calculating and managing risk remain largely unchanged. Understanding risk management is the absolute bedrock of trading survival. It is ignored by many people, which is one of the reasons why the failure rate among private traders is so high.

Risk comes before trading, not after it, and so too in the structure of this book.

We have been publishing a weekly trading newsletter since 1996. Called *Tutorials in Applied Technical Analysis*, the newsletter is designed to illustrate the methods and approaches relevant for current market conditions. It does not give stock picks, but it does provide ongoing trading education. Articles are written by myself, by staff writers and by other contributors, some of whom have gone on to become established authors. The case study portfolios start each financial year with a nominal $100 000 and each trade is around $20 000. Each of the case study examples uses strict risk control methods defined by the 2% rule. A significant number of the trade examples are personal trades. In every year of publication the newsletter case study portfolio has substantially outperformed the market, including the 2008 bear market period. The success comes from the strict application of risk management discipline.

The chapters in this part have been condensed, but they remain much the same as the original chapters because these trading foundations do not change. These foundations protected traders in the Global Financial Crisis while large institutions that told investors they knew better were going down in flames. These management methods protected traders against the damage from the foolish advice from many brokers and commentators who told investors to hold on in January and March 2008 because the market was 'irrational' and things would quickly return to normal. They said it was a bargain of the century and became a good example of the collective failure of established investment analysis. With notable exceptions, such as Bear Stearns and some other casualties of the Global Financial Crisis, these are the same people who tell us nothing significant has changed following the market rebound in 2009.

Risk does not have new fancy names. It remains unchanged. Modern markets have given traders some new tools and trade execution methods which help reduce the risk in trading, but they do not change the fundamental nature of trading risk.

Trading methods

Trading is more than just finding an opportunity. Successful trading includes a range of skills that revolve around specific trading situations. Traders use their knowledge of order flows and order systems to enhance the opportunity, to improve entry and exit prices and to implement modern tape reading tactics. In this section we look at nine specialist trading situations. They build on the analysis of markets, but these are the nuts and bolts of trading execution and activity. They bring together exact understanding of price volatility and match this with better trade execution to collect better profits from the underlying opportunity. We show how derivatives are used to maximise returns from short-lived, or otherwise small, opportunities. And we show how these trades are handled when things go wrong.

This is not technical analysis. We do not introduce advanced or complex technical indicators. We apply some very basic price chart analysis, but this section is about the skills of trading. It's based on the close observation of behaviour in the market and oddities or contradictions in behaviour that point the way to opportunity. This is information garnered from reading the tape — from understanding the messages delivered in the ebb and flow of buying and selling activity revealed in the order lines on the screen.

Beating the world

Australia is geographically a long way from anywhere, and this geographic isolation has affected Australian thinking. It's been easy to ignore the world despite the close relationship between the behaviour of the DOW and local indices. For decades these relationships existed in every market as the DOW lurched from rally to retreat. In the early years of the 21st century this relationship changed because of the growth of China. By and large Australians saw only one aspect of this relationship, which came from the positive impact of Chinese demand for resources. Like many other markets, we were slow to understand the full impact of the tremendous growth of the China market and the increasing internationalisation of market behaviour.

Investor protection became a much broader problem, moving beyond the boundaries of individual markets. New trading instruments and platforms brought the world within fingertip reach, and a new world of risk. Contracts for difference trading made it possible to pursue opportunities wherever they could be found. If your favourite trading style was a rally breakout based on volume leadership then why restrict yourself to the relatively small Australian market? It was just as easy to trade the same behaviour in European markets, or Asian markets, as it was to trade the limited pool of opportunity in Australia.

Traders who were not comfortable with direct exposure to overseas markets using a derivative were given a choice of a much more friendly-sounding derivative as exchange-traded funds (ETFs) bundled the world into a single instrument that was given the legitimacy of trading just like a stock on the traditional stock exchange. These investing products gave instant access to global diversity. Like most investment stories, if it sounds too good to be true, then it's probably not true. The ETF story hides the significant changes, and increases in risk, that have developed around these products. They have shifted from investment diversity into trading instruments, but most retail users have not come to grips with this change. Used effectively, ETFs give us a tool to beat the world, but used without caution they become a tool the world uses to beat us.

Behind the borders of China is a financial market already rivalling the size of the US markets in terms of turnover and number of listings. This is an entirely domestic market which does not yet have foreign company listings. It is closed to foreign traders and investors, apart from limited access through qualified foreign investment funds. The quota of shares they can buy, and their impact, is small. This market has behaviours and trading patterns specific to the China market. It is a very foreign market, made more difficult by language and writing barriers that make investors entirely reliant on the quality and timeliness of translation. Despite this, the foundation of market behaviour is tracked and analysed most effectively using the methods of technical analysis and charting to capture the thinking of market participants.

The independent markets of Shanghai and Hong Kong with co-listed stocks provide a real-time case study of the effectiveness and validity of technical analysis and the way price behaviour is determined more powerfully by investor and trader thinking than it is by the fundamentals of a company or organisation. This is important for understanding China market behaviour, but it also points the way to how traders and investors can manage their home market and international market risk with the tools discussed in earlier chapters.

International cooperation

This book is also an international cooperation project, coordinated from multiple locations in Australia, China, Singapore and elsewhere. My friend and colleague Chen Jing assisted with insights, and her analysis of China markets has influenced my thinking and analysis of markets outside of China. Writing this book would not have been possible without the support from my staff in Darwin—Alan Lim, Jenny Lin and Ryan Guppy—whose work makes my time available for this task. My wife Marion shows unending patience for the process of writing in addition to the demands of her job as a high school principal. Proofing is enhanced again by my mother Patricia, with a correction pen still endlessly supplied with red ink despite her decades-long retirement from teaching English.

I started trading in 1989 and the markets have changed a great deal since then. Some of the methods I use have stood the test of time, and they are discussed and updated here. Other methods became less useful as time and market conditions changed. Old tools have been re-sharpened to deal with new instruments, and new opportunities created by increased market transaction efficiency. New techniques have been added to profit from opportunities that did not exist in the last decade of the 20th century or the first years of the new century. This book brings together battle-tested methods and indicators. It summarises the most enduring and important chapters from my eight books—sixteen if you count editions re-written and modified for international and Chinese markets. It combines them with other methods developed in recent years to take advantage of new market conditions and processes. This is a combination that works for me. It is a combination I know from reader feedback that works for many others. This is not the only way to trade the market. It is not a masters guide to market success. It is a collection of methods and understandings which have helped me. You should take from this those elements which will help you to improve your current trading results.

Trade to the best of your ability.

Daryl Guppy
Darwin, Beijing, Singapore, 2011

Part I

Modern
trading world

Chapter 1

Different sea— same sharks

The 2008 Global Financial Crisis was a wake-up call for those who thought the sharks were friendly and the financial waters welcoming. Now it is much easier for the sharks to get into our pool and savage our savings. Easy access to the internet and modern technology have broken down the barriers between private traders and the large institutions, but some things never change. Now more than ever it's survival of the smartest.

This book is about the changes wrought by modern markets, and we look at the Guppy trading methods that have stood the test of time. We introduce modifications and new methods designed to prosper in markets irrevocably changed by the Global Financial Crisis. This is the modern world and some things have changed forever. Before we are overwhelmed with change we revisit some of the foundations, which have not changed.

Trading is tough, but traders who work with smaller amounts of capital have an advantage over traders who must work with larger amounts of capital. This size advantage allows the smaller trader to outperform the market. It is an important trading edge and a foundation of the Guppy trading methods.

Everybody who trades or invests in the market looks for a trading edge. Most times they look in the wrong places and it may take many years and a lot of cash before they discover their mistake. A trading edge is an approach, a tool or a technique providing you with an advantage in understanding how the price of your stock is most likely to behave. There are four stages in developing a market edge, and the last is the most important because it gives part-time and private traders a gift to make their edge super sharp.

The first stage is the most simplistic edge based on a variation of insider trading. This relies on finding out information before others do. Insider trading is illegal, but the search for secret information is not. Understanding the price activity shown in figure 1.1 may provide clues to the insider information used by others. This clearly looks illegal, although it's rarely enough to trigger a query from market regulators. One popular market approach is based on the idea that hidden somewhere in the company accounts and the details of the business is a fact or interpretation undiscovered by the rest of the market. This is not considered a suspect activity and this search method forms a foundation of the investment industry. These gems do exist but they are rare.

'Find good companies that are undervalued' appeals to our sense of the simple, but it rarely provides an investment edge for anyone other than the most skilled professionals. Knowing what is happening is important, but it usually does not provide the edge needed for success.

Some people try to use charting and technical analysis in the same way to find early information. Good chart analysis identifies developing patterns that may be created by traders with more information than the general public. These patterns are discussed in chapter 26, Patterns of informed trading.

The least harmful aspect of this is the search for leading indicators. These are technical analysis approaches claiming to provide advance information of trend changes, of exact market turning points, and at times they claim to tell the future. These are the least harmful because they usually only involve wasted time.

The most harmful development of this idea is found in very expensive trading programs, secret systems and other trading schemes sold to customers desperate for a trading edge. These promoters play on the belief there is a 'secret' to the market, and that exclusive information is required for success.

Figure 1.1: possible insider selling

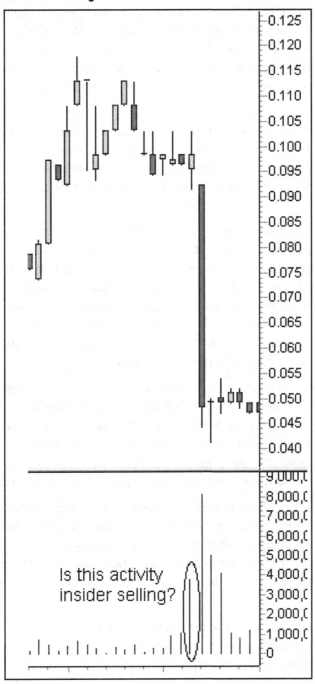

The second stage of developing a market edge comes with our understanding of personal trading techniques. Not only are there multiple markets to choose from, but there are also multiple useful trading and investment techniques. We could choose to trade only stocks, or banking stocks, or work in the derivatives market. Depending on the market or market segment we select, there is a specific range of techniques that work well. Our task is to find the techniques, or combinations of techniques, we can use successfully.

Our market edge is sharpened when we understand there is no single magic trading approach. Each of us is different, and our personality influences the way we see the market, the way we identify opportunity and the techniques we prefer to use. We sharpen the trading edge by specialising in a single market, or a small group of trading techniques.

The third stage comes when traders apply money management to every trade. Losing is an inevitable part of winning and cannot be separated from our trading activities. This hungry, unwanted partner often consumes all our trading profits and much of our trading capital. We control these devastating impacts by using a risk management rule based on the 2% rule. The chart in figure 1.2 shows how these calculations and discipline protect the trader from devastating losses. It is tamed by techniques to safely grow our trading capital and protect trading profits. The exact combination depends on the market you select and the trading techniques you prefer.

To the novice, this solution seems a long way from the real business of buying and selling shares. The successful trader builds her success on close attention to the details of these techniques. They provide the most important aspect of her trading edge. The professional, full-time trader develops an edge from knowing her selected market, honing her technique and applying disciplined, accurate money management. In this book we discuss the combinations necessary to provide our trading edge.

The fourth stage is perhaps the most important of all and contributes to superior returns. The part-time trader has one additional edge that allows her to outperform her professional counterparts because it gives her a super-sharp edge. It comes in two parts. The full-time professional trader has to trade every day. The part-time trader does not. She simply waits for the absolutely best opportunity to develop, and then trades it.

Our small size, trading in thousands of dollars rather than hundreds of thousands of dollars, is also an advantage. We can trade smaller stocks and enjoy the advantages of price leverage. Using price leverage, the Australian stock IVA in figure 1.3 offered a

378% return over eight weeks. This low-volume stock turns a $10 000 position into $37 872 profit. The trading volume is large enough for the part-time trader, but too small for the professionals.

Figure 1.2: protection from large losses

Time and small size are gifts given to part-time traders. Many foolishly squander these gifts with impatience and by taking good, but not excellent, trades. Use the gifts of time and size to make careful selections suitable for your preferred trading style. This is the super-sharp trading edge we use. Used correctly it gives an additional 20% to 30% on top of the underlying market performance. Traders who do not acknowledge their small size or use it incorrectly will deliver returns at about the same level as those delivered by the funds, which are constrained by their large size.

Figure 1.3: opportunity for the part-time trader

Stay in touch with reality

The financial markets are like an ocean full of sharks where large financial institutions, mutual funds, savvy institutional traders and brokerages prowl for profits. The survival rate for the small fish, the private trader—the minnow, or the guppy*—is very low.

We are all part of a financial food chain, but the guppy does not have to provide a protein feast for the shark. The ocean is big enough for both of us. Let them eat someone else. As a small fish, I need to survive in order to grow into a bigger fish. You, as a private trader, need to learn and master those strategies most suitable for your size.

We need to consider survival strategies suited to the guppy of the markets. This is not to disparage the skills of professional traders, nor to underestimate the importance of the institutions and funds in providing liquidity. The purpose is to understand we are not them and their rules cannot be ours.

The private trader has a tremendous capacity for self-delusion. Many beginners assume they ought to follow and imitate large professional traders. They believe and hope that Warren Buffett's investment objectives can also be theirs. We really do not understand Berkshire Hathaway's objectives, but we know they consistently make money over a long period and we want to do the same. Warren Buffett attracts perhaps more than his fair share of myths. They include:

- long-term investing is for dividends—but his company Berkshire Hathaway does not pay dividends. It's a pure capital appreciation investment

- Buffett has always been an investor—but his initial stake was built through takeover and merger arbitrage trading as revealed in *Buffettology* by Mary Buffett

- derivatives are dangerous and should be avoided—but Berkshire Hathaway turned in a second quarter profit fall of 40% or US$1.97 billion in July 2010 due to derivative losses.

The danger in these myths is in the way the unsophisticated believe them and then go on to make fundamental investing errors.

We confuse the activities and image of professional traders with success and try to imitate their behaviour, hoping success will follow. The foolish amateur feigns indifference as if he had a million dollars because he believes the market will soon give it to him.

---

* For those with a curiosity about the history of the word, the fish *Girardinus guppyi* or *guppy* was named in 1866 after Dr Lechmere Guppy, a distant relative of the author and an Amazon explorer.

All of this is, in a word, wrong.

Success does not require you to imitate the methods of institutional traders. There are important differences between us and them. Before we enter the water as private traders we need to know who we are and, just as importantly, what we are not.

What is the difference between Warren Buffett and us? What is the difference between a trader working on the floor for Morgan Stanley and us working for ourselves?

Our answers determine our trading techniques and even more importantly our money management techniques. The mutual funds and institutional traders make *our* money work for *them*. Our challenge is to make *our* money work for *us*.

There are eight significant areas of difference between traders and the big institutional investors. We look at each in turn.

Transaction size

The first difference is that Warren Buffett, George Soros, Jim Rogers and others all control several hundred million dollars of capital. Not only does this provide them with more capital to trade, but it provides a cushion against losses. The transaction size of each trade is routinely large.

Michael Lewis describes his first steps in the London office of Salomon Brothers in *Liar's Poker*:

> My first order. I felt thrilled and immediately called the US Treasury trader in New York and sold him three million dollars worth of Treasury bonds.

Quite clearly we are not in the same league. The most inexperienced, junior, untried and untested institutional trader moves more capital in a day than many private traders do in a lifetime.

Their size allows institutions to diversify, buy the best research and have a cushion against trading losses. When we trade with small capital we rapidly become shark food if we play by their rules. The first step is understanding this basic difference. The second step is accepting the difference. The third step is choosing a trading method to fit your size.

The margin of profit

The net profit of a trade depends on entry, exit, transaction size and expenses. Institutional traders control millions of dollars, but generate shark-sized returns from many trades with small margins. They scalp the market by shooting for just a few ticks of profit and make money, thanks to their huge size.

For private traders, profit margins are more realistically measured by the percentage return on capital.

Michael Lewis talks of narrow margins:

> Dash knew what [the bond prices] should be ... If a price was off by an eighth of 1 per cent, he'd pile half a dozen institutional investors into a trade to make that eighth of 1 per cent. He called his technique nips for blips.

Institutional traders generate huge profits, but their margins are thin. They scalp the market by skimming a small return from each trade. They succeed in this because of the volume of capital.

Can we play the same game? With stocks, two ticks might be as low as $20. And these are profits *before* brokerage commissions. Every trade also has to cover slippage and overheads such as data costs. After these bills get paid we need to make a return better than the rate of inflation.

These figures are the bare survival margin. To prosper, we have to add enough further gain to be competitive with the return from a riskless cash account. We require a premium for the additional risk we take by entering the market. If we are trading with leverage, then factor in the cost of borrowed capital also. Only after these calculations comes the real profit.

A few ticks is good money for institutions but murder for the private trader. To survive, to prosper and to succeed, the private trader needs a different strategy and different tactics. Changes in modern markets mean we can now use similar tactics in some situations, and we discuss these in chapter 29, Derivative gold.

The 'no risk' boss

Trading means choosing and then managing risk. What can we learn from institutional traders? Forget the collapse of Lehman Brothers and Bear Stearns. We are told these are the result of rogue traders but in reality institutional traders often lose a great deal of money—only their bosses usually step in to prevent lethal bleeding. Jim Paul provides a starting point. He writes in *What I Learned Losing a Million Dollars*:

> The market ... started down that Monday and I proceeded to lose on average about $20 000 to $25 000 a day, every day for months. By the middle of October I was under

water. I didn't know how far under I was, but I knew I'd lost most of my money ... On November 17th one of the senior managers from the brokerage firm came into my office and proceeded to liquidate all my positions.

Overcoming fear and bailing out of a trade as soon as it goes against you is the greatest challenge for every trader. You, as a private trader, have no boss to take you off a sinking ship and put you into a lifeboat. Nobody will step in to help you maximise a winner or exit a losing trade.

Your ability to handle risk and take the tough decisions is what will make you a successful trader. If you copy the institutional traders you will be washed out of the market very quickly because you cannot have losses like them. This is one of the most fundamental differences between yourself and company traders. It is your major weakness, and only by acknowledging and confronting it can you overcome this handicap.

Trading the news

On reflection it is easy to accept that if we do not have the capital size to survive on the small profit margins generated from each trade then we cannot afford to let our losses get out of hand. But do the basics of trading remain the same for the big players and ourselves? Let's take George Soros as our guide as he writes about Saturday, 28 September 1985 in *The Alchemy of Finance*:

We live in exciting times. The emergency meeting of the Group of Five finance ministers ... constitutes a historic event ... after the meeting of the Group of Five last Sunday, I made a killing of a lifetime. I plunged in, buying additional yen on Sunday night (Monday morning in Hong Kong) and hung onto them through a rising market.

Soros was trading news. He was using his knowledge and his understanding of the market, and he made a judgement to anticipate the way the crowd would react to specific news.

It is difficult for private traders to compete on this level. As the smallest fish in the food chain, they receive the news last. If they hear market rumours from a newspaper or a chat room the market has already moved. Even watching CNBC it is difficult to trade news unless they are able to interpret the news and its impact on the market. In chapter 28, Indexing the news, we look at the way private traders trade some news events.

The intelligent private trader concentrates on movements in price action and is prepared to take advantage of this after the news event has nudged a trend to change.

The private trader enters the market armed with the tools of technical and chart analysis. These inexpensive but powerful tools help counteract the advantage institutions enjoy with their access to fast-breaking news. The Guppy methods we discuss show how these tools are deployed to our advantage.

Entering and exiting trades

Everybody closes out a trade to make a profit, or to cut a loss. This assumption ignores two additional factors that make institutional trading fundamentally different from private trading.

Institutions often enter positions for reasons that have nothing to do with their views of the market. A bank whose customers are buying Japanese yen may find itself short yen and start buying yen futures, simply to protect itself from market risk, while working to unwind its cash position.

Institutions also exit positions for reasons that are alien to private traders. One of the largest sectors of the financial industry is the retirement or superannuation fund sector. By law, these funds must keep balanced portfolios, prudently weighted in several investment areas. Their decision to sell a particular stock may be driven by the need to adjust portfolio weightings and have little to do with the health of the stock.

Our objectives as private traders do not include the legal need to keep a balanced portfolio, nor a requirement to wind down sector positions based on fear of being out of step with Wall Street.

When law or circumstance forces sharks to spit out good food, we can find trading opportunities. By learning to swim a short while with the crowd the guppy can benefit and still avoid becoming shark food.

Trading environment

Most of the men were on two phones at once. Most of the men stared at small green screens full of numbers. They'd shout into one phone, then into the other, then at someone across a row of trading desks, then back into the phones, then point to the screen and scream, 'F– – –!' Thirty seconds was considered a long attention span.

Does this office portrayed by Michael Lewis sound like your trading office? I trade from home, from a quiet room overlooking the garden. There is no overt emotion associated with entering a trade, although grinners are winners and it is pleasing to see it go as

13

planned. It is disappointing to see a trade go against me, but with proper risk control, it is never depressing.

Until we are able to trade and make a living from our trading, it is the cash book and the journal, the classroom, the hospital office, the agency or the shop floor that defines our working environment.

Private traders tend to trade alone. They lack the support of peers and the support of other people who are involved in trading. Private traders work alone and they are easy prey to their emotions, particularly fear and avarice. Isolation is severe and its effects—depression and impulsive trading—can be harsh.

The solitude of home is not a good place for those who are desperate for human contact with the market, its crowds and the excitement. Internet chat rooms are a poor substitute for peer support because they are populated by so many losers hiding behind false names, imaginative boasts and time-wasting, ill-informed tips. It's an amusing sub-world, but not the real market.

The solitude of home is a fine place from which to observe the crowd, to trade with discipline and without distraction or pressure to act constantly. The ability to trade with confidence and keep focused is a strength the part-time private trader needs to cultivate. It is one of our advantages over institutional traders.

Offices and equipment

I had a special desk that was on a copper pedestal coming out from the floor. On top of the pedestal was a giant 3' × 6' × 7' piece of mahogany. The table top looked like it was suspended in mid-air. The credenza didn't touch the floor either. It was a matching piece of wood bolted to the wall, also looking like it was suspended.

Did this help Jim Paul trade? Given he lost over a million dollars, a handsome office wasn't particularly useful.

Institutional trading is characterised either by traders jammed side by side in a bedlam of noise, heat and limited space in a single trading room, or by a symbolic power arrangement where the office is dominated by THE DESK.

A private trader does not need extravagance. Nor is he forced into the worker-ant colony, battered by the need to trade all the time. Simple, comfortable space is an advantage enjoyed by a private trader. You are likely to have one to three computer screens and a reliable broadband connection.

The length of the internet connection between our trading business and the market has no effect on our ability to trade. It's the key foundation advantage of the 21st century.

Access to research and information

Institutions have many advantages when it comes to research. They have large support staffs for ferreting out information. They pay for information by directing commissions to its sources. Who is likely to receive market-moving news first—a reporter earning $60 000 a year or a fund manager who throws $60 000 commissions to a good source in one day? Access to hot information gives institutions an edge. Private traders are always further down the line for the up-to-date research.

Access to research and information is an undisputed edge enjoyed by the mutual funds and institutions. However, it is only an edge if you are trading on their terms.

To survive we have to step outside the traditional pool and make much more use of technical analysis and charting tools to identify the mood of the market, to find the twitches in the stock price and to trade the profitable entry and exit points.

Swimming with sharks

We need to compete with the sharks of the financial markets. We have to do it on our terms, not theirs. Savvy institutional traders leave their marks as they move money in the markets, and we identify them using technical analysis.

The institutions have their edge in the market. Their size allows them to ride out losses and buy the best research. Their traders survive and prosper on narrow profit margins by trading very large pools of capital.

As private traders we have a very limited ability to withstand losses, and we need to get a good profit margin from most of our trades. If we compete with the institutions on their terms, we lose. We win only if we capitalise on our strengths.

What main advantages do we have as private traders?

Our first advantage is time. The institutions, like all sharks, need to eat very often and they must move all the time. Their traders have to trade when they come to the office in the morning. Private traders are under no such pressure—we have the luxury of deciding whether the risk–reward ratio is attractive enough to trade. We are able to take our time in establishing trading as a business. The progress from start-up to survival is usually spread over years.

The second advantage is that technology provides us with the tools to even out the playing field. Inexpensive powerful computers, better software and cleaner electronic data help close the gap between us and them. Information flows more freely, more rapidly and at a lower cost.

A third advantage is that by identifying where the big money is moving, we can follow the sharks to trading opportunities. The person on the other side of the trade is not always smarter than we are.

A final and most important advantage is the understanding that the same information can be used simultaneously by many people to make money in the market. The institutions may trade news, but they buy and sell price. As private traders we have access to price data we can analyse in depth using technical analysis software.

We should copy what is appropriate and relevant from the institutions, but we should not copy slavishly. A guppy that stakes out the middle of the ocean is instant shark food. We must plan for survival and growth. Nobody else cares about your survival as much as you do.

The more things change, the more some things remain the same. Conquering greed is a market constant, and we look at these challenges in the next chapter.

Chapter 2

Behavioural finance for crowds

GREED stands for Greater Returns Expected Every Day. It is the strongest unfettered emotion felt by every trader and it is a pole star constant in the investment universe. It stands at the centre of behavioural finance, but its impact is more important than the simple parlour tricks created by superior mathematicians to show logic flaws in everyday thinking. It keeps us in losing trades and paradoxically helps turn winning trades into losers because we delay the exit in the hope of recovering lost profits. It gives shape and substance to markets and market behaviour because the market is our personal behaviour extrapolated.

Greed is home grown, but it is triggered by the crowd we mix with. Greed distorts our thinking, harms our reactions and drives us into a self-deceiving financial suicide. Harnessing greed requires balancing the difference between personal behaviour and the behaviour of the market crowd. Increased market communication speed has accelerated the swings of greed and fear. Catching and profiting from the turn in sentiment requires better trade management. The behavioural triggers remain largely the same and they create a foundation for our trading methods.

We profit from understanding these differences and the way the differences impact on market behaviour. We need to refresh our broad understanding of these differences so we can use them to analyse market behaviour. Then we set achievable trading goals for individual stocks.

Difference between traders and investors as groups

Broadly speaking, investors see market investing as calling the long-term market trend. Called correctly this is very profitable, but it is only suitable for cash you can afford to tie up for years. This market approach places a strong emphasis on dividend returns as well as capital gains.

An investor is seldom alone and can draw on plenty of support. There is a financial support industry—herds of financial advisers, fund managers and brokerages, all of whom sell support to the investor. These are guides in the financial jungle. Investing, by its very nature, is a long-term venture. Any doubts about temporary dips in port-folio value are dispelled by members of the financial support industry. They bring out charts that reduce the 1930s depression to an insignificant dip. They conveniently ignore the fact it took 25 years and a world war for the DOW to regain its 1929 highs. The investor rarely feels he is alone. The hands-off approach feels acceptable because 'everybody else' is doing it. This is a comfortable feeling for many market participants.

The investor favours a comfort zone created by having a professional guide to run the adventure. Some investors run their own adventures, but they listen to the profes-sional guides—they run when they run, and bluff when they bluff. These common characteristics give body and form to movement in the market. A real jungle guide can distinguish between a venomous snake and a harmless python. Uninformed investors often run away from both.

Again, broadly, trading is about taking advantage of short- and intermediate-term price differences, managing risk and understanding that reward is determined not by your choice of stocks but by your exit from good and bad trades. Trading is always about making a capital gain from the trade. The objective is to take a profit from the changes in price.

It is about recognising when a move has started, and getting out before the move has finished. It is not about calling the market correctly, but about trading the market. A position is neither right nor wrong—it is either profitable or unprofitable. Completing a successful trade does not require forming a precisely accurate view about the market's direction. It does mean recognising a trading opportunity and taking advantage of it.

The trader's temperament favours independent decision-making, self-reliance and low-risk situations where risk is effectively managed by the action the trader takes. By the time the jungle guide has steered his party away from the threat, the trader has already discovered new paths to opportunity.

Many smaller market participants are confused about these essential differences between investing and trading. Their confusion leads to poor decision-making and then to substantial losses. They trade by taking a position in a number of stocks, then, when a position goes against them, they hold onto it as an 'investment'.

The hopes and fears of the small unsuccessful trader are no different from those of the successful trader. Success lies in the self-discipline of the latter. These hopes and fears drive the market. Our task is to recognise these characteristics—these comfort zones—as they are manifested in the market by various groups, and to take advantage of the opportunities presented. The characteristics show up in price movements and these movements seduce many investors into thinking they want to become traders.

All of these groups—investors, private traders, funds, banks, institutional traders and others—make up the market crowd. Every crowd member has four choices. She can buy, or sell, or consider buying or selling. These choices define membership of the market crowd and are reflected in the activity of the crowd.

Unlike individuals, crowds tend to behave in a common fashion, and when we talk of the crowd in this and later chapters we refer to this characteristic. The investigation of crowd behaviour is the foundation for Guppy trading methods. A crowd is more than a group of people assembled in one place at one time. A restaurant may be crowded, but it is full of small groups of people who do not interact with others. But as soon as the smoke alarm goes off and somebody yells 'fire!', the people in the restaurant behave as a crowd. United by a common emotion, strangers become linked with other strangers by virtue of the event and their reaction to it. These united crowd reactions also drive the market.

Buy low, sell high

Crowds hang out around prices. Hope coupled with greed creates the highs, and fear shapes the lows. Every stock chart reflects this when it makes new highs followed by new lows several weeks or months later. This up-and-down pattern is reflected in the old trading-from-the-long-side adage 'buy low and sell high'. Many in the crowd take this as a holy grail, meaning 'buy at the absolute low and sell on the absolute high'.

They waste small fortunes trying to catch such extremes, and having missed them, let go of the trade. Experience suggests that catching the top, let alone the bottom as well, is due mainly to luck.

As indicators of group hope and fear, these price extremes are useful as absolute benchmarks against which trading techniques and performance can be measured. These are the theoretical goal posts.*

The very bottom and the very top of each price move provide the theoretical maximum price move we may catch. Note the words 'theoretical maximum'. Whatever trading system or technique we use, it is unlikely to consistently have us enter at the very bottom and exit at the very top. In reality our entry is more often some distance above the bottom and our exit some way below the top. Understanding and accepting this is an important step towards better trading and better trend trading. Modern market volatility makes it even more difficult to catch the bottom and the top of a price move.

When we accept that catching 100% of the move is absolutely unlikely, we give ourselves permission to concentrate on catching the section of the move that is possible. We should only use this theoretical maximum spread as a measuring rod for our own gains taken from the market and not as a stick to punish ourselves with.

Why should we accept that catching 100% of the move is unlikely, particularly if moves have become smaller and of shorter duration?

Crowds create tides of market movement by acting together in pursuit of profit. Crowds united by common characteristics—their comfort zones—have similar reactions to any given event. Just as the ebb and flow of waves spreads above an ocean tide, the surface of the market is rippled by individual waves with their own peaks and troughs. In the ocean, a gust of wind may whip up the waves, increasing the distances between the peaks and the troughs. These wind gusts are not usually sufficient to change the direction of the tide.

In the market there are similar gusts of wind. The causes are diverse. The collapse of a major American bank, an earthquake, speculation about an early election, rumour of a higher-than-expected inflation figure—the list of possible causes is endless and well explored by television commentators and others.

---

* Charles Le Beau and David Lucas take this concept further and use this 'efficient exit' benchmark to develop a measure of trading efficiency against which they assess the performance of any trading system. This is discussed more fully in *The Technical Traders Guide to Computer Analysis of the Futures Market* (Business One, Irwin, 1992).

We can model the impact of these gusts, but we cannot duplicate them. It is difficult to find a market gust that can be isolated, taken apart, analysed, reassembled and tested for validity in a live market. Yet in individual stocks, the price spikes and catastrophic dips seem to suggest there are gusts at work. This is where the trader wants to work.

The market forces producing these gust-driven waves are reflected as price differences. We can best observe market forces through the action of price. We recognise their existence through inference based on price movements and volume.

Our understanding of the forces at work may well be forever incomplete, but this does not prevent us from recognising such forces exist and from taking advantage of them. We are compelled to accept the uncertainty of the cause, but at the same time we can act upon the certainty of the effect.

What we need to understand is that the multitude of attitudes and reactions that cause the market to hesitate, to lurch or to leap in one direction are almost invariably reactions of a crowd nature. There is a logic to this behaviour, but does this imply predictability?

Using crowd behaviour

Understanding the reasons for crowd behaviour is useful, but more important is the ability to recognise common behaviour patterns of market crowds and the trading opportunities created for us by them.

The skilled, but illiterate, fisherman is at home on the sea because he understands the tides and the seas without reference to a tide chart. Irrespective of whether he believes the flow of the tide is caused by the Gods or by the moon, he recognises the common and repeated behaviour of the sea. He makes his living by knowing the big fish feed at the top of the tide.

Traders take advantage of ripples in the tide, or trend, in the same way. As traders we attempt to reasonably anticipate future market price movements of individual stocks in a reduced time frame.

The fisherman knows the next day's tide will be a little bit higher than today's because it usually is at this time of the year. The trader knows the next day's price is likely to be higher because—well, because he has faith in the indicators he is using. Both are less confident about their ability to forecast the exact height of the tide—or the price high—in a year's time.

Prediction is where the trader and the investor truly part company. The trader understands that the longer the time frame, the more difficult it is to forecast an event with detailed accuracy. Trading profits come from exploiting the detail of short-term price fluctuations that present trading opportunities.

This is where the trader differs from an investor. The investor plans to take his profits from capital appreciation and dividends over a much longer time frame. He takes comfort from the knowledge that historically the market has always trended upwards, so the detail of short-term price fluctuations is of less consequence. He chooses not to explore the details of the myth that the market always rises. We dissect this myth in chapter 31, Capturing the world, and show how it is used to improve our portfolio returns.

The investors claim the long-term trend is easier to identify and to follow than the gyrations of the market in increasingly shorter time frames. The idea that investment is somehow more comfortable if you ignore the short-term swings, and count only the long-term gains by continuously extending your time frame, has great emotional appeal to many. It comes as a rude shock when market heavyweights such as Enron, Bear Stearns and Lehman Brothers are no longer household names and they can now only be whispered with distaste.

For people of this investment temperament, time in the market is more important than timing the market. Everything will be okay in the long run. They are supported in this belief by the fund managers whose handling fees are not performance-based.

This group, by its inertia, helps to maintain market trends by providing substantial levels of support or resistance. Only major storms will shake them into action. We track their behaviour with the long-term group of averages in the Guppy Multiple Moving Average indicator display. This is a foundation analysis method discussed in chapter 10, Trading with the GMMA.

Private traders are paid on performance alone. The luxury of an extended time in the market is not available. We buy in the expectation of a short-term gain on our capital base.

Can we predict common behaviour?

The illiterate fisherman cannot read a tide chart and so he cannot predict the tide by this means, but he can recognise, and take advantage of, the common behaviours that indicate the tide is turning. This may be as simple as seeing his boat stranded on the beach by the departing sea. Recognising repeated behaviour patterns doesn't mean we can predict them. There is no tide chart for the market and we have stopped looking for it. Our analysis methods concentrate on quickly recognising trend change.

As traders we must be careful not to confuse the ability to recognise common behaviour with a power of prediction. On the other hand, once we recognise a common behaviour, we can take useful action. When the fisherman's boat refloats on the rising tide he knows he can go fishing.

Any fisherman can tell when the tide is rising, but putting a precise time on the turn requires much more skill. Any fool can tell it's winter, but it takes a bit more skill to forecast the rainfall on any given day. I can predict with reasonable certainty what I will be doing tomorrow, but I have great difficulty in predicting what I will be doing this time next year. So too with the market.

We base our trading decisions on the repeated behaviour patterns of each group. This is the foundation of chart pattern trading. Traders post gains by exploiting the price differences in the short term, even if the trade eventually continues for many months or a year.

Figure 2.1: trading with the crowd

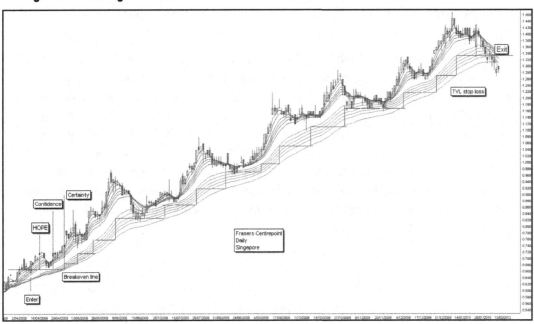

The trade in figure 2.1 with Singapore-listed stock Fraser Centrepoint started life as a short-term trade. It was a case study trade in our weekly Asia newsletter, taken at a time when this was an unloved sector in a nervous market battered by the 2008 market collapse. It was entered in April 2009 and closed in February 2010. There were no exit signals, so the trade remained open for 11 months and delivered a 102% profit. It was managed with a new trading method discussed in chapter 11, Trend Volatility Line analysis. This is the essence of walking a mile with the crowd.

The key trading feature of market crowds

We take advantage of crowd behaviour in the markets only if we have a thorough understanding of the repeated behaviour patterns found in crowds. The tendency of any crowd to move in a single direction for a period of time is the one fundamental repeated characteristic of crowd behaviour and our trading success depends on it. Most of the time crowds are impassive, waiting for something to happen, milling in place, but at times they burst out of apathy in a sudden jump that expands the waves on the market tide.

The key feature of market crowds is repeated common behaviours. Taking advantage of a repeatable pattern does not mean its occurrence can be predicted, nor its causes fully understood. As a trader I am interested in effects, whatever their causes.

The market collapse in early 2008 required action rather than a prolonged debate on the causes of the rapid fall. The DOW index chart in figure 2.2 shows how the 'economically illiterate' traders were able to move more quickly than the qualified economic analysts who continued to insist well into 2008 that the market was irrational and recovery was imminent. Traders exited as the head and shoulder pattern developed. In early January 2008 I gave an interview with *The Edge* newspaper in Singapore which was headed 'Guppy is a Bear'. At point A many commentators told investors not to panic. At point B they told the public the market was irrational. At point C commentators blamed short sellers for company stupidity. Those who used chart analysis quickly recognised the shift in crowd sentiment and acted to collect profits and protect portfolio values.

Trading requires us to stand aside from the crowd and observe its behaviour without becoming part of the crowd. We cannot tell when a market crowd stampede will start, but we recognise the symptoms. Unless you are incredibly perceptive, or lucky, day in and day out, you are unlikely to be able to call the beginning of a trend change, or the beginning of a short-term reversal in an individual stock. I am unlikely to be able to call the exact point in time when a passive crowd of investors in an obscure stock starts running wild.

We need to know enough about this behaviour of market crowds to recognise it, and to take advantage of it.

Figure 2.2: DOW 2008 collapse

Just give me a mile

The task is to identify the direction of the market mood about an individual stock and to decide how likely it is to persist. As a trader I do not wish to be caught in a reversal. Since I cannot reasonably predict the long-term outcome of a stampede, other than that it will end, I have no choice but to manage my position very defensively to limit risk.

We cannot accurately select the turning point that ignites the crowd into a buying or selling frenzy. We cannot tell exactly when it will start, nor exactly when it will end. Yet we need an entry point and an exit point if we are to profit from the stampede.

This dynamic creates our trading opportunity. We recognise stampede behaviour, and our understanding of the power of the crowd and its unpredictability defines the distance we are prepared to travel with it, and hence our time of exit.

The question we need to answer is: how far is too far?

I am content to run a short distance — a mile — with the crowd, and then leave it. The crowd may already have run a mile before I am comfortable in joining it, and it may well run another mile, or several miles, after I have left. On the other hand, it might run only a few more price ticks before collapsing on itself.

Exactly how long will your 'mile with the crowd' be? This will depend upon your evaluation and judgement of the probability of the crowd maintaining its direction. In later chapters we will explore several tools that help us refine the decision. Remember that no tool is a substitute for emotional maturity — when the time comes you have to get out of a trade with dignity, without haggling or whimpering.

Different traders use a different combination of charts and indicators to signal the end of the crowd move. The choice of specific tools will reflect the individual temperament of each trader. Whatever indicators you use, do not fall prey to 'what if?' calculations based on raw greed or fear. What if I stayed a bit longer and took the last 3%, or what if the price falls tomorrow before I have time to get out with my profit? Take a chunk from the action rather than ride the wave completely to the top. Take what the market gives you in relative safety.

If I find a stock with typically short trends, I might run barely a mile with the crowd before I sell the stock. If my reading is that the stock tends to move for longer periods, then I manage the position more defensively by taking partial profits at rising levels of return so I benefit from as much of the move as possible while limiting my downside risk. If the crowd continues to show strength then, like the Fraser Centrepoint trade in figure 2.1, the trade remains open for much longer than I anticipated. The technique depends upon the temperament of the individual trader and targets for the specific stock. Greed always lurks behind and you must be careful not to fall prey to this immensely dangerous emotion.

The objective is to trade the price move, not to call the top. Once we put on a trade, coping with greed and fear—managing our position—separates professionals from amateurs. This is the time of maximum danger because we must observe the crowd impartially while running with it.

Earlier, the problem was that we could not accurately predict when the crowd would start to run. Now our problem is different. We cannot accurately predict when the crowd will stop, nor how it will stop. The crowd may slow down and mill around in a lethargic series of price jabs we broadly describe as a consolidation pattern. Or the crowd may get badly spooked by a real or imagined event, dumping the stock with a ferocity often exponentially sharper than its rise. Specific trend behaviours—such as the parabolic trend discussed in chapter 23, Getting ahead of the curves—put a travel and time limit on the trade.

Greedy traders who make a successful entry near the bottom of a strong short-term uptrend often get hooked and attempt to defy the odds by staying with the trend, trying to milk the last few ticks at the top. At the end of each day, they count the money on the table and congratulate themselves on their perceptiveness and judgement. If you are counting profits at the top, you are set to ride that stock all the way back into the valley—and perhaps even lower.

Leave insurance on the table

Trading is not about the opportunity of a lifetime. It is a consistent approach to taking profits from the market time after time. Mark Weinstein in *Market Wizards* talks of watching the sparrows in his garden when he trades from home. He feeds them bread and they keep flying back and forth, taking small bits of bread each time, until all the bread is gone. He approaches trading the same way.

> *For example … when I am sure the S&P is going up … I don't try to pick the bottom, and I am out before it tops. I just take the mid-range where the momentum is greatest. That, to me, is trading like a sparrow eats.*

In the great bull markets just before and after the turn of the century this approach seemed inappropriate. In *Trend Trading* we showed how this was modified and applied to trading long-term trends. In the market massacre of 2008 the sparrow approach was vindicated. In current markets the increase in volatility makes for fat sparrows while roasting greedy pigs.

This trading philosophy leaves money on the table because unrealised gains may continue as the crowd surges further before collapsing. The margin between the exit price and the final top price is the insurance premium I willingly pay to avoid financial disaster. A good trader constantly hones and refines her entry and exit techniques, but a good trader also recognises she can destroy a good trading system by trying to make it perfect.

We enter trades because we recognise the crowd has started to move in a particular direction and we reasonably anticipate—not guess—it will continue in that direction. We select a mix of tools and techniques that allow us to reach valid and sustainable conclusions about the start of the short-term trend. Our enthusiasm, or our caution, will help to determine the entry point to the trade. The more we want from the trade, the sooner we will enter, and the later we will exit as we try to grab a bigger bite from the move.

The amateur trader thinks success comes from selecting the right stock. The professional trader knows success comes from developing the right attitude to risk and trade management. There is always a danger we will undermine our own success, and we look at this in the next chapter.

Chapter 3

Self-inflicted injuries

It's very easy to get distracted by the day-to-day excitement of the market. It's a distraction facilitated by 24-hour business news channels and a media focus on short-term news with little long-term analysis. Traders need to step away from the daily action of the market and consider the broader strategic situation. This prevents you from trading from the long side in a viciously falling market. Strategic thinking also helps traders to place other behaviours into context.

One of the enduring features of trading is the way we sabotage our success. The Chinese call this 'replacing superior beams and pillars with inferior ones'. It's one of the classic 36 strategies of the Chinese, and originally it was designed to make the enemy change its formation frequently so their main strength is exhausted. If features critical to success are weakened, or replaced with inferior quality, then the battle is lost. When we replace good habits with bad habits, the trading battle is lost because excellent trade analysis is destroyed by poor trade implementation. The market world has changed but traders continue to sabotage themselves, although not in new ways.

Good traders make money in almost any market conditions. Bad traders make serious mistakes in all market conditions. Aspiring traders fail because they have become skilled in replacing the superior beams of their own analysis with inferior trade implementation influenced by fear, greed, poor trading discipline and emotion. The mechanics of trading are not difficult nor complex. Developing superior beams is not a time-consuming task. Hundreds of books explain in fine detail the exact information required to implement successful trading strategies.

Inexpensive software programs effectively search the market to identify particular types of trading opportunities. These same programs allow you to back-test the selected trading system to assess its profitability. There is simply no shortage of superior analysis beams, so why do so many traders fail so consistently?

They fail because they cannot trade. Their trading skills are inferior and do not match the strength of their analysis skills. Replacing superior beams is a deception strategy designed to be used against others. When it comes to trading, it is often a strategy we use against ourselves. Understanding how this strategy operates gives us some awareness and protection so we can ensure our superior analysis beams are not supplanted by inferior trade execution.

Our mistakes start when we do not understand risk. People often spend a lot of time avoiding even the thought of risk. Instead they look for something to reduce the anticipated pain. They believe just one winner will compensate for all their losses. They plan for success without contemplating failure and unknowingly make a start with inferior beams.

Sabotage errors

Here are the top nine mistakes standing between traders and success. These are like stop signs. Of course you can drive straight on through but you risk death and injury. It is no different in the market except you risk financial death and injury.

1. Only use money you can afford to lose

This piece of common financial advice is fatal. It suggests losing all or most of your investment capital is acceptable, and this develops a poor attitude to risk. If we believe, even subconsciously, we can 'afford to lose' all this capital then we will lose it simply because we do not care about it. With this attitude there is little opportunity to develop adequate measures for risk control, or even understand risk because it is money we believe we can afford to lose. Good risk control means limiting losses to a small amount of capital.

2. Investing for the long term

The idea it is acceptable for an investment to lose money because we are holding it for the long term is the most significant barrier to achieving good returns from the market. This excuse gives the investor and trader permission to ignore the terrible destruction of their market capital in 2008.

Time alone will not turn a bad investment or investment management decision into a good one. Bear Stearns was once one of the top investment banks, but time will not bring it back to a market listing. Bank of America and General Motors are a shadow of their former listings, with the stock price so diluted by share splits that recovery of original capital is doubtful for many long-term investors. Only the names remain, giving the illusion of market continuity.

Holding on to 'quality' stocks in bad times does not compensate for the loss of capital, or the opportunity cost. When prices rise we watch others make money while we are still waiting to recover our losses.

3. Treating the first analysis step as the last step

Many people believe success is possible if they make a better selection before the stock is purchased. They feel risk is eliminated, or significantly reduced, by better fundamental analysis before buying. This is a comforting thought, shown in figure 3.1, but in any market even the best analysis can be destroyed by changing market conditions. Good analysis and research is necessary, but it is the first step in developing a trading and investment strategy. It is not the last step. Trade success comes from the management of risk because risk cannot be eliminated by analysis. It is your reaction to price behaviour that defines and mitigates risk.

4. Buying quick solutions

Making money in the market is hard work because there are so many other people who are trying to take it off us. Some people prefer to spend quite a lot of money, rather than time, to find quick solutions to market profits. They buy trading programs and systems and seem to believe a more expensive product is better. Quick solutions are no substitute for proper risk management. Learning from others is necessary but it takes time and effort.

Figure 3.1: where is the risk?

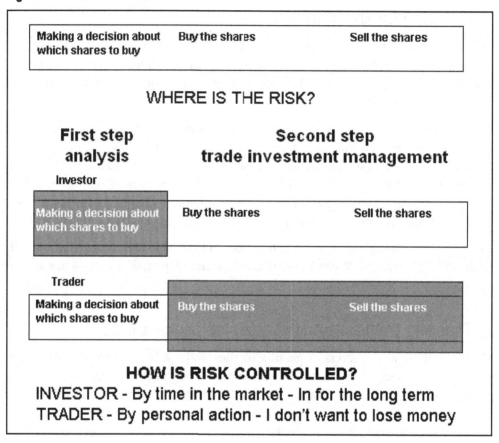

5. Stop what?

Long-term survival depends on understanding the concept of a stop loss and learning to apply it. Learning this skill is sometimes hampered by well-intentioned advice from brokers who ask, 'Why sell it? It is a good company and it will recover. Remember, the market is about the long term.' The market is here for the long term. Your money may not be, so it pays to manage risk carefully. We define acceptable levels of loss in advance using the 2% rule.

6. Profits do not look after themselves

Many traders and investors ignore losses because they believe just one good winner is needed to compensate for all the pain. They watch the raw price figures and fail to understand how money management is used to help profits grow and limit losses. Trading and investing are about protecting capital and adding to it. Money management is the key to this success. Without this knowledge there are people who get most trades right but still end up with a massive loss at the end of the year from just a single losing trade.

7. Trading discipline

It takes discipline to develop a trading plan that accurately reflects both the expected losses and the anticipated profits. A trading plan establishes the reasonable profit targets for every investment and trade. It sets specific exit conditions designed to protect your capital. Planning means anticipating a range of possible outcomes before stock is purchased. Discipline means having the ability to act on the trade plan to lock in a profit or limit a loss. Discipline does not mean sitting on a losing investment for a long time.

8. Counting paper profits

Greed has a corrosive impact on superior beams. People count paper profits and believe this is a record of their investment success. The only record of investment success is the real money in your bank account. Anything else is false, so we should avoid counting paper profits in open positions and using them to bolster real profits lodged in our bank account.

It is easy to talk about mistakes but much more difficult to stop making them. A problem for many traders is they know they are losing money but they are not sure why. Trading requires a combination of analysis skill and trading skill. Success demands both of these pillars are of superior quality.

9. Betting against your analysis

Trading is difficult because we complete accurate analysis—a superior beam—and then distort the entry decision to match our own particular biases and fears—replacing the superior beam with an inferior beam of trade execution. Often the entry decision bets against, or discounts, our original analysis. As a result we miss out on profitable trades, or buy into unprofitable trades. This error is magnified with increases in trend volatility and the speed of rally reversals.

Consider this straightforward trend trade in figure 3.2 as an example of how this analysis discount process works. The uptrend is defined by the accurately placed straight edge trend line. Prices find support on the line and bounce away, so this is a very easy trend to trade. In this example the trader's plan is to wait for prices to pull back to the proven trend line before entering at the best possible price. It is a sound strategy based on good analysis—a superior beam.

Figure 3.2: strong uptrend

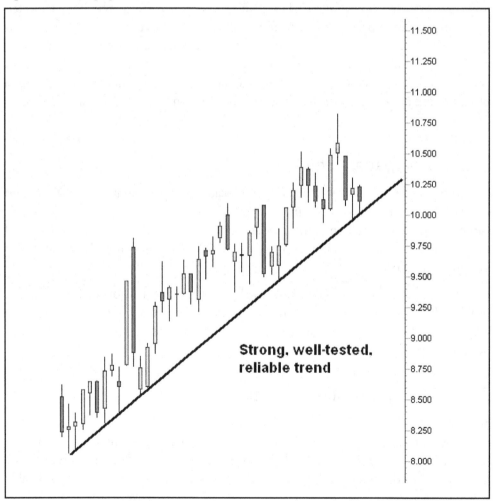

The entry signal is generated on the chart by the price dip down to the trend line. The day closes higher as prices rebound away. The key question is: how much will the trader pay tomorrow?

The trader has three choices, shown in figure 3.3. The one he consistently chooses has a significant impact on trading success.

Our first trader sets his buy order in the zone shown by circle A. He wants to buy this stock at yesterday's lows, or even lower. He looks for temporary weakness in the new uptrend. His order, placed below the current value of the trend line, totally discounts his trend analysis. This is a weak beam.

Figure 3.3: possible entries

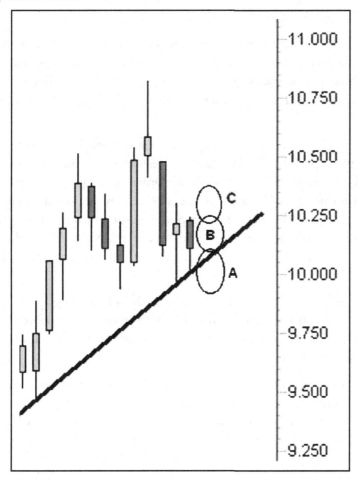

He wants to buy the stock because it is bullish, but he delays until the stock stumbles below the very trend line he is using to define the trend. His analysis and his action are inconsistent. Once the trade is open he plans to use a close below the trend line to generate an exit signal because there is an increased probability of a trend collapse. Yet, this is the very condition he wants to see before he agrees to buy the stock in expectation of the uptrend continuing.

Now, success depends on the trend behaving exactly opposite to the way his analysis suggested it should. This is bargain hunting, and it is surprising how many traders pursue this strategy. If prices do not pull back to yesterday's lows then they miss out on entering the very trend they want to join. If prices pull back, these same traders often hesitate to buy because now they worry it is a sign of trend weakness. This is the most extreme example of replacing superior beams with a weak beam. Less extreme examples still have the same effect.

The second trader who puts an order in area B has taken some steps to avoid betting against his own analysis. This trader does not want to pay much more than yesterday's high price. Preferably he wants to pay less. He might start off the day with an order at the bottom of the circled area, and then lift the order during the day if his initial order is unfilled.

Superficially this is an attractive strategy. Look deeper though and it is just a variation of the strategy followed by the first trader. In restricting the buy orders to area B, the trader is still discounting his own analysis. Orders placed in this area cannot take advantage of further bullish activity as prices bounce away from the trend line. If his analysis is correct, and the trend line is a powerful support point, then prices should rebound. The price rebound shown by the most recent bar should lead to a rebound continuation and a confirmation of our analysis. If this happens, the order placed in area B is not filled.

Again, this trader discounts his own accurate analysis by betting against the strength of the trend. He wants the strong trend to weaken so he can get onboard. This desire replaces a superior analysis beam with a weaker beam of trade execution and often the trend leaves without him.

The trader who respects the accuracy of his analysis places an order in area C. He expects prices to keep on rising as they rebound from the trend line. This expectation is consistent with his analysis. He may use a variety of order structures or timing to get the best possible entry on the day. He is happy to pay market price, or a price higher than yesterday's high. The rebound is additional evidence his analysis is correct, so if necessary—and within limits—he chases the price.

Strategies designed to get the best entry price on the day should not be confused with those buying intentions that effectively discount our initial analysis. This replaces superior beams of analysis with inferior trade plan implementation.

The challenges in trading are more than just finding the right advice, trading system or method. Our capacity for self-sabotage should never be underestimated, and traders should always be alert for the first signs of this destructive personal behaviour. Caution is also required when pursuing market education because it is an area populated by a different type of shark. We will consider this in the following chapter.

Chapter 4

Modern market education

In the fast-moving modern world of trading we simply do not have time, or the money, to learn from our mistakes. Traders need education, but all too often education is just a fancy wrapping to disguise poisonous self-interest, poor advice and serious conflicts of interest. The growth of trading services that also claim to offer free education has further blurred the line between advice and education. It has also made it more difficult for genuine independent educators to do their work and get paid for it. Free is always attractive, no matter how much it eventually costs the student.

The snake oil of previous generations has been repackaged on a microchip and sold from impressive-looking websites. The photo-shopped label reads 'education' but it has been pasted over 'fraud' or 'scam'. The antidote to the poisonous multi-billion dollar frauds like those created by Bernie Madoff is education.

How can you separate true education from a sales pitch that masquerades as education, or which is really investment advice? It is an important question for traders because we need to learn about the market if we are to survive. It is also an important question for regulators because many financial services regulators do not recognise genuine investment education.

Investors are not in a position to make the best use of licensed investment advice unless they have a level of investment education. Investment education is not investment advice, but the distinction is often uncertain. The importance of education is indisputable, but its delivery is clouded by the activity of licensed advisers, marketeers and genuine educators.

The best learning teaches us how to understand the financial market and how to use various tools to help make better investment and trading decisions. Education is essential for an informed decision, and it is important that the regulatory environment recognises the difference between education and advice.

The key practical distinction comes from the manner in which income is generated from the client. The key philosophical difference is that advice tells the client what to buy, while education teaches the client how to independently evaluate recommendations.

The role of the investment adviser is to provide advice on the appropriateness and suitability of a range of selected financial products, or buying and selling decisions. There may be an advantage in providing some level of education in relation to the specific product being recommended or advised upon. However, this education is peripheral to the primary task of the investment adviser. Her primary task is to generate an income via the investment and trading activity of her client. This is the sole reason for providing advice, and any peripheral education is only necessary to facilitate the uptake of the recommended product or course of action.

The most significant problem faced in a regulatory environment is the delivery of financial advice by marketeers who masquerade as educators. These marketeers are active in the financial markets. This 'education' has an important conflict of interest because the real objective of the marketeer is to lock you into using their products or services. Instead of providing education that allows you to make an informed choice, they carefully direct you towards a single investment solution or product.

The objective of this group is usually to on-sell an additional product such as software, an integrated 'system' that locks the client into a single commission- or revenue-generating stream, or an arrangement that provides financing. Some of these products or services are characterised by unrealistic claims of ease of use, unrealistic returns, undisclosed commissions, secret operating procedures and suspect systems.

Many people believe that 'education' delivered by those who stand to benefit from your trading activity, such as brokerage houses and investment advisers, includes multiple areas of irreconcilable conflicts of interest. They also believe marketing and sales promotion that uses 'education' to lock customers into specific software products, programs or ongoing courses—usually very expensive—is not genuine education.

Our long-term survival in the markets and our longer term investing success rests on better education. Books and magazines are a very useful starting point, but there is a large gap between reading about the market and actually participating. Education seminars can fill this gap, giving the opportunity for participants to ask questions and explore issues.

So how do you separate education from product promotion, marketing or hidden investment advice? Education is distinguished from investment advice by several key issues and points of difference. They include:

- educators do not generate or receive commission flow from the trading activity of participants once they have completed the 'course' or read the magazine or book

- education material is platform independent; that is, you do not *have* to buy an expensive software system to implement the learning

- education units, articles or books are stand-alone—not part of an extended marketing plan designed specifically as a lead-in to very expensive programs, services or products

- educators and writers are independent. Education, not financial advice, is their business

- educators and writers teach skills that allow the student to replicate and apply the technique or process being taught. An accounting course teaches the skills so the student can learn the procedures and processes. It gives no guarantees the student will become a CPA

- educators teach how to use investment and trading tools that are already in the public domain. You can use the tools with many programs, or buy the software or books from many different shops

- all examples are lagged in time and designed to illustrate techniques. The stocks used as teaching examples cannot be traded in the same way in tomorrow's market

⊞   claims of returns, ease of use and the focus on risk management techniques are substantially different from marketing promotions. Investing in the market is not so simple that 'you need no previous knowledge' to make a fortune. Nor is investing so difficult that you need 'a secret only traders know' to be successful. Educators are realistic about returns and risk and teach you how to manage both these aspects of investing.

Defining the difference between education and advice is not insurmountable. It has already been highlighted and resolved in the accounting profession. If you learn accounting at school you are not taught by an accountant. If you want to learn how to use accounting software you go to a teacher who is generally not an accountant.

But if you want accounting advice, you go to an accountant. If you want accounting services, you go to an accountant.

If you want to learn about investing then the best educator is someone who has the experience and knowledge of trading and investing. This is available through books, articles and live education courses. This is valuable knowledge, so you should expect to pay for the presenter's experience delivered in a book or a seminar.

If you want investment advice about which stock to buy or sell, then you need investment advice. The best person to get this from is a licensed investment adviser, or your broker. Some brokerages offer very good educational products for their clients, and we would be foolish not to take full advantage of them. However, these educational products have an inevitable bias. The company is trying to sell you a product, or give you some skills so your trading continues to generate commissions for them. This makes these offerings more suitable for people who already have independent learning and knowledge. They can assess and evaluate the information more effectively.

Education is about acquiring knowledge. Education allows investors to understand and evaluate the advice provided by licensed financial advisers and others. Education provides information that requires skills to be used in an environment independent of the learning centre or facilities.

Education underpins all effective investment decisions. It is essential that the regulatory environment develops a mechanism to recognise the difference between education and advice. Until this happens the new trader remains potential shark bait. The complexity of modern markets and trading instruments attracts bigger sharks and they eat more.

In the next chapter we look at essential survival rules.

Chapter 5

Rules to stand by

The financial landscape began to shift after the Tech Crash at the turn of the century. The landscape shattered with the Global Financial Crisis in 2008. A significant portion of accepted thinking was shown to be either incorrect or inappropriate. Like dinosaurs after the meteorite crash, some market participants and regulators struggled just with the effort of survival, and continued to do the same things in much the same way. In this first section we have suggested markets have changed significantly at the margins in terms of trade execution, the flow of information and the rapid aggregation of risk that brings the famous butterfly effect into real life.

The modern market environment looks the same as the old market environment, but lurking beneath the surface are important changes. They include faster trade execution, genuine algorithmic trading and its nasty offspring, flash trading. It includes the cancerous growth of dark pools of anonymous liquidity provided by off-market exchanges where there are increased opportunities for manipulation to slide undetected beneath the waves.

The status of individual traders, the need to work with the crowd and avoid self-sabotage and the need for genuine education have changed in emphasis and become more important. Traders ask, 'What rules stand true in this new environment?'

When I first started trading I studied and learned from other master traders. Then as my skill grew I developed my own thinking and my own approaches. I shared these in my books so others could also learn. Then I became too confident and the market reminded me my skill always needed to be updated to survive in developing market conditions. The foundation trading rule was always humility.

Humility means you understand and acknowledge that other people in the market know much more than you know. They understand what is happening in the business for a particular company. Other people understand what is happening in the economy, or in government. Other people have much better analysis skills, or much better information. It is not possible to personally develop this knowledge. You cannot be smarter than the market or the people in the market.

Humility means you appreciate their knowledge and you learn to follow their conclusions in the market. All of their information and analysis skill is revealed in the chart of price activity. Every day intelligent people buy and sell in the market. You measure their knowledge and opinion by watching the price activity.

The rules standing true are the rules that have always stood true. They are rules for the activity of trading. They are not prescriptive rules or instructions for specific trading techniques, methods or instruments. My rules are developed from experience to suit my trading style, my personality and to compensate for my weaknesses. The specific rules you adopt will be different, although they may well be drawn from the same type of observations. These rules offer protection in an evolving market, but they are not shark-proof.

Rule 1: Understand trading discipline — trade development

This is most commonly understood to mean the discipline to follow our trading system and approach. Better traders understand it also includes meeting the challenge of cutting losses and taking profits cleanly.

As traders with less experience slip into the fast-moving areas of derivative trading with contracts for difference (CFDs) and other instruments, trading discipline becomes even more important. Hesitation loses a fortune, particularly with leveraged trading instruments.

It takes time, experience and observation to make the best use of real-time information such as that provided by CFD vendors. It is too easy to forget the minute-by-minute relationship between the bid and the ask may change quite quickly and quite dramatically. The novice is better equipped for position trading based on end-of-day data, where decisions are made without the interference of the market froth and bubble.

The discipline the novice must master is the discipline to act on his entry signals even if it means being out of the market for a long time. Just because this is the first skill learned does not mean it is the least important. Without it, a trader cannot grow.

Trading discipline is the ability to exit a trade under one of two conditions. The first is to realise a loss and the second is to take a profit.

Selling is more difficult because we can never be sure which way the market will perform in the future. We buy for one reason, but we sell for many reasons. This side of the trading process is much more complex and challenging. Unless traders develop a disciplined approach to the exit their trading suffers.

In understanding the way discipline applies in this trading rule we build on our understanding that a loss is not the same as losing. Until we accept this distinction it is difficult to exit a trade at a small loss. This lack of discipline rapidly destroys all our accumulated profits, assisted by the most discouraging market law of all: a 10% loss cannot be made up by a 10% gain.[*] This is the toughest market law. Developing the discipline to take a profit sounds so simple that it is almost irrelevant. Yet failure in this area has destroyed many trading accounts.

Rule 2: Understand trading discipline — emotional development

The very successful traders have another understanding of discipline separating them from the average. They do not let their emotions, their temper or their frustrations get in the way of their trading.

A novice trader talks of losses as being caused by a mythical beast — the market. Then they go on: 'I was so annoyed that I bought more as they fell'. This is revenge trading,

---

[*] Starting with $100 and taking a 10% loss leaves the trader with $90. To bring this up to $100 the next trade must make at least 11%. Over 12% is needed when brokerage is included.

aiming to get even with the market. These traders let their emotions dictate their trading strategy.

Sometimes our broker encourages this emotional deception, particularly during the Global Financial Crisis. 'Remember those shares you bought last year at $18.00? They are trading at $1.80 today. It's a good opportunity to get more at even better prices.'

This attack on emotional discipline is seductive and successful. Instead of exercising the discipline to get out, we go for emotional comfort, trading for revenge. This explains the last trades in Bear Stearns on the day it was suspended from trading.

More frightening, because it is less frequently acknowledged, is the impact of anger and frustration on our trading performance. Trading rage is even more deadly than road rage.

Take a moment of quiet reflection. How many times have your losing trades been driven by external emotions—by anger, frustration, revenge or the need to prove something to somebody else? How many of these trades have been used to satisfy emotional needs that have absolutely nothing to do with the market? Finding the answer takes some hard searching through your soul rather than your trading records and contract notes. All of us have been guilty. It is part of the process of moving from novice to journeyman to craftsman. The essential factor separating the skilled journeyman from the craftsman is this emotional discipline.

Rule 3: Accept total responsibility for your actions

Trading is an activity where personal responsibility is unavoidable. Despite the efforts of the regulatory authorities to coddle and protect investors from the consequences of their decisions based on investment advice, the trader has no such protection, and ultimately seeks no such protection.

Exploring and understanding different trading approaches is one of the first steps towards developing trading responsibility. Each trader brings her own experience and interpretations to every approach. Having assembled the pieces herself, the trader accepts the responsibility for the outcome.

When your broker gives you trading advice that turns into a loser, accept responsibility. After all, you took the advice and acted upon it. It was you who chose not to initiate any stop loss procedures.

Although you may decide to use the proceeds of trading to improve your lifestyle and the lifestyle of your family, you are ultimately trading for yourself. You cannot trade to meet the expectations of others.

Responsibility is nourished by trading discipline. It is difficult to develop true trading discipline without accepting responsibility for trading action and outcomes. Surprisingly, this is the major obstacle standing between many traders and success.

Why we succeed or fail in the market depends more on ourselves than on any other factor. Work towards understanding this every day, and when you can accept it, work on understanding why you are succeeding or failing.

Rule 4: Plan the trade, trade the plan

The trading cliché above my computer reads: 'Plan the trade and trade the plan'. If only trading were so simple.

Everybody plans to trade, but only the successful traders have a trading plan. This is often reduced to just a few notes, small enough to stick on the side of the computer screen. What goes into the reduction is important. This single rule has many sub-clauses, including:

- have a clear reason for being in the trade

- know your exit conditions in advance

- ride winners

- cut losses quickly

- use strong money management

- keep positions small.

Rule 5: Have a clear reason for being in the trade

Why am I in this trade? Traders are often reluctant to probe the reasons for each individual trade, even though it is an essential part of the planning process. A selection of good answers includes the following:

- to exploit this short-term rally

- I am trading momentum

- I am trading the long-term trend and this is the best entry point

- a major news event—the budget—will probably cause a rally. I am trading the rally

- this is a recovery trade to rescue a position already under water

- I am trading the triangle breakout

- this is a trading channel trade.

All of these answers, and others like them, are a useful part of the trade planning process. Answers like these are less useful:

- I have spare cash so I feel I ought to be in the market

- everyone else is making money

- this broker/magazine/newspaper recommendation sounds so good that I would be a fool not to trade it

- after the last loss I need to get some money back

- the stock is now worth half what it was when I bought it. I will average down

- I need some money for a holiday/boat/car/tax bills

- at this price it is a bargain or it has to be a bottom

- if I wait much longer I am going to miss out

- the margin loan facility has been cleared. What can I buy?

These do sound far-fetched in cold hard print, but if there is a tiny twinge of recognition, then take the time to put in writing the answer to the question that begins every real planning process: 'I am in this trade because ...'

Rule 6: Know your exit conditions in advance

The first exit condition is designed to cut losses quickly. This rule is up there with the hardest trading rules of all. Ignore it and it becomes the mass murderer of market nightmares. Our protection is in the trading plan.

The summary impact of this plan is to ride winners and cut losses quickly. It is the public core of trade planning and usually the starting point for the progression from novice to better trader:

- the first exit condition is designed to cut losses quickly

- the second exit condition is to protect and lock in profits.

Rule 7: Money management

Money management is the key to trading survival. We can get almost everything else in the planning process wrong, but if the money management aspect is right, we will survive.

Conversely, even if every other aspect of the trading plan is perfect, we fail if money management is incorrect. Without money management all the wins, big and small, may be destroyed in just a few losing trades.

One money management model does not suit all, but without some form of money management we are extremely vulnerable in the market.

Rule 8: Keep positions small

Traders with limited capital often think this trade planning rule does not apply to them. Although they readily agree it is foolish to take a million dollars of trading capital and put it into a single stock or position, they are less agreeable to applying it to their own trading. All $6000 of their trading capital sits with a solid blue chip such as Bank of America or Goldman Sachs because their adviser told them it was a safe investment. The same advisers failed to deliver sell advice as these stocks collapsed or were delisted.

The small private trader is locked into greater risk because he has limited capacity to diversify his risk profile across the market. No matter how large our trading capital, the objective is to match position size with risk. Each position puts at risk only 2% of total trading capital, and our exit is based on this figure.

Amateur traders, and amateur gamblers, bet big. Survivors take many small positions and many small losses in pursuit of the winner they ride for major wins.

Rule 9: Trade the market, not your opinion of it

There is only one right answer and the market has it. We are paid for trading the market, not our opinion of what the market should be. This is an essential rule when traders start with index trading.

This rule is mostly ignored by experienced traders. Quite suddenly they lose touch with the market, and losing trades begin to accumulate. If trading discipline is strong, the losses don't amount to much in dollar terms, but the losing trades still hurt in emotional terms.

This rule is rarely broken by the novice because she has a clear understanding of her position in the market. Ego grows only when we gather some success and with it a dangerous certainty we can pick the market direction. The private trader is generally food for larger market sharks, and those who forget these limitations become shark food.

Rule 10: Take what the market will give you rather than what you would like it to give you

Many times the market does not behave as anticipated. Carefully calculated profit targets are nearly reached, but the momentum slides away. By monitoring open positions we make a better judgement about the probability of our sell, or buy, order being filled.

Here we ride in dangerous territory. There is a fine balance between micro-managing the trade and paying too much or accepting too little. For the position trader, this micro-management can be unproductive. Generally it is more useful to set our parameters and wait for the market to meet them, particularly on the buying side of the equation. If we do miss out it means we have the cash to commit to the market elsewhere.

In selling, the advice is less useful. If we do not sell, our open profits are eaten away by falling prices. If there are clear reasons for exiting the trade below our initial profit targets, then we should act on them.

Rule 11: Manage every trade, every day

Every single open position must be monitored and managed. Many times management is no more difficult than looking at the chart at the end of the day. At other times more serious action is required. Some trades require minute-by-minute management, and they take a chunk out of your wallet if they are ignored. If we lock the trade away in a bottom drawer we cannot tell when emergency action is needed.

Management comes from planning. At the end of each day bring up a new chart of each open position and ask the following six questions.

▦   What is my trading plan?

- Is it still valid?

- If no, then what is my amended plan?

- What are my exit plans?

- Have these been triggered?

- Are they close to being triggered?

A *yes* answer to one of the last two questions means we spend more time looking at this trade to decide whether we need to take action on the next trading day. Most days this is a five-minute exercise. It's not much to ask, but it is a life-saver.

Rule 12: Always analyse winners and losers, but never agonise

We need to learn from our mistakes because we have paid real money to make them. Study your trading errors so you can avoid repeating them.

Assemble the objective circumstances and conditions of each successful trade, whether it turned a healthy profit or incurred a small loss. Study these as well, and reward your successes.

When we agonise over what could have been we lose sight of the very real success of a trade in locking in a profit. Each trade is an island in an archipelago of our own design, so we step from one to the next, but without regret.

Rule 13: Be humble

Never forget where you came from. The market can send you back there very quickly. Your trading approach should work for you. Beyond that is only uncertainty and the market.

There is a risk of loss

These 13 rules come with no guarantees. There is not a lucky rabbit's foot hiding among them, nor is there the financial equivalent of a loss-proof Kevlar vest. Trading success is a constantly expanding mixture of knowledge and skill. We make an error if we confuse rule-based trading with market mastery.

Rules offer a guide and some degree of protection but they do not guarantee a consistent result. Every trader is different, and although we work with the same information, our conclusions and results will be different.

Recently I was involved in a trading training class. I taught the class a single trading method. The final activity for the class was live trading. They knew the theory of the trading method but now they were trading with a small amount of money. I identified the entry conditions for the index trade. There was enough time for all the students to evaluate the trade suggestion and enter an order. All the students had the same computers, the same software and a similar knowledge of the trading methods I had been teaching.

Logically we think all the students should obtain similar results. In fact, the results of the students were very different, as shown in figure 5.1.

When I identified a profitable trade, some of the students made more money than me. They entered the trade early because of their greed. Some students made less money because they waited to get extra confirmation before entering the trade. Other students lost money because they entered too late. A few students did not trade because they had experienced losses and were 'afraid' to have another loser.

When my trade suggestion was not successful, the same variety of results also occurred. Some students lost more money than me. Some students lost less money than me, and some students had a profitable trade.

The most important difference in results came from the way students acted on their stop losses. Students who acted quickly had good success. Students who did not act quickly on the stop loss were less successful and their trading was not profitable. Every student was looking at the same chart and the same market index. The students all acted differently and their trading results were all different.

These experiences in the training class confirm psychology is an important part of trading success. A good trading plan and rules are important but the psychology of the trader decides whether the trade plan is successful.

American trader Mark Douglas said: 'You must be rigid in your rules and flexible in your expectations. Most traders are flexible in their rules and rigid in their expectations.' This advice is important because it covers two of the most common problems experienced by new or struggling traders.

Figure 5.1: different trade entries

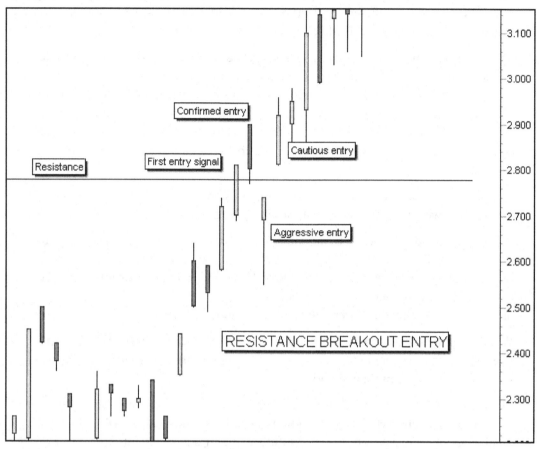

The first problem is that most traders are flexible in their rules. Many traders do not have a firm set of rules for each trade. Many traders say they have a stop loss plan and they set exit targets. But this is not a trading plan, so they can be very flexible in their rules. Very few traders have the rules required for a quality trading plan. A quality trade plan includes rules explaining how the trade will be managed.

The second problem is that traders are rigid in their expectations. They develop a market bias, or a feeling about a particular security. They do not change this opinion even when the chart of price activity is telling them something different, as shown in figure 5.2. Some traders fall in love with a security and they refuse to believe the price will continue falling. When good news is released they buy the security and ignore the price chart which shows a strong downtrend.

Figure 5.2: long-term downtrend

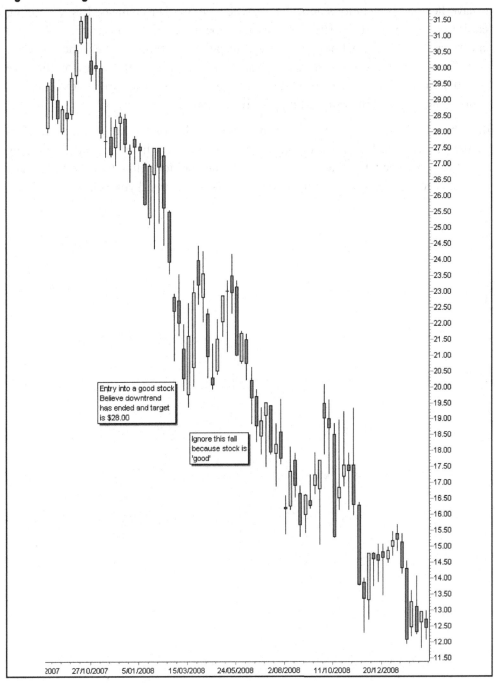

Some people say you cannot follow rigid trading rules, because trading requires you to have flexible expectations and change when the market changes. I agree trading requires you to be flexible. The flexibility must be included in your trading plan and your rules. You should define how you will recognise a change in the trend and then define how you will react to the trend change. You could exit the trade, sell half the trade or adjust the stop loss method to protect profits. This is the correct flexibility and it should be included in your trading plan rules.

Treat these trading rules as guideposts on the side of the road. They set the conditions for analysis discussed in the next chapter. They show you where the road is, but they do not tell you where the road is going. These rules cannot define your destination or your fate because those are a decision between the market and yourself.

Part II

Analysis

Chapter 6

Easy to learn, hard to master

With contributing author Ryan Guppy

Analysis is the foundation of trading, but it's not a solution. Analysis methods are easy to learn but the application of those methods to develop a stock pool of opportunity and then select the best of those to trade is much more difficult to master. Changes in modern market volatility force us to revaluate the nature of trending activity and this impacts on the way search results are assessed. Historically traders have assumed price volatility is the same as trend volatility. This is no longer the case, where large intraday price moves shake the normal definition of the trend but do not disturb the underlying trend behaviour. We call these volatility wipes, and we examine these in more detail in chapter 11, Trend Volatility Line analysis.

As a result we need to apply measures of price volatility with more caution. Traditional methods of identifying trend behaviour require modification to manage the more numerous false exit signals. Some measures of trend behaviour, such as the Darvas method, become more useful in modern markets because they define the trend in a different fashion. A new indicator, the GMMA Trend Volatility Line, takes a different approach and sets the conditions for tighter trade management.

These are all analysis tools. They define the way we look at the market and define the way we search for opportunities and develop an initial stock pool. This is the strategic framework of market analysis, and at times it tips easily into tactical applications. A close above a Darvas box is a strategic signal, but also a tactical entry signal. We have tried to keep the focus of the chapters in this section on the construction of these analysis methods and why they are relevant in the modern market.

We start with the most powerful analysis method of all: eyeballing. Although it sounds so 20th century, this method has become even more vital in modern markets. It quickly sorts through the mathematical flotsam and jetsam produced with automated market scans or explorations. We use the scans to quickly develop a small stock pool of opportunity. Then we eyeball the stocks in the pool to identify the better trading candidates. The eyeball is confirmation that trading is an art aided by science. Mathematical science creates the stock pool, but it's an art to select the best trading candidate from the pool. We take you through the steps involved in an eyeball search and evaluating five potential trades. We do not ask you to agree with the analysis conclusions. Our purpose is to demonstrate the process involved in eyeball evaluation.

There are many ways to find opportunity in the market. The most common technical methods are:

- search the market using a technical scan using construction methods discussed in the next chapter

- use stock selections identified by other sources, including brokerages, magazines, newspapers and other media. These are a starting point and provide a small group of preselected stocks which are subjected to further technical analysis

- do an eyeball search of the market. This means looking at the chart of many stocks and identifying those showing strong trends, breakouts or chart patterns.

A regular full eyeball scan of the market helps the trader to develop a feel for the market. It develops an understanding of the normal current behaviour of trends, breakouts and retracements. It makes it easier to identify abnormal situations. It assists in identifying the chart patterns currently enjoying a higher probability of success.

We use three types of eyeball approaches to assess the market:

- *a casual eyeball.* Whenever we look at a stock for whatever reason, we then also eyeball search through the other stocks in the same alphabetical folder.

This takes five or six minutes. This is a haphazard approach, but over a short period of time it covers most of the stocks in the market

- *a systematic eyeball.* This is a long process, ideally suited to a weekend. The objective is to eyeball every active stock in the market. Even at speed, this is two to three hours' work, and fatigue—and boredom—is a problem. Even for dedicated traders it's not particularly exciting flipping through mountains of charts

- *a selected eyeball.* Every trader should do this. It is applied to a pool of stocks selected using some other method, usually a technical scan of the market. This is the method we discuss below because it captures all the essential elements of this analysis method.

Eyeballs

For new and seasoned traders alike the process of deciding if one trade is better than another is a process that is repeated over and over again. Whether you are trading an end-of-day or a one-minute chart, and trading regularly or irregularly because you are in for the long term, the process of determining one potential opportunity from another is ever present.

Trading can be a dangerous affair if you dive straight into the deep end with no direction; so often new traders find the only direction they head is down. Before entering the market, traders need to know how they wish to trade and what kind of trading they are going to undertake. In current markets, time in the market increases your risk. The longer you are in a trade, the greater the risk of the trade failing. This may be due to the increased volatility created by the head and shoulder patterns in the DOW, the FTSE and the XJO. It may be a result of wild swings in currency markets, teasing the dollar with the promise of parity and then plunging 20% or more. It may be because of the looming trade war with new tariffs and duties on imported products. In all these environments, traders get twitchy fingers, buying and selling out of fear rather than sound technical analysis, and this creates very volatile markets. This produces short-term momentum trading opportunities, and these are the opportunities we look for in this eyeball search application.

Short-term momentum opportunities are usually news-driven, but we can see the activity on the chart by looking for momentum days. These are days far exceeding the daily price action of the previous days, creating a strong solid green candle. This is the trading condition we are looking for on our charts using a technical scan. Once we have preformed our search we do a quick eyeball of the stocks and note the stock codes for the trading opportunities that appear profitable. We don't spend more than two or three seconds on each chart before determining if we want to trade it or not. This may seem like a short period, but by already deciding we are looking for a momentum day it is easy to see possibilities on a chart in this amount of time.

Distraction is dangerous, and any collection of charts contains multiple different opportunities. Traders need to be careful not to be distracted from what they are looking for. If you are looking for long-term uptrends, then keep an eye out for long-term uptrends. If you are looking for short-term momentum opportunities, do not get distracted by long-term uptrends. It is hard enough picking a good trading opportunity from a list of stocks exhibiting your preferred trading features without being distracted by other situations that appear profitable. There are always going to be opportunities that will pass you by when you look at the market, but this is not important. What is important is that when you put your money into the market, it has a greater probability of creating money rather than losing money. Staying focused on the job at hand is an important part of this process. We will show you how this process is applied.

Tools for eyeballs

Equipped with our shortlist of stocks from eyeballing the charts, we go back and examine each potential trade in detail, using our preferred trading tools. Keeping our trading tool set simple is a hard concept to get across to many traders. Many people believe that because the market appears complex it can only be traded with complex indicators and mathematical equations. At Guppytraders we use a small set of trading tools for our trading strategies, and the newsletter case study portfolio has consistently shown they are successful. For our shortlist analysis we use the Guppy Multiple Moving Average (GMMA), trend lines and support/resistance levels to determine whether a trading opportunity is worth taking. These are discussed in detail in the following chapters.

These searches were performed the day before the last traded day shown on the chart extracts. Figure 6.1 was a momentum rebound off a historical support level. After the initial rally and gap up, price entered into a trading band. A trading band develops when price moves sideways, bouncing between a support and a resistance level. Traders confidently trade these rallies and retreats as they provide a high-probability price target at the resistance level.

The breakout above the resistance level is a little weak as the initial price action was above the resistance level. In areas A and B traders see price used the resistance level as a support level before breaking through at the end of area B. Price has made several attempts to break through both the top and the bottom of the trading band, but the support and resistance levels have held strong. The GMMA shows expected behaviour in a trading band. The short-term and long-term groups are both fairly compact as neither the traders nor the investors are sure which direction price should go, and the groups are weaving back and forth between each other. This is indicative of sideways price action.

Figure 6.1: support and resistance levels

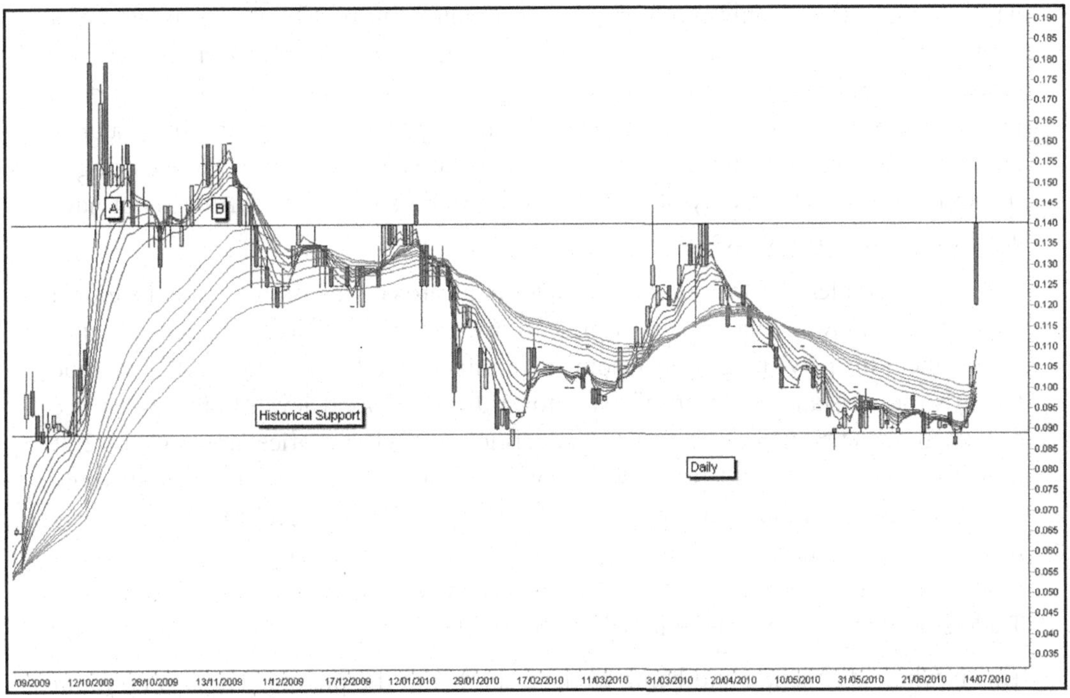

Patience is a vital part of trading. Very rarely will traders find a stock ready to be traded the next day, and they often must wait several days for a trading opportunity to fully develop. In figure 6.1, price has acted explosively at the right of the chart, gapping up and closing at the resistance level. If price breaks through the resistance level with upwards momentum this is a buy signal and traders will enter ready to ride the new rally. It is more likely price will fall back towards the support level, where traders will be able to trade the rebound back towards the resistance level.

Figure 6.2 shows a strong rebound with three full green candles (or light-grey candles here). This is a very strong rally with good sustainable momentum. The short-term GMMA group has begun to separate and push through the long-term GMMA group. Additionally the long-term GMMA group has started to compress and has turned upwards. This is a sign of a trend change and a possible trading opportunity. There are however several problems with this chart that take away from its tradability.

The first is setting the support level. There are three possible positions for the support level: A, B and C. Support level A captures two points of the price action and is the starting point for the momentum rally, however it does not capture the three days that closed below it. Support level B captures four lows and the high of the lowest day, while support level C only captures the lowest point. Support level C is in fact not a support level at all as it only captures one point, leaving support level B as the most correct support level, even though this is not the starting point of the rally. A rally does not need to rebound directly off a support level. Support level B captures the majority of the price action, even though there is one day that opened below it before closing at the support level. The variety of support level options shows the chart does not have as strong a base as other stocks.

The second problem is time. After three days of upwards momentum, we see the fourth day has closed lower. Traders expect price to pause at this level as it consolidates after the momentum rally. This critical point determines whether this rally will continue towards the resistance level or fall back towards the support level. Using past price activity, traders project how long it will take price to reach our price target of $1.92. It took about two months for price to fall from the resistance level to the support level, and it has taken a month for price to move from the support level roughly half way back to the resistance level. Therefore we can reasonably expect it may take another month to reach the resistance level. A month is a very long time in a volatile market. Traders need to decide if the time risk is acceptable.

This is where distraction and being realistic come into the picture. There is no room for wishing in the market, and the '*but if*' scenario only works in traders' dreams. '*But if* price moves up to here, I'll make a 100% profit' is great to hope for. In figure 6.2, if we entered at the most recent close of $1.59 and exited at the resistance level of $1.92 we would make 20.8% profit before brokerage, in 30 days. A 20% profit sounds like a good trade, but do not get distracted by the amount of potential profit. In 30 days would you be able to make the same or more with your capital trading other stocks? What is the probability of price reaching the resistance level? The answers to these two questions are for each trader to decide; many would conclude that in a volatile market 30 days is too long to wait for a 20% return.

Figure 6.2: price rally

This chart is discarded due to these reasons.

Figure 6.3 shows a parabolic trend line chart pattern. A parabolic trend line is a special trend line capturing fast momentum rallies. It is covered in more detail in chapter 23, Getting ahead of the curves.

The important feature here is the resistance level at $0.33. This level is the beginning of price action after the gap down, and is the level price is pushing towards as it follows the parabolic trend line.

Once a parabolic trend line has been broken, price has a high probability of falling between 50% and 80% — or more — of the price move. Fail to act on the sell signal and it takes all your hard-earned profits with it. Traders plan to exit before price crosses the parabolic trend line. Trading a parabolic trend line is a balancing act between keeping profit and being able to exit the trade.

Figure 6.3: a parabolic trend line

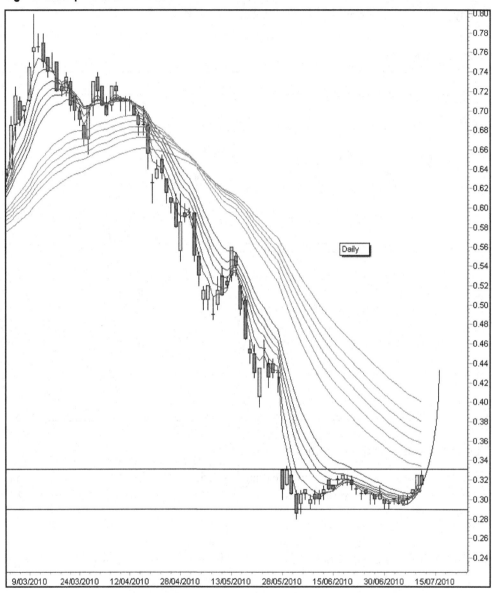

Our other concern is the long-term GMMA, which is very separated, showing strong downward pressure. There is a low probability price will push above the upper levels of the long-term GMMA. This confirms the probability of a rapid collapse when the parabolic trend fails.

Figure 6.4 shows a momentum day. Price activity has been shallow after price rebounded off the support level at $0.39, but then price made a determined move towards the resistance level at $0.58.

The GMMA relationships show the short-term group has turned upwards and pushed above the long-term group, which has also begun to contract and turn upwards. This shows buyers are coming back into this stock. The momentum day closes at the high of the day. This is a strong bullish signal.

Figure 6.4: momentum day

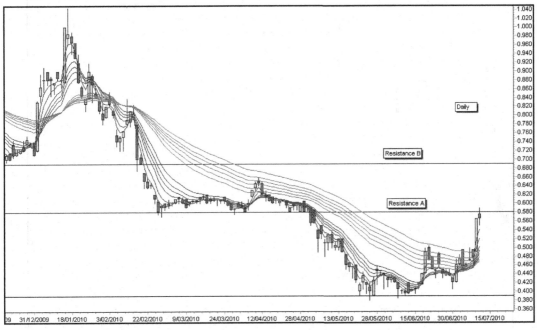

Traders wait for price to push above resistance A before entering this trade. In a bull market traders enter this stock in anticipation of price continuing upwards, but in a bear market traders are more cautious. Bear markets quickly separate the foolhardy from the prepared, and entering a trade prematurely in a bear market is a good way to get eaten. Once price pushes above resistance A traders place their buy orders.

The final selection from the technical shortlist is shown in figure 6.5. The GMMA groups are excellent, with the long-term group widely separated and heading upwards, and the short-term group consistently separated and a consistent distance from the long-term group. This is the kind of chart traders dream about. So why was it discarded?

There are two reasons. The first is time, and the second is liquidity. This chart is a relatively new stock, listed for only six months. This means there is not a long period of price action on which to make historical comparisons.

Figure 6.5: spotty price behaviour

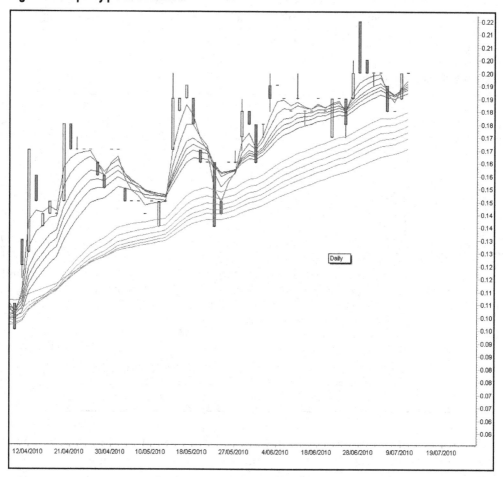

The price action confirms this stock has low liquidity. Spotty behaviour is a sign of low liquidity. Spotty behaviour occurs when the open and the closing price are the same, and there is no price movement during the day to create wicks or tails on the candle. The result is a single horizontal line. Traders avoid charts showing a lot of spotty behaviour because it is very difficult to enter and exit a trade.

Out of the five stock selections from an eyeball analysis, only three remain on our watchlist: figures 6.1, 6.3 and 6.4.

These eyeball selection and evaluation skills are the foundation of trading, and although easy to learn they are hard to master.

For the next step in evaluation of the eyeball search results we apply our preferred trading analysis methods quickly. These include:

⊞ count back line trend analysis

⊞ GMMA analysis

⊞ saucer and parabolic pattern analysis

⊞ traders ATR analysis.

Your analysis methods may be very different. You might include volume, MACD, RSI or some other analysis filter. This is not important. It's the process of finding and eliminating opportunities that is important.

In the next chapter we look at how technical searches are created, before considering more advanced methods for analysing the results of the search.

Chapter 7

Building stock pools

Eyeballs are connected to brains, and traders need to use both. There is no reliable substitute for eyeballs, but there is a partial substitute for brains in computing power. However, traders must be wary of the power of computer analysis to enable traders to make stupid decisions more quickly. This is facilitated because market data is a collection of numbers and this looks like a fruitful field for a variety of mathematical analysis techniques. It's an area where the computer is uniquely enabling.

The market is not a set of mathematical conditions, although it can often be described using mathematical models. The increase in computer power means traders can quickly search a universe of stocks and develop a stock pool of candidates meeting a set of mathematical conditions. This should not be confused with trading advice or success.

The development of algorithmic trading and flash trading is a natural extension of computing power. Algorithmic trading is not restricted to the large institutions. Private traders began using algorithmic trading as soon as the desktop computer was linked to market price data. The methods of creating a stock pool discussed in this chapter are the first steps towards creating an algorithmic trading system. Linking these to automated trade execution completes the trading process, taking it from analysis to action. Anyone who uses automatic stop loss orders and conditional entry orders has taken the first steps in algorithmic trading. But be warned. Just because the solution is mathematically elegant doesn't mean it is a successful trade.

The list of compatible stocks might range from 10 to 200, and ultimately the trader must decide which single one of these compatible stocks he will trade. This is where skill trumps mathematics. Constructing performance searches is a shortcut to quickly reduce the list of stocks requiring further investigation. It is an essential tool, and in this chapter we look at the family of indicators and search approaches based on price performance.

These performance indicators suggest a strong probability price action is developing but we need additional analysis to confirm the opportunity. We cannot tell you which combination of performance indicators is best because your trading style is individual. Instead we show you how your choices determine the search results. If your choices are inconsistent with your beliefs about market activity then opportunities will be elusive. Understanding the process builds a better search mechanism for identifying the balance of probability.

An indicator takes price data and manipulates it to reveal additional 'hidden' information about the development of price action. For instance, by comparing the standard deviation range to previous trading days we build details about the speed and momentum of price that are not readily available from eyeball searches.

An indicator reading is not a market price. It is a numerical value obtained from the result of a calculation. This difference is the key to working with technical analysis indicators.

Indicators fall into one of three categories: trend-following, oscillators and miscellaneous. This chapter concentrates on the way we use the first two without discussing a host of individual indicators in significant depth. Every software program seems to have a different coding language so we deal with the concepts rather than the formulas. Additional reading references are noted where appropriate. Later we provide a test for indicator success.

The way the indicator is constructed tells us what it is trying to measure. If it measures the same factors we want to measure, then it is safe to use it to set our scanning criteria. If it does not measure our preferred factors, then we should not use it because the results may become a dangerous threat to our trading. Powerful indicators give enticingly complex results and it is too easy to second-guess our otherwise sound analysis. Many traders succumb to the temptation to use a range of sometimes contradictory indicators because the names sound interesting, they are available on the software or other people talk about using them.

Very broadly, these two groups of performance indicators—trend-following and oscillators—are designed to answer two simple questions:

⊞   *Where are we?* These are the trend-following indicators.

⊞   *Are we breaking the speed limit?* These are the oscillators.

The first part of this chapter considers trend-following indicators. These are all based on moving average concepts and we show how this simple idea is layered into some of the most complex of indicators. All of them are designed to answer a single question: where is price now in relation to price in a previous period?

From zero to one and beyond

Using the power of the computer to search an extensive database of securities is as simple as a few mouse clicks. Understanding the report results is more difficult.

Depending on the software used, some scanning results deliver a numerical value. Others use boolean logic, returning either a 1 = YES or a 0 = NO. By using the 'sort' function the responses are ranked from highest to lowest. This groups all the 1's —yes responses—together, making it easier to develop a useful list.

No matter how they are displayed, the 'yes' results suggest turning points where the balance of probability begins to tip in our favour. These points are not always supported by the bar chart price action, but the idea is that the indicator either confirms or anticipates the shift. The initial task is to find the securities at turning points where an entry is signalled.

Where are we? An average answer

The trend-following group of performance indicators plots the current position of a stock against some previously calculated average position. The result tells us where we are.

Prices fluctuate, sometimes erratically. A plotted price line is constructed by snapshots of one price element—perhaps the close—and is a little like joining the dots. This line is made more useful when compared against past prices, on average. We want to know where we are in relation to a range of previous price activity. Simply looking back at history is one solution.

Another plot compares today's price with the moving average of prices. Unfortunately price has four parts—open, high, low and close—so we must choose one to base the average calculations on. Most times we take the close, and create a predefined average range from this data. Many traders use 3-, 4-, 5-, 7-, 10-, 21- or 30-day moving averages. Choosing a single element—for example the close or the high—immediately reduces the amount of information available.

An alternative solution combines the four price parts into a single 'average' figure. Choosing the median price—the mid-point between the high and low for the day—captures additional information about price, more than any other single data point, such as the open. This price data relationship has a value plotted on a chart as a single point. Calculate the value for each day in the past, join the dots, and the screen display plots a line in the same way as a closing price line.

We can further manipulate the median price by plotting the 10-day or 15-day moving average of the value. Then we have a data point against which we compare today's median price. Conceptually this is the same as a closing line display plotted against a 20-day moving average. But the difference is in the detail. We plot a median price against its 10-day average and learn something different about price behaviour.

This is essentially a simple calculation concept using an average of an average. The mathematics is more complex but this calculation task is ideally suited to the computer's form of high-speed idiocy. Often we make this calculation even more complex by the calculation method chosen for the moving average.

Data manipulation

The choices include a simple moving average (SMA), an exponential moving average (EMA) and a weighted moving average (WMA). Your choice may be based on simplicity and ease of use, or it may be more closely related to a specific belief about the market. With modern software all choices are equally easy so it pays to think carefully about the impact of each approach.

Does it really matter? Figure 7.1 lists the results of three MetaStock Explorer searches using an EMA, SMA and WMA. The database of securities searched are the same, but the membership of each list is subtly different. New additions are shown in bold italics.

One of these lists gives you a head start. Which one it is depends on how you match your choice with your beliefs. The search results should support and reinforce your trading strategy.

Figure 7.1: MetaStock Explorer searches using an EMA, SMA and WMA

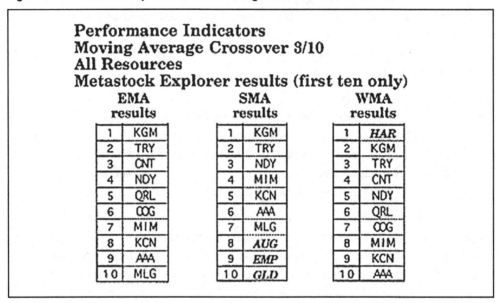

In *The Lion King* film the wise old monkey belts a young lion across the head with his staff. He tells the angry lion that the attack was in the past, so, according to the young lion's philosophy, it doesn't matter. Rubbing his head, the lion concedes the past does have an impact on current and future events. In a similar way, I believe recent price data is more significant than less recent price data.

What happens today has a greater immediate impact on what happens tomorrow than do events of 10 or 20 days ago. As a result, I use an EMA calculation because it is consistent with my understanding of the market. My trading list comes from the first column in figure 7.1.

Applying any of these styles of average calculations to a single data element—open, high, low or close—gives useful results, but they are not a simple traded market price.

The level of complexity increases when we use a relationship between price data. We might manipulate the data by selecting a median price. For example, if the low is $0.40 and the high is $0.80 then the median is $0.60.

Others prefer to use the mean price or what we commonly call the average. Continuing the example above, if the open is $0.42 and the close $0.64 then we have four observations—open 42, high 80, low 40 and close 64. The total is 226. To find the mean the total is divided by the number of data points, giving a result of $0.565.

Plotting the mean against the median leaves a $0.035 gap. This is not insignificant if your trading method relies on signals generated by moving average crossovers.

The levels of complexity are almost infinite, and addictive. Other manipulations calculate the standard deviation and compare today's price activity with past activity. Some use the mean deviation to find the average absolute value of the difference between the population of data points and the mean.

Again, does it matter? The answer is yes. Figure 7.2 lists EMA crossover search results from the All Resources sector using the close, the median and the average, or typical, price. The results are ranked by the value above or below the crossover point, with zero values identifying the exact crossover. We have only shown the candidates' names. The difference in the make up of and order within the lists reflects the relationship between the price data selected as the basis of the EMA calculation. Opportunities noted in one list sometimes do not appear in either of the others.

Figure 7.2: EMA crossover search results

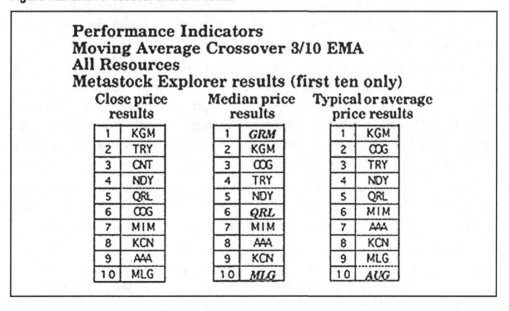

	Close price results		Median price results		Typical or average price results
1	KGM	1	*GRM*	1	KGM
2	TRY	2	KGM	2	OOG
3	CNT	3	OOG	3	TRY
4	NOY	4	TRY	4	NOY
5	QRL	5	NOY	5	QRL
6	OOG	6	*QRL*	6	MIM
7	MIM	7	MIM	7	AAA
8	KCN	8	AAA	8	KCN
9	AAA	9	KCN	9	MLG
10	MLG	10	*MLG*	10	*AUG*

Performance Indicators
Moving Average Crossover 3/10 EMA
All Resources
Metastock Explorer results (first ten only)

When Walter Scott lamented, 'O, what a tangled web we weave, When first we practise to deceive', he wasn't talking about price data manipulation but the effects are the same. If you use an indicator based on complex calculations and price data manipulation, make sure you understand and agree with the reasoning behind the structural choices.

Complexity is not always the best answer so do not select an indicator just because it is complex. Nor should indicators be selected purely on simplicity. The computational power of modern software makes the mechanics of calculation an insignificant factor in our ability or inability to construct and plot indicators. The choice of indicator should be made on the basis of the combination and approach which most closely matches your understanding of the market, and which brings out the relationships you think are important.

Crossed signals

Averages, in all their forms, help establish where today's price is in relation to prices as they were, on average, in a predefined past period. They help build the balance of probability and show the trader if her contemplated entry price is a bargain or fully priced when compared to a previous period of price behaviour.

Traders are a suspicious lot. Among the rabbits' feet, lucky coffee mugs and winning routines is a strong feeling that more is always better. Within reason this is true. Confirmation of any indicator result helps 'prove' the initial conclusion. For confirmation many traders plot two moving averages, using the crossovers as trading signals.

By overlaying a longer term moving average — one that gives very reliable signals — with a shorter term average — one that gives less reliable signals, but which is more responsive to changes in the market — the trader gets confirmation and, she hopes, the best of both worlds. When the current price is higher than the short-term average, and when the short-term average has crossed over, or turned above, the longer term average, a buying opportunity is signalled.

This simple strategy identifies a bulge in the balance of probability and, as expected, we can make it more complex in steady degrees. The moving average convergence divergence (MACD) indicator explores changing relationships between averages.

This impressive-sounding and popular indicator measures the distance between two averages, usually a 12-day and 26-day EMA. The difference between the two values is calculated and plotted as a solid fast MACD line. Then a 9-day EMA of the fast MACD line is calculated and plotted as a dashed signal line.

Briefly, the trading rules for MACD are as follows.

⊞   Buy when the fast MACD line crosses above the signal line.

⊞   Sell when the fast MACD line crosses below the signal line.

Building further complexity gives the MACD-histogram indicator. This takes its name from the vertical histogram bars used to plot the value of the fast MACD line minus the signal line. Figure 7.3 is an example of this indicator histogram plot in a MetaStock format.

Figure 7.3: MACD-histogram indicator

In screening the database to identify stocks meeting these crossover criteria MetaStock users can select the default MACD buy signal. A selection of results of an entire market using an EzyCharts search for MACD crossovers in the last 10 periods are listed in figure 7.4 in three groups of 10. Out of a universe of 2638 securities, this scan identified 374 meeting the criteria. This list must be reduced further, either by comparing it with another list, preferably one based on a different group of indicators, or perhaps the trend-following performance indicators discussed below. Ultimately, we cannot get away from the task of eyeballing the final candidates.

Our intention is to show how these groups of performance indicators are used to find specific types of information about market activity and build a list, or stock pool, of trading candidates for closer study. Readers who wish to further explore the construction and use of this and other related trend-following performance indicators are referred to Colby and Meyers's *The Encyclopedia of Technical Market Indicators*, or Elder's *Trading for a Living*.

Figure 7.4: selection of results of market search for MACD crossovers

Performance Indicators Moving Average Convergence Divergence (MACD) Entire ASX market EzyCharts Analyser results (first thirty only)		
MACD crossover	**MACD crossover**	**MACD crossover**
1 ABR	1 AJI	1 BAE
2 ABT	2 ALA	2 BAH
3 ACH	3 ALM	3 BGF
4 ADF	4 ALO	4 BHT
5 ADH	5 ANI	5 BKS
6 AFD	6 ARP	6 BLK
7 AGL	7 ASH	7 BMX
8 AGN	8 ASL	8 BNM
9 AGS	9 ATE	9 BOG
10 AIG	10 ATI	10 BRL

The trend-following indicators tell us where we are. From simple beginnings, where we recognise the neighbourhood, we layer levels of complexity until we reach the equivalent of a GPS positioning system. The objective of the search remains the same: find securities where, on balance, the current trend is changing. Effective screening using indicators has clear objectives and a clear understanding of the message each indicator is delivering.

From zero to one hundred per cent

The remainder of this chapter deals with the second group of indicators, the oscillators.

Knowing the position of today's price relative to a previous range of prices is useful, but the market does not stand still. Good trading moves in the same direction as the market, and at the same, or greater, speed. The momentum of price movements is important, but so too is the speed. These indicators answer the second question: are we breaking the speed limit?

When we drive beyond the speed limit we run the risk of making an involuntary contribution to reducing the state debt and this encourages us to slow down. Put on a broad-brimmed hat, chain a dog on the back of the utility and drive below the speed limit and some road rage maniac will encourage us to accelerate to match the flow of traffic. The smooth flow of traffic is bounded by those who drive too fast and too slow. A driver may oscillate between these extremes, but the pressure is always to return to a middle speed.

This pressure represents a probability bulge. At extremes of oscillation there is increased probability events will swing in the opposite direction. This observation is at the core of the way oscillator-based indicators are used in trading and the way we include them in performance-based screening criteria. Trading presents two problems for oscillators. First, how to measure the speed limit; and second, how to find the middle or equilibrium point when extreme speed limits change.

There are no absolute terms in trading so we measure momentum, or speed, results as a percentage—lower limit 0%, and upper limit 100%. In a percentage calculation the equilibrium point is always 50%. In extreme situations these indicators sometimes give readings above 100 and below 0, but this is unusual.

Within these upper and lower limits, experience, and testing, suggests most price activity takes place within a very broad band. The software standard stochastic indicator is ideal for this measurement. It compares where today's price closed relative to its highest and lowest trading range over the last 10 trading days. By adding a slow period we select an average figure for the high and low over the last 10 days and compare today's against the average range. This gives %K slowed by, for instance, five.

Some stochastic plots step straight into complexity by plotting a %D line. This is an average of the %K line and conceptually no different from any other 10-day moving average. Except—it is a moving average (%D) of a smoothed moving average (slow period) of an average calculation (%K).

Simple or complex, the stochastic plot sandwiches these values, expressed as percentages, between an upper and lower band usually placed at 20% and 80%.

The relative strength index (RSI) uses the average upwards price changes and average downward price changes. This value is compared with today's price range. The RSI sets speed band levels at 30% and 70%.

Most price activity, or speed, is within an equilibrium range. The stochastic plots the current calculated position within this range. The upper and lower chart bands define the areas approaching the extremes, rather like the thick lines in the high-speed areas on a speedometer. The momentum or velocity of price is also limited within an equilibrium range. The RSI style of performance indicator red-lines the extremities.

In the equilibrium range the buyers' mood almost exactly matches the sellers' mood so there is high agreement about current market value. There are fewer trading opportunities in this equilibrium range. All things being equal, prices will return to this state of rest, and when activity reaches extremes there is increased probability it will swing back towards, not the other extreme, but the point of equilibrium. Just like the speeding driver, speed slows to within the normal speed limit and his location changes.

Speed bumps

Oscillator indicators surrender information about speed, but not about location. Activity in the lower extremities is termed oversold. On the balance of probabilities price will move upwards. The indicator suggests an underlying shift in the demand and supply situation.

In trading terms, there are fewer sellers and more buyers.

An overbought reading, above 80%, suggests the current price will return to normal. This implies prices will steady within their established range before moving out of equilibrium again. In trading terms, there are now more sellers than buyers, altering the balance and forcing prices down.

Securities moving towards extremities are candidates for a return to equilibrium, and perhaps even overshooting towards the opposite extremity. Figure 7.5 lists a full market RSI search result of candidates moving into the oversold area in the last 10 periods. This full market search of 2638 securities found 22 candidates. This list is further refined against stocks that have started to recover from oversold positions and move upwards towards the equilibrium point. This distinctive signature points to possible nuggets of opportunity.

Figure 7.5: market RSI search result

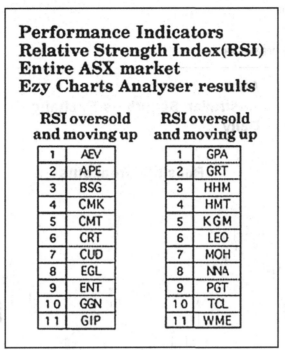

**Performance Indicators
Relative Strength Index(RSI)
Entire ASX market
Ezy Charts Analyser results**

RSI oversold and moving up		RSI oversold and moving up	
1	AEV	1	GPA
2	APE	2	GRT
3	BSG	3	HHM
4	CMK	4	HMT
5	CMT	5	KGM
6	CRT	6	LEO
7	CUD	7	MOH
8	EGL	8	NNA
9	ENT	9	PGT
10	GGN	10	TCL
11	GIP	11	WME

Oscillator performance indicators show three bulges in probability, and search criteria are adjusted to identify them. With a bulge at each extremity and a very large bulge in the middle, the trader can position all trading candidates on a performance curve. Most securities spend most of their time in the middle area and this suggests a strategy based on fading the trend. This trades from the extremity towards a return to normalcy. Charting this, as shown in figure 7.6, is the first step in assessing the further viability of the trade. Knowing where we are, and how fast we are travelling, sets the scene for a trade. A database search based on performance indicator results provides this information.

Oscillators revel in complexity. By manipulating the calculation parameters, price element, and time periods, percentage or point change, the user builds more subtle indicators. Some traders look for disagreement, or divergence, as an additional distinctive oscillator signature. When the bar chart price makes new lows and the RSI plot does the opposite, developing a series of new highs moving up from the oversold level, the indicator signals divergence as shown in figure 7.7. This is a leading trend change signal, both at market tops and bottoms, where it uncovers performance relationships obscured by the bar chart. We discuss this powerful relationship in the next chapter. The road to complexity is easily found but users are warned of blinding clouds of confusion.

Figure 7.6: possible breakouts

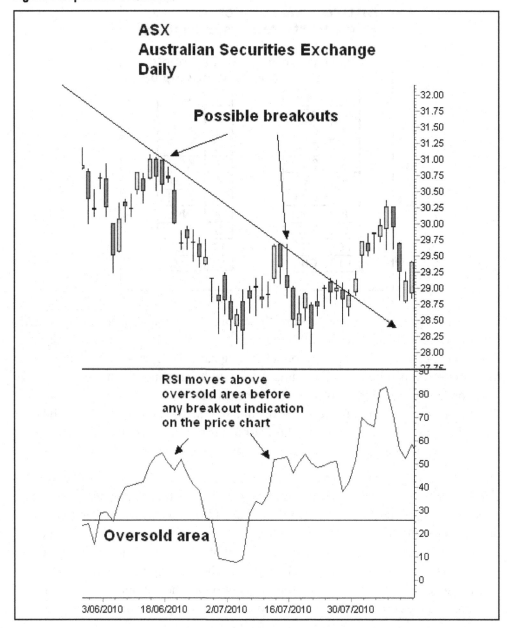

Figure 7.7: RSI divergence

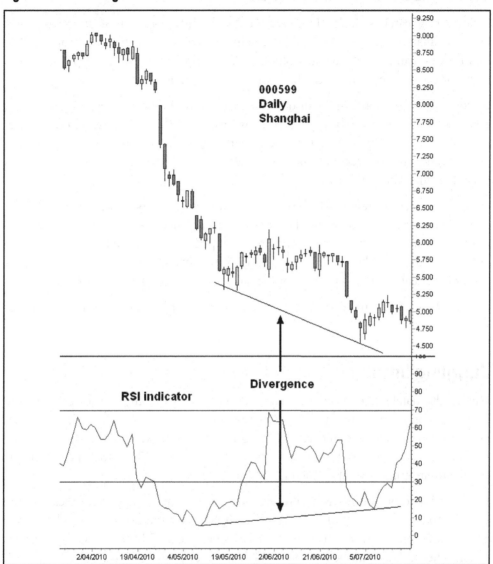

In selecting indicators, the choice between a specialised, flighty thoroughbred or a robust general duties stockhorse is yours. The market yields winning outcomes for each, but whether you ride them to the finish depends on your trading style. Complexity is not a panacea for profits so do not confuse the search for increasingly subtle signatures with the search for opportunity.

The indicator success test

Performance searches clarify the trend and its strength. Use them to find candidates for closer analysis, or to confirm initial conclusions based on eyeball observations. The lists provide candidates, but not solutions. We build better lists by applying search tools correctly rather than on the basis of complexity alone.

By comparing a screen display of our chosen indicator, and parameter settings, with a bar chart of the stock being analysed, we assess the effectiveness of our choice. All indicators must pass this test. Past chart activity shows the very best trading opportunities. If our selected indicator signals these historical opportunities then it is likely to signal future opportunities.

Traders must get this relationship correct. The indicator reflects decision points already on the bar chart. Indicator signals fit the bar chart, not vice versa. It is a sad trader who moans, 'The indicator signalled a trend break but price continued to fall'. Price validates indicator results, and the further you move away from market price — the more complex the indicator calculation — the greater the danger of losing touch with the market.

If your chosen indicator does not pick historical turning points it certainly will not select future ones.

Juggling lists

Mining the database using performance indicators to identify particular signature activity is not a substitute for further analysis. Like the previous searches, this search helps to manage our time effectively by eliminating irrelevant price activity. Those candidates passing the test are not necessarily good trades. The stock pool contains candidates meeting a set of mathematical criteria.

Each candidate on the list is finally eyeballed on a chart. There is no escaping the eyeball. You either start with the eyeball or finish with the eyeball. The chart gives additional information and the first set of numbers needed for any trading decision. When other market numbers confirm the balance of probability the trade is opened, or closed.

These classic methods remain the foundation of the search for opportunity in modern markets. The eyeball has become more important because it quickly captures the nuances of behaviour which slip through the mathematical net. In the next chapter we consider the nuances of indicator messages which also improve strategic analysis and trade execution.

Chapter 8

Divergence in a smile

Traders with basic chart analysis skills identified the collapse of world markets in January 2008 several weeks before the end of 2007. In the first week of January 2008 I was interviewed by *The Edge* financial weekly in Singapore. The article was headed 'Guppy is a Bear'. The analysis used the head and shoulder pattern to set downside targets for the DOW. The flow of disbelieving emails stopped two weeks later when the market collapsed 17%, before going on to fall more than 50% and exceed the reversal pattern targets.

Traders with these basic chart analysis skills also identified the rapid 2009 rebound from the Global Financial Crisis several months before it was acknowledged by other analysis methods. This early identification gives traders a massive advantage, putting them on the correct side of the trend at a time when markets develop major trend reversals. In 2008 they saw the dagger sheathed in a smile.

The concept of divergence is a foundation of analysis because deception is a fact of life in financial markets. Despite the failure of market transparency which contributed to the 2008 Global Financial Crisis, the regulatory responses, if anything, have increased the lack of transparency in the market. The growth of dark pools created by off-market exchanges openly selling anonymous trading is a direct challenge to transparency in the market. Divergence suggests where ulterior motives may lie. The Chinese call this a strategy of 'A dagger sheathed in a smile'. In the market we detect this with divergence analysis.

This dark side of trading is discussed in chapter 12, Dark side trading analysis. Divergence analysis helps shine a light into some of these dark corners. The most dangerous dagger sheathed in a smile comes from the market itself. As traders we need to be aware of situations where the strategy is applied against us.

The flow of misleading information from companies is unceasing. If the information was accurate, reliable and trustworthy then we would have little need for the financial press and the hordes of analysts who fill brokerages and fund management companies. It sounds a harsh statement, but not when we consider these media and analytical activities in more detail. One of the primary tasks of the financial media is to discover, uncover and report the difference between the purported performance of a company and the actual performance. The general public relies on the auditing profession to highlight these gaps. This trust is misplaced, as the ongoing sudden collapses of companies with 'audit'-approved balance sheets attests.

Early identification of trend changes has always been one of the primary achievements and objectives of technical analysis. The volatility of modern markets has increased the speed and frequency of trend changes so it has become more important to identify changes early. The growth of dark pools and the way they suck liquidity out of the market and into less transparent trading environments also contributes to tsunami-like trend changes. The trading behaviour is hidden in the dark pool just as the initial surge of displaced water is hidden in the deep ocean after an earthquake. The tsunami develops only when the surge hits shallow water, or in this environment, when the buy or sell orders are revealed to the public market.

Subtle warnings of the market tsunami are delivered by divergence behaviour. The RSI divergence and the chart pattern head and shoulder behaviour are key leading indicators of developing trend change. The market looks good, apparently smiling on investors and traders, but the divergence signal reveals a dagger hidden behind the smile. These strategic analysis tools give traders the opportunity to protect profits and prepare to trade the opposite side of the trend.

RSI oscillator divergence

Divergence is an early warning sign of a trend change, revealing the dagger sheathed in a smile. It is most useful when applied to a daily chart, as shown in figure 8.1. Divergence is used to confirm a sudden drop, or indicate when a slow trend change is the start of a new downtrend rather than just temporary trend weakness. The trend development and divergence by point 2 had already alerted traders to prepare for a trend collapse at point 3.

Tactics

⊞   Provides early warning of trend weakness. This may change the tactics applied to a particular trade, or the stop loss methods used.

⊞   RSI is the dominant indicator, overriding trend strength signals from other indicators.

⊞   Primary usefulness is to alert the trader to trend weakness. It is not useful for timing.

Rules

⊞   Trend lines are based on joining the peaks or valleys of price activity. Trend lines are not applied to the detail of intervening trends.

⊞   Trend lines join the peaks or valleys of the RSI but only those peaks or valleys appearing above or below the trigger lines. Valid signals appear above 70 or below 30 on the RSI.

⊞   Peaks and valleys within the body of the indicator between 70 and 30 on the RSI are unimportant.

⊞   Divergence occurs when the peak or valley trend line on the price chart moves in the opposite direction to the peak or valley trend line on the RSI display.

⊞   Divergence appears in several different configurations, shown in figure 8.2.

Figure 8.1: RSI oscillator divergence

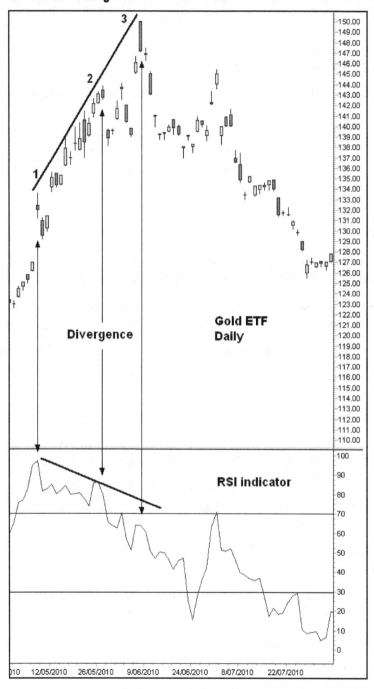

Figure 8.2: divergence configurations

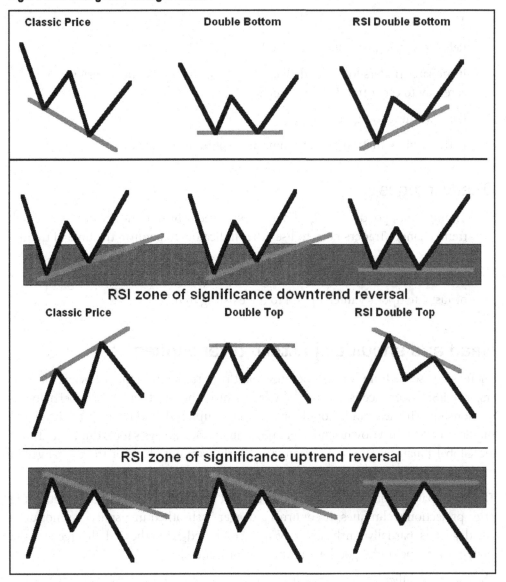

Advantages

- This is a leading signal.

- Reliable signal, particularly with RSI.

- It prepares traders for a trend change and tells them it is time to listen more carefully to other trend change signals.

- Early warning to tighten stops.

- Early warning that time has become an important risk factor.

Disadvantages

- Timing is not good. The signal may appear weeks or months ahead of the actual trend change. Traders need to use other indicators to confirm the time of trend change.

- Does not indicate the degree or level of trend reversal. This may be significant, or just a temporary interruption to the existing trend.

Head and shoulder pattern divergences

There is no escape from eyeballs because chart patterns capture the behaviour of traders. The RSI divergence is a statistical relationship. The chart pattern is a behavioural relationship. The head and shoulder pattern in an uptrend, and the inverted head and shoulder pattern in a downtrend, were powerful market analysis tools during and after the Global Financial Crisis. They provided early warning of major trend changes in markets. They also apply to individual stocks.

This three-part pattern signals a trend reversal. It is used to set downside targets using price projection techniques. It confirms a dagger is sheathed in a smile, but not until the dagger is partially unsheathed. When combined with the RSI divergence, the analysis gives the trader good warning of major trend changes.

The pattern is difficult to recognise until it has been almost fully completed. This makes it a confirming indicator. The full pattern is shown in figure 8.3. It is most usefully applied to setting future downside targets. When prices reach the target level, the trader may decide to close short positions or look for long-side trading opportunities.

Figure 8.3: head and shoulder pattern

Tactics

- Use other indicators to confirm the end of the trend and exit as the right shoulder forms on a rally.

- Definitely exit once the right shoulder has formed and the neckline has been penetrated.

- Use the downside targets to manage short-side trades.

- Use the downside targets to prepare for possible long-side rebound trades.

Rules

- The shoulders and head are clearly defined rally and retreat patterns.

- The neckline connects the bottom of the left and right shoulders.

- The neckline may slope up, down, or remain horizontal. The degree of slope has no influence on the degree of reliability of the pattern.

- Pattern is confirmed first by the rally and retreat forming the right shoulder.

- Pattern is confirmed secondly by the inability of price to rise above the neckline after the retreat below the neckline.

- The distance between the neckline and the head is measured.

- This distance is projected downwards from the neckline to set the downside targets. Projection is most reliable when it matches an existing support level.

- Targets should be regarded as minimum targets.

Advantages

- Reliable for setting downside targets when they match an existing downside target.

- Useful for trading the short side.

- Helps to define potential rebound points.

Disadvantages

- Difficult to recognise in advance. Recognition usually only comes, at earliest, as the right shoulder forms.

The market has an essential rule: trust no-one. Divergence analysis, either with an oscillator or using a reliable chart reversal pattern, helps traders make better strategic decisions. Suspecting a market is about to turn determines the trading methods. The selection of methods is further supported with a clearer understanding of just who is driving the market and this requires better trend analysis, which is the subject of the next chapter.

Chapter 9

Market trend foundations

The core of our trading approach is the Guppy Multiple Moving Average. In terms of its chart display it is a deceptively simple indicator that summarises a complex set of market relationships. This indicator allows us to develop a better understanding of what is happening in the market. This analysis method is the foundation of the global market analysis work we do with CNBC in Asia, Europe and the US. It is the foundation of the analysis support we provide to fund managers in the US and elsewhere. It is also the strategic foundation of our own trading. The next two chapters explore the basis and construction of this indictor. The following chapter then explores advanced applications to intraday trading and a new analysis of trend volatility.

Some trends turn out to be nasty characters with concealed weaknesses leading to sudden trend collapses. Others just plod along slowly, adding to your profits day after day. Identifying the difference in the nature of the trend—fast, slow or parabolic—and the character of the trend—well supported and dependable, bedevilled by trading activity, dominated by a trading bubble—provides us with a significant trading edge. It allows us to select the most appropriate trading strategy and the best trading tools for managing the selected trade. It is foolish to treat a rally in a prolonged downtrend as the beginning of a new uptrend. When the rally collapses there is a tendency to hold onto the stock because we convince ourselves the rally retreat is temporary and the uptrend will resume. Such hopes pave the way to financial disaster. Understanding the nature and character of the trend is essential.

The stocks in figure 9.1 are clear examples of different types of trends. Not every chart you look at has this clarity. We use the Guppy Multiple Moving Average (GMMA) to define the character of the trend. This is much more useful than using just two moving averages because the GMMA captures the character of the trend and the relationship between two dominant forces in the market—the traders and the investors. The GMMA was introduced in *Trading Tactics* and expanded on in *Trend Trading*. Since then the indicator has remained the same, but the range and sophistication of its application to a variety of trading situations, markets and financial instruments have increased substantially.

We apply the GMMA to each candidate on our stock pool selection list. Those without good trend character and a suitable nature for our purposes are dropped from our final list. The GMMA is a standard tool in Guppytraders Essentials, MetaStock, OmniTrader, EzyChart, BullCharts, Chart Nexus and other end-of-day charting programs. It is included in MetaStock Professional and NextVIEW intraday charting packages and can be programmed into many of the platforms used by CFD providers and into Gousen and other Chinese charting programs. The GMMA is included as a systems selection test and exploration option in OmniTrader, giving users advanced and sophisticated screening and filtering capabilities. The indicator is constructed by combining the groups of moving averages as discussed below.

Tracking inferred activity

The GMMA indicator tracks the inferred activity of the two major groups in the market. These are investors and traders. Traders are always probing for a change in the trend. In a downtrend they take a trade in anticipation of a new uptrend developing. If it does not develop they get out of the trade quickly. If the trend changes they stay with the trade but continue to use a short-term management approach. No matter how long the uptrend remains in place, the trader is always alert for a potential trend change.

Figure 9.1: examples of different types of trends

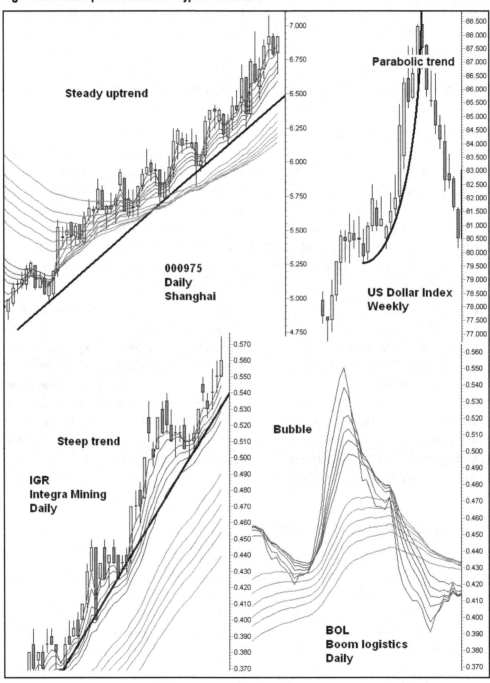

We start with analysis of a daily chart. For reasons covered later, the same analysis is applied to intraday charts. We track the traders' inferred activity by using a group of short-term moving averages. These are 3-, 5-, 8-, 10-, 12- and 15-day exponentially calculated moving averages.

The traders always lead the change in trend. Their buying pushes up prices in anticipation of a trend change. The trend survives only if other buyers also come into the market. Strong trends are supported by long-term investors. These are the true gamblers in the market because they tend to have a great deal of faith in their analysis. They believe they are right, and it takes a lot to convince them otherwise. When they buy a stock they invest money, their emotions, their reputation and their ego. They simply do not like to admit to a mistake.

The investor takes more time to recognise the change in a trend but he always follows the lead set by traders. We track the investors' inferred activity by using 30-, 35-, 40-, 45-, 50- and 60-day exponentially calculated moving averages. The length of each average is increased by one trading week. We jump two weeks from 50 to 60 days in the final series because this is a reference average used by many fundamental investors.

The GMMA grew from two observations about moving averages. First is the lack of clues about future behaviour from moving averages, and second is the lag in the moving average crossover signal.

The classic uptrend signal is generated when the short-term moving average crosses above the long-term moving average. The perfect examples shown in trading books are just too perfect when they show a moving average crossover followed by a new uptrend. Real trading is often much messier, and the chart extracts in figure 9.2 highlight the problem. When a moving average combination converges almost to the point of a crossover it provides no useful information about the probability of future behaviour.

We cannot tell which of these convergences is most likely to lead to a collapse of the trend or a continuation of the trend. Make the correct choice and we get to stay in a trade where the trend continues steadily upwards. Select the wrong chart, and the trend collapses very rapidly. These two charts show a decision point based on a 10- and 30-day moving average crossover. They both look exactly the same. Had we purchased stock previously, then this signal would have us reaching for our sell orders. Unfortunately one of these stocks goes on to add 80% in the following weeks. The other loses 32%. Can you select the winning stock based on the moving average display? It is a matter of luck, not judgement.

Figure 9.2: moving average examples

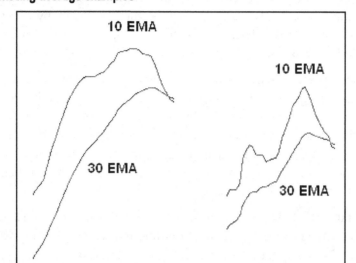

Despite the so-called power and reliability of a moving average crossover, at significant turning points we cannot usefully choose between chart A and chart B because we cannot understand the nature of the trend using this indicator combination. A pair of moving averages is a useful trading tool but it simply does not give the trader enough information to decide where the balance of probabilities lies.

The GMMA provides a clear view and understanding, and this is the information we use when applying it to the exit question posed above. The eventual developments for charts A and B are revealed in a note at the end of this chapter.

The second starting point for the development of the GMMA was the lag between the time of a genuine trend break and the time a moving average crossover entry signal was generated. Our focus was on the change from a downtrend to an uptrend. Our preferred early warning tool was the straight edge trend line, which is accurate and simple to use. However, some breakouts were false and the straight edge trend line provided no way to separate the false from the genuine. The count back line discussed in chapter 21, Counting back the profit, was one solution.

On the other hand, the moving average crossover based on a 10- and 30-day calculation provided a higher level of certainty the trend break was genuine. However, the crossover signal might come many days after the initial trend break signal. This time lag was further extended because the signal was based on end-of-day prices. We see the exact crossover today, and if we were courageous, we could enter tomorrow. Generally traders waited for another day to verify the crossover had actually taken place, delaying the entry until two days after the actual crossover. This time lag often meant price had moved up considerably by the time the trade was opened.

The standard solution calls for a shorter term moving average and this moves the crossover point further back in time so it was closer to the breakout signalled by a close above the straight edge trend line. Some combinations are shown in figure 9.3. The drawback is that the shorter the moving average, the less reliable it becomes.

Figure 9.3: moving average combinations

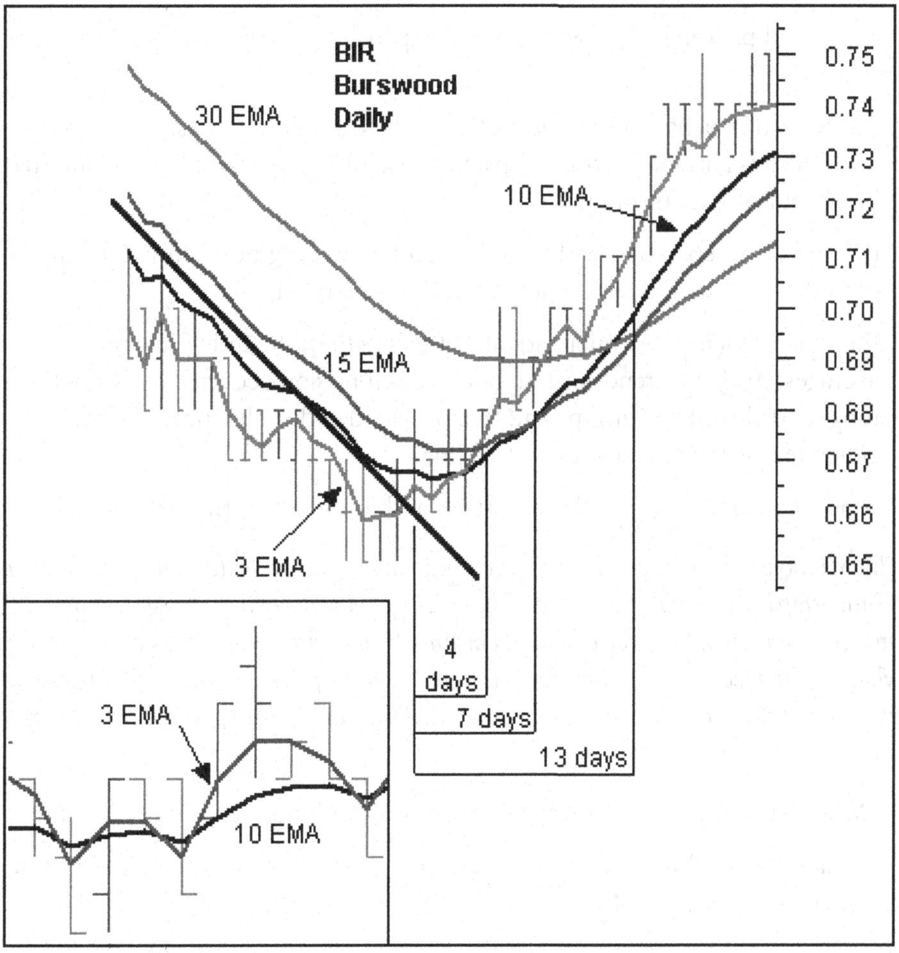

Finding the GMMA

Serendipity and luck had a role to play in the development of the GMMA. In exploring these combinations I initially worked with a single test stock. The charting program I had at the time limited the number of simultaneous moving average plots on the screen. For convenience I used the maximum number of six short-term averages. Later I cleared the screen display, leaving the original bar chart intact, and applied six long-term moving averages. When these multiple short-term and long-term exponential moving averages were placed on the same underlying bar chart five significant features emerged. They were:

- a repeated pattern of compression and expansion in a group of six short-term averages

- a repeated pattern of compression and expansion in a group of six long-term averages

- the pattern of behaviour was fractally repeated across different time frames. These short- and long-term groups were useful in understanding the inferred behaviour of traders and investors

- the degree of separation within groups and between groups provides a method of understanding the nature of the trend and trend change

- the synchronicity was independent of the length of the individual moving averages. At major trend turning points compression occurred across both long- and short-term groups and this provided early validation of signals generated by the straight edge trend line.

This conclusion emerges from these features and it underpins the GMMA:

The relationship between moving averages and price is better understood as a relationship between value and price. The crossover of two moving averages represented an agreement on value over two different time frames. In a continuous open auction, which is the mechanism of the market, agreement on price and value was transient and temporary. Such agreement often preceded substantial changes in the direction of the trend.

The GMMA became a tool for identifying the probability of trend development.

These broad relationships and the more advanced relationships used with the GMMA are summarised in figure 9.4.

Figure 9.4: GMMA relationships

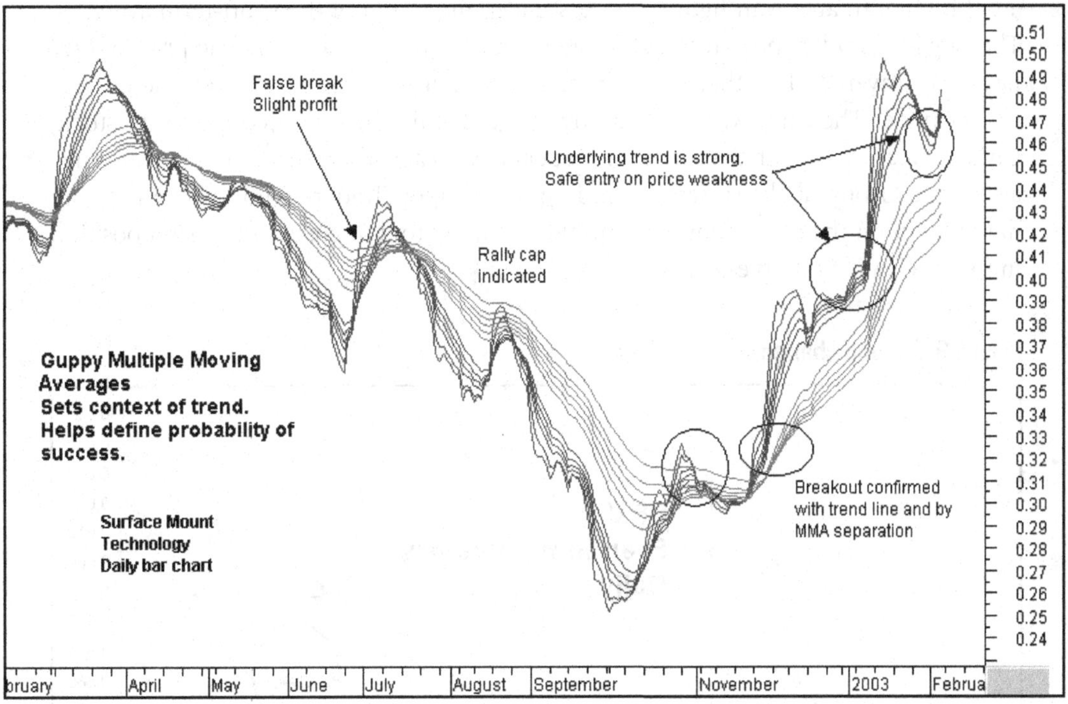

The chart illustrates the most straightforward application of the GMMA, and it worked well with 'V'-shaped trend changes. It is not about taking the lag out of the moving average calculation. The GMMA is used to validate a prior trend break signal by examining the relationship between price and value. Once the initial trend break signal is validated by the GMMA the trader is able to enter a breakout trade with a higher level of confidence. The GMMA is about understanding relationships between the dominant participants in the market.

Finding character

The GMMA is used to assess the probability the trend break initially shown by the straight edge trend line is genuine. The vertical line in figure 9.5 shows the chart decision point. We want to know at this point if the stock is a buy signal for a continuation of the trend breakout above the trend line. The GMMA assists in this decision, and to highlight this we only show the GMMA without the background price candles.

We start by observing the activity of the short-term group. This tells us what traders are thinking. In area A in figure 9.5 we see a compression of the short-term averages. This suggests traders have reached an agreement on price and value. The price of PRV has been driven so low that many traders believe it is worth more than the current traded price. The only way to take advantage of this 'cheap' price is to buy stock. Unfortunately many other short-term traders have reached the same conclusion. They also want to buy at this price. A bidding war erupts. Traders who believe they are missing out on the opportunity outbid their competitors to ensure they get a position in the stock at favourable prices.

Figure 9.5: trend change

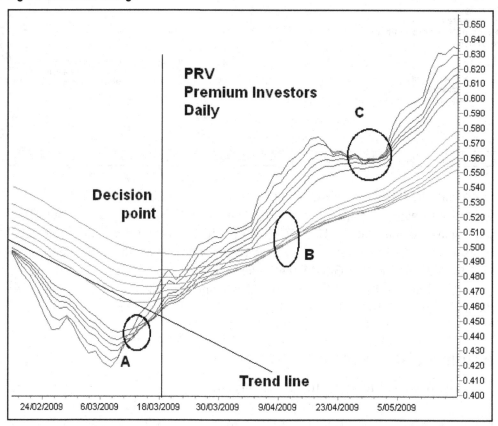

The compression of these averages shows agreement about price and value. The expansion of the group shows traders are excited about future prospects of increased value even though prices are still rising. These traders buy in anticipation of a trend change. They are probing for a trend change.

We use the straight edge trend line to signal an increased probability of a trend change. When this signal is generated we observe this change in direction and separation in the short-term group of averages. We know traders believe this stock has a future. We want confirmation the long-term investors are also buying this confidence.

The long-term group of averages at the decision point shows signs of compression and the beginning of a change in direction. Notice how quickly the compression starts and how this signals the decisive change in direction. This is despite the longest average of 60 days which we would normally expect to lag well behind any trend change. This compression in the long-term group is evidence of the synchronicity relationship that makes the GMMA so useful. This compression and change in direction tells us there is an increased probability the change in trend direction is for real and sustainable. This encourages us to buy the stock soon after the decision point shown.

The GMMA picks up a seismic shift in the market's sentiment as it happens, even though we are using a 60-day moving average. This compression and eventual crossover within the long-term group takes place in area B. The trend change is confirmed. The agreement among investors about price and value cannot last because where there is agreement some people see opportunity. Many investors missed out on joining the trend change prior to area B, and now the change is confirmed they want to get part of the action. Generally investors move larger funds than traders so their activity in the market has a larger impact.

The latecomers can only buy stock if they outbid their competitors. The stronger the initial trend, the more pressure to get an early position. This increased bidding supports the trend and is shown by the way the long-term group continues to move up, and by the way the long-term group of averages separates. The wider the spread the more powerful the underlying trend.

Even traders retain faith in this trend change. The sell-off in area C is not very strong. The group of short-term averages dips towards the long-term group and then bounces away quickly. The long-term group of averages shows investors take this opportunity to buy stock at temporarily weakened prices. The degree of separation in the long-term group remains relatively constant, confirming the strength of the emerging trend.

The temporary collapse of the short-term group comes after a 30% appreciation in price. Short-term traders exit taking short-term profits, and this is reflected by the compression and collapse of the short-term group of averages. As long-term investors step into the market and buy PRV at these weakened prices, traders sense the trend is well supported. Their activity takes off, and the short-term group of averages rebounds, separates, and then runs parallel to the long-term group as the trend continues.

The GMMA identifies a significant change in the market's opinion about PRV. The compression of the short-term and long-term groups validates the trend break signal generated by a close above the straight edge trend line. Using this basic application of the GMMA, the trader has the confidence necessary to buy PRV at or just after the decision point shown on the chart extract.

Probability and GMMA

When we apply the GMMA in figure 9.6 we gain a better idea of the probability of the trend line break actually being the start of a new uptrend. Again we have shown the position of the trend line but deleted the price chart display so you can concentrate on the GMMA relationships. The key relationship is the level of separation in the long-term group of averages and the trend direction they are travelling. At both decision point A and decision point B, the long-term group is well separated. Investors do not like this stock so every time there is a rise in prices they take advantage of this to sell. Their selling overwhelms the market and drives prices down so the downtrend continues. The trend line breakout is quickly identified as false.

The degree of separation between the two groups of moving averages also makes it more difficult for either of the rallies to successfully change the direction of the trend. The most likely outcome is a weak rally followed by a collapse and continuation of the downtrend. This observation keeps the trader and investor out of BKN.

Looking forward to the right edge of the chart we do see a convergence between the short-term group of averages and the long-term group of averages. Additionally the long-term group begins to narrow down, suggesting a developing level of agreement about price and value among investors. At decision point B the 10-day moving average closes above the 30-day moving average, generating a classic moving average buy signal.

Using the GMMA we ignore this signal and the other GMMA convergence relationships. This decision is based on a more advanced understanding of the relationships revealed by the GMMA, and we examine these strategies in the next chapter.

Figure 9.6: false breakout

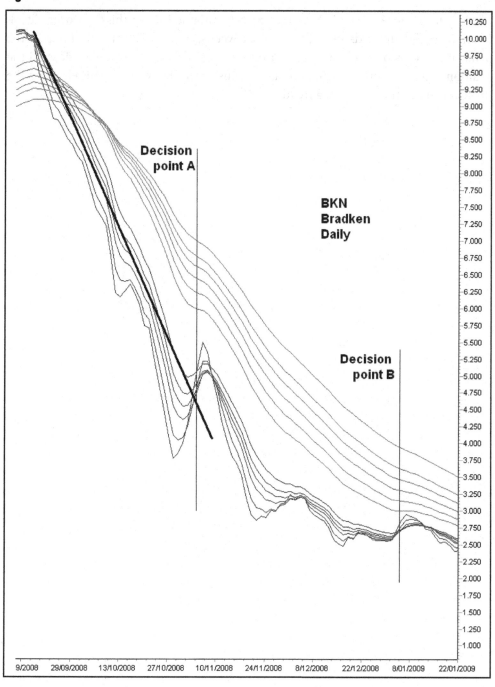

Note:

Chart A in figure 9.2 lost 32% in the three months following this crossover signal. Chart B moved upwards over the next six weeks, adding 80% to the price at the point of this crossover. If we focus just on moving average crossovers we lose all the additional information a moving average tells us about the way the market values the stock and supports the existing trend.

Annex to chapter 9

Volatility cluster behaviour

Analysis by Adam Cox originally published in our weekly newsletter, Tutorials in Applied Technical Analysis

Some technical indicators seem to be more robust than others. Some seem to work fine, only to fall apart at the most inopportune time. But why? Is there a specific reason? Is the answer simply to use more indicators? Like most traders I have asked these same questions over the years. To satisfactorily answer these questions, however, I had to start off at what I call step number one — develop a 'market philosophy'. In other words, start the trading equation from the bottom up to understand the share price time series. Although share price time series may be classed as having a type of random walk, they have a rich texture. We start with a brief look at one of the elements that gives 'body' to some of this texture.

'Heteroskedasticity' describes a fairly simple concept and in essence means variance or volatility changes over time. I am using the term volatility loosely here in lieu of variance or standard deviation. The Greek word 'hetero' means to be different, while 'skedasticity' simply means variance.

This phenomenon may be called 'volatility clustering'. Share price time series have a rich texture. To examine volatility clustering we may take the difference of each price as illustrated in figure 9A.1. This technique is used a lot by econometrics to create what is known as time series 'stationarity'. This stationarity simply allows the time series' mean and standard deviation to be measured. Westpac's return series displays a familiar bell-shaped distribution curve, shown in figure 9A.2.

Figure 9A.1: return transformation illustrated

Time	Price	Return		
1	10			
2	10.20	(10.20-10.00)/10	= 2%	
3	10.50	(10.50-10.20)/10.20	= 3%	
4	10.35	(10.35-10.50)/10.50	= -1.4%	

Figure 9A.2: asymmetric volatility

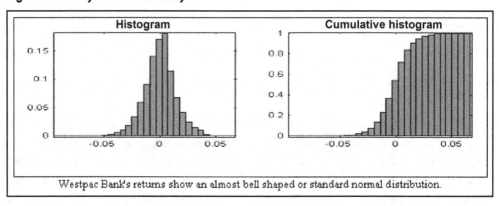

Westpac Bank's returns show an almost bell shaped or standard normal distribution.

Share price time series also display another phenomenon: asymmetric volatility, related to heteroskedasticity. Shares tend to display more volatility on the downside than the upside. This phenomenon may be explained by the leverage effect. Volatility appears to be higher on the downside because margin loans are called in when the share price falls. Margin loan–based selling drives price lower and with more momentum than upside price raises. This phenomenon cannot be attributed to short selling alone. An investor with a current long position may exit that position at market, whereas the short seller may not make a new low by his selling.

The GMMA captures the behaviour of heteroskedasticity and auto-regressive processes at 'levels' rather than being an oscillator. The GMMA describes this phenomenon in an effective and deliberate manner shown in figure 9A.3. Daryl Guppy writes in *Trading Tactics* '… the signal we read is not price, but behaviour'. This indicator has the advantage of showing these phenomena or behaviours at levels, as well as displaying long and short directional characteristics; something a pure volatility indicator does not indicate. Many oscillator-based techniques, including the stochastic oscillator, are simply averaging processes, and cannot reconcile the effects of volatility clustering.

Figure 9A.3: volatility expansion and collapse

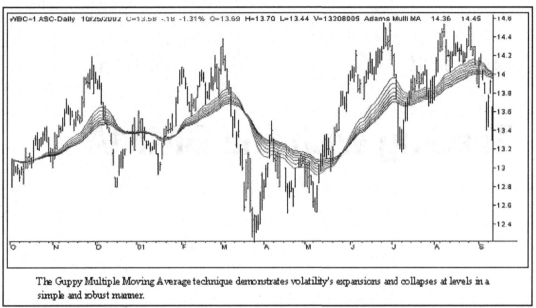

The Guppy Multiple Moving Average technique demonstrates volatility's expansions and collapses at levels in a simple and robust manner.

The GMMA describes heteroskedasticity and serial auto-correlation in a simple and robust manner, while retaining price direction qualities, something a pure volatility indicator cannot do. This indicator also has the advantage of dynamically illustrating these phenomena or behaviours at levels, as well as displaying long and short directional characteristics; something a pure volatility indicator cannot do.

Chapter 10

Trading with the GMMA

The market in all time frames is dominated by investors and traders. Bulls and bears are irrelevant because they only describe our emotions. Investors and traders are significant because they have very different, but consistent, behaviours in the market. They are the anchor points providing continuity between market behaviour before and after the 2008 Global Financial Crisis. In the next chapter we show how they contribute in a new approach to trend analysis, but we start with the way the GMMA captures investor and trader relationships. The analysis of these relationships enables traders to make a better decision about the most appropriate trading tactics to apply to the trade.

These basic trading environments provide the foundation for more advanced applications of the GMMA in intraday trading, and for the trading of more volatile derivative instruments including CFDs, currencies and indices. Our preference is to use the GMMA to identify a trending environment so we can join an established trend. This is not breakout trading. The trade-off for the loss of potential profits available from an earlier entry into the trend is an increase in the reliability of the trend. This means fewer false exit signals. However, increased modern market volatility has seen a surge in false exit signals so a better understanding of underlying trend strength is essential. The foundations of the GMMA trading application are used to create a Trend Volatility Line, discussed in the next chapter. But first the GMMA trade foundations, which have become more important in modern markets where price volatility has become more erratic. We need better analysis of the underlying trend strength to know if it is safe to enter a trend showing high levels of price volatility.

How we decide to trade these trends and select the entry tactic depends upon our understanding of the relationship between traders—the short-term group of averages —and investors—represented by the long-term group of averages. We focus on the activity of the traders because the trends are underpinned by committed long-term investors.

These trend trading opportunities use the clearest of the GMMA relationships. We are not concerned with how the trend change was initiated. We are not called to make a judgement about the degree of compression at the point where the old trend changes to a new uptrend, nor is timing a vital issue.

Our interest is in the nature and character of the established trend. We look for low-risk, high-probability trend trades. Our intention is to either take a bite from the trend or to get out of the trend *after* it has started to deliver trend weakness or end-of-trend signals. The GMMA helps our analysis of the trend, but trading discipline turns this analysis into trading success. For comparison we also examine the effectiveness of a standard two moving average combination indicator.

Fast-moving steep trend

We do not have to be among the first to see an opportunity to be able to benefit from it. Often we see trends that developed over several weeks and we have just one question: is it safe to join the trend?

Often traders rely just on two moving averages for trading entry and exit decisions. The 10-day exponential moving average is shown as the thick black line in figure 10.1. It is well above the 30-day moving average. The current price action is above the 10-day moving average but this just confirms this is a strong, fast-moving trend. Price volatility has expanded with daily price moves of 7% to 10%. Is it safe to buy on the next day for a continuation of the uptrend or is this retreat the beginning of a trend collapse? The combination of two moving averages gives us no additional information about the strength of the underlying trend and the probability of the trend continuing. Once we move beyond a simple crossover analysis, the information provided by two moving averages is limited.

Figure 10.1: fast-moving trend

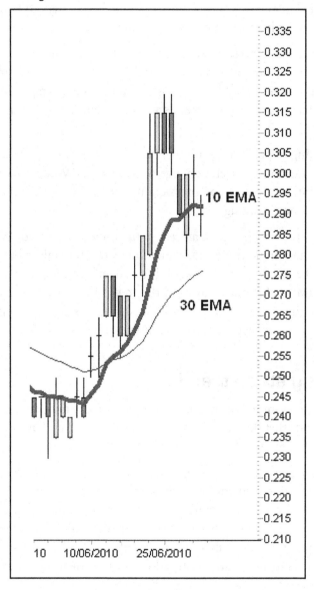

Figure 10.2: GMMA confirmation of breakout

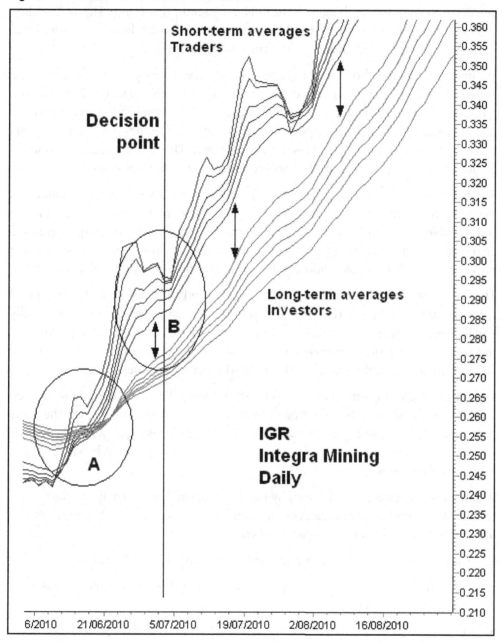

The information we extract from the GMMA display in figure 10.2 is much more detailed and useful in making a decision about joining this trend. The vertical line shows the decision point on the previous chart extract. The first feature we note is that the activity of the GMMA in area A confirms the trend breakout.

We first want to know how the long-term investors are thinking. This is an optimistic crowd. Once the uptrend had started the long-term group of averages quickly separated into a broad band. The wider the band, the more stable the trend and the more strongly it is supported. Although the slope of the trend is steep, the long-term group suggests there is a scramble among investors to buy this stock. The development behaviour of the long-term group duplicates the way the short-term group has spread out.

The behaviour of traders also provides important information about the stability of the trend. If the trend break is dominated by speculative trading then we expect to see considerable expansion and compression activity in the short-term group of averages as traders sell and collect quick profits. Prior to the decision point we see trading activity is limited. This observation is also confirmed by future trend developments.

The short-term group of averages quickly separated and remained separated by around the same amount. By the time they reach area B the averages are moving broadly parallel to each other. The expansion has slowed. This trend is well supported by investors, and by traders who may have entered with a short-term time frame but who are now inclined to hold onto the stock while the trend continues.

Finally, the degree of separation between the averages, shown by the double-headed arrows, has stabilised. The two groups of averages are maintaining much the same degree of separation and moving parallel to each other. Looking forward, the second double-headed arrow shows how the degree of separation remained relatively constant as the trend continued.

Although this is a steep trend driven by momentum, the GMMA analysis shows it is a low-risk trend trade entry at the decision point. In summary the GMMA provides this identification information for a mid-trend entry:

- short-term group is well separated and moved into a parallel pattern
- limited compression and expansion activity in the short-term group means less speculative trading
- long-term group separated quickly and develops a steady parallel relationship. Group is widely separated

⊞ distance between groups of averages has started to stabilise, confirming trend continuity.

Longer term steady trend with limited trading activity

Trend stability depends on two factors. The first is the level of support offered by long-term investors. This is shown by the degree of slope and the degree of separation in the longer term group of averages. The second is the level of speculative trading activity. This is shown by the frequency of compression and expansion behaviour, and the degree of rally and retreat shown in the short-term group of averages. The GMMA indicator provides a lot more information about the character of the trend and the most appropriate trading tactics.

We start the analysis by examining the activity of the long-term investors in figure 10.3. The vertical line shows the decision point. The long-term group of averages is well separated and moving in a broadly parallel pattern. There is no expansion in the averages. This has already taken place so now there is just steady buying when prices weaken. This strong parallel pattern with good separation indicates investors are still prepared to accumulate stock.

It is clear the trend in BOR is less steep than IGR in figure 10.2. This gentler slope is a characteristic of long-term enduring trends well supported by long-term investors. This strong underlying trend has a low probability of a sudden collapse. Our primary focus is on entry analysis for joining a trend. When this type of trend ends it is most likely to involve a slow rollover, giving investors ample opportunity to make a dignified exit.

The second feature of interest is trading activity that is revealed by the level of compression and expansion in the short-term group of averages. There are four complete examples of compression and expansion on the chart prior to the vertical decision point line. This is gentle trading activity. There is no fast and dramatic run up in prices followed by an equally dramatic collapse. Instead we see a steady, slow, almost cyclical expansion and contraction like waves constantly lapping at the coastline during a rising tide. The limited nature of this trading activity confirms there are no wild swings in volatility in this trend. There is no excitement, but there is a steady, rising trend.

The final feature we assess is the degree and nature of the separation between the two groups of averages. The thick vertical lines are all the same length. Prior to the decision point, the degree of separation remains approximately the same. The short-term group and the long-term group are moving parallel to each other. There is a greater level of trading activity, but it is not strong enough to pose a serious threat to the integrity of the trend. When prices pull back, investors step in. When traders sell there is barely a falter in the uptrend. Looking forward on the chart we see the degree of separation remains relatively constant over the coming months.

Figure 10.3: GMMA showing steady trend

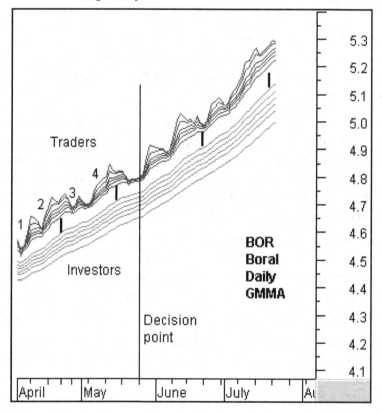

These GMMA relationships show BOR is an excellent stock for position traders and investors who want to join a well-established, stable trend. Both benefit from regular opportunities to buy the stock as prices make a temporary retreat within the context of the trend. These retreats may trigger an exit signal based on a straight edge trend line analysis, but they are unlikely to pose a serious threat to the continuation of the underlying trend. GMMA analysis confirms a low-risk trend trade at the decision point

114

and stocks with these GMMA relationships pass the fourth stock selection test. In summary the GMMA provides the following identification information for a mid-trend entry:

- long-term group is well separated in a parallel pattern. Investor support is strong and steady

- the compression and expansion activity in the short-term group occurs over a small range suggesting low volatility and limited trading activity

- traders are not probing for a change in the trend as dips do not carry the short-term group down to the long-term group of averages

- distance between groups of averages is constant. A parallel separation confirms trend stability.

The GMMA provides the trader with a greater level of information about the nature, character and stability of the trend than information obtainable from other analysis methods. This information allows the trader or investor to develop a more appropriate strategy. In a sound, well-established trend, less management supervision is required and the entry price is not as critical to the success of the trade. In an unstable trend subject to high trading activity the entry price is important and these conditions call for more frequent management, making them less suited for longer term investing.

The comparative steepness of the trend behaviour of figures 10.2 and 10.3 has been deliberately selected because it is significant. The trend in figure 10.3 was common in markets prior to 2008. The trend in figure 10.2 is more typical of market conditions following the rebound from the Global Financial Crisis in 2009. Trends are steeper, move more quickly, collapse more suddenly and contain higher levels of price volatility which may trigger many false exit signals. These are the new challenges for traders. Overcoming these challenges requires a change in thinking about the way a trend is defined.

The GMMA captures the fractal behaviour of markets, and in the next chapter we show how this is applied on smaller time scales to trade intraday markets. We also show how the foundations of the GMMA are used to understand trend behaviour and trend volatility. This separates trend volatility from price volatility and provides an effective method for managing a trade.

Chapter 11

Trend Volatility Line analysis

Price volatility or trend volatility? What is the better measure of understanding the trend? Before the Global Financial Crisis these were not questions traders worried about. Now it is one of the defining questions and challenges for traders and investors. Market volatility is not an aberration. Market volatility is an integral part of the new market conditions.

Understanding the behaviour of price trends used to be simple. Using a variety of methods traders analysed price volatility. Some of these methods look very different, but in reality they were measuring the same features of trend activity in different ways. A simple trend line measures price volatility in the trend. When the volatility increases to the extent that price closes below an uptrend line the trend is considered to have finished. While price and price volatility remain above the line the trend is intact.

The Guppy count back line, discussed in chapter 21, Counting back the profit, also captures price volatility. It creates a changing, self-adjusting range of price volatility, and sets a stop loss or protect profit stop based on the most recent significant price volatility. In many trends this measure of price volatility alone is enough to provide long-term exposure to a rising trend and a successful trade.

Indicators such as the traders' application of Average True Range, discussed in chapter 23, Getting ahead of the curves, use a time-based measure of price volatility. The true range of price is calculated, and movements beyond these levels are considered as harbingers of trend change. It's the change in the volatility of price that triggers the change in the trend.

Even techniques seemingly quite different in their approach to defining the trend have their foundations in price volatility. They include Darvas trading methods, which define a boxed range of price and use this as a trigger signal for trend continuation or end-of-trend behaviour. Stepping into more exotic areas we include Renko and Kagi charts.

There is a rich history of using price volatility as a substitute for defining the trend and, by inference, as a definition of trend volatility. These analysis methods continue to give good results for many stocks, but increasingly these methods also deliver many false exit signals. The reliability of these indicators has been challenged now that volatility wipes have become a regular feature of modern markets.

The volatility wipe is a fast price move lasting for one or two periods that delivers classic end-of-trend signals, as shown in figure 11.1. These are large-range price days. Call them spikes or dips, the character remains the same. They are unexpected in terms of trend strength, and they fall well outside the range of the previous price activity. The volatility wipe takes out stop loss positions and many traders close their trades. Then the price recovers just as dramatically and the pre-existing trend continues.

We think these volatility wipes are facilitated by the changes in trading execution. They are facilitated by algorithmic trading, by flash trading and the ability of traders to act immediately on their fears and emotions. The speed of trade execution increases the speed of reaction, and the size of the reaction and counter-reaction. This creates a permanent and erratic increase in volatility and it gives a new structure to market behaviour.

This increase is seen in end-of-day trading and also in intraday trading. It becomes a major threat when positions are being established because a volatility wipe destroys the opening position. This is a type of stress test. The stress is countered by simply using a wider stop, but this has consequences for position sizing. It makes for smaller trades with good risk management, or larger trades with poorer risk management. Or people just trade as they have in previous markets and accept the increasing number of volatility wipe knockout blows. These reactions remain in place while traders continue to rely on measures of price volatility as a substitute for a measure of trend volatility.

Figure 11.1: volatility wipe

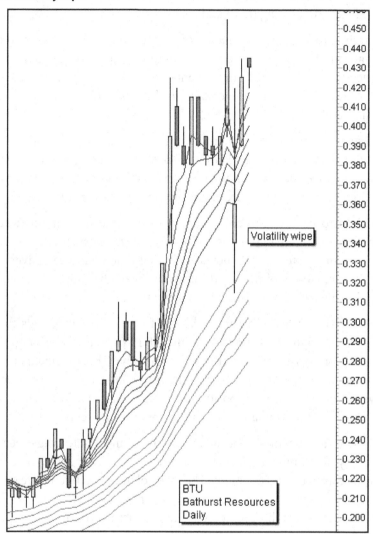

Volatility wipe

BTU
Bathurst Resources
Daily

Nature of the trend

The volatility wipe problem was highlighted in the extreme volatility days in early 2008 as the Global Financial Crisis began to develop. When the first leg of the recovery developed, traders assumed the volatility wipe would disappear. It did not. It remained in place, and the tactics we developed in 2008 were extended and modified to remain relevant in new market conditions inundated by volatility, decreases in trend stability and a decline in trend persistence. Trends do not last for extended periods, and they deliver an increasing number of false exit signals.

Before we look at solutions we need to take a small foundation detour. The Guppy Multiple Moving Average indicator is designed to understand the behaviour of traders and investors. This behaviour is independent from the price behaviour, but it is derived from price behaviour. The structure of the GMMA captures the fractal behaviour in the market and the way this behaviour repeats.

The essential GMMA analysis methods rest on the relationships between each group of moving averages, and between the two groups of moving averages. Compression shows agreement. Expansion shows disagreement. When the long-term group is widely separated it shows strong investor commitment to the trend. When the two groups of averages are consistently separated it shows trend consistency because traders are not prepared to let prices retreat too far before they become buyers again.

The relationship in each group of averages and the relationships between the groups provide the primary analysis for the application of the GMMA. This analysis is independent of price. This is underlined in our preferred GMMA display. Although many users overlay the price chart with the GMMA, this is not our preferred display option. We prefer to use just a plain GMMA display without any underlying price display. This allows for clear analysis of the trend without the distraction of price activity.

Figure 11.2: GMMA display without underlying price display

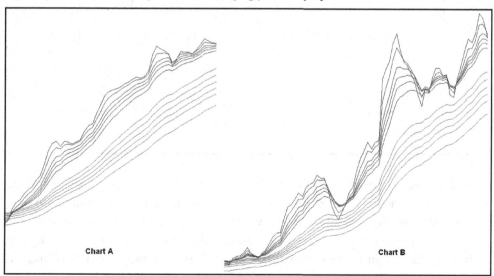

The two chart extracts in figure 11.2 show a GMMA display without price information. The nature of the trends is quiet clear just from this display. Both charts have a stable trend with good separation between the two GMMAs. Trading activity is slow in chart A and more frequent in chart B. Investor support is strong and stable in both charts. Both of these stocks provide good long-term trend trading opportunities.

Here in figure 11.3 are the two price charts underpinning the GMMA display. The picture and the story are very different. Chart B has a much higher level of price volatility with large dips and fast rises. Setting an effective stop is very difficult. Chart A has more manageable price activity. A price volatility–based stop loss gives a good trading solution and makes for easy trade management. Yet both of these trends, in terms of the GMMA, are stable, well supported and show sustainable trending activity.

Figure 11.3: price charts underpinning the GMMA display

Chart B has been selected to highlight the distinction between price activity and the way the trend is measured or defined with the long-term GMMA. We could also have used a chart showing multiple volatility wipes, as in figure 11.1. The key point is the disconnect between price volatility and trend volatility. It was a disconnect highlighted in the price behaviour in the early parts of 2008. This disconnect continued, and has become an established feature of modern markets. This signals that traders need to change their thinking about the behaviour of trends and the way trends are defined.

The trader and the trend

The chart extracts showing just the GMMA allow traders to develop effective analysis about the strength of the trend based on the degree of separation in the long-term GMMA. This observation is the foundation of the GMMA Trend Volatility Line. This trend trade management technique is built on a change in the way we view the relationship between the trader and the trend.

Step back into history, and the land of hope again. Investors and traders have been fixated on establishing the beginning and end of trends. Collectively millions of man hours have been devoted to developing indicators designed to locate the start and end of a trend. Less time has been allocated to understanding how to manage the trend. It's a legacy of investment thinking where there is a focus on the identification of the trend rather than the management of the trade.

Entering as a trend changes is a higher risk proposition because we are betting against the direction of the previous trend. The rate of selection failure is high and this in part leads to increased concentration on the concepts of stop loss and the 2% rule. These concepts were applied reluctantly to mid-trend entry conditions. Traders who joined in mid-trend, as discussed in my book *Trend Trading*, were often considered to be less skilled than traders who joined the trend earlier. As we have suggested in chapter 2, Behavioural finance for crowds, there are considerable advantages in joining the trend after it has started and taking just a large chunk out of the trend, exiting before it has finally ended.

Changing our focus away from finding the beginning of a new trend pays good dividends in modern markets. Our focus is on rapidly selecting the best entry point in a developing trend, and then managing the subsequent trend behaviour and our exposure to it.

This distinction is particularly important. The focus is on managing our exposure to the trend based on the point where we entered the trend. This is a subjective judgement. If I enter the trend at $15.00 and you enter the same trend at $25.00 then our management of our exposure to the trend may be very different.

This is counter to the historical understanding of a trader's relationship with the trend. In the past traders have believed there is an objective measurement of the trend used by all traders. The position of a count back line or a trend line does not change depending on the trader, or on the point where the trader enters the trend. This is an excellent solution if we believe price volatility defines trend behaviour. It's not so good if trend behaviour is different from price volatility.

The GMMA provides an alternative way of understanding trend behaviour and delivers a method of managing the trader's exposure to the trend based on her entry point.

Trend volatility

The concept of using trend volatility to manage the trade starts with the trader's selected entry point. In this example we show the entry point at $50.00 in figure 11.4. Here is the first divergence with the traditional trend management based on price volatility. The entry point at $50.00 is used as the initial stop loss calculation. Based on the entry point we project a line to the right. We call this the breakeven line. Later we explain the detail of this line. For the moment we concentrate on the way it is used to manage and define the trend in relation to the trade.

Figure 11.4: entry point at $50.00

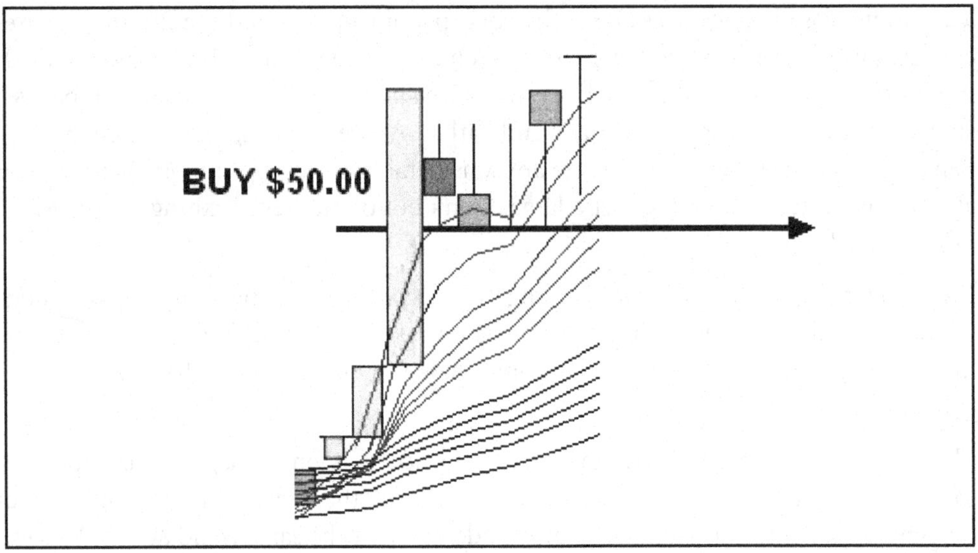

BUY $50.00

The objective is to enter the trend in such a way that the probability of a price volatility retreat—a volatility wipe—is substantially reduced. The objective is to treat volatility as a welcome friend rather than as an unwanted enemy. We use the increase in upwards volatility to protect the entry against the probability of a downside volatility wipe. The exit signal is a close below the breakeven line. The breakeven line is used as the stop loss until the next set of conditions are met. Any price volatility indicator exit signals generated in this period are ignored. In the chart example in figure 11.5 we show a CBL exit signal generated early in the trade development.

Figure 11.5: CBL exit signal

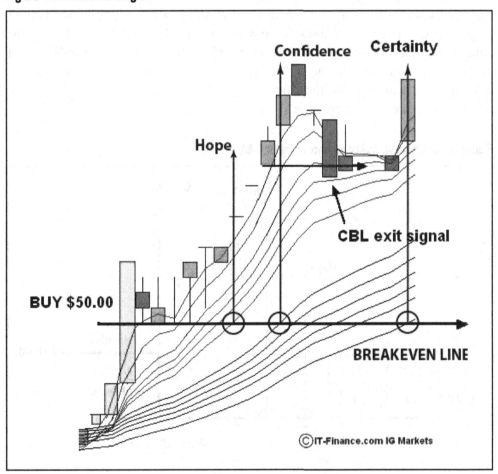

The relationship between the value of the breakeven line and the development of the GMMA is the important feature of this trade management. When the value of the breakeven line crosses the lower edge of the long-term GMMA then the trader has confirmation of trend sustainability. We call this development process Hope, Confidence and Certainty (HCC), and this is discussed in more detail below and in chapter 21, Counting back the profit. The GMMA is used to measure the trend strength. The horizontal cross-section of the long-term GMMA defined by the breakeven line is an exact measure of trend strength. It's an extension of the foundation concepts of the GMMA and allows the trader to take two important steps.

The first step is the calculation of how high to lift the stop loss to follow the developing trend. The usual solution was to measure price volatility using a CBL or ATR calculation. The new solution is to measure the volatility of the trend as shown by the GMMA in figure 11.6. The vertical distance between the 30 EMA and the 60 EMA—the long-term GMMA—shows the current amplitude of the trend. This is independent of the volatility of price. In the early stages of the trend the amplitude is small. As a sustainable trend develops the long-term GMMA develops wider separation. This shows an increase in the amplitude of the trend.

Figure 11.6: trend volatility as shown by GMMA

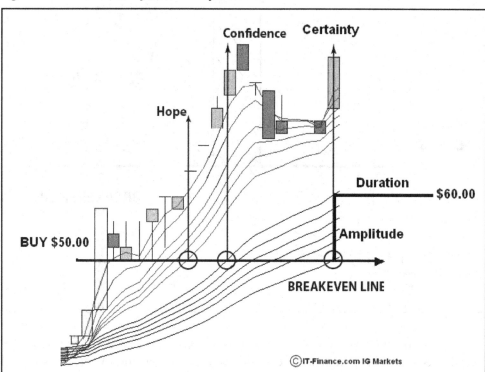

The current amplitude provides a solution for how high the stop loss should be adjusted. In the chart example the stop loss is lifted from $50.00 to $60.00.

Classic trend analysis uses a measure of price volatility to determine how high the stop loss should be lifted. The method uses a measure of the amplitude of the trend—not price—to determine the appropriate stop loss adjustment level.

The vertical projection is halted when it reaches the value of the 30 EMA. From this point a line is projected to the right. This is used to define the period of time for which this new stop loss value is appropriate. This line defines the duration of the stop loss at this level. The duration is not known in advance. The time to recalculate the stop loss is signalled when the value of the horizontal line next intersects the 60 EMA. This defines the duration of the stop and signals the recalculation of the amplitude of the trend. The value of the stop loss is adjusted to match the value of the 30 EMA and a new line is projected to the right to define the duration of the stop loss.

This combination of amplitude and duration creates the Guppy GMMA Trend Volatility Line (TVL). Amplitude plus duration equals trend volatility. It is used to follow the developing trend. The exit signal is delivered when the price closes below the TVL. The exit is taken in the next candle period. The chart extract from a case study trade in our Asian newsletter shows the difference in the understanding of the trend. The extract includes many price volatility–based exit signals. They include CBL exit signals and trend line exit signals. These are circled on the chart in figure 11.7. We have not shown the ATR exit signals. These are all false exit signals. However, the long-term GMMA shows no weakness in the trend. Using the TVL trend management method the false exit signals based on price volatility are ignored.

This indicator is used as a trend management tool. It is not used as an objective definition of the trend. Traders looking for objective end-of-trend signals will be disappointed. Traders looking for effective methods to manage their trend exposure in a trade will find this a very useful tool.

It is important to note these caveats:

⊞   the TVL does not define the start or end of the trend

⊞   the TVL is not an objective trend definition tool

⊞   the TVL is a trade definition tool.

The TVL defines how you will manage the volatility risk based on the price and time of your entry. It's an uncomfortable concept for people who look for certainty in the market. It is a familiar concept for those who study the behaviour of turbulence in areas such as weather forecasting.

Figure 11.7: false exit signals

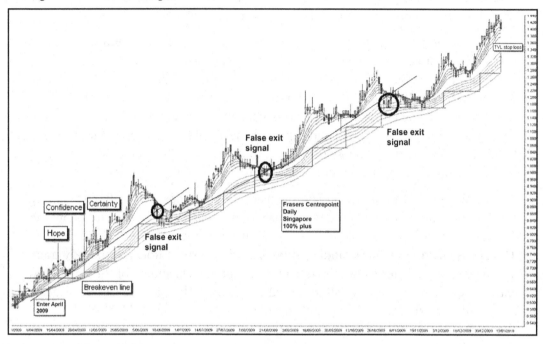

A weather forecast uses a user-defined starting point within a dynamically evolving chaotic system. The three-day weather forecast developed on Monday does not begin with an event defined by the weather. The start point for the forecast analysis is defined by the user, and so uses an analysis of turbulence the user has selected as a starting point. The TVL applies the same concept to an evolving market condition with a focus on survival based on a user-defined entry point. It shows how we survive within an environment of uncertainty.

TVL development for intraday

The TVL concept was developed in the volatile markets of 2008 for intraday trading of indices. The chart in figure 11.8 is a real-time index trade with a CFD. The points A, B and C show the calculation points for the TVL.

126

The chart in figure 11.8 is a one-minute chart and uses the same TVL technique to manage the long-term trade. The GMMA is built of fractal repetition, and the TVL method is also fractally applied across multiple time frames.

Figure 11.8: real-time index trade with TVL

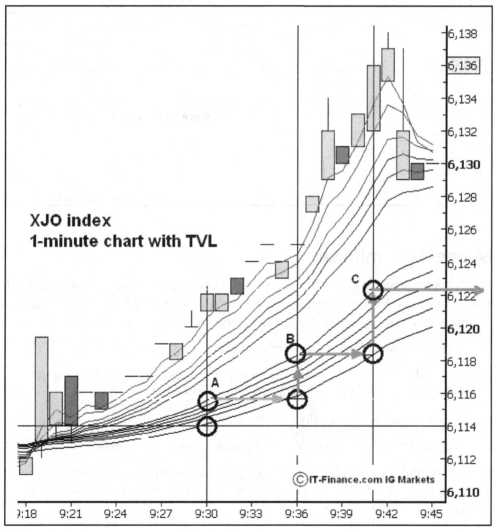

The chart extract in figure 11.9 shows how the TVL line signals an exit on a one-minute chart.

Figure 11.9: TVL exit signal

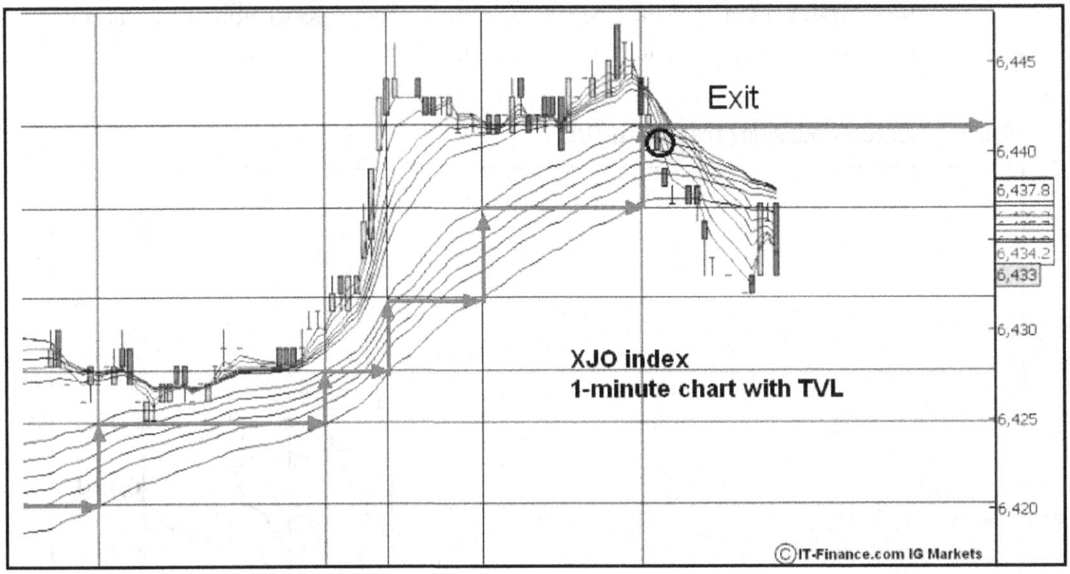

Momentum minute

The TVL concept was originally developed for intraday trading of indices. It was designed as a scalping tool. Market conditions were so volatile and unstable that carrying trades overnight was very dangerous. Traders faced several problems, including:

- very large and sudden price volatility that came without warning

- repeated failure of classical price volatility measures as a way of defining trend behaviour or short-term trend behaviour

- increased multi-day volatility with price gapping

- increased intraday volatility with sharp down moves and reversals.

All of these problems signalled a developing disconnect between price behaviour and trend behaviour. The first development of the TVL started with the observation of the impact of momentum minutes.

A momentum minute, shown in figure 11.10, is observed on a dynamically updated one-minute chart as provided by some CFD providers. A dynamically updated chart shows the growth of the one-minute candle in real time. The trader has already made a decision to enter the trade but waits for opportunity.

The opportunity came when a momentum minute developed. This was a one-minute period where the price range increased substantially. In the first 10 seconds the price already moved further than the range of price activity in the previous 5 to 10 minutes. These momentum minute candles are easy to see as they develop.

Figure 11.10: momentum minute candle

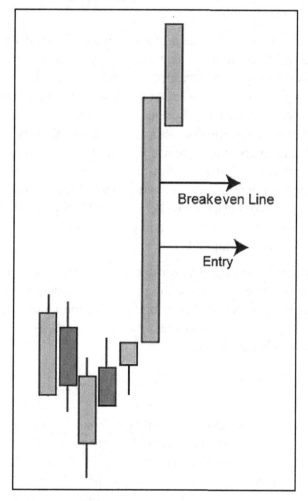

Generally the momentum continued, with only minor retracements. This created the momentum minute entry designed to ride the momentum so price was carried well above the entry point and the planned stop loss. The initial stop loss is based on the financial calculation so no more than 2% of trading capital is at risk.

Increased volatility meant the slippage between the planned exit price and the actual exit price was significant. The impact was increased when using leveraged trading instruments such as CFDs.

The trader planned to get out at $45.00, but by the time his exit order was executed the exit price was $43.00. This is slippage. With derivative trading the risk rapidly became much larger than 2%. The solution for managing slippage came from the breakeven line and the momentum minute.

The momentum minute increased the probability price would continue to move upwards in a rising trend breakout. An entry during this period protected against the potential for a volatility wipe. The breakeven line was calculated using the entry price and the minimum price necessary to exit at a breakeven for the trade. This included the cost of brokerage, commission or spreads. The practical application of this meant an exit at breakeven price also involved slippage in volatile markets, however the final exit price has a higher probability of remaining within the parameters of the 2% risk rule. Aim for an exit with 2% risk in a fast-moving, volatile market with a $100 000 trading capital and the trader usually lost between $2500 and $3000. Aim for an exit at breakeven and the trader usually lost between $500 and $1000. The momentum minute and the breakeven line combination initially provided a practical way to keep losses within the necessary financial limits.

The momentum minute concept is also extended to a daily chart. Here the entry is made during the day when it is clear the price is developing a much larger range than the previous days. This was the method used in the Frasers Centrepoint trade shown in figure 11.7. The extension of the breakeven line as a component of the Trend Volatility Line offers other opportunities.

HCC

When the trade is first entered traders hope they have made the correct decision. Later, as the trade develops, the trader becomes confident she has made the right decision. At this point the trader may decide to add to the position. As the trade develops further the trader is certain she has made the correct decision. At this point she may decide to add a third position. We call this the HCC method. This is scaling, or pyramiding, into a trade. These trend development points are shown in figure 11.11. The HCC entry philosophy is explained in more detail in chapter 21, Counting back the profit.

Figure 11.11: trend development points

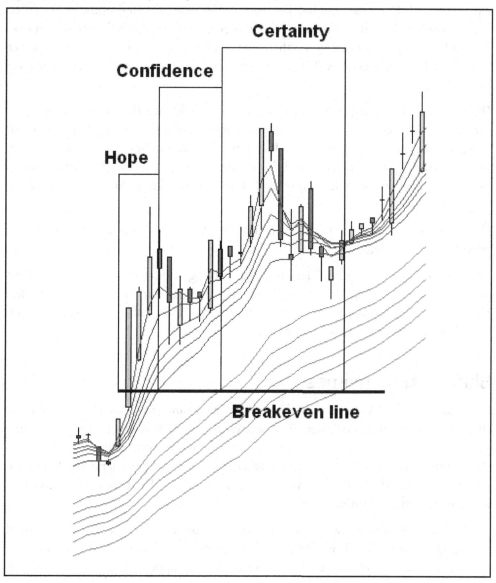

The relationship between the breakeven line and the GMMA provides clear points showing when the trade shifts from hope to confidence and from confidence to certainty. Adding new positions at these points carries a reduced probability an exit from the trend would be signalled.

The trade moves to the first scale-in point when the value of the lower edge of the short-term GMMA crosses the breakeven line. The second scale-in position is added when the value of the upper edge of the long-term GMMA crosses the breakeven line. The trade is fully confirmed when the value of the breakeven line crosses the lower edge of the long-term GMMA. This is also the signal for the first important calculation for the TVL.

These scale-in position points reflect increasing confidence the trend is moving in our preferred direction. They reflect the increasing probability of trend continuation. However, the position of the stop loss—the breakeven line—does not change. The increased risk for trades 2 and 3 with an exit based on the breakeven line is counterbalanced by the reduction in probability the breakeven line stop loss will be triggered.

The stop loss for all three positions is adjusted when the first new TVL stop loss calculation is completed.

This was originally a method designed for scalping short-term trends. As markets stabilised the method was extended to develop one-day and later multi-day trades. The development rests upon the fractal nature of the GMMA and trending behaviour. It is a logical extension of the features of the GMMA.

Shifting time frames

Classically the GMMA shows the behaviour of traders and investors. On a one-minute chart this relationship is adjusted. The new values are 3, 5, 8, 10, 12 and 15 *minutes*, and 30, 35, 40, 45, 50 and 60 *minutes*. For convenience we now think of the short-term group of averages as showing the behaviour of intraday traders. The long-term group of averages shows the behaviour of position traders. The behaviour of investors is not shown on a one-minute chart.

The GMMA captures the fractal repetition of behaviour and this enables the enhanced application of the TVL. The objective of the momentum minute and the TVL is to develop profitable trades in emerging trends. What happens when there is an exit signal on the one-minute chart?

If our intention is to scalp, the trade is closed. If our intention is to develop this into a longer term one-day trade then the time scale is adjusted to confirm if the fractal relationship is repeated. This is only applied if the trade is already in profit. An exit signal on a one-minute chart that triggers a loss is immediately closed.

If the trade is already in profit the trader opens a second screen and applies a GMMA to a three-minute chart. The next time frame is three times higher than the initial time frame. The breakeven line is placed on the three-minute chart at the same value as the one-minute chart. The TVL calculation is added to the three-minute chart. Figure 11.12 shows the application of TVL in a short trade where the time frame has been changed to a three-minute chart after the initial entry on the one-minute chart.

Figure 11.12: application of TVL in a short trade

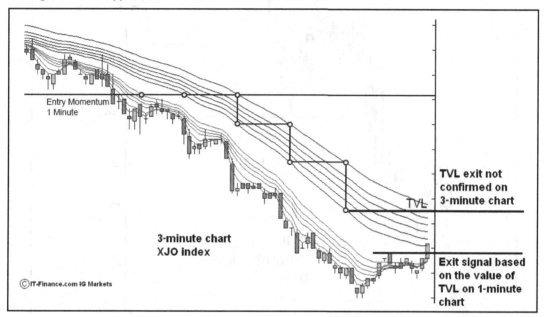

This captures the trend development in a higher time frame using the same logic of GMMA trend analysis. An exit signal on a one-minute chart that is confirmed on a three-minute chart is acted on. An exit signal in the lower time frame that is not confirmed in the higher time frame is ignored. This provides a method of extending the trade in a higher time frame in a way consistent with the development of trend volatility. This eliminates false price volatility exit signals.

An exit signal in the three-minute time frame is verified against an exit signal in the next higher time frame of nine minutes. This process can be duplicated as many times as necessary during the trading day. In practice we found that usually shifting up just a single time frame — from one minute to three minutes in index trading — was enough to capture the significant trend for the day.

Figure 11.13: TVL line

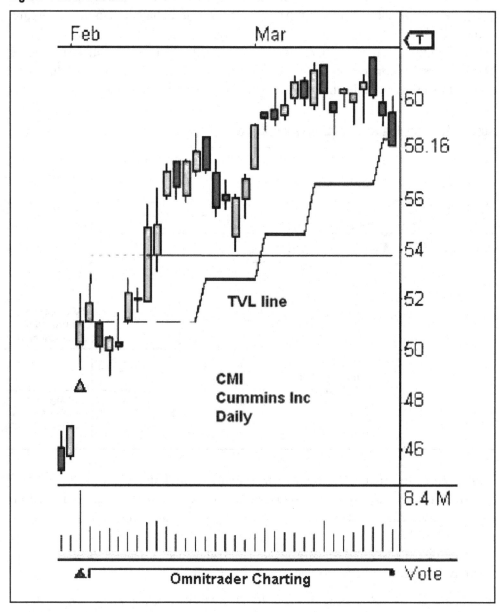

If at the end of the day the trade remains in profit then the trader can choose to move this to a multi-day trade. The same principle is applied. The position of the breakeven line does not change. The TVL calculation is also applied to a one-day chart, as shown in figure 11.7. Figure 11.13 is the OmniTrader display of a one-day chart. It uses only the TVL value without showing the underlying GMMA display. The TVL is calculated using the one-day chart. This now becomes a long-term multi-day position trade. The exit signal is given when price closes below the TVL line on the daily chart. The exit is taken on the next day.

TVL trading conclusion

The TVL is a trade management method designed to reduce the incidence of false exits triggered by changes in price volatility that are irrelevant to the stability and continuation of the trend. It is applied to intraday and end-of-day trading. It is used in trading long and trading short. It is a solution to the increase in volatility seen in modern markets. It is an effective trading solution for indices, commodities, currencies and also ordinary stocks. The TVL is a trade management method applied by measuring trend volatility. The TVL is a tool for managing the trader's exposure to the trend. It crosses the boundary, moving from analysis into action.

Chapter 12

Dark side trading analysis

Insider trading started with the first stock market and it is unstoppable. It is the dark side of trade analysis. This doesn't mean regulators should not try to stop insider trading, but we do need to recognise the fact that insider trading will continue to be with us for as long as there are markets. In this chapter we want to look at insider trading from an analysis perspective. We use genuine examples where the regulators have obtained convictions for insider trading. In chapter 26, Patterns of informed trading, we look at some detailed trading techniques in Early Warning System trading that allows traders to identify informed trading by others.

This discussion blurs the edge between analysis techniques and trading methods but it is an essential aspect of modern markets. We believe the growth of dark pools which offer anonymous trading facilities in an off-market environment will increase the opportunities for insider trading so it pays to learn how to recognise the potential signs.

What is a dark pool?

Dark pools change the way you trade. It is a fundamental change to the market landscape. A dark pool is the name given to the pool of money created by independent off-market trading markets. Some are listed in table 12.1. These operators offer a trading platform where large institutions, banks and funds can trade anonymously with each other. These are stealth markets. They allow participants to buy and sell large blocks of stocks in secrecy and at lightning speed. Think flash trading and algorithmic trading where liquidity and anonymity are essential.

Dark pools started in the US. Today, by some estimates, they account for 64% of all the trading done on the New York Stock Exchange — except this trading is not done on the NYSE during the day. It is done outside the NYSE during the trading day and reported to the stock exchange after the market has closed.

The dark pools splinter the marketplace and create private marketplaces for trading in publicly listed stocks. This gives the big banks and the funds an advantage over the retail investors who cannot participate in these markets.

This is part of the creation of the after-hours price often quoted on CNBC. For example, Apple closed today at $54.00 but was trading at $56 in the after-hours market.

Table 12.1: examples of dark pool markets

Independent Dark Pools	Broker-Dealer-Owned Dark Pools
Instinet Group Inc	BLOCKalert
Investment Technology Group	Citi Markets and Banking
Liquidnet Inc	Credit Suisse Group AG
NY/FX Millennium	Fidelity Capital Markets Services
Pipeline Trading Systems	Goldman Sachs Executive and Clearing
Pulse Trading	Knight Capital Group
Major Dark Pools	Lehman Brothers Holdings Inc
BNY ConvergEx Group	Merrill Lynch & Co Inc
Exchange-Owned Dark Pools	Morgan Stanley
International Securities Exchange Hld Inc	UBC Investment Bank
The NASDAQ Stock Market	Chi-X
NYSE Euronext	**Consortium-Owned Dark Pools**
Direct Edge	BIDS Trading
NYSE Euronext	eBX LLC
Direct Edge	

The dark pools allow for the anonymous matching of prices. You don't know who you are dealing with so large positions can be unwound in secrecy. The essential feature of dark pools is that trading takes place during the trading day, but the trading is not executed on the ASX, the SGX or the NYSE. It is only after the close of the market that the outcome of this trading—not the process—is reported to the public exchange.

The Global Financial Crisis has underlined the importance of market transparency. Dark pools are the exact opposite. The creation of competing exchanges is favoured by regulators, who see the benefits of competition and appear to be blind to the disadvantages of secrecy in the marketplace. The 2010 'flash crash' was created in part by this splintering of exchange trading floors.

There are nine main impacts of dark pools trading.

Market secrecy

Significant sections of the market are closed off from public participation. They are also largely outside the effective control of market regulators simply because of the secrecy. Think about the large Australian bank CBA. Consider the action it took on a placement in 2009 where it discovered at 3 pm that its bad debt expenses had increased by $640 million—about 6% of the bank's net profit. *The Australian Financial Review* reported that CBA decided it was not important enough to tell ordinary investors who were buying stock in the market. It delayed releasing the information until after the market close. CBA later told the stock exchange regulator the amount was not material to its share price.

However, CBA felt the information was important enough to immediately tell investors soon after 3 pm who were about to buy the stock in an off-market placement.

CBA was fined a small amount for this. Traders will need to get used to this two-track flow of price-sensitive information. This type of action is the way of the future and is facilitated by dark pool trading.

Reduced efficiency

Dark pools reduce the efficiency of price discovery. There is a public board, and several private dark pools boards. The essential function of the market is price discovery. This is where sellers try to meet buyers at an agreed price that reflects an agreed value. It's all very academic, but it's the core function of the market. In a central order book on a single trading exchange this price discovery occurs in one place and it's instantly available to all market participants at the same time. It's an efficient matching process. In a dark pool environment there may be three or four separate trading markets all trading the same stock.

Multi-market trading screens

Finding the best bid and best ask is no longer a matter of going to a central order book operated by a single exchange such as the Australian Securities Exchange. There will be several order books. What is happening in the parallel dark pool market may not necessarily reflect what is happening in the public market, partly because the information available to each is different. Dark pools do not operate under the same continuous disclosure rules as the public stock exchanges.

Locked out

Retail traders usually are unable to participate in dark pool trading. Trading is limited to institutions only. Even if we wanted too, private traders cannot participate because of barriers of minimum trade size.

Less liquidity

There is less liquidity in the public market. Dark pools suck the liquidity out of the public market because the fund and institutional trading migrates to the dark pools. With more than 50% of trading in the US taking place outside of the public exchanges this has a significant impact on the liquidity of larger and mid-size companies. Traders need to brush up on the techniques used to trade companies with lower liquidity. We look at these skills in chapter 24, Modern tape reading.

Secret trading

Dark pool trading is secret trading and it is reported to the public market after the market closes. All we see is the after-market price. The large Australian telecoms company, Telstra, is an example of the difference between public and dark pool trading.

When the Australian sovereign wealth Future Fund sold down Telstra in 2008, traders could see this activity on the trading screens. They could choose to participate in this sell down, sell short or buy because they believed the price would rebound.

If Telstra had been dumped using a dark pool then the Australian ASX public market would probably not see any of this activity. Telstra would continue trading around $3.70 during the day on the public ASX screen. On the following day, after this dark pool trading had been reported, we would see an opening price at $3.40 or lower, which reflected the impact of the dark pool sell down. This makes the gap down behaviour seen in figure 12.1 more common. Traders would be left handling the consequences of this action rather than being able to evaluate their participation in this action as it happened.

Greater potential manipulation

Secrecy and anonymity cover a multitude of sins. The ability to trade anonymously automatically gives the power to manipulate the market and market pricing. This can be as simple as arbitraging between the public and dark pool markets. It may work like this: dump shares in the dark pool market so this sale is reported to the public market after the public market close. Short the public market at the same time and close out on the next day as the public market becomes aware of the activity in the dark pools. Or watch the bullish buying pressure in the dark pools and buy on the public market for a quick profit. The public price will rise when the dark pool trading prices are released to the public market after the market has closed. These are not arbitrage opportunities. They are market manipulation and front running. Secrecy makes this not only tempting but achievable.

Conclusions only

Dark pool trading takes place during market hours, but it is not always reported to the market. Only the final results of trading are reported, not the process. In the public market you can see when a price is being sold down by large investors as they unwind a position. You can see when the price is being pushed up. These observations form the foundation of some trading strategies. We participate in the activity initiated by others.

The dark pool environment means we do not see the activity. All that is reported to the public market is the final result. When the price rises from $30.00 to $36.00 in dark pool trading we do not get to participate in the price rise. We only know the next day that price closed at $30.00 and opens the next day at $36.00. We miss the opportunity to participate in rises and falls.

Figure 12.1: possible dark pool selling

More gaps

A major consequence of dark pool trading is the increase in gapping activity when dark pool activity is reported to the market. Gaps reflect news events. They should not reflect secret trading events. Gapping activity makes it more difficult to effectively use stop loss points to manage a trade.

Traders need to learn how to trade in the new environment. Many assumptions about pricing behaviour will need to be revisited and new tactics developed. It changes the nature of public investing for the long term because the price of a share can be significantly impacted by activity in a secret market. One rule becomes most important in the dark pool environment: trade what you see on the charts. Do not trade what you believe because there are things going on that you will never know about and which cannot be discovered by any fundamental analysis method. Welcome to dark side trading in modern markets.

Old-fashioned insider trading

A persistent rumour suggests true market success rests on insider trading. It is a pervasive idea infecting investment theory as well as trading. At heart the concept suggests advantage comes from knowing something before the rest of the market is aware of it. In investing this means finding undervalued companies before the market discovers them. This is considered an acceptable, if not admirable approach to investment. In short-term trading, it is supposed to mean catching the news minutes or seconds before it breaks. Again, this is acceptable and explains why access to newswires and better TV coverage from CNBC and Bloomberg is an essential feature of all trading rooms. In trading it implies access to confidential company information before it is released in a note to the stock exchange. Trading on this information is illegal.

When we start to trade the market there is a sneaking suspicion information counts and that we can turn this into a profit. There is a little bit of Warren Buffett in all of us. Somewhere in the back of our mind lurks Benjamin Graham and his belief about buying sound companies that are temporarily undervalued. We believe if we identify a bargain situation when we have access to news before other market participants, then we have a profitable trade. All we do is buy ahead of the crowd. This is a useful investment strategy for stocks.

Access to this early information is considered so powerful that it provides an unfair opportunity for a small group to profit at the expense of the broader market. Our stock exchange regulations reflect this concern with heavy penalties for insider trading. The inability to achieve many convictions for insider trading suggests the problem may be more complex and difficult to define than the simplistic rumours suggest.

The true insider, perhaps a company executive, acts by himself and tells no-one. The nasty insider allows family and friends access to shares at preferential prices prior to the listing of a new company. This practice was widespread with IPO—initial public offer—launches in the US at the height of the technology boom at the end of last century. Neither of these insiders interest us. Our concern is with the insider tip, which is one variation of the early release of market-moving news.

Insider trading is not the same as informed trading. The difference between insider trading and informed trading is slim, but important—the former is illegal. In the real world some people start to suspect important information before others. This opinion is insignificant until they take a market position. When people back their suspicions with cash, or by taking unnecessary losses, then other traders listen. The informed buyer or seller has, at best, a one-day advantage because as soon as she takes a market position it shows up in the volume and price information. Other traders read the intent more quickly on a price chart than in the morning newspaper. This type of chart interpretation is a profitable skill and is worth developing, and we discuss this in chapter 26, Patterns of informed trading.

From the inside

We could update this chapter with many examples of chart patterns where we have good grounds to believe insider trading took place. In 2008 and 2009 several markets with previously sound reputations developed new unfavourable reputations for a high level of insider trading and regulatory inactivity. There was a lot of international focus on 'rumourtrage', where rumours were circulated by email or internet chat rooms. Significant sections of the market have always run on rumour and the attempt to reduce the role of rumour was ultimately unsuccessful. It was a politically acceptable distraction, diverting attention from both clear examples of insider trading and from the poor decision-making in many companies that made them vulnerable to the activity of short traders. Some of these incidents are winding their way through court actions, and until we have proof from judicial conviction rather than good grounds for suspicion we will stay with known confirmed examples of insider trading.

This real insider trading story starts with a weekend backyard BBQ, and we can speculate how some participants may have behaved. The BBQ was attended by a small group of friends, and a company insider. In the course of conversation over burnt sausages authorities alleged the guests were told of a news release timed for the coming Wednesday prior to the open of the market. We need to be realistic about news. It does not spring ready-formed from thin air. Somebody is responsible for creating the news and company PR officers prepare the news release. By the time we get the news it has already passed through many hands and been available in one form or another for many days, or even weeks. Top-secret government agencies leak news on a regular basis despite the best security that taxpayers' money buys. When we talk of company secrecy, news embargoes and continuous disclosure we kid ourselves if we believe news comes as a surprise to everybody when it is released.

The proposed news release informed an unsuspecting market the company had signed agreements in principle to create a global market for its product. This is the stuff of giant profit dreams and, not unexpectedly, some of the people who attended the BBQ promptly reached deep into their wallets and purchased stock when the market opened on Monday.

Our concern in this example is not with morality, but with the impact of this alleged insider trading. If this technique is successful then it is worth our time legally chasing news and news sources. If the technique does not yield a substantial advantage, then we employ our time more effectively by learning to use the news in different ways, such as those discussed in chapter 28, Indexing the news.

Imagine how the BBQ participants react. They jump into the market on Monday, buying the open. They worry that if they do not buy the open, other people may come into possession of this same knowledge and take advantage of it. They fear paying a higher price on the open. Even with inside information, speed is an advantage. This is the way the novice trader, and even sometimes the experienced trader, thinks.

The chart shows exactly how the market reacted to this development. The chart extract in figure 12.2 covers the period before, and after, the news release. Take a moment to identify the point on this chart where you believe the news was released to the market. Work back three days from this bar, identify the Monday open and the date of the weekend BBQ.

You have a choice of leading price action at point A with a 20% increase in price for the day, or point B with a 29% rise. Perhaps point C is stronger evidence of this excitement with a 41% rise. Point D, with 22%, is only slightly worse than point E with a 23% rise for the day. Choose point A and you get to ride a 240% rise, which would truly illustrate the advantages of insider trading, despite its illegality.

Figure 12.2: period before and after news release

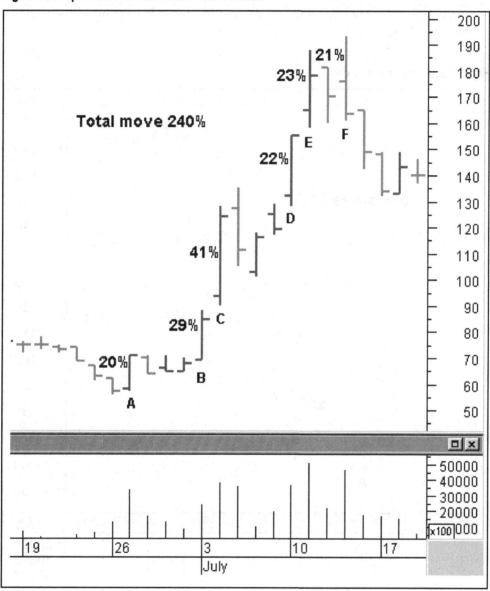

Somewhere on this chart is the inside advantage. Can you find it? The answer is over the page.

The news hit the market at point F, shown in figure 12.3. Prices climbed rapidly on the release, and then fell back to close lower than the open. They continued falling over the next few days.

Figure 12.3: news release day

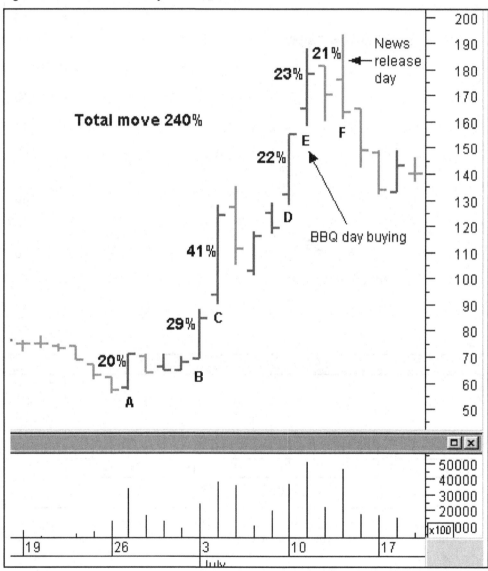

The total price move from point A to the high at point F is 240%. Those armed with the insider BBQ information entered some time during bar E and captured around 23% based on their hot tip. Even capturing this return called for good trading skill to exit at the very top price of $1.95. Failure to act on the day of the news announcement drops their hot tip insider trade back to around breakeven.

This example highlights three important points. The first is the non-exclusive nature of news. Many people knew, or suspected, good news was developing for this company. Their buying started around $0.55 and drove prices up to $1.50 before the insider's BBQ occurred. Does this mean all the previous buying was based on inside information? It would be highly unlikely. It is a fair assumption some of the buying made use of specialist knowledge not available to the broader market. This does not disadvantage other buyers, nor does it confer a major exclusive advantage on those who knew the information first.

This leads to the second point. The last-traded price reflects all that is known, or rumoured, or suspected, or proven about the company. The price incorporates the thoughts of the most informed and the least informed investors who are prepared to back their judgement with money, either through buying shares or refusing to sell their existing shareholding. Their emotions are reflected as crowd psychology and captured in the activity of price.

The significance of this news is tracked, not by a BBQ invitation, but by chart analysis. The breakout above the resistance level around $0.70 provided ample evidence of a new rally. It confirmed the bullish break above the upward-sloping triangle. Based on this price activity alone a technical or chart-based trader joins the developing trend at $0.80. An exit at the top delivers a 143% return.

The impact of news does not depend on its exclusivity. News is rarely unexpected or exclusive. Most times it is comprehensively leaked by rumour, or deliberate release, before the formal announcement to the market. We have the opportunity to follow the progress of such a leak by closely observing price action. This provides an important day-trading and short-term edge. News leaks provide a fruitful hunting ground and introduce the trading skills required for short-term trading.

The third point shows clearly how those who trade on hot tips play a loser's game. It is a fair assumption many of those who bought after the weekend BBQ still held shares when they dropped back to $1.30. Why? They entered the trade based on information from a third party without undertaking any real analysis for themselves. Typically they wait for the same third party to tell them when it is time to get out. Usually it's a long wait.

Hot tips do not only come from weekend BBQs. They come from brokers, sometimes hot and sometimes cool. Hot tips come from investment newsletters. Many investors follow these recommendations and, like the BBQ hot tip trader, they also wait for an instruction to sell. As the market collapse in 2008 showed, it can be a long wait for sell instructions. Those who follow any type of buy tips tend to wait for sell tips but, as brokerage records show, buy recommendations outnumber sell recommendations by ten to one. Tips are for waiters—and very few waiters are successful traders.

The most important lesson from this chart is that inside information or hot tips, even if accurate, very rarely give us a significant advantage in the market. We should assume there are always others who have far better knowledge than we do about what is happening, and that their buying and their rumours show up in the price action long before we get to hear about it. We need to know our place in the information chain. Accept this and we turn our attention to areas where we get a real edge in the market rather than wasting time chasing an imaginary edge.

Readers' dumps and bumps

Every week I receive a number of well-intentioned tips about stocks. Some come from reputable sources such as brokerage reports and newspapers. Some come from less reliable sources, such as emails and phone calls, and some come from suspect sources, such as chat rooms.

A few tips I subject to further charting and technical analysis and this sometimes tells me about the impact of the report on other readers. These bumps or dumps provide short-term trading opportunities because the report attracts an emotional crowd in search of easy money without hard work.

There are nearly 2000 listed companies, and only a handful receive coverage from the financial press, or from brokerages. Naturally our attention is attracted to those mentioned, and we are more likely to take a look at them. This can develop into a readers' bump, which is a temporary change in the overall trend and a fast trading opportunity.

It's very rare for a magazine or a writer to publicly acknowledge the impact of their work on the price of a stock. All too often the writers or magazine deny any influence, despite the surge in price of a selected stock in the hours following the publication of an investment newsletter. Again there are many interesting examples of this relationship — too many to dismiss as coincidence — but until the writer acknowledges the impact our conclusions remain more difficult to illustrate with direct evidence. Instead we draw on an old event which stands as a universal example of this type of relationship.

The Speculator column in the weekly magazine *The Bulletin* was used by many people as a source of stock 'tips'. For a while the column tracked AI Engineering and the coverage had an undoubted impact on individual stocks. 'This column probably had a lot to do with the instability that developed in the AIE's share register during the past 12 months', the column's author acknowledged. Several short-term trading opportunities developed from these readers' bumps, including the bump in figure 12.4.

Figure 12.4: readers' bump

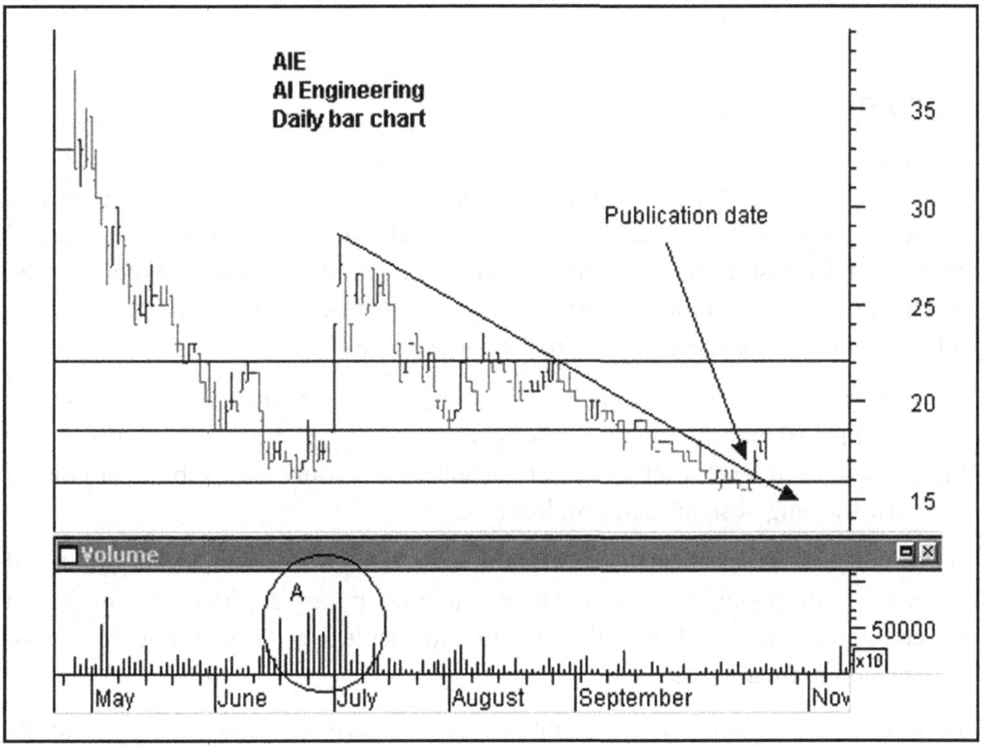

Is this rise a trend change or just a short-term opportunity? The AIE chart is dominated by a long, slow downtrend defined by a straight edge trend line moving towards a new double bottom based on the low in June. We assess this without knowing anything about the article in *The Bulletin* by observing the resistance level at $0.185. Prices are likely to run into problems here. A close above this resistance level suggests the breakout is for real and sets targets at $0.22 and $0.26.

This is a weak breakout compared with the June rise supported by a significant increase in volume in area A. The current breakout is a weak up move with low trading volume. Basic chart analysis suggests this is a weak rally.

Now add the impact of *The Bulletin* article. The rise starts on *The Bulletin* publication day. This can be a trap. When we are aware of these 'tips' we should treat the price activity with additional caution as with low-priced and low-volume stocks the impact is often short-lived. If we are not aware of the news story then good chart analysis still protects us by distinguishing between a trend change and a rally. The downtrend was confirmed in the following weeks with prices slipping to $0.11. Readers' bumps are very short-term opportunities.

Nasty news

The opposite of a readers' bump is a readers' dump after nasty company news. The readers' dump inflicts severe financial damage, so there is an important protective advantage if it is recognised early. This brings together those who follow the financial press, the relationship between rumour and news, and the sudden rumour-driven price drops which catch the uninformed and unskilled by surprise. News often leaks, and we do not need to be an insider to catch the leak early.

We use SOH in figure 12.5 as an example of this process. SOH had been in a steady downtrend for 10 months and many thought it was drifting into bargain territory. The temporary support levels provide important signals. The dip below support at point A is the first warning of significant problems.

The financial press speculated about SOH, and this shows up in the beginning of the readers' dump pattern with the break below temporary support at point B with accelerating volume. People read the rumour and decide to act. The rumour is the first confirmation of their worst fears.

The second stage of the readers' dump is when the facts are actually released to the market. SOH made its announcement on Monday, and those with access to intraday screens, live news feeds or who had read the well-informed article in *The Australian Financial Review* were ready to exit SOH at almost any price.

Figure 12.5: readers' dump

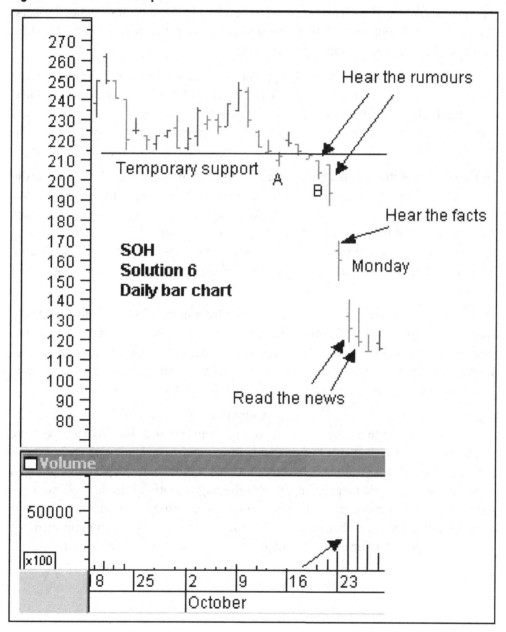

These well-informed people are not the general public. They are professional or semi-professional traders. They are valued clients who have been contacted by their brokers. They are probably not you, or the mums and dads. We get to hear the facts as a news report on the TV, or read about it the next day.

This is when the readers' dump really accelerates. We see substantially increased volume and a significant gap down in prices. This action confirms the new and accelerated downtrend. The dump is a three- to five-day pattern. It starts with rumour, accelerates with the release of facts, and plummets as the news spreads more widely in the general public.

This is not a conspiracy. It is a typical reaction to rumour and news. The fall below the temporary support level on increased volume is like a flashing ambulance light. We know there has been an accident but we do not know the details. It is a signal to take defensive action if we own the stock. If we ignore the chart signal we run the risk of being dumped as rumour turns into fact and then into news. In short-term trading we try to act before the news and often there is no shortage of advance warning shown in the charts.

Chasing early or inside news distracts the trader from more effective trading methods. Rather than jogging down the inside trader's path and attempting to find unexpected news events before they happen, the trader benefits from news events which companies are happy to leak in advance. Our short-term trading advantage comes from the way we use our skill to exploit the same information known by everybody else.

The reality is we cannot identify when insider trading is taking place but we can recognise chart activity that offers either an opportunity or a warning. We can speculate on the causes of price activity, but unless there are court convictions we cannot prove our suspicions. Insider trading is background noise in the market and it's not going to go away. Modern markets, particularly with the fragmentation into dark pools, make insider trading easier because of their anonymity. Our response as traders is to go for harm minimisation, and that means developing analysis tools and trading methods that take the potential for insider trading into account in our trade planning.

Chapter 13

Past into future tense

Finding and defining stable, sustainable and long-term trends is one of the biggest challenges with new market volatility. The GMMA TVL discussed in chapter 11 is one solution to the problem of volatility. In *Trend Trading* we introduced a modified concept from the 1960s based on Darvas trading methods. The modifications were designed to take into account changes in market volatility that had developed before the 2008 Global Financial Crisis. The logic behind the development of trends based on a defined range of price volatility has stood the test of new market developments. Aggressive traders adapted this Darvas method to successfully trade breakouts to new six-month highs in 2009.

How do you define a trend? A rising trend reflects changing perceptions of value over time and many indicators concentrate on tracking this behaviour in linear fashion. At their most basic, these indicators have a simple rule: if price stays above the indicator or line value, then the trend is upwards.

The Guppy Multiple Moving Average moves away from the classic linear understanding of the trend and it is used to understand the nature and character of the trend. The GMMA is a behavioural tool for understanding the activity of traders and investors. Their competitive buying or selling establishes the nature of the trend and we use this information to select the most appropriate trading or investment strategies. This is further extended with the Trend Line Volatility concept.

The count back line discussed in chapter 21, Counting back the profit, takes another step away from linear trend interpretations. Used purely by itself, the count back line defines a downtrend by the ability of price to close above a short-term resistance level. This is re-calculated every time there is a new significant bar. It relies on a measure of ranging activity in price and becomes a volatility-based indicator.

Ignore the classics

In this summary of the Darvas method we discard completely the classic linear analysis of the trend and examine an approach based entirely on dynamic support and resistance concepts. This has become increasingly relevant in markets where volatility is the defining feature. This detour provides a completely different way of identifying, understanding and trading the trend. This is a complete and stand-alone trading approach of Darvas-style trading. The concepts remain valid in new post-GFC market conditions.

Darvas defines an uptrend by constructing a series of imaginary boxes based on a price chart. Each box contains a set of price moves. Each new box sits on top of the previous box like a set of rising stairs. The continuation of a trend is confirmed when price moves above the upper edge of the box. The trend ends when prices close below the bottom of the current box. These upper and lower limits create a Darvas box—D_box—and define the acceptable bullish and bearish range of prices.

The starting point for this Darvas approach is defined by stocks making new highs for the selected period. Look for the list of stocks making new highs for the rolling 12-month period. Look at the price history for each stock. If you had acted on the first Darvas box plot, would you still be in the trend? If the answer is 'yes' then this suggests the stock is effectively traded using a Darvas approach. If the answer is 'no' the stock is dropped in favour of those compatible with Darvas trading techniques.

Figure 13.1: Darvas box breakout

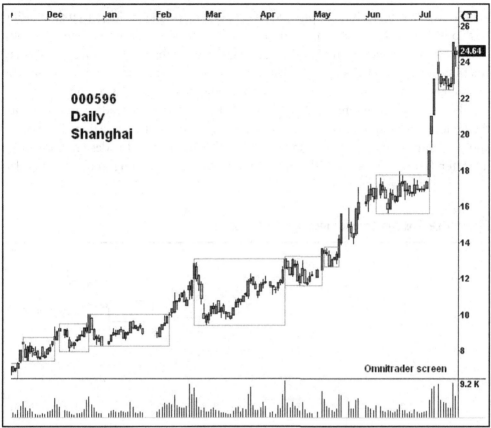

000596
Daily
Shanghai

Omnitrader screen

This process is automated with the Darvas plug-in for OmniTrader. The Shanghai-listed 000596 chart in figure 13.1 shows a breakout identification. The prior history for 000596 confirms the D_box approach is compatible with the trending behaviour as 000596 moves to make new highs.

Final selection of the trading opportunity depends on the position of price within the Darvas box and price leverage. Performance management is built on strict stop loss management directly related to the Darvas box calculation. This is the foundation of the strategy. The stop loss calculation is inviolable and directly related to the logic underpinning the construction of the box. There is no room to manoeuvre here. There is no arbitrary selection of a percentage-based retracement figure below the box because management is locked into the very structure of the Darvas box construction.

Darvas trading

The Darvas trading technique provides a useful way to manage longer term trending positions. It is designed as a method of capturing the strength of the trend. The buy signals are generated on new bullish strength and managed by using the six-day volatility range to set a stop loss. The limits of this strength and weakness set the perimeters of the Darvas box. The bottom of the box is used as a stop loss point. Ideally, as shown in figure 13.2, the box construction moves steadily upwards with the trend, with a trailing stop loss lagging just behind current price action. The Darvas approach uses a unique understanding of trend behaviour and is designed for long-term trend trading. It is a bullish approach most suited to trending stocks but it is also applied to breakout markets.

Figure 13.2: box construction moving with the trend

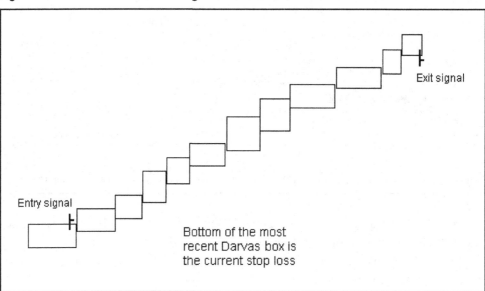

Darvas is able to follow and trade stocks without the need for intraday prices or even to have access to daily prices. This makes the approach particularly useful for readers who have full-time jobs, or who travel.

The D_box uses a range-based measure of bullish and bearish sentiment to set the parameters of significant price action. The importance of a price breakout to a new high is confirmed when price overcomes a measure of immediate bullish strength.

This combination provides greater certainty about the trend continuation, which is counterbalanced by an immediate measure of bearish strength. A close below this level set by the bottom of the Darvas box suggests not just an exit from the trade but a significant decline in trend strength and the potential for a trend collapse.

The unique feature of the Darvas approach is the way it uses a measure of both current bullish and bearish strength to define trend continuation. The Darvas approach uses its own internal logic to understand trend behaviour. When applying this method traders ignore all other indicator-based signals.

This is a strategy based on buying breakouts to new 12-month highs. The approach developed by Darvas uses the new high as a starting point, and then waits for several confirming conditions to develop before acting on a buy trigger. These confirming conditions create the rules for constructing the Darvas box. There are two important variations to this strategy. In the next chapter we show how the classic Darvas approach undergoes a modern adaptation. The differences, marked by squares, are summarised in figure 13.3.

Figure 13.3: Darvas adaptations

CLASSIC	MODERN	BREAKOUT
● Trade initiated by a new high for the rolling 12-month period.	■ Trade initiated by a new high for the rolling 12- or 6-month period.	■ Trade initiated by the second valid Darvas box after initial downtrend breakout.
● All decisions based on the high or low of the series.	● All entry decisions based on the high of the series.	● All entry decisions based on the high of the series.
● Action triggered by first trade at the trigger price.	■ All exit decisions based on the close of the series.	● All exit decisions based on the close of the series.
● Method of stop loss calculation remains constant.	● Entry action triggered by first trade at the trigger price.	● Entry action triggered by first trade at the trigger price.
● Volume increase with breakout.	■ Exit action managed on the day after the trigger close.	● Exit action managed on the day after the trigger close.
	■ Stop loss calculation uses 'ghost' boxes where necessary to handle modern volatility.	● Stop loss calculation uses 'ghost' boxes where necessary to handle modern volatility.

In adapting Darvas for markets at the turn of the century we countered the increase in market volatility by changing the trigger for the exit from an intraday price move to an end-of-day close. The increase in volatility after the 2008 Global Financial Crisis has confirmed the importance of this modification.

In Darvas-style trading a filter is applied to price movements to help determine which price moves are significant, and which are not. The objective is to determine what is a minor price move and which is a significant price move. The significant price move is significant because it signals the end of a current trend, triggers a stop loss condition or tips the balance of probability away from the current trend conditions continuing.

The classic Darvas application looked for an increase in volume with a price breakout. Our research indicates this is no longer an important identification or verification feature. This is shown in figure 13.4. There is no consistent correlation between volume behaviour and the D_box breakout

Modern markets are deep and liquid enough for massive and sustainable volume to follow price movements for extended periods. Even in stocks with modest turnover, there is often enough trading activity to make good-sized trades achievable. In modern markets volume follows price, like a crowd gathering around a school-yard fight. As a result we only consider volume in terms of our ability to purchase the number of shares we require. We ignore volume in its original classic role as a breakout confirmation.

Darvas trading is a method developed more than half a century ago. It was modified for trading markets in the early part of the 21st century. It requires no modification for use in modern markets. It is a logical process uniquely adaptable to the increase in volatility in modern markets. The classic Darvas approach, where the signal is generated by an intraday price move, is less suitable to modern markets because exits are triggered by intraday volatility. The modern Darvas approach which acts on the price close remains well adapted to the increasing volatility of today's market. It takes from the past and applies the method successfully to the future of developing markets. In the next chapter we look at the details of building and using the Darvas box.

Figure 13.4: modern Darvas boxes

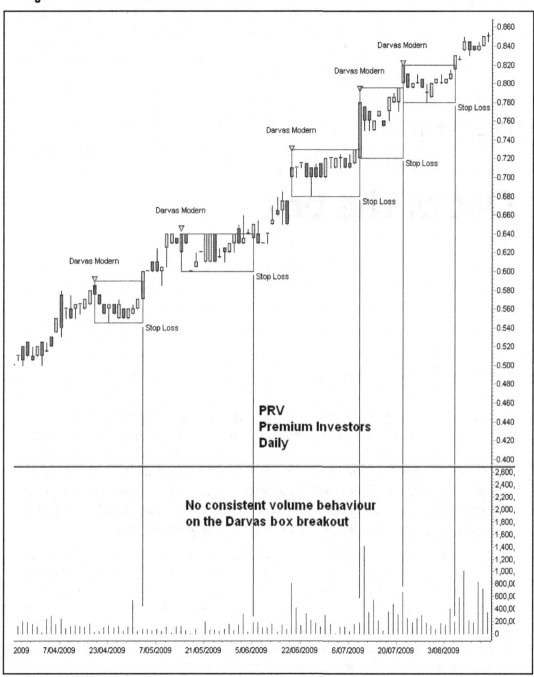

Chapter 14

Out of the box

Long and stable uptrends have become more difficult to find. The Darvas box is more usefully applied in the breakout environment with stocks making new six-month highs. If the previous six-month period has been compatible with Darvas trading then there is a good probability the trend will continue to be compatible with this method. However, the duration of the trend has a lower probability of lasting for another 6 to 12 months. It's the nature of the modern market. Despite this, Darvas analysis provides good trading opportunities which capture the progress of shorter trends.

The shortening of trade exposure and the reduction of trend trading investment horizons is an important change in the nature of the market. The long continuous uptrends that characterised the market in the first decade of the 21st century have largely disappeared. Trends have become shorter. It's both a function of volatility and a result of volatility. Darvas has the advantage of also capturing the longer term trend continuation, but just because a stock shows early compatibility with Darvas trading it does not mean this will become a trend lasting many months.

The classic and modern Darvas approach uses a new 12-month high. We use either the results in the financial media or the results of a database search to find these candidates. The MetaStock formula for this is detailed at the end of the chapter. This is a good tactic for a strong and established bull market and has a good level of reliability of around 80%. In modern markets we found using a new high for the six-month period also returned good results with an acceptable level of reliability of around 70%, which puts this technique in the select group of very successful trend approaches.

Unless you are using software such as Guppytraders Essentials or OmniTrader you will probably have to construct the Darvas box yourself. This means most other charting software users must plot the boxes by hand. Fortunately it is not difficult or time-consuming. It's worth the time and effort because this analysis technique successfully captures the increase in volatility behaviour in modern markets.

Setting the top

When applying a Darvas approach, traders start with a new high for the selected period. This has the capacity to set the top of the D_box if the correct conditions are established by subsequent price action.

Setting the top of the box takes exactly four days of price action. The high must be followed by three days of lower highs. This does not mean the highs are all descending highs where each one is lower than the previous high. The deciding factor is the three highs must all be lower than the initial high—bar 1 in figure 14.1—that triggered the start of the pattern. In the example shown, the first two days show a pattern of descending bars but the last day in the extract has a high that is higher than the previous day's bar. This is acceptable because the three most recent bars have highs that are all lower than bar 1.

The upper edge of the new box is always a four-day pattern. If one of the three days after bar 1 sets an equal high the calculation is abandoned and a new calculation commences. The new, most recent equal high is used as a new starting point. Alternatively, if one of the three days after bar 1 sets a high that is higher than bar 1, the current D_box construction is abandoned and the new highest high for the period is used as a starting point for plotting a new D_box.

The objective is to capture the high for the period and then plot the bullish strength over the next three days. No move is made to start calculating the bottom of the Darvas box until the top of the box is confirmed. Once the top is verified our attention shifts to plotting the correct placement of the bottom of the box.

Figure 14.1: establishing the top of the box

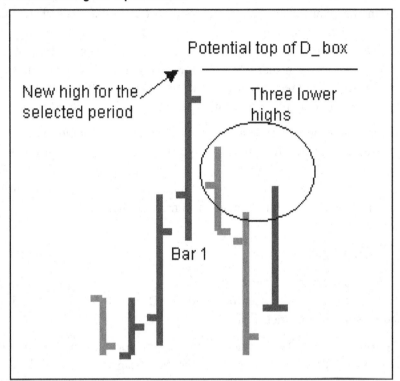

Setting the bottom

The bottom of the D_box defines the limits of bearish strength. When the box is completed it captures the bullish and bearish range of price, so breakouts above or below the box limits are particularly significant. This underpins the trend-following and stop loss strategies of the technique.

As soon as the top of the box is confirmed the trader looks for the most recent low occurring after and including bar 1 because this is the starting point for the calculation used to set the bottom of the D_box. In most cases the lowest bar is below the low of bar 1, as shown in this example in figure 14.2. The lowest bar is used as the start of the calculation point for setting the bottom of the Darvas box and is set when the bar is followed by three days of higher lows. The starting point of the calculation captures the limits of bearish strength. After this low the bulls take charge and prices lift steadily.

We do not look for three consecutively higher lows where each low is higher than the low of the previous day. The defining feature is the way subsequent lows are higher than the low of the bar used for the starting point of the calculation of the D_box bottom. In the example shown, the three bars have lows higher than bar A. The low of the last bar in the series is lower than the low of the previous day. This is acceptable because the lows of the days following bar A are all higher than the low of bar A.

Figure 14.2: lowest bar below the low of bar 1

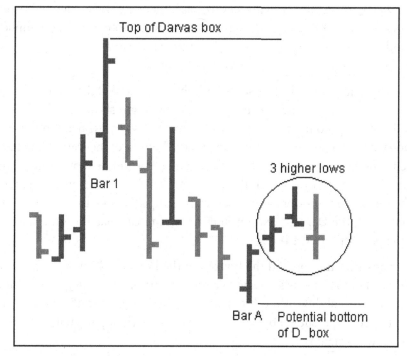

We have used this example because it shows that once the top of the box is set it may take a few more days before we set the bottom of the box. Once the top of the box is set, the bottom of the box does not automatically start from the most recent low, ignoring any further lows. The bottom of the box is only set once the specified conditions have been met. If a new equal or lower low appears within three days of bar A, the current bottom-of-the-box calculation is abandoned and a new calculation starts from the most recent equal or lower low.

The final completed Darvas box includes a high resistance level based on a single price point high. The low support level also swings off a single price point. These levels define the expected ranging activity of the stock over any given four-day period. This sounds restrictive, but the size of the box is determined by the low of the box. This low may take a week or more to establish. It may be significantly lower than the new high, and provides a considerable range for price activity before any stop loss exits are triggered.

Tricky bits and warnings

Although the D_box is plotted with relative ease, there are three potential trip points. The first is a hangover from the way we treat equal highs in other indicator applications. The second relates to the application of the automatic Darvas tool. The third resolves a contradiction in some of the notes written by Darvas.

We start with equal highs. The box starts with the placement of the upper line to define the top of the box and we use the most recent equal high, shown on the left of figure 14.3, as the starting point. This is the same process used with many other indicator calculations but this changes once the top and the bottom of the Darvas box have been confirmed. The Darvas box consists of a resistance line and a support line, and once confirmed they remain in place until they are broken by a move above the resistance line—the top of the box—or a move below the support line—the bottom of the box. Once confirmed, the Darvas box plot lines are not re-calculated until a break occurs beyond the perimeter of the box.

What happens after the top and the bottom of the box have been set is at the core of the application of the Darvas strategy. The box perimeter sets a trigger level for action. The placement or validity of the box is not affected by days with lows equal to the bottom of the box—as shown by bar X—or by days with highs equal to the top of the box—as shown by bar Y.

Once set, the perimeter of the box remains in place. New equal highs are only important if they appear *before* the top of the box is set and validated. Same with the bottom of the box, where new equal lows are only important if they appear *before* the bottom of the box is confirmed. The situation shown in the chart example does not call for the setting of a new D_box. They are potential signals for a breakout as both the bulls and the bears test the limits of their previous range. Once the top and bottom of the Darvas box are set, they remain unchanged until there is a price move beyond the confines of the box.

Using the automatic Darvas plot calculation tool in the Guppytraders Essentials charting package makes Darvas trade selection very easy. However, it carries an important warning. Once the tool is selected, it automatically places a box around any series of bars which meets the Darvas construction conditions—and this has one disadvantage.

Figure 14.3: setting the top and bottom of the box

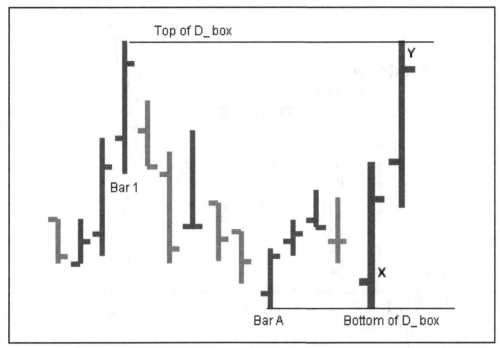

The chart extract in figure 14.4 shows two Darvas boxes, one as a heavy black line and the other as a thinner line. For clarity, both are shown just outside their calculation points. Both boxes meet the construction rules, but the light box is not a valid D_box. The reason lies with the starting point for the construction calculation.

The D_box starts with a new high for the selected period. In the classic application, this is a new high for the year. In some modified applications, this is a new high for a six- or three-month period. The choice is left to the user, so the D_box tool simply completes the calculations from any point selected by the user.

Trader A has selected a new high for the year as the starting point for his D_box, and the resulting calculation and plot is correct. Trader B has selected a starting point that is not a new high. Her D_box is structurally correct, but practically incorrect. When using an automatic Darvas tool it is important to select a starting point that is a new high for the chosen period.

Figure 14.4: different starting points

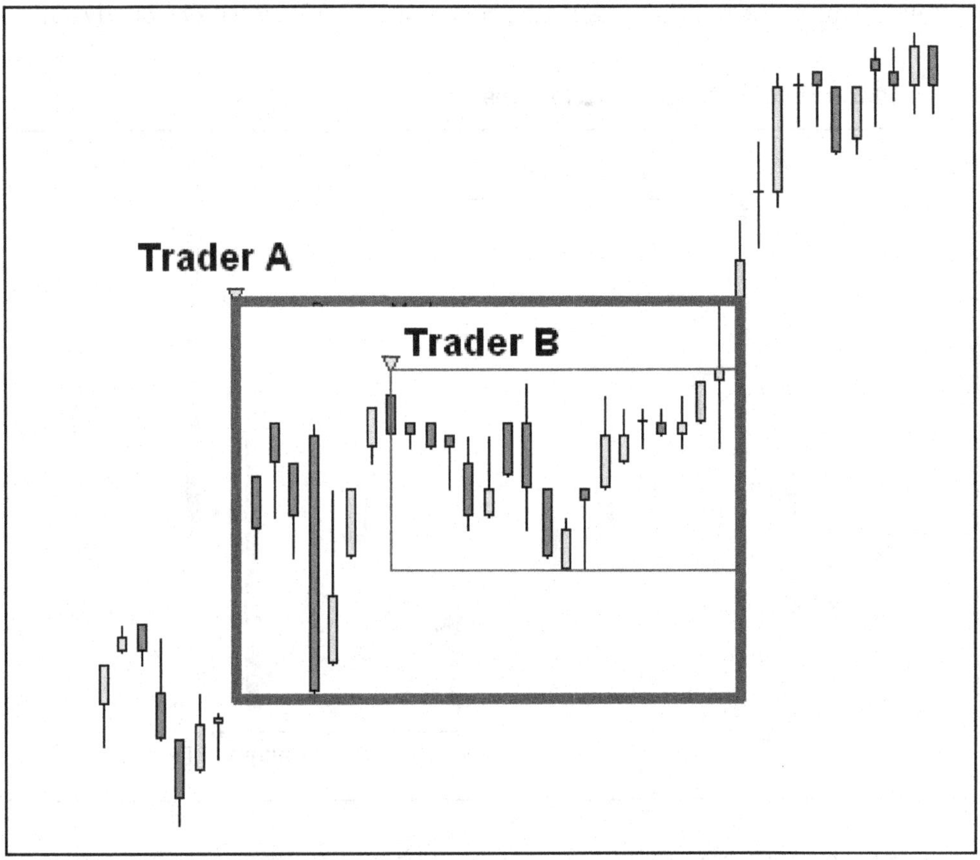

Trader A

Trader B

Special case

Darvas recognised one special and unusual case. It was unusual in the market behaviour in 1960 but it has become much more common in modern markets. In this situation the starting bar of the calculation—bar 1—is used to form both the high of the box and the low of the box. The construction of the box proceeds in the normal fashion, but setting the bottom of the box is slightly different.

We start with a new high for the selected period—call it bar 1. We look for three days of lower highs, as shown. The top of the box is plotted. As soon as the top of the box is in place we start looking for the lowest low of the period, starting with and *including* the low created by bar 1.

In the example shown, bar 1 also has the capacity to become bar A used in the calculation for the bottom of the Darvas box, where we look for three days of higher lows. We have used an extreme example in figure 14.5. In this case the first three days of lower highs also show three days of higher lows. Once the top of the D_box is set and the trader turns to the most recent low, he finds bar 1 is also the lowest low for the period. In this case the following three days also show a pattern of lows that are higher than the low of bar 1. In this extreme example the top and the bottom of the box are set simultaneously.

It is not uncommon in today's volatile markets for the initiating bar—bar 1—to also act as the confirming bar—bar A—for the bottom of the D_box.

Figure 14.5: bar 1 has the capacity to become bar A

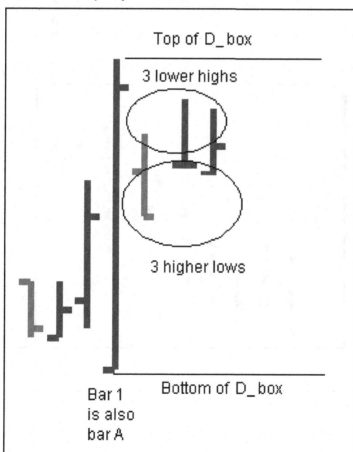

167

Box limits and modern triggers

The triggers for action using the Darvas technique are set by price moves above the top of the box or below the bottom of the box. In response to modern volatility, we find the reliability of the method is improved if we wait for a close above the top of the D_box. The default Darvas tool in the Guppytraders Essentials charting package is programmed for the classic Darvas approach. Users can also select a modern Darvas application.

Figure 14.6: price move above the top of the box

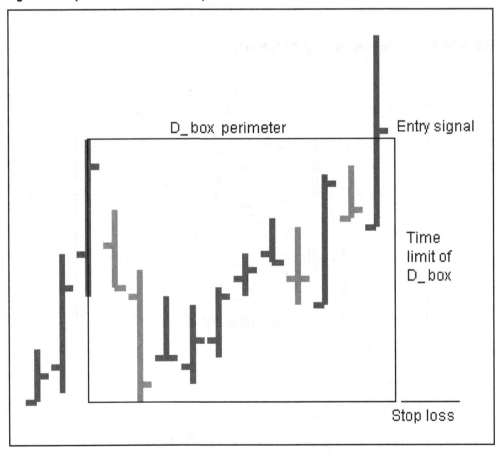

Two important things happen once we have a price move above the top of the box, as shown in figure 14.6. The first happens immediately and we use the bottom of the box as a stop loss level for the new trade. Aggressive traders act in anticipation of a D_box breakout. They buy stock once the bottom of the box has been confirmed. They buy in anticipation of a breakout above the top of the D_box and use the bottom of the D_box as a stop loss point.

The second feature is a charting convenience. Once the breakout takes place, the Guppytraders Essentials charting package plots a vertical line at the start and the end of the D_box. This helps to visually confirm the concept of a 'box' and also reminds the trader this pattern has now been fully completed. Depending on the choice of line thickness, the D_box vertical sides may obscure the underlying bars. In this extract we show the D_box as thin lines.

The breakout above the top of the D_box, by definition, sets a new high for the selected period. Traders immediately start to apply the conditions necessary to set a new D_box. Once the new high is followed by three lower highs the top of a potential new D_box is established. Once the bottom of the new D_box is created the stop loss level is lifted to match the new D_box. This is the essence of Darvas trade management.

The final D_box configuration in figure 14.7 is a D_box failure. This happens when prices close below the bottom of the D_box and signal an exit as it suggests the prevailing uptrend has come to an end. The classic application of the technique signals an exit as soon as there is a price move below the bottom of the D_box. In modern markets we use a close below this level as a signal.

Once the D_box is established there is no guarantee prices will provide an entry signal by closing above the top of the box. Some prices just continue to drift lower. Once they break below the bottom of the D_box, the trade is closed or the potential trade is abandoned. No new action is taken until the stock is able to make a new high for the selected period. Once this occurs the trader applies D_box construction techniques again.

The Darvas trading technique is easy to apply, either using an automated plotting tool or by hand. It provides a useful way to identify trends and to trade breakouts to new highs with a good level of confidence the high is not a blow-off top but part of a strong bullish trend.

Figure 14.7: D_box failure

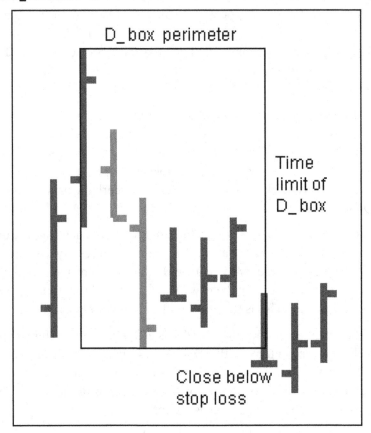

Stops define the trend

The Darvas box and trailing stop approach is designed to keep the trader in a long-term steady trend. In modern volatile markets the rules are given below. Modern Darvas rules are shown in bold.

▦ **Trade initiated by a new high for the rolling 12- or 6-month period.**

▦ All entry decisions are based on the high of the price series.

▦ **All exit decisions are based on the close of the series.**

▦ Entry action is triggered by the first trade at the trigger price.

⊞ **Exit action is managed on the day after the trigger close.**

⊞ **Action is triggered by the close.**

⊞ **Stop loss calculation uses 'ghost' boxes, explained below, where necessary to handle modern volatility.**

The chart in figure 14.8 shows a modern implementation of the Darvas trading strategy to Singapore-listed stock Giant Wire. The stop loss points move smoothly upwards. The entry at $0.15 is an example of modern Darvas trading applied to a breakout situation. It's an eight-month steady trend that has become uncommon in modern markets. We retain this example because trend length will stabilise as markets continue to recover. In this environment the Darvas method will become more compatible with these longer trends. Until then the Darvas approach will look more like the current example shown in the next section.

Figure 14.8: modern implementation of Darvas trading strategy

Ghost boxes

The Darvas trading approach was developed in the late 1950s and worked in a market where high volatility was unusual. The original approach used the bottom of the most recent D_box as a stop loss point. The stop loss point was only raised after a new D_box had been formed. This was a fine strategy in a low-volatility market, so in many of the examples Darvas uses in his book *How I Made $2 000 000 in the Stock Market* the D_boxes overlap each other. The stop loss is lifted upwards on a regular basis and does not lag far behind the current price action.

This is not the case today, and modern market volatility has made this problem more frequent. Prices often move upwards very quickly in a typical momentum-driven sharp trend. There is no threat to the underlying trend in this action. But the speed of the move is not adequately managed using the Darvas stop loss approach. We use a 'ghost' D_box to overcome the impact of volatility, as illustrated in figure 14.9. This type of fast-moving trend is more typical of the modern application of Darvas trading.

The ghost box uses the height of the last D_box, measured in cents, to capture the current volatility of the stock. If a new D_box does not develop quickly then we use a stepped trailing stop loss based on the height of the last box. To understand the reasoning behind using a ghost box we return to the original D_box calculation, which essentially establishes the three-day bullish range — the top of the box — and the three-day bearish range — the bottom of the box.

Our solution uses the most recent calculation of these combined ranges. This calculation is easily identified by the most recent D_box. The height of this D_box is an important guide because it captures the bullish and bearish range. We project this range upwards above the existing D_box as prices move. We do this by simply duplicating the box, and stacking it on top of the previous valid D_box. This captures the permissible range of price activity.

The ghost D_box is activated by a close above the value of the ghost box. The close tells us what the smart money is thinking. It is a useful calculation point that provides a margin of safety when changing the stop loss point. If we stay too close to bullish activity we may get shaken out of the trade too early. The Darvas strategy is to stay with trends.

Darvas trading remains an essential method of managing the increased volatility in new market conditions. It's a classic trend analysis technique that has been successfully modified to deliver consistent results in new conditions.

Figure 14.9: Darvas ghost boxes

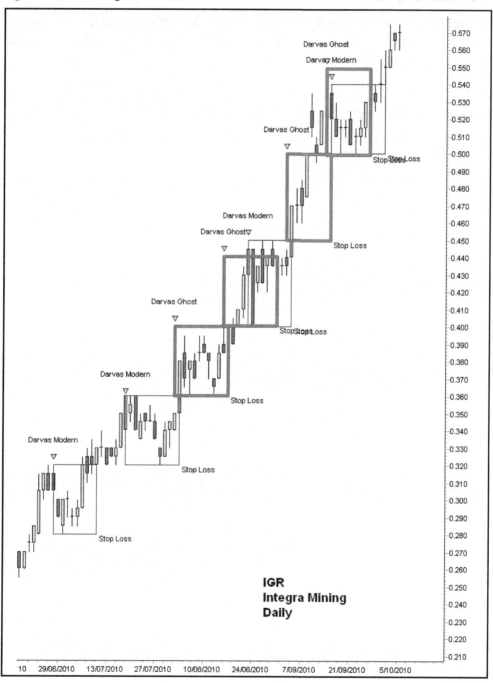

Darvas exploration for MetaStock

This search finds stocks which have made a new 52-week high anytime over the last week. It is run once a week to find all stocks that have made a new 52-week high in the past five trading days.

Col A: close (CLOSE)

Col B: prevH {Previous 52-week High} Ref(HHV(H,52), -1)

Col C: curntH {Current 52-week High} Col D: vol {Volume} V Col E: high (HIGH) Filter colE>colB

Chapter 15

Go straight to profit

Some features of chart analysis never change. The trend line, drawn simply on the screen, remains one of the most powerful methods of trend analysis. It's often over-looked in favour of more complex measures, but the power and profit of simplicity should not be ignored. Trend lines are also an important foundation of pattern analysis, considered in the next chapter.

Trend lines can make you a fortune, or cost you a fortune. This is not restricted to your personal inaccurate use of trend lines. Often the large damage comes from investment advisers and analysts who use trend lines incorrectly and so get your superannuation or fund investments into the market at the wrong time, or not out of the market quickly enough. Incorrect use of trend lines is responsible for millions of dollars of damage to trading and investment portfolios.

Does this judgement sound a bit harsh? Later we consider three examples of trend line placement taken from one of the top two financial news services and used in analysis in major financial media. You can decide, but first some background about trend lines.

Lines and the market

Chartists are skilled in understanding price charts. They use the information from the chart alone to understand what is happening in the market. Their most common tools are straight edge trend lines, and this is where we start. In contrast, the technical analyst uses an indicator, such as a moving average, to analyse the market.

Not all charts yield useful information when these charting techniques are applied. Be wary of any attempt to force charts to comply with preconceived ideas. Look hard enough, and with enough imagination, and any chart will display fanciful patterns. Charting skill avoids this wishful thinking and doubtful application of charting tools. The chartist's tools dismantle crowd action. They are not tools for building a new market in our own preferred image.

All lines are at first tentatively plotted, and we wait for further market activity to prove, or validate, the placement of them. If this doesn't occur, then we must change, plotting the lines again, or removing them altogether until they do define market action. With practice the lines are plotted accurately with just a few reference points to work from. This skill starts with straight edge lines.

Straight edge trend lines

A trend line starts at a single point. This point is not necessarily the peak of the previous trend. The starting point may be based on a rebound point. The starting point is selected because the projection of the line meets other criteria.

A tentative or potential trend line touches two major points. In a downtrend this is the peaks of two significant rallies. In real time it is difficult to determine what is, or is not, a significant rally. The significance of the rally is only confirmed historically. This is not a big problem at the beginning of a trend because our focus is on the end of the trend many days or weeks away.

The trend line is first confirmed when it touches three rally highs, or three significant rally highs. How do we identify a significant rally high? A significant rally high is a high that is not exceeded by another rally high above the trend line in the immediate future.

The trend line is treated with growing confidence when the trend line acts as an accurate rebound area for the fourth and subsequent touch points. This means a move above the downtrend line becomes much more significant and has a higher probability of developing into a genuine trend change.

The trend line starts as a tentative plot that may be adjusted in the light of subsequent activity. Once three anchor points are defined the trend line is used to define the developing trend, as shown in figure 15.1. Once four or more rebound points have been proven, the trend line is used as a trigger to signal the end of the current trend.

Figure 15.1: developing trend line

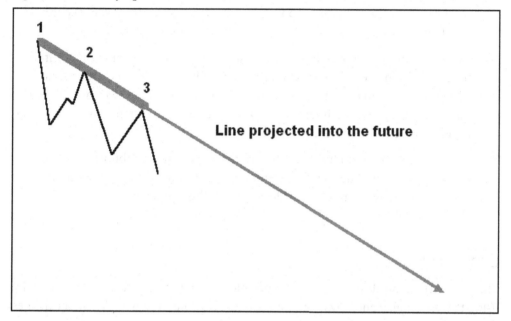

In other words, once the trend line is anchored on three points it is projected into the future. If the trend line placement is correct then we expect any future rallies will touch the trend line and then retreat. If a rally breaks above the trend line then this is the first signal of a potential change in the trend.

Rules for straight edge trend lines

The line is placed along the lows of the price bars in a rising trend. An uptrend is defined by higher lows each day. This is the price element we want to track, so the line goes underneath. If prices fall below this then the trend may change into a downtrend.

A falling trend is defined by the failure of prices to make new highs each day. We track this by placing the downtrend line along the highs.

- The trend line starts with the extremes of the price bars—the high or the low. These extremes really count because a close beyond the extreme tells us the trend might be changing. This is an entry, or an exit, signal. Trend lines placed on line charts are of little use because a line chart only tracks the closing price value.

- The trend line starts at the very extreme high, or low. This is called a trend pivot point. The trend pivot point is only determined retrospectively after the trend has developed.

- The trend line should touch the maximum number of price bar extremes from the available choices. This means we do not exclude too many extremes, nor do we go for the maximum number of hits. We want to use the trend line as a trading signal, so we are interested in closes beyond the extremes of the existing trend because these give the best trading signals.

- The more often a trend line is hit by price extremes, but not broken, the more powerful the trend line signal. A trend line hit 10 times, but not broken, is very strong. So when price does close beyond this it is a very strong trend change signal.

Crowd rules

These construction rules work because they plot the changing nature of the crowd. By using the price highs and lows—the bullish or bearish opinions—the trader defines the way the crowd acts.

Often a crowd acts no differently from us, and nor should this be surprising. A crowd is just a wide collection of individuals. When we see a petrol station with fuel at a $0.10 discount we think about filling up the tank. For many reasons we might miss the opportunity. Later prices return to the old levels and we regret the missed opportunity. Next time fuel is on special we jump in quickly, believing this is probably the best price we are going to get and we do not want to miss out a second time.

Investors and traders watch stock prices in the same way, waiting for prices to fall. When they believe the stock is likely to increase in price they jump in quickly on any price weakness. Prices do not fall very far before buyers snap up the bargains.

Buy a new car and the opposite is true. Perhaps we want the current model but we know a new model is due to hit the market very soon. The run-out sale is predictable so we circle a date on the calendar in advance.

The decline in prices—the decline in our expectations—is defined by a straight edge trend line sloping down. We plot it in advance by observing the extremes of market behaviour using the straight edge trend line construction rules.

Trend line tests

At the beginning of the chapter we said incorrect trend line placement can cost investors a fortune. Here is the evidence. Consider these three examples of trend line placement taken from one of the top two financial news services and used in analysis in major financial media. The purpose is to highlight the dangers of incorrect trend line placement. We start with trend lines drawn on the charts taken from the financial media.

Figure 15.2: incorrect trend line placement—AUD/US dollar

Figure 15.2 is the AUD/US dollar. The analysis conclusion provided with this chart was that the price at $0.88 is 'above the trend line'. This conclusion is meaningless from a trading or investment perspective and provides no indication of how the current price activity could be managed.

Figure 15.3 is the oil chart. The analysis observation that $80 is above the trend line is meaningless because it does not accurately define the current trend activity, where the focus should be on the potential collapse of the uptrend rather than any break in the downtrend.

Figure 15.3: incorrect trend line placement—oil

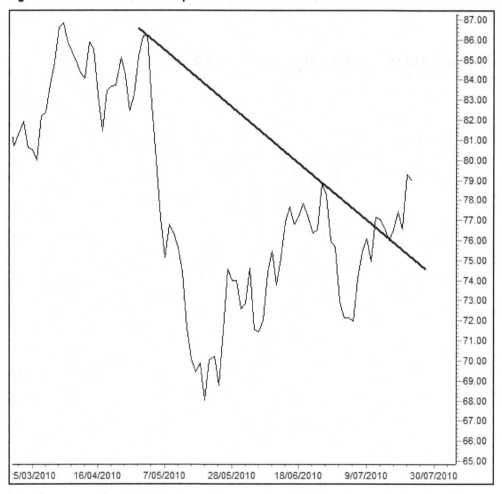

These two charts use trend line placement to conveniently support the conclusion the analyst has already reached. They are used as supporting evidence for a prior conclusion rather than as initiating evidence. If the trend line was used as initiating evidence then the trend breaks in May and June would have been highlighted and the analysis focus would be on the sustainability of the developing uptrends. The incorrect placement of these trend lines means the analysis is focused on a trend line breakout—months after the event—rather than on trend line continuation. Incorrect use of trend lines sets up a great opportunity to lose money.

Here is our placement of the trend lines on these charts.

Figure 15.4: correct trend line placement—AUD/US dollar

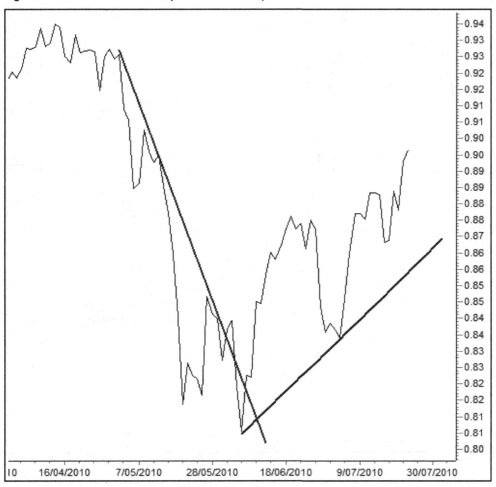

In figure 15.4, the new trend line defines the primary downtrend and captures the breakout in June. This in turn allows the placement of the second trend line to define the new rising trend.

Figure 15.5 defines the trend breakout in May. The initial uptrend from May to June can be defined with a trend line. We use a tentative trend line based on two points to define the developing uptrend. This trend line touches three points, but we treat it as tentative because the second point is not created by a major retreat and rebound in price.

Figure 15.5: correct trend line placement—oil

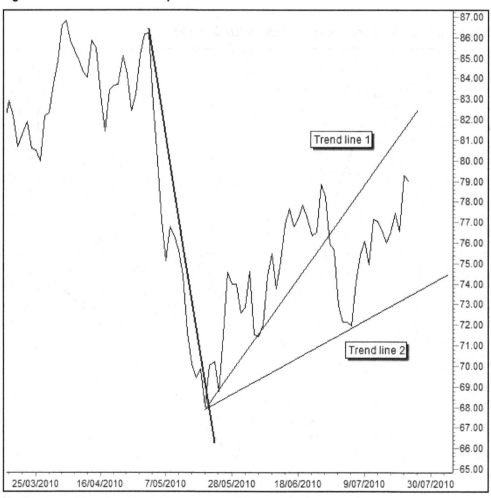

This is important from a trading perspective where exact trend line trigger prices are required.

Figure 15.6 is a final example of a fictitious trend line we couldn't resist reproducing again so we can show the problems when incorrect trend line conditions are used. It's a chart published by one of the leading analysis services. The trend line is really a fictitious trend line supposed to show 'a clean break of the key downtrend'. The trend line is fictitious because it only has two reaction points.

Figure 15.6: incorrect trend line placement—NYMEX Oil

Figure 15.7 shows alternative trend lines that use exactly the same trend line construction conditions as the trend line in figure 15.6 with two reaction points. It is just imagination to say the last trend line is the significant trend line and therefore shows 'a clean break of the key downtrend'. This conclusion is not supported by evidence. The same conclusion could have been equally as validly applied to the previous four

trend lines. The placement of these lines in figures 15.6 and 15.7 is incorrect because they exclude the obvious major change in trend in mid 2008, shown with the thick black line.

Figure 15.7: correct trend line placement, thick line—NYMEX Oil

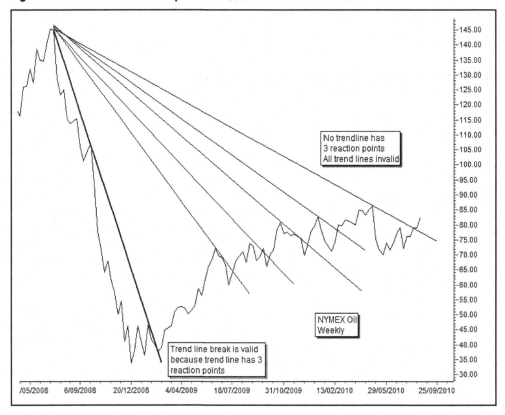

Analysts who use these types of charts to deliver technical analysis are a danger to investors and traders. You can make, or lose, a fortune using trend lines. It's up to you to decide which group you want to belong to. We use a chart as the starting point for our analysis. We do not use a chart to 'prove' our analysis.

Horizontal support and resistance lines

Up trend lines show changing valuations over time where today's valuation is higher than last week's valuation. Horizontal support and resistance lines show a consistent valuation over time where today's value is about the same as the value several months ago. The difference between a support level and a resistance level is important because it shapes the tactics used in each trading situation. The most powerful trend momentum comes from a price move above a support line. The strongest trend continuation comes from a breakout above a resistance line. The stop loss methods and trade management methods for each situation are different.

Every support level in a downtrend has the potential to become a resistance level in a rising trend. A resistance level in a rising trend has the potential to become a support level in a falling trend. Australian trader Louise Bedford calls this a change in polarity. The change in the nature of these levels provides an important way to set upside and downside targets. These levels reflect the price levels where investors and traders make important decisions about the stock. Their influence on future market development and behaviour is significant. Using support and resistance levels is a chart analysis skill. It is not technical analysis that relies on a calculated indicator such as a moving average.

Support levels

Some charts have very clear support levels. It is a clearly defined price line on the historical chart. During the rising trend, this price level acted as a resistance point. Price was capped at this level on several occasions before a breakout was finally established. In a falling market this old resistance level becomes a new support level.

The strength of the support level is confirmed when this level has acted in this way several times in the past. This requires several separate occurrences of this behaviour in both previous uptrends and downtrends. Figure 15.8 shows the ideal situation.

It is uncommon for a chart to show such a high degree of compliance and accuracy with support and resistance levels as shown in figure 15.8. Many charts show a very good degree of consistency, and these levels are used with a high degree of accuracy. The key features we look for in placing the support line at a specific price level are:

- the line captures the majority of capped rises, or falls, at this level. There may be an odd day that moves above or below the level, but these are very much the exception

- the line can be clearly placed. There is no need for fudging, and no room for dispute about the price level. The level is clear and obvious

⊞ the placement of the line also captures several historical events where the line has been valid. In a long-term rising market this may be a problem because many resistance levels would be at new multi-year highs. When price falls below these levels, the support line may include support and resistance behaviour from four to ten years previously

⊞ the line should also appear in the same position, and with a similar level of accuracy, when applied to the weekly chart. This validates the placement of the line on the daily chart and increases reliability.

Figure 15.8: well-defined support and resistance lines

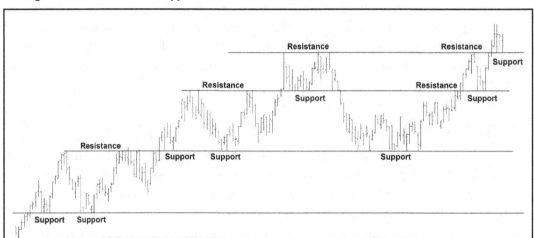

Consolidation levels

Many charts do not show support levels that can be clearly defined with a single line. Instead they show consolidation areas. These are sometimes defined as trading bands. The upper and lower levels of the bands are more difficult to place. If we use a single line we find a clustering of prices near this level, but no definitive single line or dominant price. However, on the chart we do see price has clustered in this general area for several weeks. These consolidation patterns show a pause in the previous uptrend and they have a high probability of providing a pause point in the current downtrend.

In a bull market, traders watch for a rebound from the top of the consolidation band. Temporary price weakness uses this as a support level. In a bear market the lower levels of the consolidation band are used as support. Traders watch for the price fall to lose momentum in the consolidation area. The buy signal for cautious traders is a move above the consolidation level. This is often part of a slower trend breakout and may be associated with a reversal pattern such as a saucer or rounding bottom.

Figure 15.9: long-term consolidation

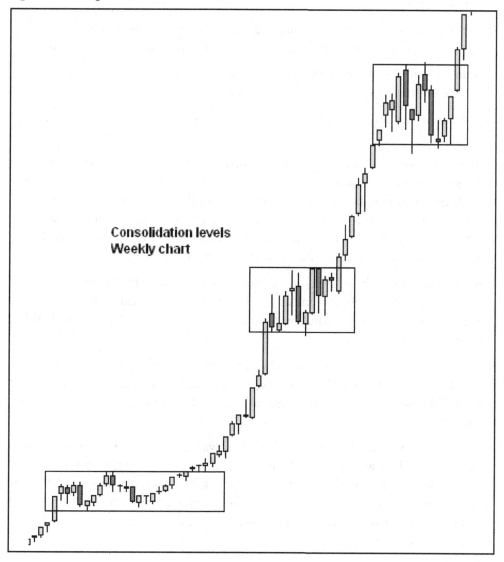

Consolidation areas are easy to see on a chart but are often difficult to pin down with exact values. Long-term consolidation is best seen on a weekly chart, as shown in figure 15.9 where consolidation develops over 10 to 15 weeks.

The key features we look for in defining consolidation levels are:

- a period of at least a week or more where price has moved sideways in the rising trend

- horizontal lines are used to define the approximate high and low limits of the consolidation. The lines are placed to capture the bulk of the price activity

- an indicator based on standard deviations, such as Bollinger bands, may be used to define the upper and lower limits of the consolidation area

- the consolidation level is stronger if it has also occurred in previous years at the same level.

Markets are dynamic, and sloping trend lines show changing market values over time. Support and resistance lines define a consistent value, or series of values, over time. These levels dominate the market more uncannily than trend lines. Just why the crowd has a focus on these areas is not clear, although some explanations make more sense than others. Patterns of resistance are seen in all markets and existed long before chartists and technical analysts drew attention to them.

Some people believe these levels are self-fulfilling because technical traders look for them and act on the signals. It is unlikely there are enough technical traders to influence the action of price in an individual, well-traded stock in this way. It is beyond belief to suggest it occurs consistently in almost all stocks in all markets.

I prefer the explanation for this crowd action developed in the crowd rules section below. Here our real interest is how we recognise and use these patterns of chart activity. These lines do not control the market, but they do help to define the action of the crowd.

Some support and resistance levels are very clear with consistent price action spanning days or weeks. These are strong levels. Weaker levels are defined with just three or four points, or, in special circumstances, just two. Strong long-term support or resistance is defined on weekly charts, or more effectively on point and figure charts. Defining and plotting them accurately is the first step towards using them effectively for investment and trading decisions.

Rules for support and resistance lines

⊞ For support levels, only the lows of price action are used. We need at least two of these joined with a horizontal line. This activity can take place at any time, say near the end of trends, or in the middle of a trend.

⊞ Two points on a daily chart are barely enough. A third point is preferred. No low should dip below the horizontal line. As soon as a new lower low occurs, the support level is invalidated.

⊞ On daily charts, strong support levels are tested many times. Price falls to this exact level, then rises again. Each time price falls it reaches the projected support level and goes no further before rising.

⊞ Short-term support levels are separated by days, or weeks.

⊞ A resistance level is defined in the same way as a support using the first four rules. Only the highs of price action are used. We need at least two of these joined with a horizontal line. This activity takes place at any time, near the end of trends or in the middle of a trend. A third point is preferred. No high should rise above the horizontal line. As soon as a new higher high occurs, the resistance level is invalidated.

On daily charts, strong resistance levels are tested many times. Price rises to this exact level, then falls again. Each time price rises it reaches the projected resistance level and goes no further before falling. Short-term resistance levels are separated by days, or weeks.

⊞ Long-term levels connect price highs or lows separated by months, or years. These are best observed on weekly charts, or point and figure charts.

⊞ Long-term levels need at least three points for validity. The more points, the stronger the impact of the level. These points are often made up of clusters of price highs or lows.

⊞ All levels are eventually broken. When this happens, rising prices are most likely to pause at the next resistance level. In a falling market, the fall is likely to pause at the next lower support level.

⊞ When price moves beyond the resistance level for a single day and then falls back to the resistance level, it delivers a bullish signal. Prices are likely to continue rising.

⊞ Resistance levels often become new support levels after price has finally broken above the resistance level. Support levels often become new resistance levels after price breaks below support.

Crowd support rules

We all belong to crowds, even though we might not gather together in the same physical place at the same time. We become part of a virtual crowd when waiting for prices to rise or fall.

In the stock market price is set by the crowds of buyers and sellers, so why does price sometimes seem to get stuck on a support level? Because one group of people think the stock, or the product, is good value at exactly that price. When prices fall, they buy at this exact level. The market sets the price floor with a common feeling the asking price is just about right.

What is important for the trader and the investor is the repeated behaviour of this crowd action. It is so repeatable that we build market strategies around it.

The market crowd appears to have a long memory. Major support and resistance levels show up on long-term weekly charts. These exact levels from the distant past appear to hold true for today's price activity. They also hold true for future activity. Please remember the line has no connection with the real world so we can only speculate on why some resistance levels are so strong, reliable and often exact. Our explanation rests on common individual behaviour repeated many times in the market crowd.

We expect the value of our shares to increase over time. We are disappointed if they don't and we make the profit and loss calculation based on the price we paid for the shares. If there are many other new shareholders who bought stock at around the same price, then they also use this price as the basis for their profit and loss calculations.

Losses hurt, and if price goes down the new shareholders remember just how much they paid for the stock. As prices rise back to these levels many people decide to bail out, taking a small loss, or perhaps a small profit. They are relieved to just break even on the trade or, in the longer term, on the investment. When lots of people bought at about the same level, and then later sold their shares at about the same level, a resistance line develops.

It works in reverse as well. Perhaps the many new buyers were right, and prices do rise. Most of the new shareholders do not sell. They wait for even more profit. When prices do fall back to the original purchase level many of these shareholders buy more. After all, the price has rallied once, so a price fall gives them an opportunity to buy even more. Using their original buy price as a reference point, these people are buyers again at this level. They provide support, or a floor, under the price retreat.

The key factor in developing support and resistance levels is the way the crowd of new stockholders use a common price point as a basis for their profit and loss calculations. More formally, this is a result of 'anchoring' where traders reference future developments based on an initial anchor point that determines value. I believe this is the most effective explanation for support and resistance patterns. We may never know the real reasons for this activity, but this does not prevent us from using this repeated crowd action profitably.

Support/resistance breakout

The defining feature of a support/resistance breakout is the existence of a previous strong support level. This support level appears several weeks or months before the current trend reversal and breakout. The support level is well defined, as shown on the following chart extract. During the downtrend the price has tested and retested this level of several weeks. This is a clear and well-defined support level. When the market begins to rise there is a high probability this level will also act as a strong resistance level.

The chart in figure 15.10 shows the important difference. The price rebound pauses briefly near the old support level. The support level does not develop into a strong resistance level. Price moves easily above this level. This signals strong trend momentum. There is a low probability the price will retreat and retest the support level and develop a bounce. There is a higher probability any collapse of this trend momentum will allow prices to easily fall below the old support level.

When price moves easily above the old support level it suggests the old support level no longer has a strong influence on market behaviour. In this strong trend momentum trade the stop loss is a momentum stop loss. Traders use the momentum and the volatility of the trend to set the stop loss and protect profits. They do not use previous support or resistance levels to set the stop loss point.

This type of situation is best described as a support/resistance breakout because the most important character of the horizontal line is its function as a previous support level.

Figure 15.10: support/resistance breakout

Resistance/support breakout

The chart extract in figure 15.11 shows the reverse situation where the resistance level is the most important feature. The downtrend has ended and a new uptrend has developed. The key feature is the development of a resistance level. This is clearly defined. Price rises to this level, retreats, then rises again to the resistance level. This resistance may continue for one to two weeks. The resistance level is easily defined with a horizontal line. A move above this horizontal line is a resistance line breakout and shows trend continuation.

When the line is projected backwards we see it corresponds to a weak support level. The market has paused near this level, so it does show support behaviour because the downtrend paused near this level. Weak support is shown in several ways:

- price activity is confused near this level. Price does not develop a well-defined support at this level. Compare the support activity on this chart with the support activity in figure 15.10. The support level is not clear

- this level may be defined as a short-term consolidation. Short-term activity does not indicate a strong support level

⊞   the consolidation area lasted for several weeks, but included confused
      price activity.

Figure 15.11: resistance/support breakout

The most important feature on the chart is the recent resistance activity. The price breakout is a move above strong recent resistance so we prefer to call this a resistance/support breakout. There is a high probability price will retreat and use the resistance level as a new support level. The value of the resistance level is used as the first stop loss in managing this type of trend continuation breakout. As the trend develops it is useful to use previous support and resistance levels to set the stop loss for the developing trend trade.

Strong support/resistance breakout

This features a well-defined price level that acts as strong support and strong resistance. This type of support/resistance relationship may also develop as an inverted head and shoulder breakout pattern as shown in figure 15.12. This was a common feature in the

2009 market recovery. When a falling market is developing a new uptrend this pattern is usually identified as an inverted head and shoulder even though its main component is the very strong support/resistance level. The key features are:

⊞ strong, well-defined support level tested many times. This level is also confirmed on historical charts. For example, a support level in 2008 was also a support level in 2001 and 1996

⊞ the support level has consistently acted as a resistance level when the new uptrend develops. This resistance level is well defined and tested many times. This level is also confirmed on historical charts. For example, a resistance level in 2008 was also a resistance level in 2001 and 1996

⊞ the price fall below the strong support level rebounds quickly and then uses the support level as a resistance level. The rebound is often from a previous historical support level.

Figure 15.12: strong support/resistance breakout from inverted head and shoulder pattern

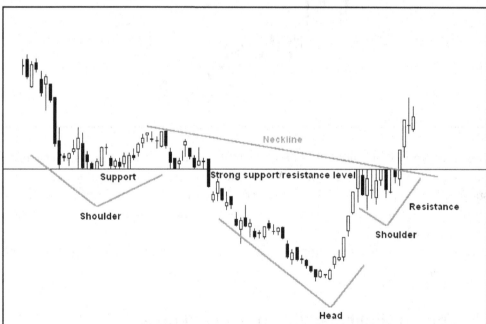

The defining feature of this chart pattern is the consistent strength of both the support and the resistance activity. It is the leading clue telling traders to look for the potential inverted head and shoulder pattern. This inverted head and shoulder pattern is used to set price targets. The distance between the neckline and the head—the bottom of the downtrend—is measured. This value is then projected above the neckline line to set the first price target for the new developing uptrend.

The price breakout above the resistance level is often very rapid and the price target is achieved quickly. This breakout is traded as a rally trade.

Resistance breakout

Markets fall in different ways and the price rebounds and trend recoveries also develop different characteristics. For some trend recoveries we look for resistance breakouts. The chart in figure 15.13 shows this situation. It is different from the previous example because a support or consolidation area does not develop during the market fall. The new resistance area is not related to any previous support or consolidation area.

Figure 15.13: resistance breakout

The resistance level is a new feature in this price activity. The value of the resistance level does not relate to any previous historical price activity. The breakout above resistance is part of a trend continuation trade. The first breakout above the resistance level may be very rapid, but there is a higher probability the breakout will fail and test the previous resistance level as a support level. Traders watch for a successful test and retest of the old resistance level. It may act as a new support level. This is part of the development of a new uptrend but it is not strong and it does not show strong trend momentum.

When we define the breakout our preference is to identify the first strongest feature. If support is the strongest feature then we talk of a support/resistance breakout. However it is more important to use these relationships to understand if the trade is a strong trend continuation trade, or a strong trend momentum trade. The stop loss methods and the trade plan targets are different for each of these trades.

These distinctions are combined in chart pattern analysis in the next chapter. Chart patterns provide a window into the behaviour of the market crowd. They capture crowd emotions. Many chart patterns are defined with trend lines, support and resistance lines and, in some cases, with curved trend lines. Accurate recognition and placement delivers a steady flow of profits.

Chapter 16

Patterns of opportunity

Markets change but human behaviour does not. Chart patterns continue to provide wonderful trading opportunities. These are not the obtuse and difficult-to-identify patterns often listed in compendiums of patterns. Most of these are statistical patterns, not the patterns of human behaviour. Turn off the lights in a crowded room, shout fire, and there is a predictable human behaviour reaction. The number of people who survive the crush to get out the door is a statistical pattern of behaviour. We trade the first situation, not the statistics.

Many behaviour reactions are instinctive and they have not disappeared from modern financial markets. The development speed of these behaviours has increased, so it becomes more important to accurately define and recognise a handful of very profitable chart patterns. There is an increased need to move quickly as the pattern develops. The near 50% fall in the DOW in six months in 2008 and the more than 50% rise in the DOW in 10 months starting in 2009 are evidence of the changes in market reaction speed.

Chart patterns point the way to high-probability outcomes. When we see the chart pattern developing the trader knows there is an increased probability price will behave in a particular fashion. When the pattern development is confirmed there is a high probability—often in the order of 70% to 80%—the price will achieve the targets calculated from the chart pattern. It is this shift in the risk and reward relationship that makes chart pattern trading so useful.

Chart patterns are the intersection of market behaviour and trading as an art. Traders who have good pattern recognition instincts apply this method with consistent success. If you do not have the ability to quickly recognise chart patterns then this trading method is both a frustration and a mystery. Despite many claims, this is not a problem that can be solved by computer software. In this chapter we provide the pattern recognition rules.

Charting uses the behaviour of price, observed directly from the price chart, as a basis for understanding the behaviour of the crowd. This remains one of the most consistently powerful and reliable methods of market analysis. It forms one of the cornerstones of our trading approach. Modern market behaviour has not sidelined these time-tested techniques. Modern volatility has often made the breakout moves more rapid. Targets are achieved more quickly, and the pullbacks from targets can be more sudden and severe. These are developmental differences. They do not diminish the core behaviours and analysis conclusions created by the combination of resistance levels and trend lines. These line convergences and intersections capture the most basic and reliable of human behaviour in the market.

The technical analyst uses a calculation of the price data to reach a conclusion about the potential future behaviour of price. This is an advanced form of statistical analysis. It is very useful and highly effective in markets where there is a high level of financial engineering. This includes derivative markets such as options, warrants and CFDs. These are 'created' markets, and the market makers try to keep price activity within the ranges of their statistical models. The warrant market maker's calculation of fair price drives his buying or selling activity as a market maker. He has the market power to make this happen in most cases. Financial engineering is less useful in the rumble tumble of publicly traded stocks. Here we want to follow human behaviour more closely, and chart analysis provides a long-term advantage.

Statistical coincidence

Chart patterns are not a statistical coincidence. The chart patterns we look for are a product of human behaviour and not the product of number behaviour. The closer a market is to the behaviour of willing participants the greater the validity of a chart pattern. Some markets are dominated by unwilling participants, and although they sometimes throw up apparent chart patterns, these cannot be used reliably.

Some analysts identified a head and shoulder reversal pattern in the US dollar index chart in figure 16.1. They point to the left shoulder developing in March 2010 and the recent rally and retreat activity forming the right shoulder. The head and shoulder pattern does appear on the dollar index chart but it has no analytical significance.

The head and shoulder pattern appearing in a stock chart or an index chart is significant because it captures the psychological behaviour of willing participants in a market. The stock market, and by proxy, the index, is created by a crowd of buyers and sellers who make a decision to participate. They back their opinions on market direction with money. Their fear, greed and expectations create the psychology of the market. Their behaviour in turn creates a number of high-probability chart patterns which are used to evaluate the changes in the balance of probability.

Any number series, such as a record of the weather, or a series of randomly generated numbers, will throw up 'chart patterns'. They are meaningless coincidences because they are not a reflection of the decision-making of participants. The weather cannot choose today to be 30 degrees rather than 29 degrees. A random number generator by definition cannot choose to select 100 rather than 99 as the next number. A trader, or investor, can and does make a decision to buy or sell when price next moves to 109. This gives a behavioural component to pricing and this makes chart patterns of behaviour a valuable analytical tool.

The foreign exchange (FX) market is dominated by unwilling participants. Every time a bank customer buys or sells in a foreign currency the bank is obligated to take the other side of the trade—irrespective of the bank's preference. The bank is held hostage to the demands of its customers so it lacks the freedom of behaviour found in stock markets. The FX market is effectively analysed using statistical technical analysis and this includes moving averages, trend lines and support and resistance levels.

The chart patterns that emerge in FX markets are largely the product of statistical coincidence and are not analytically significant. The head and shoulder pattern exists on the dollar index chart, but it is essentially meaningless from a behavioural perspective. Traders must be aware of the dangers of statistical coincidence.

Patterns by themselves do not necessarily lead to consistent outcomes. The development of chart patterns alerts the trader to a selected range of more probable outcomes. As price moves towards a well-established resistance level the trader pays more attention to the stock, ready to place a buy order if prices move a few ticks above the level. She cannot buy until others have bought because she wants to follow the action, not create it. When prices retreat into the body of the support and resistance band, or other chart patterns, the trader shifts attention elsewhere.

Figure 16.1: US dollar index

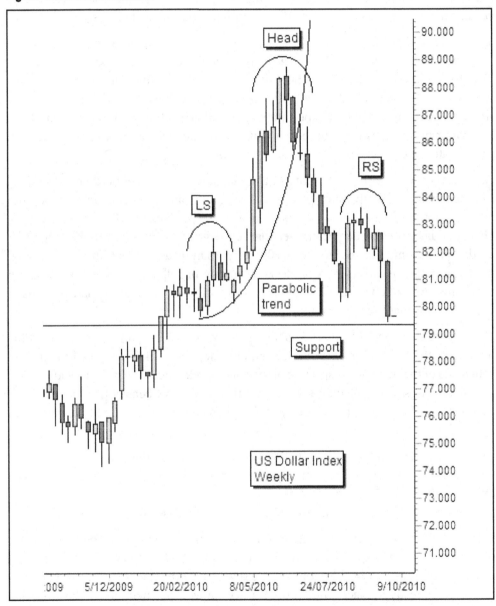

Chart patterns signal the probability of action, and in this chapter we consider the essential and most reliable analysis patterns. We look at trend reversal patterns, the major triangle patterns and how they are used in analysis. We start with end-of-trend support and resistance behaviour as a base for changes in trend direction.

Double bottom and double top

These are trend reversal signals found at the end of a trend. Here we concentrate on the 'double bottom'. The same conclusion, but in reverse, is applied to a 'double top'.

The classic double bottom is sometimes called a W-shaped recovery and it has quite precise construction rules. These deliver a very high probability of successfully selecting the future direction of price. Other double bottom rules are less rigid, and have a lower level of probability. The rules you decide to use will determine how reliable the double bottom is as an indicator.

A single bottom in a falling trend is the point where the trend reverses direction. Sometimes prices rise and then fall back again to retest the low. This is the beginning of a potential double bottom. When the pullback in prices is exactly equal to the earlier single point low, or is within a few ticks, we label it a double bottom, as shown in figure 16.2. Increased volatility means there are more intraday dips below support in this pattern. The key feature is the position of the close in relation to the support area. This is a powerful signal when the two bottoms are separated by several weeks. It is still a powerful signal when separated by just a few days, but the reliability is reduced.

W or double bottom recovery features

- A sharp rebound from a historical support level.
- A sharp rebound following an overshoot of a support level.
- A short-term rally, four to six weeks, followed by sharp retracement.
- A second sharp rebound from a historical support level. This should not include any large overshoot.
- Pattern is confirmed when price moves above the high set by the initial rally.
- Short-term, three- to six-week rally trades.
- Long-term long-side trades when the second rebound is proved.

Figure 16.2: double bottom

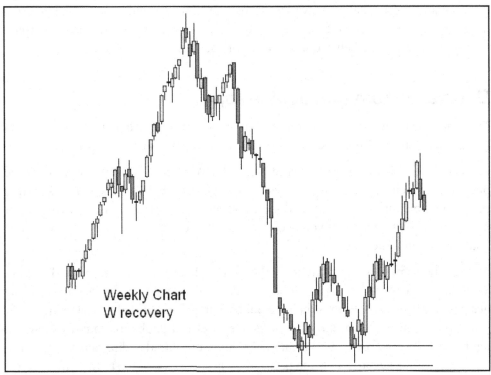

Weekly Chart
W recovery

V recovery features

The V-shaped recovery develops from a single rebound point. A single bottom in a falling trend is the point at which the trend reverses direction, as shown in figure 16.3. It has these recognition rules:

- fast rebound from a historical support level

- fast rebound after an overshoot below a historical support level

- minor pullback after an initial three- to six-week rally

- strong uptrend continuation after pullback

- trade the first rise as a rally

- use the pullback to add to positions, or open new long-term, long-side positions.

These are bottom patterns. They do not occur in the middle of uptrends or downtrends.

Figure 16.3: V-shaped recovery

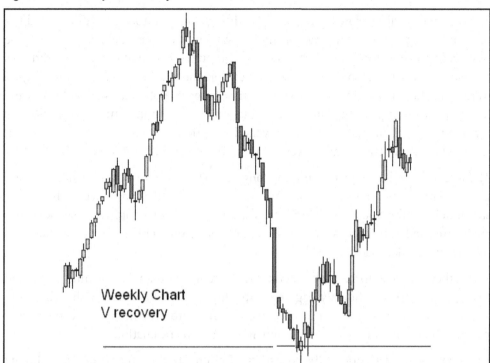

Significant double tops occur in stocks with strong trends. The first top is a significant and clear high. The price levels at the second top must be very near to the first top price. The two tops must be separated by at least several days of price action falling from the first high to a low point then rising to the second high.

Longer patterns where the highs are separated by several weeks are much more reliable indicators. Trading volume must be steady and consistent. Double tops in thin markets are not strong indicators. These are top patterns. They do not occur in the middle of uptrends or downtrends.

Triple bottoms or tops are constructed in the same way as double bottom or top patterns. The triple bottom includes another failed rally with a price retreat to the same levels, followed by another uptrend. Although many traders feel these triple patterns are more reliable, they sometimes signal the start of a channel trading opportunity. Cautious traders wait for the trend break from these triple patterns to be fully confirmed before taking action.

Crowd rules

These patterns reflect crowd behaviour. The first definite bottom in a falling trend is a bargain buying opportunity. Traders and investors wait on the sidelines, watching the price collapse at a steady rate over weeks and months. Eventually, company fortunes change. The actual reason is not as important as the action it initiates from buyers waiting in the wings. Now the stock is a true bargain, not because it is historically low, but because it is potentially undervalued in relation to its future prospects. This turnaround in fortune is rapid, and buyers drive prices upwards in a scramble to get stock. These smart traders and investors jump on the trend break very early.

The less informed have given up hope long ago. They have read, and believed, every good news story put out by company management during the long price decline. They stop looking at the stock price every day because it is so depressing. These stockholders are hurting and avoidance is one way to ease the pain. When prices do move, they miss out. They are asleep at the wheel.

When they do wake up they take action. Prices are higher than the last time they dared to look. Some sell very quickly, frightened the downtrend will resume. Others hang off, trying for better prices so their level of loss is reduced to something they can tell their partner about without collecting too much grief and recrimination.

Early buying is beaten down by investors who already hold the stock and who are eager to get rid of it as the price rises. Some of the early inexperienced buyers see this, and worry they have made a mistake. They begin to sell, and gradually the price is forced down, overwhelmed by nervous sellers.

The final result has several possible outcomes. At worst, prices continue to fall below the previous low. If so, this rally turns out to be just an excited blip in a longer downtrend. The most useful outcome is when prices fall to very near the same low level as in the past, and then begin to rise again. Traders look for this second rally to build from a double bottom. When prices bounce off the same old level it suggests many more people have decided this is a good buying opportunity.

The double bottom can become a self-fulfilling pattern, as many traders watch for this type of chart pattern. When the second bottom is confirmed they pile on, adding to the buying pressure and pushing prices higher.

Does this matter? Probably not. Traders use the pattern to get in early on solid new uptrends. Exactly who creates the pattern is not as important as making money from it.

Up-sloping triangles

Resistance and support levels, marked as horizontal lines on a chart, act as barriers. They are static forces controlling crowd action. Trend lines, on the other hand, are dynamic because they reflect changing value over time. With these lines we get a sense of crowd movement. The real dynamics of crowd action are expressed by a combination of resistance levels and trend lines. These chart patterns capture the dynamics of the crowd and help traders select powerful movements.

Triangle patterns develop from the clash between those with rising expectations, defined by an up-sloping trend line, and those who are set in their ways, defined by a horizontal resistance level. When these two lines eventually meet they define a perfect point of contradiction. Sellers firmly believe the stock is worth a particular amount. This belief is so strong that a solid resistance level forms, extending usually for days or weeks, although sometimes for months. Buyers believe they know better. They sense future value in this stock, and effectively push prices higher. Each time price retreats, they bid a little higher just to make sure they get stock. This builds a rising trend line.

Where these two lines intersect they form a triangle, and ultimately the end point of conflict between two substantial and active groups in the market. Who wins—the crowd of buyers or the crowd of sellers—is not a foregone conclusion, although the probabilities are weighted in particular ways with up-sloping triangles. What we do say with a high level of certainty is: here is a point where the crowd is involved in some serious action.

Just like a school-yard fight, this action draws more spectators, and more participants. It quickly becomes a brawl, and in market terms we want to be on the winning side. The slope of the triangle points the way to the victor.

Rules for up-sloping triangles

⊞ The resistance level is plotted according to the resistance line construction rules in the previous chapter.

⊞ The up-sloping trend line must be accurately plotted and conform to the trend line construction rules in the previous chapter.

⊞ Single days spiking above the resistance line are ignored. These are a good sign of building strength and are a guide to price targets for any breakout.

⊞ Use the height of the vertical edge or base of the triangle to project upside price targets. Breakouts often meet these targets, and pause at this level before new trending action develops.

⊞ The same techniques are used to establish downside targets. More accurate downside targets are determined by starting the projection from the trend line slope at the actual breakout point.

⊞ Short-term triangles lasting just a few days have low reliability. Triangles developing over 10 days, or several weeks, are more reliable. Very long term triangles, constructed over three or four months, or sometimes even longer periods, have a low level of success.

⊞ The horizontal edge of the triangle is divided into thirds, as shown in figure 16.4. The divisions start at the base and end where the sloping trend line intersects the horizontal line. Price breakouts starting in the middle third of the triangle tend to be very strong.

⊞ Price breakouts from the last third towards the triangle tip tend to be weaker than middle triangle breakouts.

⊞ The up-sloping triangle is very bullish when the entire market, or market segment, is also trending upwards.

Figure 16.4: up-sloping triangle

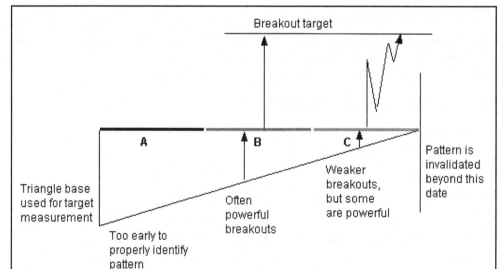

Crowd rules

This psychological crowd action develops a clear chart pattern shown as an upward-sloping trend line. Prices appear to fall back to the line, then bounce off it again. There is nothing magic about the line. It is just an aid to show us how the crowd is thinking.

In some uptrends the price rise seems to run into an area of resistance. When prices get to a particular level, a large number of sellers come into the market with stock to offer at one price. Buyers do not have to bid higher to get stock, so the price rise stalls. This is defined as a horizontal line. This shows a consistent value over time.

People sell shares for many reasons. Sometimes it is to take a profit. Often it is people who bought the shares on the way down, and now they are selling to break even on the trade on the way back up. We cannot understand all the individual reasons helping to create a resistance level. We do not need to know them. But we use our knowledge of this price action to make better trading decisions based on the evidence of a resistance level.

These horizontal and sloping lines are initially placed tentatively on the chart. We watch for future price action to confirm the placement of these lines. These lines offer us a glimpse into a potential future. If they are accurately placed then we reasonably expect price action to react away from each of the lines. Prices will bounce off the rising trend line, and ricochet off the horizontal resistance level. By projecting these lines to the right of the chart—by projecting these lines into the future—we build a picture of future price action. The trader defines a point in time when she expects certain action to have taken place. If it has not taken place, then the trade is abandoned on this basis alone.

The triangle formations are one of the few chart patterns pinpointing a deadline or timetable for price action. Crowds are excitable, and when rising expectations meet a barrier the crowd tries to push through it. This barrier is created by a wave of sellers. While the crowd can throw more money at the barrier it is inevitable the sellers will start to disperse. Most leave because they have been paid. Gradually the others realise they can get more for their stock, so they shift their section of the barrier, asking higher prices. Using a depth of market screen, traders watch these tactical withdrawals. Beyond the current frontline of trades, new resistance levels are prepared as sellers dig in at even higher prices. The order stream grows at these levels.

Finally even the most dedicated seller realises better returns are available, and when the last sell order is withdrawn from the old resistance level the line crumbles. This is a triangle breakout. Flushed with success and pushed from behind, buyers surge forward, chasing the last of the sellers. A decisive breakout happens when price closes consistently higher than the old resistance level. Everyone believes price can only increase. An indecisive, or weak, breakout sees traded prices pull back to the old resistance level, or even below it. There are still sellers who are not entirely convinced the rally is for real.

Every market crowd has its bullies, its weaklings, its fearless idiots armed with more money than sense and the nervous losers who refuse to believe their own good luck. The triangle formation captures all these elements in a crowd, and it captures them in action. This makes the triangle one of the most useful chart patterns.

Traders use these chart patterns to understand how the crowd is thinking. They try to get in ahead of the crowd because they know there is a high probability prices will go even higher. Investors use these patterns to confirm a stock is likely to increase in price. They add to existing shareholdings with a higher level of confidence. The up-sloping triangle pattern is very bullish in rising trends. There is an increased probability of prices continuing to rise above the pattern. This pattern is not as useful in falling trends. In this situation the trader looks for other confirming chart indicators.

Using up-sloping triangles

Chart patterns are not always as ideal as the schematic diagram above. The example in figure 16.5 shows a more difficult situation. The base of the triangle is distorted by a price spike above the resistance level. The trend line includes a hanging start. This is a successful and profitable up-sloping triangle pattern, but it's more complex.

The first recognition step is the resistance level. The second recognition step is the placement of the trend line. Combine these and you have the up-sloping triangle. The base line used for target calculations is measured between the start of the trend line and the resistance level.

The trend line placement includes a 'hanging' start. This occurs when there is a clear trend line identified with rebound points. These are shown as points 1, 2 and 3 on the chart. The trend line is drawn along these points and projected backwards in time until it intersects a price bar. This becomes the nominal start of the trend line. It often hangs in mid-air and is not related to a price low. This is most common in placing trend lines as part of a chart pattern, such as the triangle pattern.

Figure 16.5: hanging start to trend line

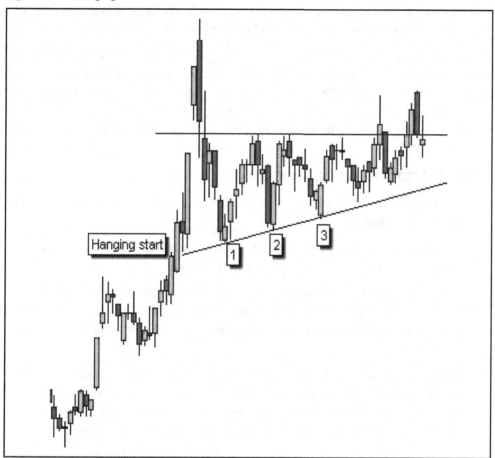

Down-sloping triangles

This chart pattern is an accurate measure of growing fear of loss. It shows the trader exactly what the crowd is thinking, and if he holds an open position—if he owns stock—then he contributes to the development of the pattern with his own selling.

The down-sloping triangle is a bearish pattern, and even more so in a falling market. True believers hold up the floor with dollar bills. Every time price falls they jump in, buying whatever stock is offered. Nervous sellers like this because they have an apparently guaranteed price from buyers who stand firmly in the order line and build this support level.

Very nervous traders worry about this, and although prices do bounce up, they sell a little early just to be certain of getting out of the stock. This is a falling trend line, and when it meets the horizontal support level traders look for crowd action.

The key advantage with this pattern, shown in figure 16.6, is the way the base of the triangle is used to calculated the first and second, and in this extreme case, the third downside target level. Prices fall more quickly than they rise, so down-sloping triangles identify ideal short trading opportunities. Traders who hold open long positions use the down-sloping triangle pattern as a warning to take profit or cut losses.

Rules for down-sloping triangles

- The support level is plotted according to the resistance line construction rules in the previous chapter.

- The down-sloping trend line must be accurately plotted and conform to the trend line construction rules in the previous chapter.

- Single days dipping or spiking below the support line are important warning signals, although they are ignored in terms of placing the line. These spikes are an accurate sign of developing weakness and are used to project the level of any future price fall.

- The height of the vertical base of the triangle is used to project downside price targets. Breakouts often meet these targets, and pause at this level before new trending action develops. These projections are also used to project upside targets, but these are less reliable when applied to down-sloping triangles. The upside targets are determined by starting the projection from the actual breakout point on the trend line.

- Prices tend to fall more easily than they rise. Short-term, down-sloping triangles lasting just a few days have reasonable reliability. Triangles developing over 10 days, or several weeks, are more reliable. Very long term triangles, constructed over three or four months, or sometimes even longer periods, have a low level of reliability.

- The horizontal edge of the triangle is divided into thirds starting at the base and ending where the sloping trend line intersects the horizontal line. Price breakouts in the middle and end third of the triangle tend to be very strong.

- The down-sloping triangle is very bearish when the entire market, or market segment, is also trending down.

Figure 16.6: using the base to calculate target levels

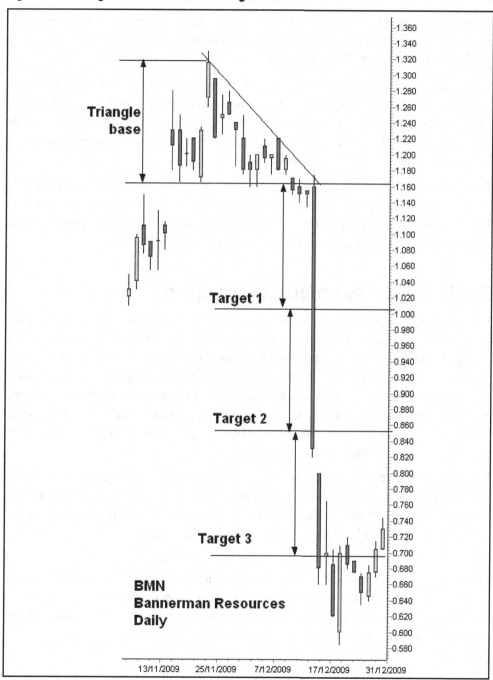

Crowd rules

We believe we are more rational than the market crowd, but reality suggests many of us act in very similar ways. It is these individual actions, each rational in its own way, that build crowd action. The down-sloping triangle captures our fear.

Traders see this pattern developing and move quickly to lock in profits. Investors also use these chart signals, particularly when they confirm other downtrend signals. The development of a down-sloping triangle in a downtrend is a strong continuation signal, suggesting the downtrend is likely to continue. This prevents investors from buying 'bargains' at inappropriate levels.

Down-sloping triangles in uptrends act as caution signs. Here the price collapse is likely to be limited by other support areas and the general strength of the trend. The downward-sloping triangle defines crowd action and, like the up-sloping triangle, allows the trader to anticipate how the action might develop.

Equilateral or symmetrical triangles

The equilateral or symmetrical triangle should be the most dynamic pattern of all. It combines two opposing sloping trend lines, each representing the way the crowd changes its idea of value over time. Instead, this pattern shows weak indecision. Both trend lines are valid, and they define an equilateral triangle. The market is uncertain as to the correct pricing for the stock. Both sellers and buyers revise their valuations over time, but in opposite directions. No single group gains the upper hand and what initially looks a sensible trading decision turns into a prolonged attempt to get out with some dignity, and perhaps even a little profit.

The equilateral triangle with its contradictory sloping trend lines is a model of market indecision. Traders and investors are trapped. It usually takes an external shock—an event not directly related to the stock itself—to open the floodgates to an escape route. When the crowd surges through the gap, prices often move very quickly in a new direction.

This indecisiveness is not a fruitful ground for traders. The classic equilateral triangle is symmetrical, as shown in figure 16.7. Triangles that slope slightly up or down are labelled wedges. The direction of the dominant slope is a guide to the direction of any breakout, but these are still weak patterns looking for leadership.

Figure 16.7: equilateral triangle

Rules for equilateral triangles

- ⊞ The up-sloping trend line is plotted according to the rules in the previous chapter.

- ⊞ The down-sloping trend line is plotted using the rules in the previous chapter.

- ⊞ The potential fall or rise is plotted using the height of the triangle base, and projecting it away from the tip of the pattern. Better targets are determined by starting the projection from the breakout point on the upper or lower trend line. These targets are indicative only because the pattern shows market weakness.

- ⊞ A break in the same direction as the general market is likely to be much stronger than a break going against the market direction.

Crowd rules

This is a restless crowd, milling in anticipation of an event. Some are convinced the outcome is going to be good, so they buy early, snapping up shares at lower prices. Prices do rise, and these early buyers feel vindicated. They are concerned when prices start to fall again, but others are starting to think the same way, so prices do not fall quite as far. The next wave of buyers is prepared to pay a little more. This is the classic buying pattern establishing an uptrend.

What is remarkable about the wider chart pattern is the way sellers are almost as equally pessimistic. As prices rise they take the opportunity to sell, locking in profits from trades initiated many weeks or months previously. Significant numbers of shareholders grow increasingly nervous and sell at slightly lower prices, just to lock in their profits. Frightened they might miss out, they lower their asking price.

These contradictory trends start to feed on each other. Smart traders who bought early watch the developing down-sloping trend line with some concern. By the time the pattern is clear, usually about a third of the way through the projected development of the equilateral triangle, some of these early buyers become sellers. Their selling reflects their indecision, and helps build the broader market indecision.

When the pattern first starts to develop, buyers and sellers are both firmly convinced they are right and the other is wrong. By the time the last third of the triangle is reached, buyers and sellers are not quite as certain of their correctness as they were a few weeks previously.

This confused and increasingly worried crowd has nowhere to go. They wait for an external shock, a jolt delivered by an event not directly related to the stock. This is most frequently delivered by a move in the general market but it may be triggered by some other, comparatively minor, event.

This is a crowd waiting to run. All they need is a starter's gun. Occasionally there is a false start and then the pattern just dribbles along trapping traders, investors and capital.

Triangle patterns point the way to high-probability trading. As with all chart patterns, the trader must avoid the temptation to build patterns where no patterns really exist. Creating castles in the sky from wind-driven clouds is good recreation for children. Using your time to build imaginary chart patterns from market data is a fatal trading error. These chart patterns are valid when they are clear. If you cannot see the pattern in the first glance at the chart, then it is probably not there.

Triangles map crowd activity. They do not map your hopes and desires. Correctly identified and used, these patterns return trading profits. If you chase imaginary chart patterns be prepared to watch your trading capital disappear in a very real way.

Chart patterns, along with other methods for understanding crowd behaviour, provide the foundation for analysis of the market. Each of these opportunities may be traded in different ways. Later we look at trading methods. These are the hard edge of analysis applied to an active and dynamic market. Before we move onto the battlefield, shifting from strategy to tactics, we must first check our protective safety arrangements. Trading is the management of risk. This is not considered exciting and many new traders skip the next section. Later, if they are lucky enough to survive the first encounters with the market, they rush back to the chapters on risk. It's an expensive way to educate yourself. It's much cheaper to read the next few chapters and then walk with genuine confidence into the trading arena.

Part III

Managing risk

Chapter 17

Breaking down risk

Despite all the wailing to the contrary, the world of risk has not changed. Markets have become more volatile, both in terms of daily price ranges and in terms of the speed of trend development and collapse. This has created more risk for those whose risk management techniques were always suspect in any market condition. Snails cannot survive in a fast-moving environment, and some of the major financial institutions have been very slow to realise this. The methods for calculating and managing risk remain largely unchanged but they must be applied more quickly and more decisively. There is no time for hesitation with modern market volatility. Understanding risk management is the absolute foundation of trading survival.

These trading foundations do not change. They protected traders in the Global Financial Crisis while large institutions who told investors they knew better were going down in flames. It is these management methods that protected traders against the damage from the foolish advice from many brokers and commentators who told investors to hold on in January and March 2008 because the market was 'irrational' and things would quickly return to normal. Forget for the moment that many of these institutions were selling just as they told their investors to hold on. Basic chart analysis provided the real story, and market analysis captured the avalanche of high-volume selling led by the fund managers and institutions. The risk management steps in this chapter provided the tactical solution that protected portfolios, profits and your wealth.

The world of risk is unchanged, but the mechanisms for managing risk have improved. Unfortunately not everyone takes advantage of these technological advances. We start with two questions. First, does the brokerage you use offer a stop loss service? If the answer is 'no' then you should read on because your risk management method remains in the dark ages. If your answer is 'yes' then proceed to the next question.

Do you use the stop loss feature offered by your broker? Around 70% of traders who have access to this feature do not use it. This is like driving a racing car without a crash helmet or a seat belt. Serious injury is inevitable. For your own safety, please read on. If your answer was 'yes' then please continue with this chapter as a revision for the calculations used to set effective stop loss points that do not shake you out of the trade with false exit signals.

Rich or poor? Boom or bust? The choice is often ours, but what really makes the difference to the result? In the financial markets the difference comes from money management, not from your trading skill. This can be learned, and it uses techniques mastered with simple spreadsheets and easy rules. The objective is to take a small amount of cash and, by trading the market, to consistently turn it into a larger pile.

We all start with some cash and we need to keep it so it can grow. The financial markets are the most effective way of putting money to work. They are also a very effective way of losing money very quickly if you place faith in blind luck, in selected blue-chip companies like Bank of America, Centro proprieties in Australia, or investment funds which focus on fees and commissions for just attempting to match the performance of the market.

Money management is the secret separating average traders from successful traders, and superstar traders from successful traders. There are many different ways to use money management techniques to increase profits and returns from trading. We look at just the essential methods suitable for smaller independent traders with limited accounts. The right money management helps your trading boom. Select the wrong, and often common, approaches and your portfolio goes bust.

We work with several traders in this chapter. The first is Trader Average. He has lots of fun in the market, making a few dollars in good times, and struggling in weak and nervous markets. He was wiped out in 2008. Shell shocked, he struggled to make any money in 2009 as the markets recovered. He still doesn't really understand how better money management would have saved him during the market crash. He thinks it's only about knowing when to sell. The second is Trader Success. He trades full time and trading is his primary source of income. You know of these people by reputation. This is where you want to be.

The third is Trader Superstar. There are not many traders who fit this category. They represent the pinnacle of trading achievement. We know them from their books and interviews in specialist publications. We use their methods to help improve our trading success. The fourth is Trader Lucky. He is a mythical trader who buys at the very bottom and sells at the very top. He is the friend of a friend whose uncle knows the managing director. This financial media creation is an urban myth but we can use his performance as a benchmark. Trader Novice also makes an appearance because it's where we all start.

How can I improve my trading?

This chapter is designed to answer just one question: *how can I improve my trading results most effectively without improving my trading skill?* The chart in figure 17.1 summarises the best answer. This is the path to success for Trader Average.

Figure 17.1: improving returns without winning more trades

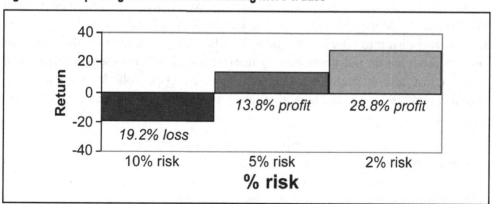

Trader Average latches onto a winner 62.50% of the time. Out of 16 trades he expects to win 10. His performance is terrible when he first starts. Each of his six losing trades sacrifices 10% of his trading capital. This does not sound a lot and many new traders lose more than this. Over 16 trades this strategy results in a 19.2% loss of trading capital. Losses are cushioned by trading successes.

Apply just one essential money management technique and Trader Average turns the same win/loss ratio into a trading approach generating the 28.8% profit shown in the third column. He does this by reducing the loss in each losing trade to 2% of his total trading capital.

Sound too hard? Just by reducing the loss to 5% of total trading capital in each of the six losing trades, Trader Average turns a losing experience into a 13.8% profit.

This is one of the most important charts in this book, and in the remainder of this chapter we look more closely at how this money management method generates success independently of trading skill.

Trade smarter not harder

When I first started trading I believed the best way to improve was to become more skilled in my trading. The more I could learn, the better I should perform. The result was a very large library of trading books, and a moderate increase in trading success. We all need to master the tools of technical analysis. Understanding how they work and when they are best applied is an important part of developing the skills of trading—in theory.

When it comes time to put this theory into action in the market we discover many unexpected psychological barriers to our success. We do not have much money when we start trading, so we take a lot of time to decide on each trade. Often the first trades are easy and turn into effortless winners. This is poor preparation for the inevitable losses because we do not know how to react to losses. When losses do come, most times we just hold on and hope. The result is a trading portfolio littered with long-term investments in the vain hope that, given time, some of these fallen stocks may rise again.

The market provides the most expensive self-education course available. Standing knee deep in blood from losing trades, we are easily distracted by the promise of trading systems developed by other people. These approaches may work very well for others, but unless they match our growing and changing understanding of risk, and our appetite for risk, the systems work poorly for us.

Smarter management

There is a shortcut for improving trading results, and to demonstrate how it works we start with a base sample of trades shown in figure 17.2. These trades were the base data for the previous chart. This Trading Performance Summary spreadsheet is available as an Excel template as part of the Better Trading pack from <www.guppytraders.com>.

Figure 17.2: sample of trades

The number of trades remains constant for all traders

This number of losses changes for each of the traders

Total trading capital remains constant with all traders

SUMMARY OF TRADING RESULTS	Total number of trades	16	Total capital $100,000	Total profit $28,796	%%% return 28.8%
	Total number of wins	10			
	%% wins	62.50			

STOCK CODE	COST TO BUY	$$$ PROFIT	%%%% PROFIT	WIN loss	$$$ PROFIT
SRP	$20,680	-$2,000	-9.67	*loss*	-$2,000
NAB	$19,933	$416	2.09	WIN	$416
SRO	$20,000	$8,000	40.00	WIN	$8,000
NABWMU	$20,100	-$2,000	-9.95	*loss*	-$2,000
CMLWAA	$20,000	$6,250	31.25	WIN	$6,250
TAH	$20,008	$3,977	19.88	WIN	$3,977
SME	$20,265	$3,423	16.89	WIN	$3,423
FBG	$20,284	$2,086	10.28	WIN	$2,086
TLSWDJ	$20,150	$7,000	34.74	WIN	$7,000
FBG2	$20,202	-$2,000	-9.90	*loss*	-$2,000
BBG	$20,081	-$2,000	-9.96	*loss*	-$2,000
SME2	$19,996	$644	3.22	WIN	$644
AGY	$19,995	$6,500	32.51	WIN	$6,500
NAB	$20,100	$2,500	12.44	WIN	$2,500
EGO	$20,425	-$2,000	-9.79	*loss*	-$2,000
ICS	$19,995	-$2,000	-10.00	*loss*	-$2,000

This loss figure changes to reflect the risk, 2%, 5%, or 10%

This losing trade shows a $3,977 profit when used for the Trader Success calculations.

The 16 trades are selected real trades and returns over a one-year period taken from our weekly tutorial newsletter. They are typical of the number of trades and the mix of returns we have every year in the newsletter since 1996. We reduced the number of wins compared to the number of losses so the results are typical of Trader Average with a 62.50% success rate. The mix of trades—ordinary shares and warrants—and the number of trades taken are also typical.

This benchmark of sample trades is used to show how money management affects three traders. Trader Average has a success rate of 62.50% with 10 wins out of 16 trades. Trader Success shows a 68.75% success rate. This is 11 wins out of 16 trades. Trader Superstar gets 13 of his 16 trades correct and has an 81.25% success rate. Each of these traders uses exactly the same series of trades as shown in the trading report. This series of sample trades has six common features:

- total trading capital is always $100 000 to allow for a consistent risk calculation

- profits for winning trades remain as shown in the base trades

- we do not add profits to trading capital. Profits are swept into a holding account and not used for trading

- we count realised and banked gains only. These come from closed trades

- the risk level is always a percentage of the total trading capital. So 2% risk always equals $2000, and 10% risk equals $10 000

- for this example we assume losing trades always lose the full amount at risk.

Our intention is to model the impact of changes in the level of risk for each of these three traders. We show what happens when the risk level grows from 2% — $2000 — to 5%, or $5000, for Trader Average. This does not change the number of losing trades. It only changes the amount lost in each losing trade.

The three traders are separated by their win/loss ratio, or success rate. Trader Average has a 62.50% success rate. Trader Superstar has an 81.25% win rate. To get from Trader Average to Trader Superstar we changed three of the losing trades for Trader Average into winning trades. We did this by calculating the median profit — $3977 — from all the winning trades for Trader Average. We then changed three of the losing trades on the base data template into winning trades, each with a $3977 profit.

The total number of trades remains the same for each trader so it is easier to compare the impact of changes in risk control. The number of winning and losing trades remains the same for Trader Success. Only the level of loss, or risk, in unsuccessful trades changes. It grows from 2% to 5% and finally to a 10% loss.

We calculate the loss in each trade using a set percentage of total trading capital. The reasoning behind this is explained in detail in chapter 19, Risk airbags. For the moment, please just accept a 2% loss of trading capital means a loss of $2000 in these examples.

In all these trades, as in real life, the level of loss is certain. We make it certain by using the automatic stop loss features available with many electronic broker platforms. If your broker doesn't offer this, then change to a broker who understands we are living in the 21st century. We set the maximum loss figure and use it as a constant in every trade. The level of reward is never certain, and the variation in the sample profits results reflects this.

If money management is really the answer to boosting portfolio returns, then how much improvement could we expect? Let's start with Trader Average, who gets it right 62.50% of the time. Often this trader risks 10% in a losing trade. Our results are based on six losing trades, each losing the maximum allowable amount. Over 16 trades, this produces a 19.2% decline in trading capital. Losses are offset by profits. This is close to the maximum amount this trader can afford to lose. If he lets risk grow out to 20% then he loses all his trading capital based on the sample trades shown.

By simply cutting losses to 5%, this trader turns in a small profit of 13.8%, as shown in figure 17.3. This does not sound much of a return, but when you compare it to average market performance as measured by the index, it is very good. In the first years of this century, a 13.8% realised return was about as good as, or better than, the market return. Many fund managers envy this rate of return.

Figure 17.3: Trader Average

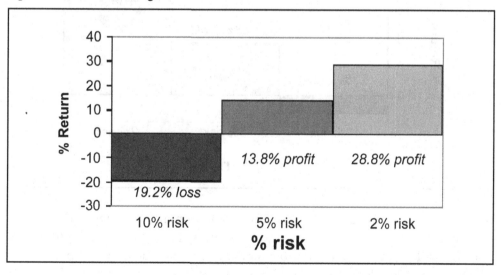

Cutting losses protects capital and allows profits to work more effectively. If Trader Average aims for a maximum 2% loss rate on each of his six losing trades then performance improves dramatically. By changing only his money management approach, using simple stop loss discipline, he boosts performance to 28.8%. These are not Trader Superstar returns, but they are achievable by average traders who get six out of ten trades wrong.

Trader Average lifts returns to become Trader Success by applying better money management. If we combine this with an improvement in skill then returns improve further. On the base data we change one of the Trader Average six losing trades into a winning trade showing a $3977 profit. This brings the success rate up to 69.75%.

Even with this win rate, Trader Success cannot afford to let losses grow to 10% of total trading capital. At the end of this sample series this blow-out in risk to 10% leaves Trader Success with trading capital reduced by 6.4%, as shown in figure 17.4. He is going broke slowly, though probably enjoying the rush from his winners. In the long run Trader Success destroys his trading capital, although it may take years.

Figure 17.4: Trader Success

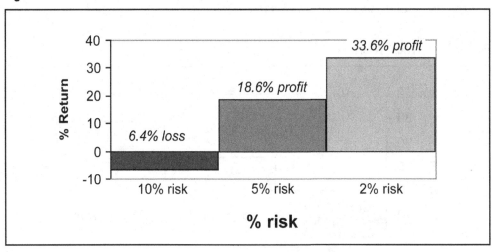

If Trader Success reduces losses to just 5% of capital on his five losing trades then he turns in an 18.6% profit. Reduce losses to 2% of capital and profits grow to 33.6%. These are still not Superstar returns, but they are more than adequate to support a full-time professional trader.

These 18% and 33% returns are possible because we are not fund managers. As we explain later, we have an advantage in size and agility. We can trade stocks with increased volatility and generate these types of returns.

It is important to note the increase in skill level from 62.50% winners to 68.75% is not sufficient to shift this trader into profit if he continues to allow losses to grow out to 10% of capital on each trade. The combination of improving trading skills and an improvement in stop loss discipline limiting each loss to 5% of trading capital is responsible for the initial move into profitable trading.

It is only Trader Superstar with a consistent 81.20% success rate who could allow losses to grow to 10% on losing trades and still survive. At this level he returns 17.6%. By reducing risk to 5% he grows profits to 32.6%.

Trader Superstar reaches this professional level because of his ability to understand and manage risk. His maximum risk on every trade is no more than 2%, and is often less. Using the base trading sample, Trader Superstar collects a 41.6% return when risk is capped at 2%, as shown in figure 17.5

Figure 17.5: Trader Superstar

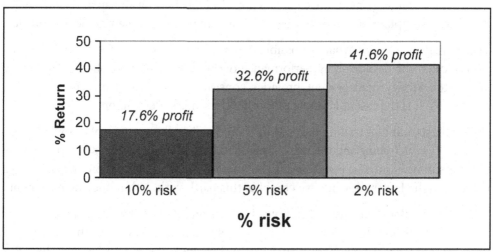

This is the essential contradiction of trading success. By the time you have enough skill to contemplate a consistent 10% loss rate, you also have enough experience and discipline to keep the losses to 2% or less.

The novice trader needs money management skills to survive, but he is the very person who is least likely to develop them. Instead he concentrates on chart analysis and trading skills, believing they hold the secret to success. He misses the 28.8% return that launches his trading onto a sustainable path to success because he lets losses grow to 10% in losing trades.

Trader Superstar generates returns of 41.6% when his three losses are kept to a maximum of 2% of trading capital. In reality his potential returns are much larger. They grow because his losses are kept small in relation to his total trading capital. His trading discipline allows him to further leverage his skill and experience.

Even with a 10% loss in losing trades, Trader Superstar returns 17.6%. This is impressive, but do you realistically think you have these skills? If you really do, then it is unlikely you are still reading this book. Reality suggests most of us are at the Trader Average or Trader Success level, so playing with 10% losses is a path to trading failure.

We do not need to be Trader Superstar to enjoy the success generated by better money management. Money management requires knowledge and an understanding of the way losses impact on capital. Applying money management requires discipline, and this is difficult for Trader Novice and Trader Average to develop. It is part of what keeps them from becoming Trader Success. It is not a lack of charting and analysis skill. It is a lack of the discipline required to effectively implement money management strategies.

These charts show you what is possible when money management is applied. They are typical of the decades-long performance of our case study portfolio in our weekly newsletter. Money management provides consistency of performance in all market conditions. It is the essential protection in modern market conditions.

The understanding of trading covered in *Share Trading*, the mastery of knowledge explored in *Chart Trading* and the tactics included in *Trading Tactics* are all steps towards trading survival and success. The path to success cannot bypass these steps, but we move onto the fast track when we combine this hard work with money management.

Rich or poor? Boom or bust? The choice is yours and it starts by understanding your reactions to trading, to sudden wealth and to sudden loss. These are the nerves and the sinews of your approach to the market, and we look at these in the next chapter.

Chapter 18

Frightened money

Traders are personally responsible for more trading disasters than any other factor in trading. When a trade crashes and burns, most times it is a result of the trader's management approach. It's all about nerves, and knowing when they should be made of steel and when they should be constructed from chicken wire. In the silence of the trading screen no-one can hear you scream when things go wrong. Equally, there is no-one to temper unbridled greed with words of restraint. It's not the trading system, the stock, the market conditions or superior analysis that makes the difference between success and failure. These all play a part, but ultimately it's how we behave that determines our success.

These reactions, and the trader's ability to control them, are the absolute bedrock of trading. The market crash of 2008 brutally exposed any weaknesses in traders' emotional approaches to the market. Many traders, including professional and experienced traders, found their skills deficient in this area. They went on to lose much of the money they had accumulated in the years before the crash. Many have never recovered from this trauma.

Exposure to large sums of money is a heady experience which magnifies emotional reactions. As the prospectors found in *The Treasure of the Sierra Madre*, wealth changes people, and for some there is an almost irresistible urge to return to the time before wealth. This sounds unbelievable to those aspiring to riches, but the consistent destruction of market fortunes suggests it happens more frequently than we imagine.

All traders lose money, and they often lose it on a regular basis. The key difference is that successful traders lose only small amounts of capital. They do this by using stop loss methods and limiting losses to a small percentage or portion of their total trading capital.

This all sounds very sensible and straightforward. In practice it is much harder. Unless you are particularly dedicated to developing trading attitudes you will find the process of losing money very difficult because we do not know in advance if our trading nerves are made of steel or of chicken wire. Most of us have an inherent inability to deliberately lose money, and this has a serious impact on our ability to trade and on our ability to set realistic stop loss points. Many of us are quite comfortable with mortgage and credit card debt, but this is not the same as taking a loss.

Taking a loss

Market myth proposes an excellent three-step traders' training course. First the student is required to put $100 on a busy city footpath and wait until a passerby picks it up and walks away with it. When the student is able to watch this happen without wincing and without tears he proceeds to the next step in the training course. The second stage is a repeat of the first—only this time using $1000. This stage is successfully completed when total nonchalance is achieved. The third step involves $10 000. The student must repeat this successfully, throwing money away without tears or fears, for several consecutive days.

Successful completion of the course entitles students to start trading.

By a variety of mechanisms, all of us consciously avoid situations where we lose money. We do not like losing money so many of us could not complete the mythical three-step traders' training course. Unless we do complete it—albeit metaphorically rather than literally—the chances of trading success are greatly reduced. Trading success demands we move beyond these attitudes.

This approach stands in contrast to the market lore which suggests you should 'never trade with more than you can afford to lose'. This well-intentioned advice misses the point by assuming our total trading capital is at risk. Better advice is: 'Never set risk levels at more than you can afford to lose'. Taking a loss is an integral part of trading, and rationally we know money lost in trading is not really thrown away. Emotionally, it just seems that way.

When we consider taking a loss it really does seem as if we are throwing money away. Lifelong attitudes to financial management subconsciously influence our decision, staying our hand when we should reach for the mouse button and exit the position. In fast-moving modern and derivative markets this hesitation dramatically increases the size of the loss. Being able to take this loss takes emotional courage and most cannot do it without a whimper. Emotionally we freeze when rationally we should act. We explore this in more detail in chapter 20, Trade shy.

Is the private trader doomed unless she develops a devil-may-care attitude to losing money? The answer lies in the difference between courage and fearlessness. The trader needs courage—an understanding of fear and the ability to overcome it. The trader without fear is a gambler who cheats financial death—for a limited time. This is not a path we want to follow.

We understand only too well the fear of losing money, and often this fear keeps us in losing trades rather than executing our stop loss. When we go too far, and too fast, fear overcomes our courage. The glimmer of an answer to the way we develop courage to efficiently execute stop loss points is suggested by the ubiquitous slot machine found in casinos and clubs. They make a business of turning chicken wire nerves into steel.

Thresholds

Casino players hate losing, even though this is an inevitable consequence of chasing jackpot rewards. The key to understanding how they run the gauntlet of loss is not the size of the inducement but the size of the wager and the way loss is limited to the wager itself.

For those with a high resistance to losing money, the 5¢ slot machine is heaven-sent. Who will miss 5¢? We all have different thresholds of tolerance and the casino operators thoughtfully provide opportunities for everyone to operate as close to their threshold as they feel comfortable. We have the choice to step up from the 5¢ machine to a 20¢ machine, or to $1 or $10 machines. We can change games and play with $50 chips at the roulette or baccarat tables, or join the high rollers at $500 a throw. By these graduated steps the casino takes advantage of differing threshold tolerances for loss.

The trader can learn from this management practice. The casino entices because the losses seem small. Many gamblers accumulate large losses, little bit by little bit. The pain is reduced as every individual loss is affordable. In some important ways the process is the same as trading, except the trader actively monitors loss levels within an overall money management scheme designed to deal with uncertain rewards by containing risk. The casinos thrive because they match the tolerance for loss with the emotional maturity of their clients—and the number of slot machines accepting bets of a dollar or less says a lot about emotional maturity.

Many traders fail because they do not match the levels of loss—indicated by their stop loss strategy—with their emotional ability to take them.

Each trader must first define how much she is prepared to lose should the trade turn against her. We use the 2% money management rule. However, the bottom line in practical terms depends on the individual trader. Some traders are comfortable with taking losses of several thousands of dollars while others feel extreme pain at several hundred.

The stop loss may be perfectly logical, brilliantly analysed and superbly placed, but unless it touches the right emotional chord it is useless because we will not execute it. And then the little loss grows into a substantial loss, further reducing our ability to realise it by selling.

The mythical three-step trader's training program proposed moving from $100 to $1000 and then to $10 000. The private trader adopts the same approach, teaching herself to tolerate larger losses. If larger losses are emotionally tolerable, then larger positions are taken consistent with wider money management objectives. As position size grows, so too does the dollar loss, even if the percentage loss remains the same.

For instance, a 2% loss on $4000 of trading capital equals $80. Losing $80 is not the end of the world, and the trader can comfortably exit the trade and move into more profitable fields. If trading capital totals $100 000 then a 2% loss equals $2000. This loss is of a different order emotionally, particularly when much of the $100 000 represents trading profits. Placing the sell order and taking this $2000 loss is much more difficult to do, even though it still represents exactly the same percentage failure as the smaller account. Beginners find it difficult to fully convince themselves it is the percentage figure that counts and not the dollar figure. Until they clear the difference they will forever remain novices in the market and potential victims of market volatility.

When they look at the trading calculation screen they glimpse the dollar loss figure on a $100 000 account and flinch. Despite having $98 000 remaining, emotionally the loss of $2000 is too difficult to contemplate. So the loss is permitted to grow, and with each dollar increase beyond $2000 the chances of closing the position and realising the loss are diminished. If they cannot act on a $2000 loss, then it is much more difficult to act when it grows to $3000 or $5000. They try to trade with frightened money. Trading success demands we turn from this grim reality and develop strategies to overcome this emotional paralysis.

Frightened money

The first factor is the relationship between winning and losing trades in the market. Professional traders know they will have many losing trades. Some professional traders have very good profits but 60% of their trades lose money. Other traders have about 50% winning and 50% losing trades but they continue to be profitable. Some traders have a higher success rate around 60%. All of these traders accept they will have between 40% and 60% of trades that lose money. When a loss develops they are not frightened. When they have many losses, they are not frightened because they know this is normal for their trading method.

Traders use calculations for 'risk of ruin' and 'maximum adverse drawdown' so they have confidence in the trade system they are using even when they have losses.

The second factor develops when traders do not have enough money to trade. Their trading capital is too small, so they cannot afford to take a loss of the correct size. The correct size of a loss is the result of the calculation based on the total amount of trading capital available. A loss in a single trade should not be more than 2% of the total portfolio trading capital available. This is the 2% rule.

Many people are confused by this rule. They think it means they cannot lose more than 2% of the money they use in the trade. The rule means the trader calculates the value of 2% of his total portfolio trading capital. This is the maximum amount he can afford to lose in a single trade, perhaps $2000. This amount will always be more than 2% of the value of the single trade. A $2000 loss in a single trade may be a 10% loss for the single trade but this is acceptable if the loss is less than 2% of total portfolio trading capital.

When traders do not have enough money to trade they are trading with frightened money. They worry too much about the inevitable losses and their stop loss is too tight. The stop loss position is not correct so they exit the trade too quickly. The trade does not have room to grow naturally with behaviour that is consistent with the normal price volatility. The chart extract in figure 18.1 shows how this works.

Figure 18.1: setting the stop loss

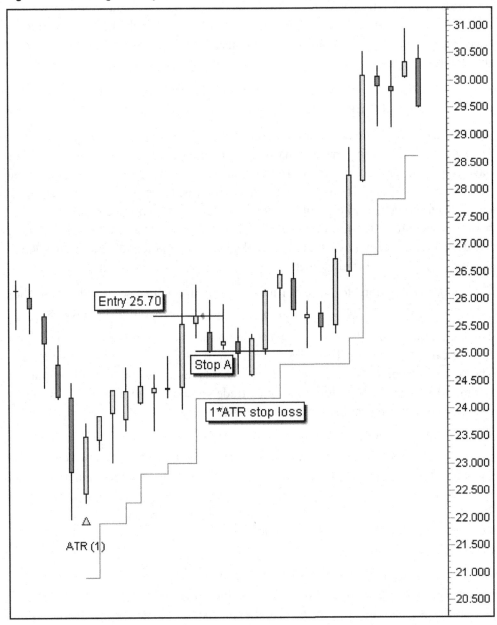

The trend is defined with the 1*ATR. The ATR, or Average True Range, indicator defines the normal volatility range of price. This means if the trader enters at $25.70 price can fall to the value of the 1*ATR at $24.19 and still be consistent with a rising trend. This is a 5.9% fall in value from the entry price. The fall from $25.70 to $24.19 should not put at risk more than 2% of total trading capital. The result of this calculation will determine the maximum position size the trader can take in this trade.

The trader working with nerves of chicken wire looks at the fall of 5.9% and is frightened. He gets nervous when the decline in the price of the trade is more than 2%. He is, of course, focusing on the wrong figure because the percentage reduction in price is irrelevant. It's the reduction in portfolio capital that is relevant. Frightened money concentrates on the wrong aspects of risk management and is distracted by the apparent loss in the individual trade.

As a result the frightened trader sets his stop at $25.08, shown as stop A on the chart in figure 18.1. This represents a 2.4% fall in value based on the entry price at $25.70. This strategy places the stop loss based on the trader's degree of fear. The more frightened he is, the closer the stop. The placement of the stop has no relationship to the natural volatility of the trend and price.

The result is that the frightened trader is stopped out by a close below his stop loss. The lower open on the next day gets him out near $24.50. Then he watches in disbelief as the trend continues upwards, staying above the 1*ATR as anticipated.

Tight stops based on frightened money kill trades and destroy profits. A trade cannot be assessed unless the trader knows the total portfolio capital being used. Every trade calculation stands on three calculation legs:

- entry price
- stop loss price based on the volatility of the trend
- the dollar value of 2% of total portfolio trading capital.

The combination of these three legs allows for the correct calculation of the trade position size so no more than 2% of total portfolio trading capital is at risk between the entry price and the stop loss price. This is the fundamental risk management rule of trading. It is the rule traders using frightened money ignore and they get stopped out of trade after trade.

The third factor is when markets change. In bad market conditions the trader has many more losses than normal. The correct reaction is to reduce the number of trades and use tight stop loss conditions. When the market conditions change then the number of trades increases and the stop loss also changes. When traders use frightened money it means they apply the methods suitable for bad market conditions to the new developing market. The result is they miss many entry opportunities, and also the trades are closed very quickly with false exit signals because the stop loss is too tight.

If you are afraid of losing money when you trade then you cannot trade effectively. Traders will always lose money on some trades, or even many trades. The solution is to keep the losses to the correct proportion of total trading capital.

Trading with maturity

Trading is not just business by another name. Despite technical mastery of trading mechanics, many novice traders still fail. All trading requires emotional maturity. Private traders tend to be more restrained, reflecting the same emotional maturity to the display of wealth as they apply to the attainment of it. Next time you attend a trading seminar try to estimate the trading net worth of individual participants. It is difficult because there are few physical clues in dress or decoration. The only clues come from the quality of the questions asked.

If we find it difficult to act decisively on stop loss points—and most of us have this problem initially—then develop this ability in small steps. In the beginning this appears to limit profits, but as we develop as traders we understand this emotional maturity acts as a brake on losses and so allows profits to flow and grow naturally. These skills allow us to trade with certainty in an environment of consistent uncertainty. They turn nerves made of chicken wire into nerves of steel.

Chapter 19

Risk airbags

When a car crashes we use an airbag to protect the occupants. When markets crash we use the airbag equivalent to minimise the damage to our portfolio. The increased speed in cars has heightened the need for an airbag and the increase in modern market volatility has made the airbag concept vital for trading survival.

We cannot remove uncertainty in the market—the risk of a personal financial crash —but we can tame risk using the airbag concept. When we enter a trade we cannot really know how price will develop in the future. The only feature we can control is our reaction to future price developments. This is the foundation of stop loss and risk control. Successful traders know the secret: the effective management of risk guarantees the reward. We look at the 2% rule, but our focus here is on the modifications to stop loss applications required in modern markets with higher levels of volatility. We show how a stop loss cushion is created that acts like a safety airbag when the market crashes. It limits the financial injury.

We also look at the relationship between risk and reward. Before you dismiss this as old hat we take you through an example drawn from a popular trading advice publication. The risk–reward ratio shows how their readers will go slowly broke.

Aladdin found wealth hidden in a cave. We find it in the financial markets, lurking on our computer screens. If there is a secret to gathering this wealth, it is this: do not allow yourself to be blinded by the glitter of profits slipping across your computer screen. Instead, concentrate closely on protecting your capital and profits will follow.

The novice trader ignores this advice and remains a novice or a loser. Professional traders focus on protecting capital every day against the risks that make the rewards of the markets possible.

Central to trading survival is the stop loss rule. Central to trading success is a correct evaluation of the risk–reward ratio. Each of these aspects of trading is considered in this chapter. Together, they provide the essential framework for trading and investment success. Trader Novice believes success lies with proper stock selection. Trader Superstar knows success lies with proper money management after the stock has been selected. This is the key to protecting capital, so we start with an overview of the essential calculations found in every trader's toolkit.

Taming market risk

How do we turn uncertainty into opportunity? How do we turn risk into reward? Successful traders have a solution, and it comes from just three numbers that accurately define and manage the risk in every trade.

As soon as we buy a share, all the risk comes down to a single factor: if price moves against us and we start losing money, then our risk has increased. Risk, in this case, is equal to loss. It is precisely estimated and measured because risk is the product of the relationship between entry price, exit price and your portfolio capital.

We start defining risk by noting the price we pay to buy the stock. Next we decide the exit price. This price is designed to tell us when we are wrong. Remember, we cannot predict what is going to happen, but we know when the trade is going bad—we start losing money.

The second important price is often called a stop loss price. The difference between our entry price and our stop loss price is the risk we take in the market. Not everybody understands this and they often go on to lose a great deal of money. They also forget the third number in the calculation: the total amount of trading capital, or account size.

When we enter a trade it is tempting to believe trading capital is equal to the amount we have allocated to the trade — that capital equals position size. This is a significant distraction because it does not take into account the relationship between each trade and your portfolio performance.

If our total trade size, or position, is $20 000, then it is highly unlikely the entire amount is actually at risk. The only way to lose the entire $20 000 is if the company goes out of business. It happens, but not very often. This is the key difference between gambling and trading. In the casino the entire $20 000 is always at risk. Lose the game, the hand or the roll of the dice and you lose the entire $20 000. The market is different. We control how much we are prepared to lose, and it's a defined fraction of the $20 000 we allocate to the trade.

This is often an area of confusion. Many people measure the loss in terms of the money allocated to the trade. Have a look at the example in figure 19.1. The entry is at $11.10 and the stop loss is at $8.10. A fall from $11.10 to $8.10 is a 27% loss. If the initial trade size is $7400 and capital is reduced to $5400 at the stop loss exit then the loss is $2000. This is a 27% loss for the trade but a 2% loss when assessed against the total portfolio trading capital of $100 000. If we measure the loss against the money allocated to the trade we exaggerate the risk. We must put this loss into the wider context of our portfolio.

The 2% rule simply states no single position, or trade, should put at risk more than 2% of our total trading capital. If we have $100 000, this does not mean each trade is limited to a total of $2000. It means the actual risk of the trade — the amount we are prepared to lose before we admit we are wrong — is not larger than 2% of our total trading capital.

We use the 2% rule consistently in all our trading calculations. We use 2% because testing shows it is the optimum size for Traders Average and Success. Trader Superstar cuts risk further, opting for 1% or less. Trader Novice treads on dangerous ground and often has no choice but to let risk grow to 5% or more because his starting capital is very small.

As we make successful trades, our portfolio capital grows, and the dollar size of 2% grows larger. As we take losing trades the dollar size decreases. Every time we enter a new trade we calculate the dollar value of 2% of our total trading capital.

This changes our understanding of risk. If risk is the amount we actually lose then we control this using a stop loss figure. Further, if the loss is measured against our total account size then we make sure no single trade has the power to destroy us.

Figure 19.1: calculating 2% loss

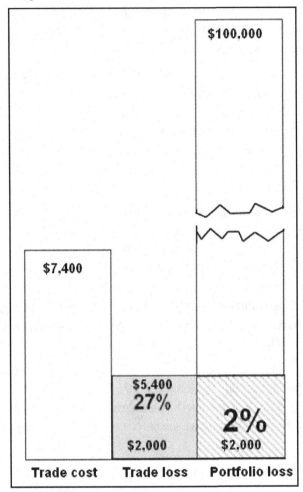

We tame market risk by understanding the amount we truly put at risk in every trade. It is the amount we choose to lose. When we control this decision using a stop loss order we tame market risk.

Setting genuine stops

Traders need to use a stop loss. There are a wide variety of methods available to calculate where the stop loss should be placed. Some traders set arbitrary stops based on a financial calculation, exiting the trade when the loss is 10%. These stops often have no relation to the logical or chart-based stop loss point. They reflect the trader's attitude to risk rather than market behaviour. Our focus is on logical stops based on defining the trend. Some are based on price volatility, such as the count back line, the ATR discussed in later chapters, or the TVL and Darvas methods discussed earlier. Others are based on trend definition tools such as trend lines, support and resistance lines or moving averages.

Setting the stop has three stages. They are:

- the theoretical stop loss calculation
- the trigger price for the stop loss activation
- the execution price for the stop loss.

These are three different figures. They are combined to develop an effective practical stop loss strategy that has a high probability of successful implementation. For this example we are going to assume the stop loss is triggered by any price move at the stop loss level. Think of this as intraday trading, but the principles and issues apply to end-of-day trading as well. We also assume the trader is using a contingent order stop loss mechanism offered by a number of brokers. At the end of the chapter we will also look at how we use intraday stops to manage trades based on an end-of-day stop loss.

Theoretical stop loss

We use FMG as an example. The strategy in this example is to trade the stock mentioned on CNBC SquawkBox as a stock to watch. These notes are taken from our weekly newsletter where this trade was added as part of the ongoing case study portfolio. The strategy for the trade is based on FMG exposure to the iron ore talks in China. The dominant pattern is the equilateral triangle shown in figure 19.2. This is a pattern of indecision. The bulls believe the outcome of the iron ore talks will be positive, so they bid up the stock, creating the uptrend line. The bears are not so confident, so they get out of the stock in anticipation of a not-so-good outcome. The CNBC SquawkBox report suggests higher iron ore prices are an inevitability so they put the stock on the bullish watchlist.

The first step is to develop the theoretical stop loss.

The stop loss is the value of the lower or up-sloping trend line on the day of the entry. On the next day, the value of the trend line is higher, so the stop loss moves upwards. Initially all the theoretical calculations are based on the current value of the trend line at $4.73.

Figure 19.2: equilateral triangle in FMG

We make three assumptions. First the total trading capital is $100 000. Second the size of the trade is $20 000. The third assumption is that the total loss on an individual trade cannot exceed 2% of total trading capital. In practice, this means any loss on this trade cannot exceed $2000.

The formal theoretical calculation looks as shown in figure 19.3.

Figure 19.3: theoretical maximum size of trade

Stock	Price	Qty	Pur Value	Close	Cur Val
FMG MAXIMUM	$4.810	25,000 $	120,250	$ 4.730	$ 118,250
		Newsletter date		26-Mar Open Profit	-2,000.00
				Percentage	-1.66

With an entry price of $4.81 and a maximum loss of $2000 the largest theoretical maximum size of the trade is 25 000 shares for a total cost of $120 250. This is much larger than we plan to allocate for the trade. The key figure in this theoretical calculation is the maximum permissible loss.

The second key figure in the actual theoretical calculation is the total planned spend of $20 000. When we start with this figure in figure 19.4 then the trade size is 4158 shares for a total cost of $20 000. The stop loss is at $4.73, which is the current value of the trend line. An exit at $4.75 delivers a loss of $332.64. This is less than 0.05% of total trading capital and smaller than the maximum permissible loss of $2000. This makes this a low-risk trade in terms of the financial aspect of the trade. The difference between the loss of $332.64 and $2000 provides a stop loss airbag cushion, and we show how this is used later in the chapter.

Figure 19.4: total planned spend

Stock	Price	Qty	Pur Value	Close	Cur Val
FMG	$4.810	4,158 $	20,000	$ 4.730	$ 19,667
		Newsletter date		26-Mar Open Profit	-332.64
				Percentage	-1.66

It is essential that all stop loss calculations are calculated using the theoretical stop loss. This allows for quick and easy comparison between potential trading opportunities. But the theoretical stop loss price of $4.73 is not used as the stop loss price in real trading.

Trigger price for stop loss

With the FMG example the theoretical stop loss is $4.73. This is equal to the value of the trend line. In other circumstances it may be equal to the value of a moving average, a count back line, an ATR line or a support level. This is the trend barrier. We are prepared to allow price to fall to this level, but no lower. At this price level we expect price to stop falling and develop a rebound. This trend line value defines the rising trend.

If the last-traded price is at $4.73 we do *not* want to exit the trade. It's okay for price to touch the trend line. It is not okay for the price to move below the trend line. For calculation purposes the stop loss trigger price is at $4.73. When we set the stop loss order—the contingent sell order—the trigger price is one tick lower at $4.72. It is only when price trades below the stop loss level that we want to take action to close the trade.

Figure 19.5: loss on the trade with an exit at $4.72

Stock	Price	Qty	Pur Value	Close	Cur Val
FMG	$4.810	4,158 $	20,000	$ 4.720	$ 19,626
		Newsletter date	26-Mar	Open Profit	-374.22
				Percentage	-1.87

The loss on the trade with an exit at $4.72 is now $374.22, shown in figure 19.5. With the lower exit price the loss grows and is now $51.58 larger than the $322.64 loss at the planned theoretical exit price at $4.73. In this example it's not a large difference, but if you are operating at the maximum position loss of $2000 with the theoretical calculation then the difference becomes more significant. The risk increases by 0.25% so the total loss is $2250. This is shown on the FMG MAXIMUM spreadsheet extract in figure 19.6.

Figure 19.6: maximum position loss

Stock	Price	Qty	Pur Value	Close	Cur Val
FMG MAXIMUM	$4.810	25,000 $	120,250	$ 4.720	$ 118,000
		Newsletter date	26-Mar	Open Profit	-2,250.00
				Percentage	-1.87

The theoretical stop loss calculation uses the exact value of the stop loss. The trigger price for the stop loss exit is just below the exact stop loss value. This lower price is the first element of slippage. Slippage is the difference between your planned stop loss exit price—$4.73—and the actual price you achieve in the market for your exit. A trade at the trigger price is a signal to execute the trade. This creates further problems when it comes to practical stop loss execution.

Stop loss execution price

The stop loss exit is triggered when the last-traded price is at $4.72. It is not useful to activate the stop loss sell order at $4.72 because there is no guarantee you will be able to exit at this level. The market may not fulfil your wish to exit at this exact price. There is a good probability the market will continue to fall. This probability is higher when the stop loss is based on a support chart feature such as a support level or a trend line. A move below this level often triggers a cascade of falling prices and a rapid price drop.

The contingent order system will rapidly put your sell order in place when the last-traded price is $4.72. However the position of your sell order will determine if it is executed.

The screen in figure 19.7 shows a stop loss execution instruction with a low probability of success. The trigger price is $4.72, and the sell order is placed at $4.73, which is the value of the uptrend line for FMG. It sounds logical. Despite the logic there is a high probability the sell order will not be executed because the price continues to fall, as shown with a different trade example in figure 19.8. The planned exit in this TOL trade was at $8.07. The price quickly moved below the stop loss price so the stop loss sell order could not be executed. The result is the sell order remains in the sell order line and the price is trading at $7.20.

Figure 19.7: stop loss execution instruction with low probability of success

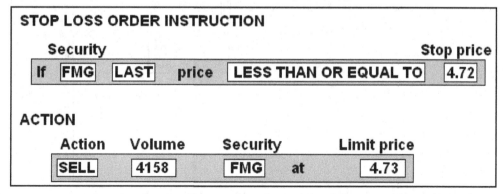

Figure 19.8: planned exit price not achieved

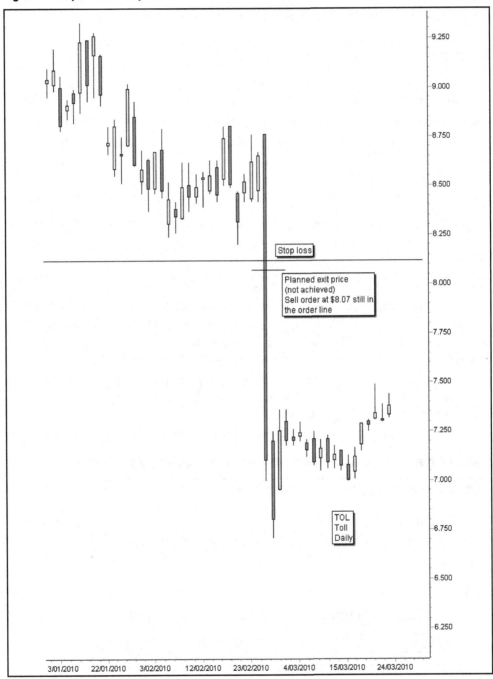

This is the danger with the FMG stop loss placement. The sell order will be in the sell line at $4.73 but the trading activity will be at $4.72 or lower. The sell order is not executed so all the careful risk management calculations are rendered useless.

A better stop loss instruction allows room to manoeuvre in a falling market. The stop is triggered by a trade at $4.72 and the sell order is placed below the trigger price. In the example in figure 19.9 we place the stop loss sell price at $4.70. This achieves two objectives.

In a fast-falling market this sell order has a better opportunity of being executed. When prices move below support you want to get out quickly. Getting out is more important than getting your preferred exit price. Placing a sell order lower than the trigger price means you increase the probability of having the sell order executed. It is very frustrating to have your stop loss sell order triggered but to then see prices fall much lower and leave your stop loss order unexecuted.

Figure 19.9: stop loss execution instruction with high probability of success

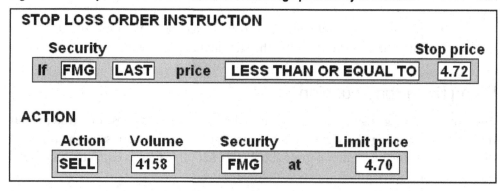

Placing the stop loss sell order below the trigger price at $4.70 means the order moves to the top of the selling line. If the next buy order is at $4.72 or $4.73 then your sell order will be executed immediately and essentially at market. It may be executed at a higher price than $4.70.

Figure 19.10: exit at $4.70

Stock	Price	Qty	Pur Value	Close	Cur Val
FMG	$4.810	4,158 $	20,000	$ 4.700	$ 19,543
		Newsletter date	26-Mar	Open Profit	-457.38
				Percentage	-2.29

An exit at $4.70 increases the loss to $457.38 or a little less than 0.05% of total trading capital, as shown in figure 19.10. This is still an acceptable result, but the slippage between the planned exit price and the achieved stop loss exit price adds an extra $124.74 to the loss.

The impact of the FMG MAXIMUM trade is much greater. The loss expands to $2750, as shown in figure 19.11. This is almost 3% of total trading capital. Consistent losses in excess of 2% of total trading capital create a significant problem for long-term survival in the market. The slippage becomes an important factor when traders operate at the maximum allowable loss levels.

Figure 19.11: result of slippage at maximum allowable loss

Stock	Price	Qty		Pur Value	Close		Cur Val	
FMG MAXIMUM	$4.810	25,000	$	120,250	$	4.700	$	117,500
		Newsletter date			26-Mar	Open Profit		-2,750.00
						Percentage		-2.29

Slippage is created by the problems of stop loss execution. We limit the impact of slippage by using the airbag cushion in the stop loss calculations.

Using the airbag cushion

The stop loss airbag cushion is the difference between the actual loss incurred in your trade exit — including slippage — and the maximum permissible loss in the trade. In these examples the maximum permissible loss is $2000, which is equal to 2% of total portfolio capital.

The spreadsheet in figure 19.12 shows the initial calculation. Entry is at $4.81 for a total cost of $20 000. The price can fall to $4.33 before a loss of $2000 is incurred. This is the maximum loss calculation. The exit after slippage at $4.70 is inside the cushion area so the loss is a smaller percentage of trading capital.

Figure 19.12: initial trade calculation

Stock	Price	Qty		Pur Value	Close		Cur Val	
FMG	$4.810	4,158	$	20,000	$	4.330	$	18,004
		Newsletter date			26-Mar	Open Profit		-1,995.84
						Percentage		-9.98

The FMG chart in figure 19.13 shows the airbag cushion area based on the position of the uptrend line and an entry at $4.81. The area between the trend line and the $2000 loss line is the airbag cushion. Any actual trade exit above the $2000 loss line will lose less than $2000 or less than 2% of the total trading capital. The $2000 loss line is always parallel to the stop loss line.

Figure 19.13: airbag cushion area

The cushion area allows for slippage on the trade exit execution price and it limits the damage to the portfolio. The FMG MAXIMUM trade does not have a cushion. The trade must be closed at $4.72—the value of the trend line—to keep the loss within acceptable limits. Slippage causes problems for the FMG MAXIMUM trade.

Where possible we ensure that the worst potential exit price, after slippage, falls within the 2% cushion area. We use the theoretical stop loss calculation to compare trading opportunities. We use the airbag cushion calculation to ensure the trade exit price actually achieved in the market is within the limits of 2% of total portfolio loss.

Using intraday stops for end of day

The cushion also gives us a method to use an intraday stop loss based on an end-of-day stop loss trigger. The stop loss for the FMG trade is a close below the value of the trend line at $4.73. We do not want to act on this stop loss until the day after the close below the trend line. The airbag cushion concept provides a way to manage this exit safely using an intraday stop loss.

If price falls below the trend line we want to protect ourselves against the possibility of a continued rapid price decline. Traders use a protective intraday stop loss even though they plan to make the exit based on the end-of-day close price.

Using the position size of 4158 we know price can fall to $4.33 before 2% of capital is lost. A protective stop placed at $4.57, shown in figure 19.14, delivers a loss of $997.92. A price dip to $4.57 would suggest the trend line has failed, so an exit at this level is warranted rather than waiting for the full exit signal based on the end-of-day close price. The airbag cushion allows for this protective intraday stop so any loss remains less than 2% of total trading capital. Setting a protective stop should also include room for slippage in the actual trade execution exit price.

Figure 19.14: protective stop

Stock	Price	Qty	Pur Value	Close		Cur Val	
FMG	$4.810	4,158	$ 20,000	$	4.570	$	19,002
		Newsletter date	26-Mar	Open Profit			-997.92
				Percentage			-4.99

You have a choice with the stop loss. You can argue with the market and place your stop loss at the exact trend line level. Or you can listen to the market and set your stop loss execution in a way that improves the probability your stop loss order will be executed.

Risk and reward

Understanding risk and reward is at the very heart of trading but few traders formally assess these relationships. The new trader, and even experienced investors, tend to focus almost entirely on the reward side of the equation. They start with an idea of how much they could make from the trade or the investment. For the trader this is often based on the price regaining old highs. For the investors, it is most often based on compounding interest, yield and dividends.

This is old hat, right? Everybody knows how to do this, right? Wrong. One of the lessons of the 2008 Global Financial Crisis was that basic risk control was forgotten, ignored or never learned. This condition persists. The extract example in figure 19.15 is taken from a buy recommendation from a trading advisory service. It's a very expensive subscription with daily buy and sell instructions. We will return to this example at the end of this chapter.

Figure 19.15: buy recommendation

Entry price		10.02
Calculation entry price		10.02
Stop loss price		9.60
Target price		10.95

One of the first steps to market survival is to understand how risk is defined by the potential downside of any planned trade or investment. What could go up could also go down. This is a simple statement, but it is often distorted. A few diehards believe the risk of something going down is very small if your stock selection is good. This is a 'picking winners' approach, and at its very heart it relies either on some type of prediction or on luck. Many others look at the risk, exaggerate it, and stay completely away from the market. They believe the market is too risky, and too much like gambling.

Between these extremes lies a more effective understanding of risk and reward. A chart of price activity provides a logical way to calculate the potential risk and reward from each planned trade or investment.

There are a minimum of three features we need to consider.

- Decide where significant resistance is placed. This acts as a cap of the price rise and defines the reward. If there is no resistance, then this calculation is based on a preferred minimum return from the trade.

    In a strongly trending stock making new historic highs, we might enter the trade with a profit objective of 20%. If the trend is still strong when the objective is reached, then we stay with the trade and the risk–reward ratio becomes even more favourable.

    As a first step we need a figure to help us reasonably calculate the reward component of the planned trade. This is the trade reward. It is the difference between the planned entry price and the planned profitable exit price. By itself, it means little. We need to combine it with the risk on the trade.

- Decide where significant support is found below the planned entry price. This acts as a safety net, and defines the level of risk in the trade.

    There are several ways to set this stop loss point. Some traders, and trading systems, use an arbitrary percentage figure. Our preference is to select a figure based on a logical chart point. These points include identified support levels. In some trades it may be the value of a moving average line, the value of an ATR calculation, or a count back line. No matter which method you select, it should yield a single figure. This is the price at which the trade or investment will be closed. The difference between the planned entry price and the planned stop loss exit price defines the risk on this trade.

- The final calculation is the risk–reward ratio. It is a calculation many traders just guess at. If the figures look good they go ahead with the trade but they rarely know exactly the risk–reward ratio. Comparing risk–reward ratios provides traders with another way to select from a variety of trading opportunities.

    The ratio is calculated by dividing the expected reward by the expected risk. The preferred result is used as a ratio. This ratio is used to separate good trades from better trades. It is used to eliminate foolish trades. But most importantly, the ratio tells us how much money we are risking in chasing a defined reward. These ratios are easily calculated on a spreadsheet available from <www.guppytraders.com>.

Successful traders aim for a risk–reward ratio above 1:2 at a minimum, and above 1:3 wherever possible. This does not mean making a 200% or 300% return on the trade.

It means the potential reward from the trade is at least three times larger than the potential risk in the trade. Achieving this is not as daunting as it first sounds. The solution is found in the stop loss point.

The spreadsheet extract in figure 19.16 shows a trade with a planned entry at $0.20 and a planned exit at $0.27. This is a 35% return which is readily achievable in this area of the market. The return on this trade is $0.07.

Figure 19.16: trade with planned entry at $0.20

Trade 3		
Planned entry price	$	0.20
Planned profit exit	$	0.27
Planned stop loss exit	$	0.18
Trade reward	$	0.07
Trade risk	$	0.02
Trade risk/reward ratio		3.50

The risk in the trade is $0.02 because the stop loss condition is set at $0.18. This gives a risk–reward ratio of 1:3.5. This trader expects to get back 3.5 cents for every cent she risks. The risk is not the total amount of cash allocated to the trade. The risk is the actual amount lost—or in this case, planned to lose. This risk–reward ratio is the minimum acceptable in any trade.

By applying risk–reward analysis the trader has an additional method to grade and rank trading opportunities. It is not enough just to select high-probability trades. We want a success rate higher than 50%, and preferably around the 70% level. However, even this rate of success will not guarantee long-term survival if the risk–reward ratio is incorrect or too thin.

The trading advisory service example we started with has a risk–reward ratio of 1:2.2, as shown in figure 19.17. For every dollar at risk you are looking for 2.2 dollars in return. Okay, it's not as bad as a 1:1 ratio (and this trade advisory service includes a number of trades with that ratio), but at 1:2.2 the long-term odds are against success. This calculation does not include brokerage costs or slippage. Slippage is when you pay more than you planned to get in, and you get out at a lower price than you had planned. This is an expensive trade advisory service in more ways than one.

Good money management, tight stop loss control and close observance of the 2% rule are all ingredients of success. Selecting trades with the best risk–reward ratio is what brings these ingredients together in a successful long-term survival strategy.

Figure 19.17: risk–reward ratio of 1:2.2

Entry price		10.02
Calculation entry price		10.02
Stop loss price		9.60
Target price		10.95
Risk and reward ratio	1/ 2.2	

Setting a stop loss price is easy in theory. It is much more difficult in practice because our emotions get in the way. None of us likes losing money so we develop a financial flinch when it comes time to act on our stop loss. The next chapter examines this and suggests some strategies for beating it.

Chapter 20

Trade shy

The Global Financial Crisis gave new meaning to the idea of gun shy, which is when riflemen develop an involuntary flinch that stops them pulling the trigger correctly. Many traders developed a permanent tic and became trade shy, apprehensive about taking the next trade. They were scarred by large losses, and this flinch tic prevented them from taking advantage of the 2009 market recovery. They were trading with frightened money. The increased use of derivatives by private traders introduced them to the concept that losses can be rapidly magnified in just a few moments. Knowing how to identify our flinch points is essential for survival.

As soon as we start a trade, all that counts is survival. In trading terms this means protecting our capital. If our capital is injured, or killed, we cannot make it to the other side of the trade. We do not get to enjoy profits, no matter how good our analysis and planning was. Success comes from avoiding being run over.

The reasons for each individual trade are not related to the success or failure of each trade. Even the best trades are destroyed if we fail to avoid significant capital loss.

This is a disquieting conclusion. It suggests the time spent on planning and analysis is not directly related to the success of the trade or investment. To a significant extent, this is true. It is also true that a better understanding of the trend and its character allows you to select the better trade entry point, but this does not diminish the impact of the loss if it hits you. Noble reasons and good analysis count for little if you are squashed.

The coward in every trader

The stop loss is the celebrity of the trading world—everyone has heard of it, but few have a close relationship with it. Individually, we need to change this relationship because a stop loss strategy is the key to long-term trading survival. This chapter explores some factors preventing us from building a closer relationship with this financial celebrity. We know the mathematical calculations, the logic of chart analysis and the arithmetic of risk. Here we look at why this so often fails when we try to apply it to our own trading.

Trading survival depends on protecting your trading capital. Disciplined use of a stop loss order is the most important step in building trading capital. When a stock is purchased, the stop loss is designed to protect trading capital. As the trade starts to make a profit, the stop loss is used to protect profits using trailing stop loss techniques. In this chapter, our main focus is on using the stop loss as a means of protecting capital and the reasons why we do not act on the stop loss.

Trading is about the management of risk. Many traders fail when it comes time to act on their risk control plans. Cowardice takes over and they back away from action. When we make money, we plot an equity curve. When we lose money we should plot a coward's curve because it identifies our weaknesses.

Cowardice thrives when we mismatch our intentions with our courage. It grows and dominates our trading when we place the blame on the mechanics of the trade rather than where it belongs. All stop loss strategies require discipline and a willingness to act. It is astounding just how many times we fail to act when stop losses are hit.

It is not a problem with the stop loss mechanism. Facing a loss, many traders seem to find so many convenient excuses for cowardice. Excuses range from 'My stop is too close so I better use a more flexible approach' or 'The price looks like it's getting better' to the more imaginative, including 'The mouse stopped working' or 'I was distracted when the telephone rang just before the close of trading'.

Try writing down your next excuse for inaction. Look at it a week or two later. Does it remind you of the dog-ate-my-homework type of excuse?

These excuses conceal the way we flinch or freeze just when action is required. The long-term prospect of financial loss is not enough to outweigh the immediate financial pain of executing a stop loss order. We back away from making the decision. The flinch factor stays our hand, and the stop loss order is never placed or acted upon.

Measuring the flinch

These flinch and freeze points are measured in the potential dollars lost, and this varies from trader to trader, but the process remains consistent. By developing a better understanding of the way our fear develops and where the flinch and freeze points are located, we improve the chances of placing and acting on stop loss orders. Our trading records provide the data to develop an action curve showing the exact area where cowardice overcomes good intentions.

Start by identifying the size of losses in old closed trades. Go through your trading records. Organised traders look back through their collected trading plans. Make two piles of contract notes—one for winning trades and one for losing trades. Our interest is in the pile of losers because they contain vital information about ourselves that we often prefer to ignore. Two important features will likely emerge.

- We are good at selling when the loss is quite small. If the loss, for example, is $500 we sell the position easily. Stop losses at this level are easy to execute.

- Although it does not make much immediate sense, we are also good at selling when the loss is very large. We use a figure of a $4500 loss and above in this example.

These losses are in trades, or investments, that have gone seriously wrong. The evidence of failure is too large to be ignored, and with a shove from the tax man or the accountant we decide to sell. The eventual sell decision is rarely related to a formal stop loss level—it was exceeded months or years ago. Once we decide to bite the bullet, we tend to dump the stock, selling at whatever price is available. These reactions turned the trickle of blood in early 2008 into a torrent by the end of the year. Failure to act bled many portfolios dry.

These are extremes of trading behaviour. Between them we expect to see our ability to act on a stop loss signal to decrease as the size of the loss increases. Small losses are easy to take. A large loss is more difficult so we expect a curve shaped like the dashed line plotted in figure 20.1.

Figure 20.1: ability to act on stop loss

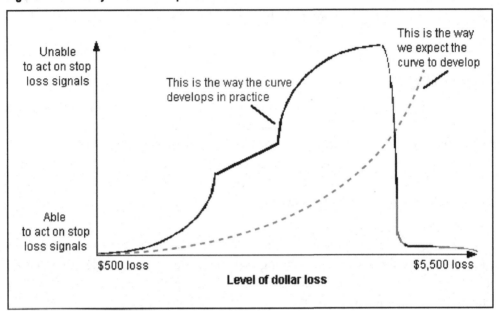

Instead, we discover the data plots a series of curves. Each section of the curve records our willingness to take action on our stop loss points in relation to the dollar loss incurred in the trade. The curve falls into four separate sections and their shapes are quite different. The combined curves in figure 20.1 belong to Trader Average. We met him in previous chapters and he is just like many of us. He trades with an account of around $80 000 to $140 000.

These curves match the size of his loss with his ability to act. It is a measure of the degree of courage or cowardice contained in each of his trading decisions.

Section 1 of this curve, in figure 20.2, is the type of curve we intuitively expect to see. It shows a steady rise from our ability to act cleanly to cut a loss to the area where action becomes more difficult. As the level of loss increases in dollar terms, our ability to act on our stop loss decision decreases.

For Trader Average, a $500 loss is easy to take. Your starting figure may be different, but the shape of the curve remains the same. Trader Average has $100 000 in trading capital. By the time the loss grows to $1500 it takes a little more thought before he clicks the mouse button to send the sell order. As the level of loss and financial pain increases, he finds his good intentions get weaker. This is a smooth process, asking for just a little more moral courage at each new and larger level of loss.

Figure 20.2: section 1 of stop loss curve

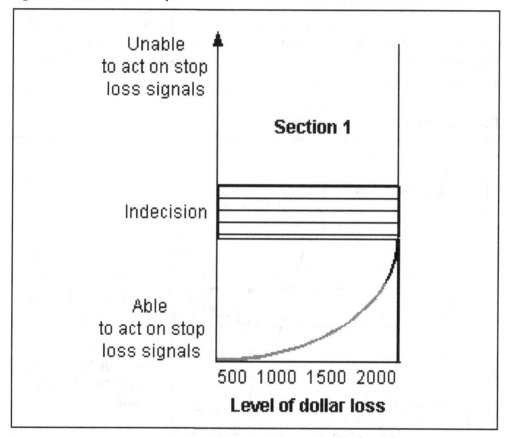

The vertical scale measures his ability to act on a stop loss signal. In the middle of this scale there is a zone of indecision. By the time the loss for Trader Average reaches $2000 it becomes harder, but not impossible, to act on the stop loss signal. All traders know the feeling; if we give the trade just a little more time to develop it may become profitable.

Our friend, Trader Average, watches the loss grow and slowly loses the willpower to act.

Phase transition

Physicists have long been aware of the phase transition phenomenon, such as when water suddenly turns to ice. Traders feel this phase transition when a loss suddenly cracks the size barrier and paralyses all action. By the time the size of the loss sneaks to over $2000 Trader Average finds his ability to act is paralysed. The shape of the plotted line, shown in figure 20.3, changes dramatically in section 2.

We hit a 'freeze' point, and this danger zone is responsible for more trading deaths than any other factor. The freeze point danger zone is at the intersection of the action indecision zone and the dollar indecision zone. It is a phase transition point where our ability to make a decision is snap-frozen.

Figure 20.3: section 2 of stop loss curve

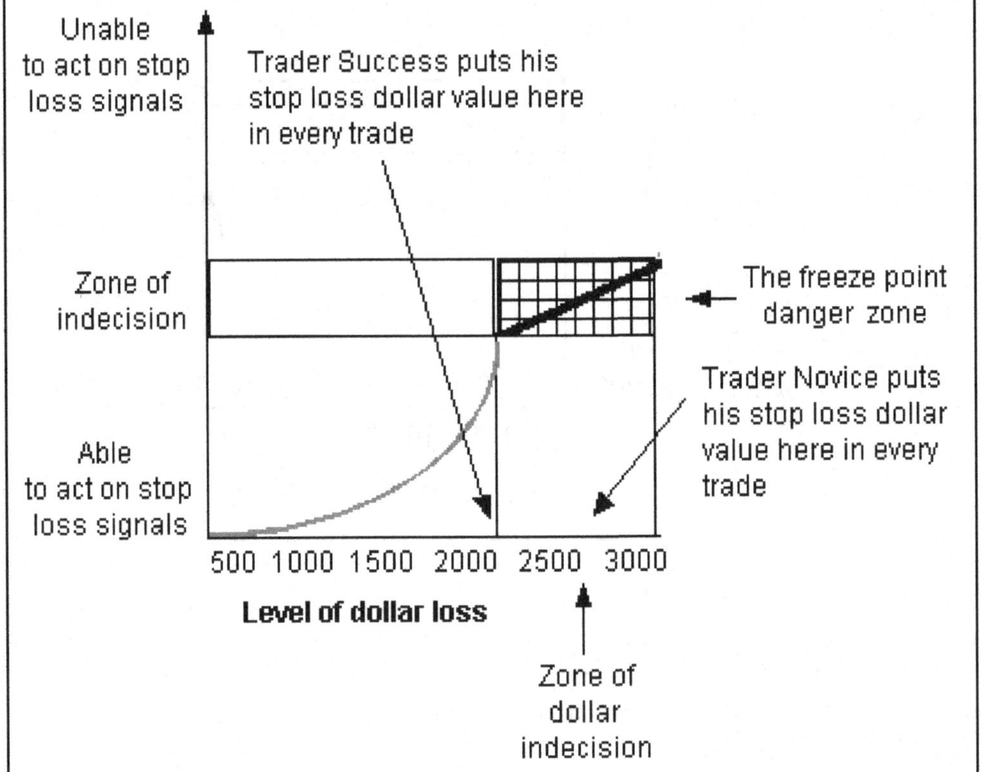

The size and shape of this paralysis zone has a direct relationship to the size of the potential loss. For Trader Average, we show the zone of dollar indecision stretching in a $1000 gap between a $2000 and $3000 trading loss. Once the loss grows to $2000 or larger, it is very difficult to act on the stop loss signal. The larger the loss grows the greater the probability Trader Average will fail to act.

Your personal paralysis point may appear at a different dollar level, and stretch wider or narrower, but there is no doubt you do have a freeze point. If you know it and understand it, you have the opportunity to avoid it. Remain unaware of it and your trading capital suffers.

The line in section 2 is shown as a straight line. It reflects the sudden phase transition that creates this freeze point. There is no gradual move from action to inaction. Our ability to act is snap-frozen. As the size of the loss grows, Trader Average moves rapidly through this zone of indecision to a stage where fatalism takes over. The exact parameters of this personal danger zone level come from your trading records.

Most traders, beginners or experienced, have a good idea of how much loss they can comfortably tolerate. Past trading contract notes put precise figures on it. These contain the trades you know you should have closed, but did not. These trades go on to become big time losers. Pinpoint the price at the time of this indecision and calculate the loss in dollar terms. This cluster of losses defines the limits of your freeze zone.

Approaching the deep end

Failure to act in the critical levels does not free us for instant action as the loss grows even larger. Although no longer frozen in indecision, we lack the resolution to end the pain.

The exit from the danger zone often has a well-defined trigger level and is usually plotted within just a few hundred dollars. Once the dollar loss breaks into section 3, the curve changes shape again, shown in figure 20.4. As the loss grows, in this case beyond $3000, Trader Average quickly decides it is so large that he cannot afford to take it.

Trader Average turns his back on the trade and walks away. Resolving not to take action comes with a rush of relief. The curve quickly climbs to the highest levels of inaction and stays there. The curve is concave because the closer it gets to the highest level of inaction, the more difficult it is to act. Cross the upper side of the freeze threshold and pain is avoidable. Like any shock victim, Trader Average blanks out the trauma.

Figure 20.4: section 3 of stop loss curve

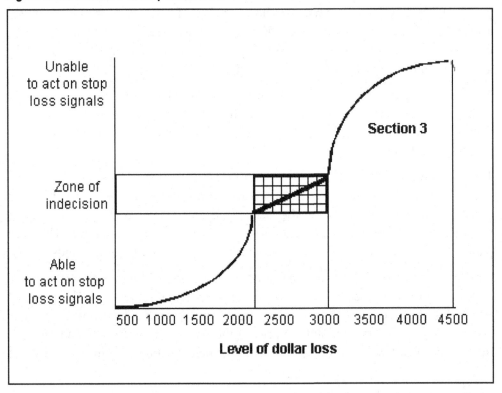

Do you act like this? Of course not—or so you hope. Take a moment to flip back through the contract notes and the last portfolio statement. Do not forget 2008. Your action here provides the most important lessons for future success by showing you the mistakes you need to acknowledge and avoid. How much is written in red? Did you discover some old stocks purchased years ago you had forgotten? What about the buy contract note at the back of your record book? The company was delisted after the 2000 tech wreck and another failed to make a reappearance after the 2008 market crash. These contact notes represent a few thousand of your dollars that went missing in action.

How many of your current stocks are in section 3 of the curve? More importantly, how did they get there? Identify the period, defined by the dollar value of the loss, when they slipped into and then out of the freeze zone. This is the starting point for plotting your personal section 3 of the flinch curve.

The deep end

In extremes of despair investors and traders sacrifice their trading capital. Section 4 of the curve is the last significant threshold. It is another sharp phase transition. This curve records the performance for Trader Average. The phase transition, shown in figure 20.5, starts at a loss greater than $4500. In reality the transition point is usually much greater, even for Trader Novice, often starting around $10 000. Losses of $10 000 or more are substantial, almost catastrophic losses. They are losses too large to ignore, and it takes a lot of courage to sell.

Figure 20.5: section 4 of stop loss curve

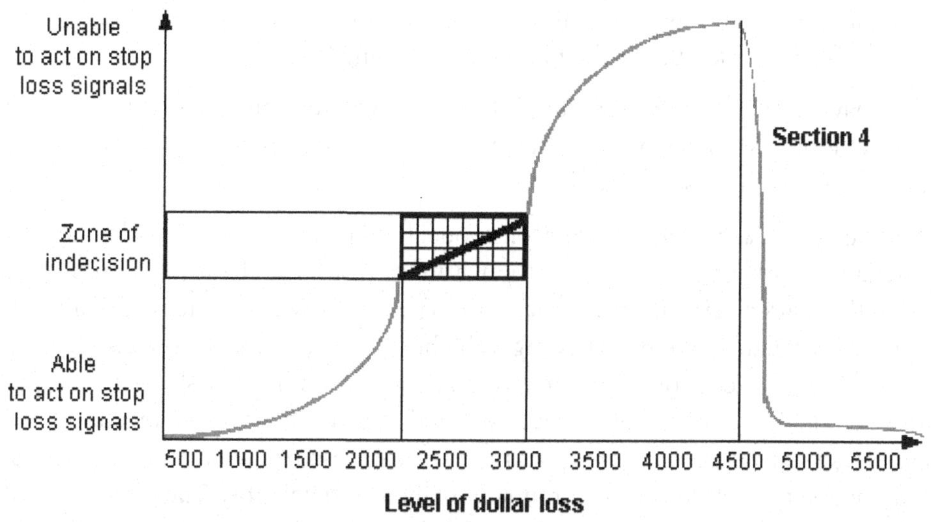

The shape of this curve in section 4 is a function of time and dollars lost. It is the shape of a financial catastrophe. After a long period in a losing trade, for some perverse reason it becomes easier to sell a stock with a very large loss. Perhaps we are so long divorced from the buying decision that our ability to act returns quickly and the large loss is locked-in with grim resolution. You may have one or two of these trades in your trading records. They should date back to your days as a novice.

Your own curve

No matter how experienced or skilled we become, the shape of the first two sections in the curve remains the same. The paralysis zone never disappears because there is always a point where losses overcome our ability to act. Successful trading is possible while we make sure our intended stop loss remains on the curve in section 1 and that our selected dollar value is less than 2% of our total trading capital. We give ourselves a better opportunity to trade successfully because the stop loss matches the reality of our ability to act.

Good intentions are easily sabotaged by the prospect of money. We welcome the distraction from a hard stop loss decision when the possibility of abandoning a good trading plan offers potentially greater profits. Real sabotage is when our trading capital is left unprotected by the failure to execute stop loss orders. Our examination of stop loss techniques is entirely wasted if we fail to match the theoretical planning with our own capacity to buckle under the pressure of growing losses.

We all have a flinch and freeze curve. If we know where our paralysis point is, we construct more effective stop loss strategies to match good planning with real trading action to protect our trading capital.

A popular conclusion promoted by professional fund managers who lost clients' money in the 2008 market is that risk and the nature of risk have changed. This is untrue. Risk in the market remains much the same. The events which increase the impact of risk have accelerated. We have trading at higher speed and greater velocity thanks to changes in trade execution. Our personal reactions to reward, to risk, to loss, to greed and the emotions generated by involvement in the market have not changed. What has changed is the need to act more quickly to ensure these behaviours do not adversely affect our ability to trade in an environment of increased volatility. The market murders trade-shy traders so it's even more essential to know in advance your flinch and freeze points, the quality of your nerves and your attitudes to risk and reward before you even consider the trading methods you may use.

Part IV

Trading methods

Chapter 21

Counting back the profit

Analysis is not trading, although sometimes the two are inextricably entwined. Successful trading calls for a range of skills that revolve around specific trading situations. Traders use their knowledge of order flows and order systems to enhance an opportunity and improve entry and exit prices. In this section we look at nine specialist trading situations. These are the nuts and bolts of trading execution and activity.

We start by applying some basic price chart analysis with the count back line, the Average True Range and parabolic trend lines. These are the tools of trading methods, and this section is about the skills of trading in markets where volatility is king.

Volatility and changes in volatility define the modern market. The increased speed of trade execution means the consequences of emotional thinking flow more rapidly through the market. Many old measures of volatility do not serve traders well because they are time dependent. The trader selects an appropriate calculation time, usually an average, and this remains unchanged despite changes in volatility. The count back line

(CBL) is a self-adjusting volatility indicator and it continues to serve traders well with the increases in modern market volatility.* Trader and systems developer Jeff Drake from OmniTrader describes the CBL as 'one of the best dynamic, volatility-adjusted stop methods we've ever seen'.

The CBL indicator uses three significant days to calculate the volatility barrier, which must be overcome before a change in trend direction is signalled. A significant day in a downtrend is when the previous day has a higher high than today's high. The number of days between the three significant days may be as little as three or stretch out to 10 or 15 days in a consolidating market. It is this flexibility in the time component of the calculation that makes this a self-adjusting volatility stop when a trade is first entered. It also makes it a self-adjusting volatility protect-profit stop when the trend is developing. Although the CBL can be used as a stand-alone indicator, our preference is to use it with other methods to confirm the probability of a trend break.

Originally applied to stocks, we find this volatility method is also suitable for indices, currencies and derivatives. It can be applied to end-of-day charts and to intraday charts. It captures price volatility and, by inference, trend volatility. The default calculation is three significant periods as this is a robust solution suitable for most instruments. However, in some special and limited circumstances two or four significant periods may be optimal. The OmniTrader CBL plug-in allows users to optimise the CBL for any trading instrument. We successfully combine it with the GMMA Trend Volatility Line to help with the initial entry into a trend.

The following discussion will focus on going long, but the same method, in reverse, works for going short. When the trend is up and we want to go long, we first wait for a short-term decline. Whenever prices make a new low, we draw a horizontal line from the high of that bar to the left until we hit a bar with a higher high. Ignore any price gaps and move to the next bar in the current trend. Then we draw another horizontal line from the high of that bar to the left again, until it hits a bar with an even higher high in the current trend, again ignoring any price gaps. From the top of the third bar we draw another horizontal line — but this one pointing to the *right*, forward, into the future. If the market closes above this line tomorrow, it gives a buy signal. We repeat this process each day the market makes a new low, creating a moving support/resistance line. The CBL follows the market on the way down, its placement determined by the recent highs, as shown in figure 21.1. A full and detailed discussion

---

* The count back line builds on work done by Joe Stowell in his three-bar net line. As noted in *Share Trading*, the CBL includes some modifications so the name was changed to avoid confusion with Stowell's work.

of the entry and verification process is included in *Share Trading* and *Trend Trading*. In this chapter we summarise the important features and applications.

Figure 21.1: potential pivot point low

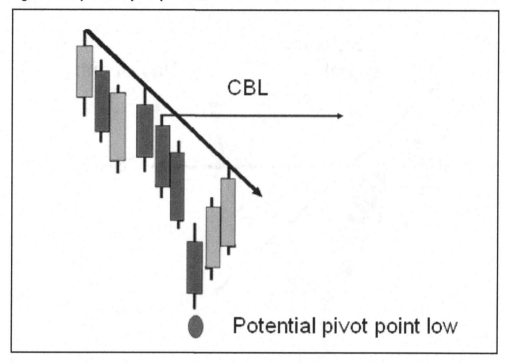

The objective is to locate the pivot point low of the downtrend as quickly as possible. This confirmation of the pivot point low is rarely going to be the next day following the pivot point low. It usually takes two to four days or more for confirmation to develop. However, this does provide a very early warning signal of a trend line trend break and, more importantly, a sustainable trend break. The CBL helps to reduce false breakout signals.

Usually the CBL is used to verify an existing trend breakout signal. In the chart example in figure 21.2 we use a downtrend line, but this could be a moving average crossover and MACD breakout or a signal generated by other analysis methods. These early signals are not acted upon until they are verified by a close above the CBL. Highs equal to the value of the CBL or closes equal to the CBL are ignored. The confirmation signal is a close above the CBL. The entry is taken on the next day, or time period. In a daily chart, entry is the next day. If each candle is five minutes, the entry is taken in the next five-minute period. It does not matter if the next candle is a down candle. In fact this gives a cheaper entry.

Figure 21.2: confirmed pivot point low

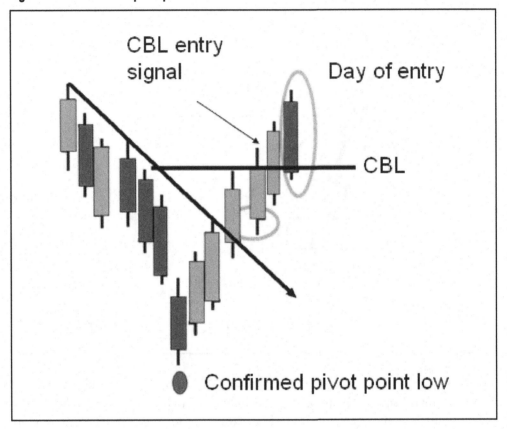

The chart in figure 21.3 shows a continuation of the breakout. As soon as there is a close above the CBL used as an entry method the CBL calculation is reversed. The day of the confirmed breakout is counted as the first new high in a new uptrend. This breakout high is used as a reference point to calculate the CBL trailing stop loss. Start with the new high, move to the bottom of the candle and across to the left to the next lower candle. Move down to the bottom of the second candle, and then to the left to the next lowest candle. At the bottom of the third significant candle draw a line to the right. This is the count back stop loss line.

Figure 21.3: continuation of the breakout

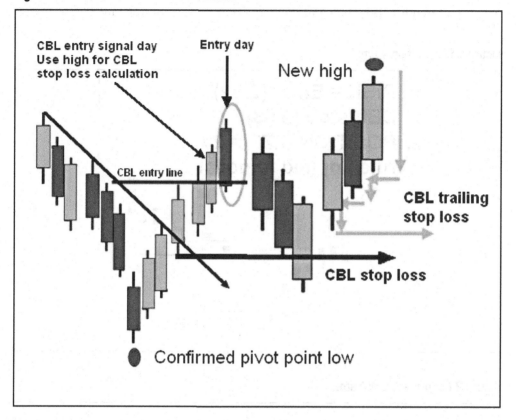

The value of the stop loss line is used for the position sizing calculation discussed in chapter 19, Risk airbags. The process is summarised in figure 21.4.

Every time a new high is made, the CBL calculation is repeated. This creates a trailing stop loss. The key change in the function of the count back trailing stop loss line occurs when the value moves above the entry price for the trade. Then the CBL becomes a trailing protect-profit stop, as illustrated in figure 21.5. It is used to define the new rising trend. The end of the trend is signalled when price closes below the CBL stop line.

The core of the CBL is the way it adjusts to the significant changes in price volatility as the trend develops. It does this by counting back three significant price bars or candles. In a downtrend, equal highs are ignored and the calculation moves to the next highest bar. Intervening bars with lower highs are also ignored, as shown in figure 21.6. The same applies to price gaps. The calculation method always uses the next highest bar in the current trend. This is shown in the right-hand illustration in figure 21.6.

Figure 21.4: position sizing

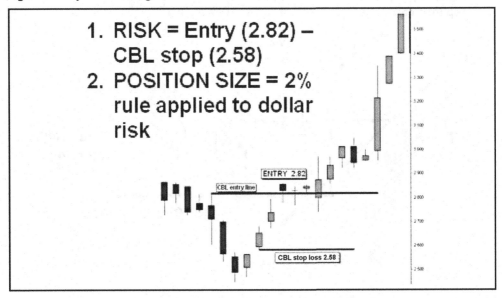

Figure 21.5: protect-profit stop

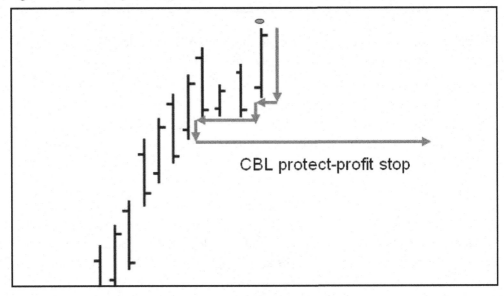

Figure 21.6: using the next highest bar in the trend

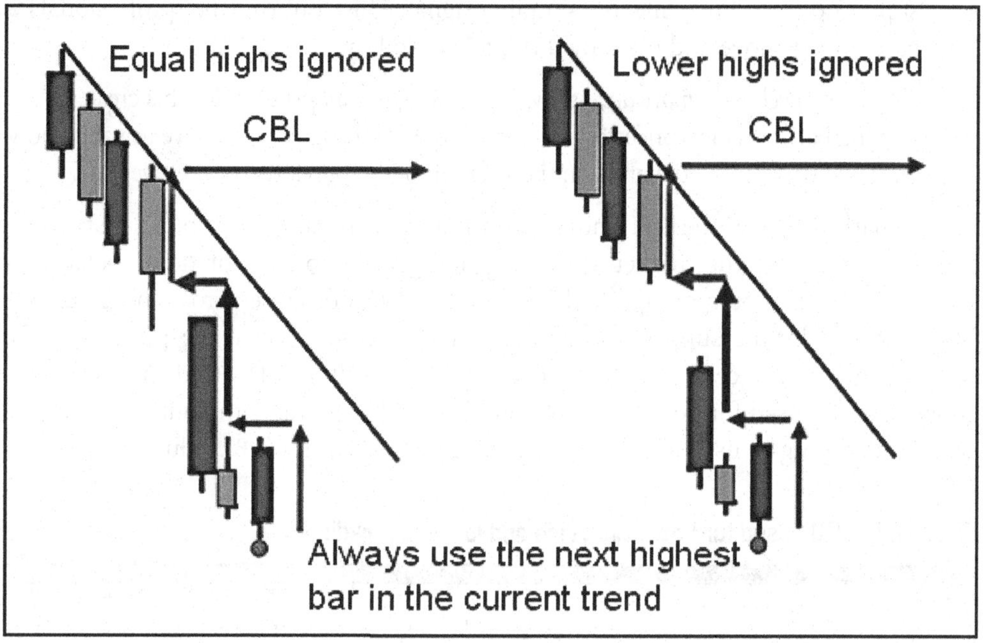

The logic of the line

When a sergeant gives a command, 'By the left — quick march', it consists of two parts: a cautionary and an executive. The first, 'By the left', alerts the troops that a command for action is coming. A momentary pause allows them to get ready, and then comes the second part, 'quick march', telling them what to do.

The CBL normally creates a pause between a warning and an action signal. A single day's move in the direction we want to trade alerts us that a breakout may be coming. A close across the CBL completes the command, telling us to buy or sell.

The CBL is readjusted whenever the market moves enough to reach a new extreme point, a high or a low. This moving support and resistance line does not travel parallel to the trend. It skips from level to level, depending on volatility, indicating new temporary areas of minor support and resistance.

The three main advantages of the CBL are:

☒   *it serves as a filter on price action.* If the market makes no new high in an uptrend or new low in a downtrend, that action is excluded from calculations

- ⊞ *it gives trading signals on close only.* It uses only the close across the moving support or resistance line as its trading signal. This confirms that professionals support the move and the crowd is likely to follow

- ⊞ *it measures each day's move against two previous significant price levels.* This creates a moving barrier which prices must jump before we recognise the move as valid. How far the barrier moves depends on the strength of the previous price moves.

As the market moves, the CBL moves with it and keeps us out of trades that would be out of line with the market sentiment. Temporary up-ticks or down-ticks masquerading as breakouts are ignored because they do not close across the CBL. The buffer created by the support or resistance lines helps to affirm the potential for a serious long-term price move, rather than a temporary flutter. The trade in figure 21.7 shows the CBL used for both short-side and long-side trading with Southern Co. This OmniTrader plug-in used a stairway-style display to show the CBL value.

Figure 21.7: CBL used for both short-side and long-side trading

Markets often narrow down before taking off in a new direction. This consolidation pattern is recognised and charted by many indicators. The CBL recognises it also and tightens its support or resistance line in tune with the market, so when the breakout comes we catch it early.

CBL trading

Although the CBL is not designed to independently track the development of a trend as a stand-alone indicator it can be used in this way.

Figure 21.8: CBL trade management

The case study trade in figure 21.8 with Singapore-listed Tianjin Zhongxin is taken from our weekly Asian newsletter. The trend was managed using only the CBL. The CBL captures the price volatility, which was a successful measure of the trend volatility in this particular trade.

Hope confidence certainty

The CBL method is also used to scale into a trade, providing clear signals for the appropriate entry time for new positions. We call this a Hope, Confidence, Certainty, or HCC, trading method. We first met this concept in the GMMA Trend Volatility Line. It is applied with the CBL in a similar fashion. It uses exact points in the CBL indicator calculation to establish when the next position should be added.

The essence of this management technique is the position of the CBL stop loss calculation. The first calculation point for the CBL is shown with the *1 in figure 21.9.

Figure 21.9: CBL and HCC

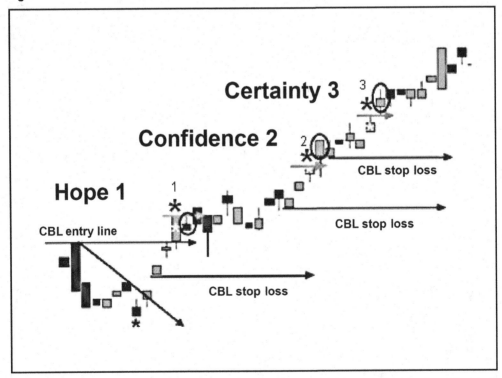

When a trade is first entered we *hope* we have made the correct decision. This is the first entry point, shown with the circled candle hope 1. The trade does not move into *confidence* until the CBL stop loss calculation has a value higher than the first entry price. This is shown in the candle circled with confidence 2. This developed with the CBL calculation from the candle marked *2.

The trade does not move into *certainty* until the CBL calculation is higher than the price used for the second trade entry. The CBL stop loss calculation that gives this result is made from the candle marked *3.

The day following the * calculation days may be an up day or a down day. This is not significant. The CBL calculation confirms there has been a change in the price volatility relationships and that an entry has a higher probability of trend continuation.

All positions are closed when a CBL exit signal is generated. This scale-in method means that when the most recent position is closed there is a higher probability the previous positions will also be closed at a profit. The trade is considered to be safely profitable when the most recent CBL calculation is above the entry price paid for the third entry.

The CBL method is an effective measure of price volatility. In the next chapter we look at the traders' application of the Average True Range indicator which can be used alongside the CBL to provide another measure of price volatility and trending behaviour.

Chapter 22

Traders ATR

Managing volatility is the most significant challenge in changed market conditions. Long-term trend volatility is effectively managed using the Trend Volatility Line but this is less suited to the increasingly common shorter, sharper trend behaviours. These extended rallies require management based on price volatility, but these measures need to be more sensitive to volatility developments to ensure profits are kept and not diminished by stops placed too far below the current price action.

The count back line with its self-adjusting stop is one option for volatility. Another is the traders' application of the Average True Range (ATR). This captures price volatility, defines the emerging trend breakout and provides a method to manage the developing trade. Our purpose is to use the ATR calculation as a stop loss designed to protect capital and identify the end of one trend and the beginning of another. We use the ATR as a method to identify and confirm trend changes. Later we want to use the ATR as a protect-profit stop designed to protect profits and identify the end of a trend. In extended rallies it is combined with the CBL to provide a series of alert and confirmation exit signals.

The ATR is an elegant mathematical solution developed by Welles Wilder. It highlights the difference between the mathematical analysis of market behaviour and the actual process of trading. Just having a good mathematical solution does not create a good trading solution. Hence we call this work the traders ATR.

Our purpose is to use the ATR to enable entry at the best point in the trend to:

- follow the trend break

- define average price volatility and price volatility limits

- adjust price volatility calculations as average price volatility changes

- set stop loss conditions related to price volatility and use this as an exit signal for trend changes.

ATR calculations

The mathematics of the ATR calculations are less important than the use to which the results are put. The ATR calculations are done automatically in most charting software. Our interest is in the logic of the calculations rather than the details. The logic is summarised in figure 22.1.

Figure 22.1: finding the ATR starting point

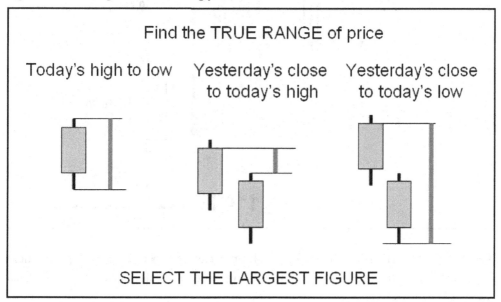

Find the TRUE RANGE of price

Today's high to low   Yesterday's close to today's high   Yesterday's close to today's low

SELECT THE LARGEST FIGURE

The true range is equal to today's high to today's low, or yesterday's close to today's high, or yesterday's close to today's low. The largest of these calculations is selected as the starting point for the calculation of today's ATR value. In the example in figure 22.2 the largest ATR calculation for today is 1.20. This figure is combined with the one-day ATR calculations for the previous four days. This provides a total of 4.90 for the five-day period. The five-day average of this calculation is 0.98, making today's ATR value 0.98. It suggests price can move 0.98 during the day and remain within the average five-day volatility range.

Figure 22.2: calculating ATR

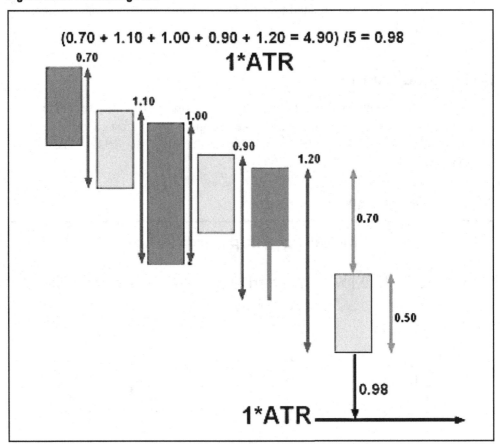

The value of the ATR is the degree to which price can be expected to move on the next day and still remain consistent with the existing trend. The trader takes the next logical step and decides a move larger than this value is outside the current volatility range and may indicate a change in the trend. The 1*ATR is often considered too sensitive so the indicator sensitivity is reduced by calculating the 2*ATR value. Usually the ATR value is multiplied to create a 2*ATR value. In this example the 2*ATR value is 0.98*2 = 1.96. This doubling is used to reduce the whipsaw, or false signals, generated by the 1*ATR.

Figure 22.3: plotting ATR

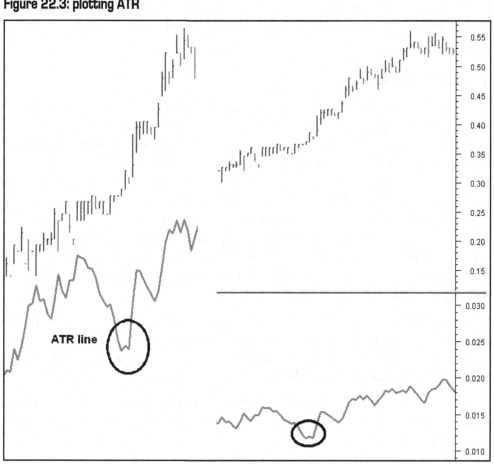

These ATR calculations provide great insights into price volatility and its measurement. The changing value of the ATR calculation is usually plotted as a line, as shown in figure 22.3. Typically the results of these calculations are shown in a separate window below the main chart display. And they are not particularly useful for actual trading.

The display does not quickly show the relationship between the ATR calculation and today's price. It is difficult to use the ATR as a trend change indicator, a stop loss or a protect-profit stop.

Additionally the ATR value moves up and down, and that breaks the first rule of a stop loss. In a rising market the stop loss should only move upwards because its purpose is to protect the profit and provide an early exit signal. A stop loss value that moves to lower values in a rising trend does not protect profit. The traders' application of ATR overcomes this problem by taking the essential calculations of the ATR process and modifying their application to prevent the erosion of profit when a trend reverses.

Traders ATR

The traders ATR takes the calculation results and displays them in a way that is useful for trading decisions. It has five elements. We start with the result of the ATR calculation and create a ratchet or stepped process. For example, we start with the first ATR calculation of 1.00. If tomorrow's ATR calculation is 1.2 then the value of the ATR is plotted at a higher level. If on the following day the ATR calculation falls back to 1.00 then the new lower ATR value is ignored. The ATR value is shown as the previous day's ATR value of 1.02. Values lower than 1.02 are ignored until a new higher ATR value is calculated. This process is shown in figure 22.4. The dots show the value of the ATR calculation. The three dots below the horizontal ATR line show ATR values lower than the value of the horizontal ATR line. These values are ignored in the traders ATR display solution.

When the next ATR value is 1.03 then the ATR plot moves higher. Using this first modification the ATR value follows the rising trend without taking any backward steps. This makes the ATR more useful as a stop loss method rather than just an interesting measure of all changes in price volatility.

In a falling trend the same principle is applied, but in reverse. The ATR in a falling trend is designed to follow falling prices down. In this environment the ATR shows only lower ATR values and ignores any higher ATR values.

The second element of the traders ATR is the relationship between the ATR calculation and the current price. How is the ATR value of 1.00 related to today's price? Unless the trader establishes a relationship the ATR calculation remains a curiosity rather than a trading tool.

Figure 22.4: traders ATR

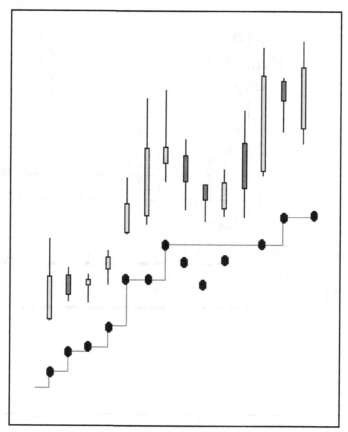

We start with a long-side trade. Here the intention is to enter an uptrend and use the ATR as a method of managing the trend. A fall greater than the value of the ATR suggests price volatility has expanded. This is a potential end-of-trend signal. To use the ATR in this way the value of the ATR must be directly related to the current price so it establishes a barrier. If the price tomorrow moves below the value of today's ATR then it creates a trading signal.

The value of the ATR is subtracted from the value of today's price. We have a choice of using the low price for the day, the close price for the day or perhaps the open, high or median price for the day. The selection of the subtraction point has a significant impact on the location of the ATR value, as shown in figure 22.5. The ATR calculation for the indicator is the same, but the subtraction point is different so the location of the ATR line changes.

Figure 22.5: selection of subtraction point

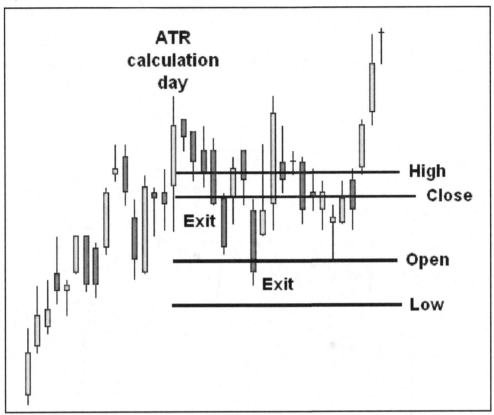

The purpose of using the ATR is to create a stop loss line that follows a rising trend and gives an exit signal when there is increased probability the trend is changing. Our preference is to subtract the value of the ATR from the value of the close to establish the correct position of the ATR exit signal. This selection is a solution to the increased volatility in the market. If we use the low as the calculation point then the danger is that the ATR line is too far away from the current price because intraday volatility ranges have increased. By using the close the position of the ATR becomes a tighter stop loss and it ignores the swings of intraday volatility. The ATR based on the close provides the better solution in conditions of high price volatility.

The third element in the calculation of the ATR is the length of the average calculation. Depending on the software you use, the default is a 14-day or 10-day average period for the calculation. In conditions of higher price volatility a seven-day average calculation is more suitable for catching rallies and extended fast-moving, short-term trends.

The fourth element in the ATR calculation is the multiplication factor. The multiplication factor is applied to the value of the initial ATR calculation. If the value of the seven-day ATR calculation is 1.00 then the 1*ATR value is also 1.00. The value of the 2*ATR would be 2.00. This can be extended to a 3*ATR equalling 3.00 but this is not particularly useful for either investing or trading solutions.

The selection of the ATR multiplication value has a significant impact on the management of the trade, as shown in figure 22.6. The 2*ATR captures the long-term underlying trend. The 1*ATR calculation is more sensitive, and triggers an earlier, and potentially false, exit.

Figure 22.6: 1*ATR vs 2*ATR

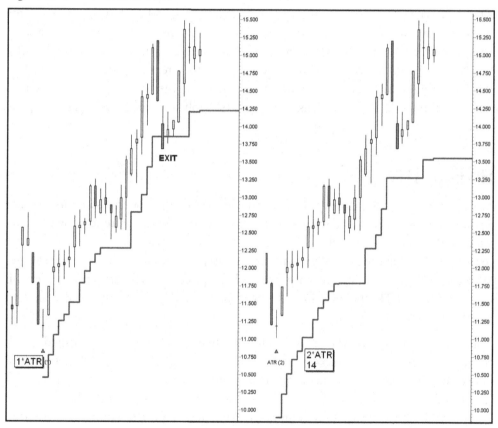

Prior to the Global Financial Crisis many traders used the 2*ATR calculation and this was very suitable to long-term rising trends. It remains well suited to these conditions, but with increased price volatility it often leaves the exit signal too far below the current price. Substantial profits are surrendered before the exit signal is triggered.

We prefer to use the 1*ATR. It's a trade-off between more frequent exit signals and collecting better profits. In figure 22.6 the 1*ATR generates a false exit signal while the 2*ATR keeps the trader in the trade. However, if the 2*ATR exit signal had been triggered then the profit erosion for this trade would be substantially larger than the profit erosion using the 1*ATR. Using the trend high at $15.80 as the calculation point, profits are eroded 13% with the 2*ATR signal compared to a 9% profit erosion using the 1*ATR signal.

The fifth element is the ATR display on the chart. This display creates the full application of the traders ATR. In a rising trend the ATR values only move up. The value of the ATR is shown with a continuous stepped line, already introduced in figure 22.6. This display is available as a default indicator in the Guppytraders Essentials charting package. When the price closes below the ATR line an exit signal is created. The ATR line is extended to the right, clearly showing an end-of-trend signal. The stepped line display provides the trader with an instant evaluation of the current price in relation to the ATR stop loss conditions. This is the traders' application of the ATR, and it opens the door to two other trading applications.

Sliding ATR

When the traders ATR is displayed on a chart using the Guppytraders Essentials charting package it provides a clear and elegant solution for managing the trend. However, the value of the ATR is often well below the current price activity. This creates a problem for trade entry planning. Ideally we prefer an entry close to the value of the ATR line. When we use the CBL for our entry method the price is often very near to the CBL value. With the ATR line used in this way it may take days or weeks for the price to move near to the ATR value.

The solution is a sliding ATR entry condition. This is applied to an established trend. It starts by identifying a compatible trend and evaluating the average distance of price above the ATR value. Price has a higher probability of moving into this area and a lower probability of falling below this area. The trade risk and reward calculations are based on an entry within the trading range. This may require a reduction in position size as the ATR stop loss may be some distance from the entry price.

Figure 22.7: sliding ATR entry

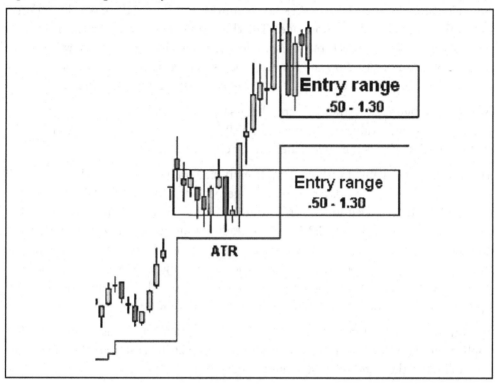

The illustration in figure 22.7 shows an example of this entry method where the entry range is always $0.80 and always calculated from $0.50 above the value of the ATR line. When the value of the ATR line changes the trade entry range is adjusted so it slides upwards in a rising trend. Traders wait for the price rebound behaviour to develop before the trade is entered. The initial stop loss is set at the lower edge of the entry range. The ATR is used as the stop loss when the value of the ATR moves above the trade entry price. Aggressive traders may decide to pay a little bit higher price if the trend rebound is strong.

Combined ATR entry

In the previous chapter dealing with the count back line indicator we showed how the CBL follows the downtrend and gives an entry signal when price closes above the value of the CBL in a downtrend. This signals a change in the volatility of price in the existing downtrend and points the way to a higher probability of trend reversal.

This same logic is applied with the ATR. The downtrend is followed using the short-side calculation for the ATR. The ATR line continues to fall until there is a closing price higher than the value of the short-side ATR. This is a signal to close short positions and the closing value of the ATR provides a reference point for a potential new uptrend. This is not an automatic stop and reverse process. A close above the short-side ATR is a signal the short trade is closed. It is not a signal to open a long-side trade.

As shown in figure 22.8, traders start a long-side ATR calculation. The entry signal is generated when the value of the long-side ATR is higher than the closing value of the short-side ATR. This is the circled area on the chart extract.

The downtrend is defined with the 1*ATR short-side trading indicator. This is a 1*ATR calculation using a seven-day moving average period. It is used to define long-term downtrends. Traders wait for the price to move above the 1*ATR short-side line. The entry signal is when the 1*ATR long-side trading indicator value is very near to or above the value of the 1*ATR short-side indicator value. The objective is to enter the trade when the price rebounds from near the value of the 1*ATR long-side line. The price sometimes dips below the ATR line but closes above the ATR line and develops up momentum on the next day. This is an entry opportunity.

Waiting for this condition increases the probability the trend change is genuine. Traders apply a sliding ATR entry technique or join the trade at the best possible price in the days following the trend breakout confirmation.

ATR and CBL verification

Both the CBL and the ATR indicators measure price volatility. We use them as a combined alert and confirmation signal combination. This guards against false exit signals and improves the reliability of the exit while still maximising profits. However, each indicator has a slightly different purpose. The purpose of the ATR is shown below and the key differences are in italics:

- to *follow* the trend break
- to define *average* price volatility and price volatility limits
- to adjust price volatility calculations as *average* price volatility changes
- to set stop loss conditions *related* to price volatility.

Figure 22.8: long-side ATR calculation

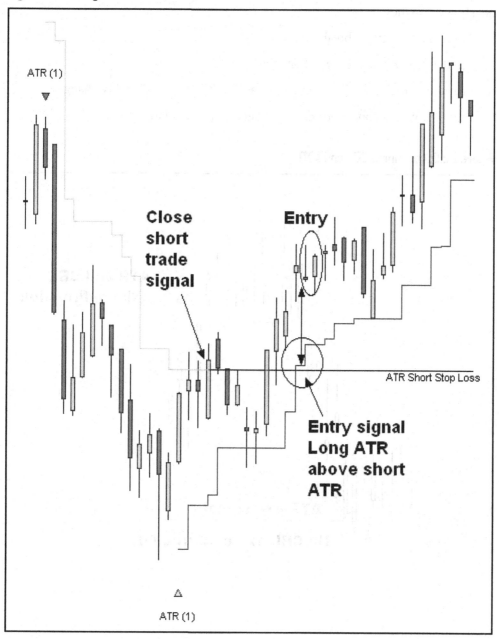

The count back line is similar, but different in some significant areas. The key differences are shown in italics:

- to *identify* the trend break
- to define *significant* price volatility and price volatility limits
- to adjust price volatility calculations as *significant* price volatility changes
- to set stop loss conditions *directly* related to price volatility.

Figure 22.9: combining CBL and ATR

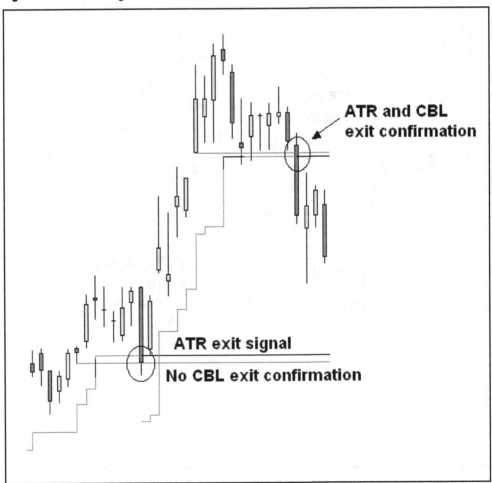

Combining these two indicators to manage a developing trend change and to confirm the trade exit, as shown in figure 22.9, provides a useful solution for the problem of false exits on volatile markets. Both indicators are displayed on the chart. A close below the highest value indicator is an exit signal. Confirmation of the exit comes with a close below the value of the lower indicator.

The first signal on the left of the chart shows an ATR exit signal but not a CBL confirmation signal so the trade remains open. The ATR calculation is commenced again from a new start point after the false ATR exit signal.

On the right of the chart there is a combined ATR and CBL exit signal which confirms the end of the trend.

The combination of methods that measure the same element of the trade — price volatility — in different ways develops a more reliable exit signal that eliminates many false exit signals.

Traders ATR application

The expansion in price volatility is the defining feature of the post-GFC market. The management of extended short-term rallies and declines provides the solution to consistent profits. The use of the traders' application of the ATR provides an effective solution for end-of-day trading in stocks, indices, commodities and currencies. The same method is also applied to intraday trading using 3-, 5- and 15-minute charts.

The traders ATR is defined as a trading solution. It is not applied as a long-term investment or trend-following solution, although higher values such as 2*ATR can be used in this way.

Tactics

⊞ In long-side trading buy while the price is above the ATR value.

⊞ Sell when price drops below the ATR value.

⊞ In short-side trading buy while price is below the ATR value.

⊞ Sell when price rises above the ATR value.

⊞ Exits are executed on either intraday alerts or at the open on the following day.

Rules

⊞   The ATR value defines the acceptable limits of volatility.

⊞   A move beyond these ATR limits signals an end to the current trend.

⊞   Stop loss is based on the value of the ATR. This is updated whenever necessary.

Advantages

⊞   A good measure of volatility.

⊞   Good for short-term trends.

⊞   Good for momentum-driven trading as a stop loss and protect-profit method.

⊞   Very useful for intraday trading.

⊞   Works well with derivatives.

Momentum and volatility go hand in hand. The traders ATR is not useful when these two features combine in extreme circumstances. Trading these extremes calls for a different approach to capturing and defining volatility, and we look at ways to stay ahead of this curve in the next chapter.

Chapter 23

Getting ahead of
the curves

With contributing author Ryan Guppy

News propels prices, although the news is not always well known when the price begins to move. Fast-rising prices attract the attention of small sharks, and later larger sharks. The news does not have to be genuine. Markets have always been partly driven by rumour, but the difference in modern markets is that rumour moves much more quickly and is distributed more widely. The result is the more frequent appearance of two momentum-based features. The first is the parabolic trend, and the second is the price gap trade. Both of these have the capacity to create something out of virtually nothing. A rapid price move is created in response to very little news.

Creating something out of nothing is one of the ancient 36 strategies of the Chinese. In its original application the objective is to create a false front to conceal your real intention. The enemy develops a misconception about the true situation. These deceptive appearances often conceal developing dangers. In the market there is usually not a deliberate intention to create a false front, but the price moves built on rumour and news have the same effect. The developing danger for unwary traders is the sudden collapse of momentum. The trading methods we consider in this chapter are designed to avoid the developing danger so profits are protected.

What causes a stock to suddenly shoot up? The answer is not particularly relevant for trading because our task is to identify the shooting star and trade it quickly before it fades. However, we improve our chances of success if we look in the correct places for these momentum trades. Finding them is surprisingly easy.

The most effective way to find these opportunities is to use charting software to scan the market looking for degrees of price change. Stocks increasing by more than 10% a day, or more than 15% in a few days, are potential candidates. They deserve closer inspection to establish if other momentum trading conditions exist.

Momentum continuation comes in many forms, but the ones we find most useful are overnight gaps and trends best defined with curved trend lines. Of these the Guppy parabolic trends offer a rapid ride to profits. The first type of opportunity appears when a stock rises quickly as a result of some external event. At the end of the trading day we find these stocks using a search to identify those that have increased by more than 10% in the day. The opportunity is confirmed if the opening price on the following day is higher than the high of the previous day. This is an overnight price gap.

The second type of opportunity is a Guppy parabolic trend. This curved trend line describes the way prices accelerate over several days or weeks. The curved trend line defines the rising trend and provides exit triggers. The rising curve has particular properties, so as it develops the curve moves towards a vertical line. This vertical segment of the curve is matched with a chronological date to give an exact ending point for the momentum trade. This is the date when prices collapse rapidly back towards the lower values prevailing before the uptrend started. We explain this trend below.

Parabolic momentum trading

The Guppy parabolic trend line is a curved trend line. It is not a mathematically 'correct' parabolic calculation. The shape of the curve is a proprietary calculation applied with the Guppytraders Essentials charting parabolic tool, and is shown in figure 23.1.

Application

This pattern was observed in the market more than 80 years ago and was misnamed a parabolic trend. It was comparatively rare then but now it has become a frequent pattern in the market. It is a reflection of the increased volatility in modern markets. This is used to define fast-moving trend acceleration where something—a good profit —can be created from nothing—a rumour that may turn out to be false but which drives price. These fast moves are unsustainable and prone to rapid collapse. A characteristic of these trends is the rapid collapse when prices move to the right of the trend line. This trend has an end date defined by the end of the parabolic curve. These trends occur in all types of stocks, in FX trading and commodities. These trends may be an additional development in an existing trend.

Figure 23.1: correct and incorrect parabolic trend definition

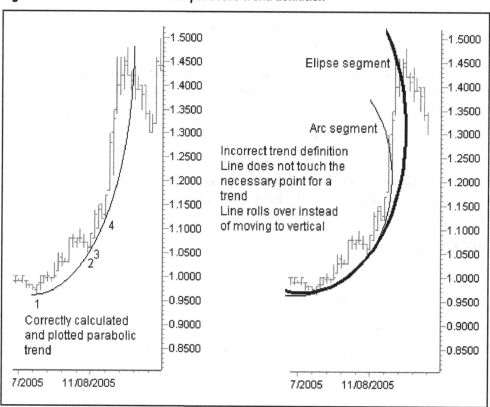

Tactics

⊞ During the middle section of the parabolic trend development, exit on a close below the trend line.

⊞ As the parabolic trend approaches the end date, exit on any intraday move below the trend line.

⊞ Exit on the day prior to the inevitable move to the right of the parabolic trend line.

⊞ Use the value of the parabolic trend line as a stop loss. This changes every day.

Rules

⊞ This pattern is traded without reference to any other indicator. It is a stand-alone indicator.

⊞ Moves to the right of the trend line signal an immediate exit from the trade. This is the equivalent of a close below the trend line.

⊞ The parabolic curve must hit at least two, but preferably three, initial low points to start the trend line plot. Once plotted and anchored on these three points, the position and shape of the curve does not change.

⊞ The curve starts from a 'best fit' point but not necessarily at the start of the trend.

⊞ When the curve moves towards vertical it sets the day on which the next price bar will inevitably move to the right of the trend line.

Advantages

⊞ Captures fast moves developing from 'nothing'.

⊞ Identifies accelerating trends.

⊞ Sets an exact day of exit.

⊞ Most effectively used with price or derivative leverage to increase the return from the trade.

Disadvantages

⊞ Trends often collapse rapidly.

⊞ Difficult to identify this type of trend in the early stages of trend development.

Using the parabolic curve

Towards the end of May 2010 on CNBC Asia SquawkBox and in my weekly CNBC Online column I identified the Guppy parabolic trend in the US dollar index. Parabolic trend analysis suggested the uptrend would finish at the end of June with a potential high near $0.89, followed by a retreat in the order of 60% to 80%.

Figure 23.2: parabolic trend in US dollar index

The Guppy parabolic trend is an unusual chart pattern. It captures a spurt of enthusiasm and it also does an excellent job of defining the end of the trend with an exact date. When the Guppy parabolic trend line is drawn the end of the parabolic curve becomes vertical. This provides a fixed reference point or date. Every day a new price candle is added to the chart, slowly moving towards the fixed end date for the parabolic trend. When the price activity reaches the date there is a high probability the parabolic trend will end because the next price candle will move to the right of the parabolic trend line.

The next most important behavioural feature of this parabolic chart pattern is the rapid collapse when the parabolic trend ends.

Parabolic trend collapses often retrace 60% to 80% of the original parabolic trend rise. The support level near $0.79 shown in figure 23.2 was the beginning of the parabolic trend and the peak was near $0.89. A 60% retracement from $0.89 had a target near $0.83 and this was exceeded. A 70% retracement of the value of the parabolic trend rise has a target near $0.82 and was also exceeded.

The US dollar index has strong historical support and resistance levels between $0.79 and $0.82. This is a long-term consolidation band and the market staged a short-term rally from $0.80. A retreat below $0.78 is more than a 100% retracement of the parabolic trend and this is unusual.

Investors who were short the US dollar index used these parabolic trend retracement calculations as target levels and were ready to cover their short positions when the rebound developed from $0.80.

The full parabolic trend pattern includes the fast rise and the fast collapse of the trend. The parabolic trend does not provide clues to the development of the next trend or chart pattern.

Finding the correct curve

Curves capture particular types of market emotions. The parabolic trend is one of a family of market curves. When traders look at a chart they must decide if they are working with a rounding bottom, a cup or a parabolic curve. Pattern recognition is an art and a skill. It is not a mathematical function, which is why it is virtually impossible to develop effective pattern recognition software. Some people have an intuitive skill in pattern recognition.

Using a common chart Ryan Guppy explains how we apply and assess pattern recognition steps. The assumption in this example is that you have decided this stock may provide a trading opportunity. You are trying to decide the most appropriate analysis method.

In each of these steps we use the curved trend tools, or parabolic curve tool, in the Guppytraders Essentials charting software. The shape of the curve is automatically adjusted depending on our starting point. The curve is extended from the start point and the objective is to find the best fit consistent with the pattern rules. To avoid confusion, we generally show only the correct best fit solution.

Step 1

In this example we are looking for patterns that involve curves. The first step is a step of elimination. Can the broad trends on this chart in figure 23.3 be defined with straight trend lines?

Figure 23.3: attempting to define the trend

We need to use multiple trend lines to adequately define the price development and activity. The downtrend lines are difficult to apply. Trend line breakouts at point A and point B are false. The trend continues to decline.

Incompatibility with a straight edge trend line is a clue the trend may be better analysed with curved trend lines. But incompatibility with straight edge trend line analysis does not automatically mean we can use curved trend lines. Some charts do not give effective solutions with either form of analysis.

Step 2

We start with the parabolic trend. We need a few definition reminders before we start to apply a parabolic curve. These include:

- a parabolic curve shows steady acceleration with price remaining near to the curve

- a parabolic curve does not exclude significant sub-trends within the pattern

- a parabolic curve needs three lows to set the position of the curve

- a parabolic curve is a trend breakout pattern.

We use the parabolic curve tool in Guppytraders Essentials. Once the starting point is selected, the objective is to position the curve so at least three significant rebound points are connected. The starting point is usually a low near to where the visual up-trend starts. The Guppytraders Essentials tool makes it easy to experiment with several different starting points, as shown in figure 23.4.

We start with the curve P1. This gives a good fit that describes the trend as it has developed. It has multiple touches on the line. But price does not show a steady acceleration. There is a fast rally at point 1, and then another fast rally at point 2. This is not steady acceleration. Additionally these are major sub-trends within the parabolic pattern defined by P1. The curve excludes these significant patterns. A 35% move from $8.58 to $11.65 is a significant trend in itself. A 28% jump from $9.21 to $11.54 also cannot be ignored as a small development within the context of a parabolic trend.

Additionally, point A is a significant rebound level. This is excluded when we position trend line P1. We cannot reasonably adjust the position of P1 to include rebound point A because this then excludes other important price action.

The parabolic trend captures the steady acceleration of a trend, so we need to consider a different starting point. We look for points where the trend has accelerated. If we select point A as a start point for the parabolic curve then the parabolic trend must use point B as the second point in the trend line. The placement of the parabolic trend line P2 fails to capture the development of price. Additionally the rally in area 2 invalidates using point A as a starting point for a parabolic trend.

Figure 23.4: experimenting with different starting points

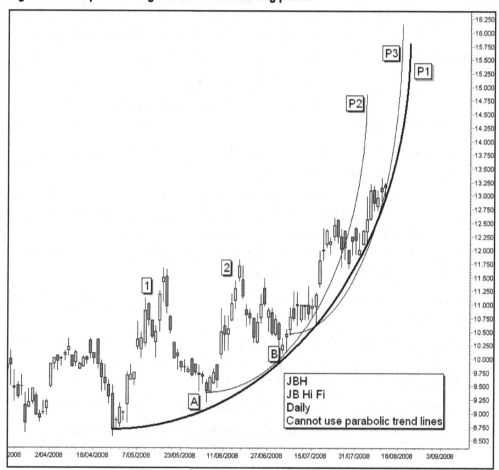

If we use the area near point B and plot trend line P3 we have similar problems to P1 and P2. Additionally this breakout trend has already developed so there is a lower probability a parabolic trend will develop. The line P3 can be used, but it is not a good definition of the character of this overall trend breakout.

Our conclusion is that this is not a parabolic trend.

Step 3

This step relies on the difference between a cup and a saucer. A cup pattern has a short duration and steeper sides than those found in a saucer pattern. A saucer is a shallower pattern that develops over an extended period. Defining a saucer pattern, or a rounding bottom as it is sometimes called, is not a simple matter of joining the lower points. The chart in figure 23.5 shows a beautifully placed curve with eight significant points all falling on the edges of the curve. This curve captures all the significant price activity—but it's not a valid pattern. The shape of the curve is determined by the initial touch points 1 to 4.

We start with the positive aspects of the pattern as drawn on the chart. They are:

- multiple touches on the curved trend line. The significant retreat and rebound points all fall on the curve

- the duration of the pattern is long term. This starts in January and ends in August so it's an eight-month pattern

- this is the best fit. The starting point for the curve is P1. This is the only starting point that includes all points 1 to 8 on the curve. A curve starting at P2 does not include all the significant price activity, and curve P3 excludes some of the significant price activity. Price activity is significant when it is a retreat and rebound point, such as points 1 through 8.

It seems all the boxes are ticked, so why is this excluded as a valid saucer pattern? There are four reasons. They are:

- the depth of the pattern. This is not a shallow pattern. It stretched from $8.58 to $16.40. This pattern has a depth of 91%. This exceptional depth is a factor that suggests this is not a valid saucer pattern

- this pattern starts from the top of an uptrend

- by definition a rounding bottom occurs at the bottom of a downtrend. It is usually preceded by a steep fall, or by a prolonged downtrend before the rounding pattern starts to develop. The bottom pattern is a specific type of consolidation pattern usually located near historical lows. This would need to be near $4.00 for JBH

- the upside target projection sets a target of $24.25. This is 83% above the current price. This may be achievable, but given the behaviour of the stock this seems to be a low-probability outcome. The projection target for a rounding bottom found near the bottom of historical price activity often matches a prior resistance level. In this situation projections of this magnitude are acceptable because historical price activity verifies the target. JBH has a blue sky target and this adds a question mark to the validity of what is normally a bottom pattern. Blue sky targets appear when a stock moves above all-time historical highs.

Figure 23.5: invalid pattern

Despite getting a number of ticks from a mechanical perspective, this is not a valid pattern for JBH. The location of the pattern and the depth of the pattern are all powerful factors which suggest this is not a valid application of a saucer pattern.

Step 4

Just as with a saucer pattern, the cup pattern can include some significant rallies. The curve of the cup captures the lower limits of price activity. The analysis starts with defining the lip of the cup. This resistance level can be defined in two ways. The first is where there has been a significant resistance level historically prior to the formation of the cup pattern. In this situation we can infer the position of the lip of the cup. This is not the case with JBH.

Figure 23.6: cup and handle pattern

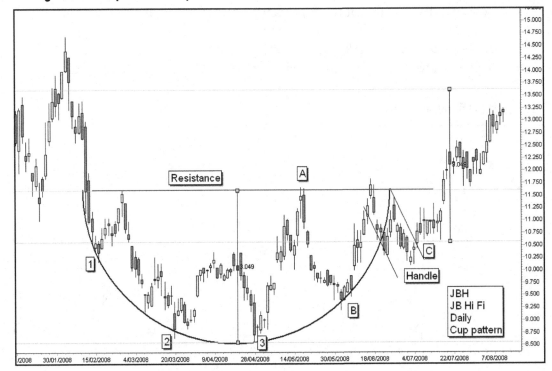

The rally peak at point A confirms the position of the resistance level and the lip of the cup pattern in figure 23.6. This also includes the peak of the rebound from point 1. The lip of the cup pattern is confirmed with the rebound from point B.

The left side of the cup is created by points 1, 2 and 3. These set the shape of the curve. We watch for future price activity to rebound from the position of the projected curve. The potential for a cup was seen prior to point B, but the point B rebound confirms the cup pattern because it gives a location point for the right side of the curve. The position of the curve is already defined by points 1, 2 and 3. This also gives a trading opportunity from $9.80 to the target on the lip of the cup at $11.60. This is an 18% return.

Cups often have handles. The handle pattern development starts inside the cup in this example and then extends to the right of the cup trend line. The breakout from the handle pattern uses a new upside target calculated at $13.58. An entry into the pattern based on the handle breakout at $10.62 creates a 28% profit. This breakout shown on the chart extract is moving towards the pattern projection target.

2

Conclusion

JBH is a cup and handle pattern. It is not a parabolic trend. The cup pattern was recognised at point B in figure 23.6. The full cup and handle pattern was recognised at point C. The drawing tools in Guppytraders Essentials give traders the flexibility to experiment with the position of the plots and the curves. This is not a random exercise. We look for specific conditions to validate the placement of the curved trend lines. When these conditions are met we can have greater confidence our identification of the pattern is correct.

Overnight and gap momentum

Curves capture emotion. Price gaps also capture emotion but they offer a different type of trading opportunity. A price gap appears when there has been a change of opinion. The value people thought was appropriate yesterday is no longer considered appropriate today. For some reason, usually related to a news event, the crowd has changed its opinion overnight.

In some stocks this is a regular occurrence, and reflects no more than the general ebb and flow of trading activity. These are the common gaps. When we look at a gap on today's price action and then compare it with the longer term chart we are likely to see many of these common gaps. If the stock has a history of common gaps, then it is not suitable for a gap trading strategy.

We want stocks that show significant gaps and which are actively traded. Additionally, when the gap appears, we want to see plenty of trading action. Some stocks show a lot of gap activity, but this is simply a move from one price level to the next. This may be a jump from $0.40 to $0.42 which shows up on the chart as a flat spot. This spot activity shows there is no trading range for the day. The open, high, low and close are exactly the same. Stocks with a history of this type of activity do not provide trading opportunities. With only a small number of trades all taking place at the one price level, there is limited opportunity to apply effective trading strategies.

We are looking for gaps driven by crowd enthusiasm, and which have attracted many trades. Without trading liquidity, we cannot implement our trading strategy.

The overnight gap strategy is shown in figure 23.7. The strategy accepts we miss out on the best price of the day. Our intention is to buy on day one and sell at a good price on day two. At the end of day one, many traders execute a routine search of the market looking for stocks posting large percentage gains with good volume.

These people act on day two with the hope of joining a trend breakout, a rally or perhaps a rebound trade. This crowd buys the stock we purchased on day one. Our strategy is based on the continuation of crowd excitement as the size of the initial price move is discovered by traders using end-of-day data.

Figure 23.7: overnight gap strategy

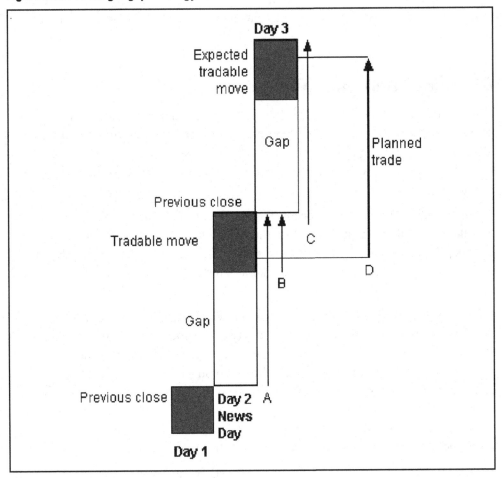

The same strategy is applied when there is no initial gap, but only if the momentum and scale of trading are outstandingly strong. We locate these opportunities by scanning for high trading volume. This captures the number of trades, not the number of shares. When there is a swirl of many trades there is the opportunity to create something out of the nothing of crowd emotion. When the high number of trades is matched with a fast price rise we have the setup for a momentum-based trade that applies the same principles as an overnight gap trade.

Here is the strategy:

- fast trading, significant price rises and good news deliver the same information as a price gap

- momentum is likely to continue over the next day of trading as those who missed the first rise identify the large price move after the market has closed

- the trader buys on day one — the momentum day

- the trader sells on day two to those people who discover the price change after the market has closed on day one

- the objective is to capture the continuation of momentum. We are not interested in trading any trend.

Aggressive traders need no extra information. They simply buy into this pool of activity. Less aggressive traders wait for confirmation of what is driving the activity. In this case, the confirmation comes from the news release. It gives some fundamental backing for the momentum apparently based on nothing.

In these trading situations there is no point in arguing with the market. The trader simply buys at market by bidding higher than the last-traded price. He may be filled with several sell orders and end up with an average price. This is an excited crowd and it is as rude and unforgiving as the rush for 'free' seating on a budget airline flight. The entry tactic is to bid high, not argue, and be satisfied with just getting a ticket on the momentum run.

Gap down trading

Gap up or gap down, the situation offers the same opportunity. In 2010 the Australian Government announced a new Resources Super Profits Tax. The result was both predictable and tradable from the short side. Traders expected a short-term rapid fall in mining stocks followed by a rebound. To make the most of this situation traders use CFDs to leverage the returns from the short-side trade. The screen shot in figure 23.8 is from the IG Markets CFD platform and uses a five-minute chart provided by IT-Finance. We explain our thinking at each of the steps in this trade evaluation to show how traders stay ahead of the curve. These notes are taken from our weekly newsletter written at the time.

The market was aware of the growing probability of a 40% resources tax on Thursday and Friday. This contributed to the existing downtrend in the RIO price. Although the daily chart shows down days, the intraday price activity was erratic without a clear trend. Getting and maintaining an entry with a reasonable stop loss was difficult on these days and no entry was taken. Aggressive traders entered a short trade in this period, but they used loose stops. Cautious traders did not enter and this means they do not reap the benefit of the Monday price gap where price fell from $72.00 to $68.00.

We apply a cautious approach. The Monday gap down does not lead to a follow-through fall. On Monday the price opens lower and then rises. Towards the end of the day the price develops a downtrend as RIO joins the broader market sell off. The CFD entry is made after the price retreats from the downtrend line. Entry is made at $69.44. This is intended as an overnight gap trade.

Figure 23.8: RIO gap down

The margin for the trade is 5%. Position size is 3600. Cash value is $12 499.20. Face value is $249 984. Stop loss is at $70.00 and gives a loss of $2016. Note that in this CFD trade the position size is calculated from the maximum loss. As with any trade the maximum loss figure is 2% of total portfolio capital. This is $2000. This is the base calculation figure for the CFD trade. The position size is adjusted until the cash loss in the trade is around $2000. The overnight stop loss is set at $69.30 based on the small support level prior to the Monday close.

Day two of the trade, shown in figure 23.9, requires stop loss adjustment. This is a loose stop loss because the gap down in price already delivers a profit. The objective in the day two trade management is profit protection. The stop loss is not hit so the trade remains open for an additional day. The most significant danger is the bargain hunting rebound as RIO approaches support levels.

Figure 23.9: day two of trade

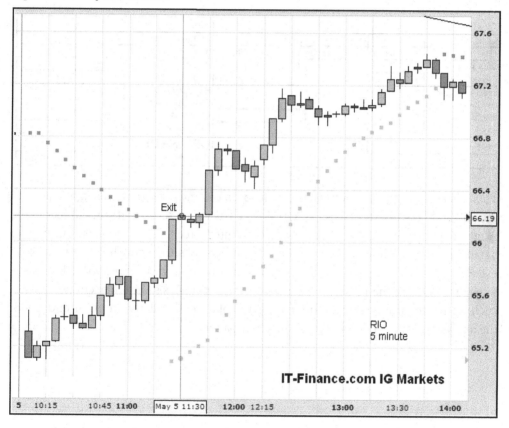

On day three of the trade we look for rebound activity from the support level near $66.00. On day three we manage the trade using the Parabolic SAR to deliver a tight stop and protect profits. This should not be confused with the parabolic trend line discussed above. The Parabolic SAR is a tool that delivers frequent whipsaw signals, with multiple entries and exits. In this situation we want the sensitivity of the SAR because we expect a rebound from the support level and need to lock in profits quickly.

After another gap down, the SAR exit signal is delivered rapidly. The exit is taken at $66.19, as summarised in figure 23.10. This delivers a $11 700 profit, or a 93.61% return on the trade.

Figure 23.10: exit at $66.19

CFD leverage	5.00	Portfolio	$	100,000.00		2% risk	$	2,000.00
SHORT		MOTHER					CFD	
Name	Sell price	qty	Total			CFD buy cost	Risk	
RIO	$ 69.44	3,600	$	249,984.00		$ 12,499.20		2,016
Stop loss	$ 70.00		$	252,000.00				
Close/Target	$ 66.19		$	238,284.00	Balance		$	11,700.00
Interest income	$ -				Buy commission		$	-
day 2	$ -				Sell commission		$	-
day 3	$ -				GSL cost		$	-
day 4	$ -				Carry income		$	-
day 5					**CFD PROFIT**		**$**	**11,700.00**
					CFD %			93.61

This is snatch and grab trading. In part it relies on understanding the significance of the ebb and flow of order lines using real-time price data screens. It's an old technique of tape reading transferred to the modern computer screen, and we look at this in more detail in the next chapter. The trading method catches the short-lived impact of an event and turns it into a profit opportunity. Sometimes, as with the proposed Resources Super Profits Tax, the opportunity rests on market analysis. In other circumstances, such as the dollar index or the dramatic parabolic trend collapse in oil in mid 2008, the analysis is derived entirely from the chart pattern.

Chapter 24

Modern tape reading

With contributing author Ryan Guppy

Reading the tape is an old-fashioned term for analysing order flow yet it's become an essential part of order management in modern markets. Getting your buy order in the right place and getting your sell order executed at your preferred price are essential aspects of successful trading. This is where analysis and strategy turn to action. Just how much of these tape reading techniques you can apply depends on your exchange.

Data is divided into three levels. Level 1 is just the current buy and the current sell. Level 2 is aggregated buy and sell orders down to perhaps five or ten price levels. Level 3 data shows the individual orders at each price level to unlimited depth. This is full market transparency and some market players do not like the glare of full light. We do. It provides us with opportunities to manage entries and exits by analysing the flow of orders. In volatile markets where trends end quickly this is an essential skill that allows traders to get out at, or near, the top of the trend.

As Ryan Guppy writes: 'What is the aim of trading?' Every time we enter a trade we use our analysis to gauge the probability of price action. Will price rebound off a support level, and will the rally continue towards our price targets? Will price reach our price target, or get trapped in a resistance area? These are all questions that our analysis can answer, but analysis does not provide answers to getting the best entry or exit price. The order screen is an important step in producing our trading plan as it has the power to redefine probability.

It is important to realise that with even the best analysis the order line is where it all comes to fruition. This is where the trading actually starts, where shares are bought and sold and profits are realised or lost. Traders know the price target for a triangle pattern but your position in the order line ultimately determines the success of your trade. In this example we are trading a hypothetical upward-sloping triangle pattern that has broken upwards with a price target of $0.40. We have entered at $0.30. We have bought our shares and are now looking to lock in our sell order to give us the best possible return.

Figure 24.1: order line

Price	Volume
39	2294
39	1000
39	6213
39	6000
39.5	40000
39.5	10000
40	3000
40	3000
40	70000
40	70000
40	20000
40	30000
40	3000
40	23000
40	1000
40	5900
40	40000
40	40000
40	6500
40	30000
40	1700
40	1000

What is the definition of the best possible return? We all judge the success of our trades by the profit margin. The higher the profit, the more successful the trade, but there comes a point when looking at the order line can redefine this objective. This is an actual order line shown in figure 24.1, and it is an example of how the order line can redefine what the best possible return for a trade is. Hypothetically we have bought into this stock at $0.30, with a price projection from the triangle pattern at $0.40. This gives a 33% return for the trade and most traders would consider this to be a good return on capital.

But if we look at the order line we see there are already 16 sell orders placed at $0.40. This means if we were to place our sell order at $0.40 we would become 17th in the order line, with 344 400 shares between us and our order being filled. We get around this problem by lowering our sell order, essentially undercutting everyone who has placed their sell order at $0.40 to jump ahead of them. Looking at the order line there are only two orders at $0.395 totalling 50 000 shares. It is more likely our order will get filled if we become the third seller at $0.395 rather than the 17th seller at $0.40.

By placing our sell order lower we reduce the potential profit by 2%, bringing it down to 31%. The trade-off is an increase in the probability of our sell order being filled as price makes its way to the price target of $0.40. Even though our trade will not give us the greatest potential profit it will give us the greatest potential to be filled. This delivers realised profits instead of theoretical profits. No-one cares about how much you *could* have made, only how much you *actually* made.

This brings another trading strategy into play, and we call it the bowl of rice strategy. If you are trading with someone your offering needs to hold value to the other person. When you place a sell order there needs to be someone who thinks the value you have placed on this stock is lower than the 'true' value. No-one buys an empty rice bowl because it no longer has value. There must still be some rice in the bottom of the bowl for the other buyer to eat. Placing your sell order lower in the price line does not cut significantly into the potential profit, but it increases the probability of your order being filled as there is still room for price to move.

Do you define the best possible return as how much you could have made? Or do you define this as making as much as possible from the trade? Every trader wants to try to get the maximum profit from every trade. There is no denying that each day we trade we work our money as hard as we can. But the difference between theoretical profits and actual profits is that your actual profits fatten your bank account. To get actual profits your sell order needs to be filled, and that may require modifying your greed.

Leapfrog orders

Leapfrog orders show desperation to get into, or out of, a trade. Sometimes it's a single large buyer, and this may be a clue to insider trading activity. Sometimes there are three or four traders all vying to get a position in the stock. This order line excitement is a momentum confirmation feature. This behaviour is often created by a small group of informed traders who are anxious to get a position in the stock. The leapfrogging of unfilled orders is an important clue to developing momentum.

Imagine a single trader. The trader puts in an order to buy 200 000 at $0.10. Her order is partly filled, with 50 000 at $0.10. The price rises. She leapfrogs the order line and amends her order to buy 150 000 at $0.11. You identify this movement on the order screen as the old residual order for 150 000—the original order for 200 000 less the partial fill of 50 000—disappears from the order line and reappears at the same order size of 150 000 but at a new higher price level. This process is summarised in figure 24.2, with her changing orders shown with an *.

Perhaps she is partially filled again with 100 000 at $0.11 before the price rises. Again she leapfrogs the order line, filling the remainder of her order with 50 000 at $0.12. The key behaviour is the desperate need to fill the quantity of the order at almost any price.

Figure 24.2: leapfrog orders

	Buy order	Price	Sell order	Price	Course of trades Trades	Price
* Trade 5	50,000	0.12	50,000	0.12	50,000	0.12
Trade 4	50,000	0.11	30,000	0.115	30,000	0.115
* Trade 3	150,000	0.11	100,000	0.11	100,000	0.11
Trade 2	150,000	0.10	20,000	0.105	20,000	0.105
* Trade 1	200,000	0.10	50,000	0.10	50,000	0.10

Original order to be filled

This leapfrogging cannot be observed unless you use a live screen. Leapfrogging is inferred from an end-of-day chart when a large price rise appears which is not accompanied by large volume. A detailed and animated explanation of entry and exit tactics using leapfrog order lines is included in the *Gold: Mining the Markets* DVD. This includes leapfrogging orders, and getting to the head of the order line for entry or exit.

Low-volume exits

How do we manage an exit when trading volumes are low? This is a strategy of 'The golden cicada sheds its skin', discussed in *The 36 Strategies of the Chinese for Financial Traders*.

Exits in a low-volume environment use a softly, softly approach, and the screenshot in figure 24.3 from the course of trade screen shows how it operates. For the purposes of this example, we start the exit on the day LRX trades at $0.175. The objective is to illustrate how this type of exit is implemented. Notionally we have 118 000 shares in this open position. Once the stop loss point is triggered the plan calls for us to sell the shares. If we place a sell order for the full amount then we 'bully the market'. This simply means our order is so large in comparison to other traders that it dominates, or swamps, the order line. If we are big buyers, this tends to push the price up. Potential sellers see the large buy order so they lift their own asking price knowing the big buyer will probably chase prices to fill the order. The reverse applies when selling.

Figure 24.3: low-volume exit

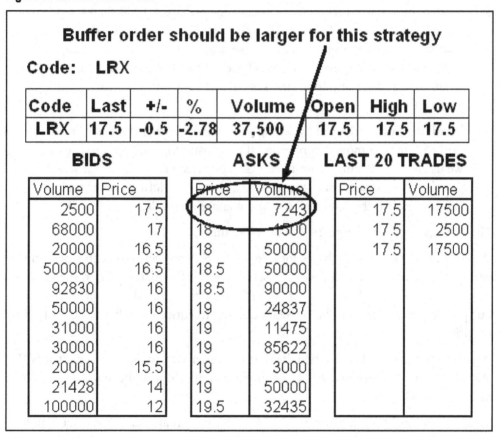

If we put in a large sell order then potential buyers hold back waiting for the price to drop. This is particularly so in a weak market where buyers are not active. The seller's solution is the same as that used by the large institutions. Like them we break up the sell order into smaller pieces. The institutions do this by placing sell orders with several different brokers. They reward those who get the best volume weighted average price, or VWAP.

We cannot do this, but we can control the number of our shares that appear for sale in the order screens. There are three ways to achieve this.

- First, simply place all our 118 000 shares for sale at $0.175. Like a big bait, there will be some small traders who will nibble away at this. It may take many days to completely sell the order. It also runs the risk of dominating the market as discussed above. This is the least effective solution.

- Second, by placing a sell order at $0.175 for perhaps 10 000 shares. Once this order is filled, a new sell order is placed at $0.175. This continues until all our shares are sold. This approach means we must watch the screen all day, and replace our sell order every time it is filled. This solution is not bad, particularly if you have a pager or phone alert system that tells you when each small order has been sold.

- Third, the exit is achieved by selling at market whenever there is a bid at $0.175. This is a more complex and time-consuming strategy. It is the one we use to exit LRX in this notional case study trade taken from our weekly newsletter. It is the most effective strategy because it attracts other traders. You must sit on the screen all day and manage each sale.

The strategy, shown in figure 24.4, works like this:

We offer 20 000 or 40 000 shares for sale at $0.18. If we get sold at this price this is very good, however the objective is to set a buffer in the market. Often the next buy order will be $0.05 below this—at $0.175. They bid up to the buffer price. This is our planned exit price, but the buyers are trying to entice the seller at $0.18 to drop his price.

If we set a sell order at $0.175 then the next buy order is most likely to appear at $0.17. We lift the bar by keeping a sell order in place at $0.18, just above our planned exit price. This is like a bait.

Whenever a buy order appears at $0.175 we hit it with an exact at-market matching order. In this example, this means we make the first sale of 17 500, followed by 2500 and then again by 17 500. If we meet the buy order for 2500 we succeed in selling 40 000 shares on this day. When we meet the market at $0.175 we also 'mark the tape' with our selling activity. Other traders see sales at $0.175.

Figure 24.4: selling with buffer order

Code: LRX

Code	Last	+/-	%	Volume	Open	High	Low
LRX	18	0.5	2.86	26270	18	18	18

BIDS			ASKS		LAST 20 TRADES	
Volume	**Price**		**Price**	**Volume**	**Price**	**Volume**
2500	17.5		18	4273	18	17527
68000	17		18	10000	18	1500
100000	17		18.5	50000	18	7243
92830	16		18.5	90000		
50000	16		18.5	32435		
31000	16		19	28417		
30000	16		19	11475		

Buffer order is hit as well

This activity has two important effects.

- First, it reassures those who already hold the shares. They see interest and trading in a stock that had slowed. This usually renews their hope and they hold off selling. This reduces the selling pressure.

- Second, this increase in activity attracts the interest of other traders. Those who have been watching this share may take the trading activity at $0.175 as an indication of increasing momentum. Sometimes they are eager enough to take out your reserve buffer order at $0.18 because they believe the buying activity at $0.175 is an indication of a rebound.

For this notional trade we show an exit for half the shares at $0.175 ($10 325) and the other half at $0.18 ($10 620) as the benchmark order is sold. Our objective is to 'unwind' our position in a low-volume environment. This calls for careful management of the way we sell the stock. There are a variety of strategies, and their success depends on the time we have available and our understanding of the way other traders interpret the price action.

Mining depth of market

Armed with financial calculations and a clear knowledge of how much we are prepared to pay, or sell for, we do battle with the market. The bid information about a stock is useful, but what is below and above the current bid and ask? Are these orders a temporary phenomena, or are they indicative of a wider selling campaign? To find the answer we need full depth of market information. The most obvious advantage of this information is that it prevents us buying at $0.25 when the next buyer is at $0.23 or less. Depth of market allows us to fine-tune our trading—and also to occasionally outsmart ourselves.

The full depth of market information is shown in figures 24.5 and 24.6. The depth of market information gives details of each bid and ask at each price level. It also lists the number, the size and position of orders in line at each level. The buy orders closest to the buy column are the first orders in line at each level and will be executed in this exact sequence. Orders remain in place until filled or withdrawn. Sell orders closest to the sell column are the first executed.

This new information represents only the potential for price action because not all these orders will be filled during the day. As prices move in one direction or another, the gaps in price levels may be filled with new orders. Someone may choose to place a new buy order at $1.57, for instance. During the day the number of orders at any level may swell as people join the rush. They also fall away as traders cancel their market orders, and perhaps place them at new levels or leave the market entirely.

And, of course, the most important caveat of all: what you see here is not what you will see in one hour's time, or in two days' time. But all this said, these figures provide a remarkably useful guide for trading activity, and they support chart analysis in some very interesting ways, considered below.

Many traders and investors use standing, or good till cancelled, orders and this gives a unique character to the market. Orders at specific price levels are lodged early and remain in place for extended periods. Unless instructed otherwise, many brokers leave orders in place for three days before they automatically expire. These semi-permanent orders provide an outline of the structure of the market and help us to identify the bulges in the balance of probability.

Going up

In mining this depth of market information the first nugget is the number of buyers and sellers. The second nugget is the order volume. It's all very well to know there are six buyers and one seller for YDN, but having decided our trading opportunity lies in an entry with YDN additional volume information helps fine-tune the entry.

Figure 24.5: depth of market, buying pressure

				YDN Last sale 1.62			
Qty			BUY	SELL	Qty		
6,300	3,050	250,000	1.62	1.63	3,097		
*0	30,000	27,741		1.64	16,900	30,000	
		100,000	1.61	1.65	25,000		
	100,000	100,000	1.60	1.67	12,000	50,000	
		200,000	1.59	1.68	2,200	25,000	3,300
100,000	1,900	5,000	1.58	1.71	2,537	8,520	10,000
		1,000			5,000	2,000	5,000
23,111	100,000	3,000	1.56		19,000	10,000	2,000
	*0	6,000	1.55		13,500	5,000	25,000
		4,000	1.54		4,000	10,329	7,300
		2,000	1.52		5,000	3,500	4,500
4,000	20,000	2,000	1.51		10,000	4,500	3,300
					4,000	6,000	700
				1.72	25,000	6,000	
				1.73	25,000		
				1.75	5,000	10,000	20,000

The six buyers at 1.62 want at least 317091 shares. The order marked *0 is for an undisclosed quantity. The seller has only 3097 to sell. Unless many more sellers come into the market at current prices, buyers will not be satisfied at this current level. Most will miss out on stock. This in itself suggests rising prices as buyers outbid each other to chase scarce stock.

Moving down the depth of market screen gives additional advantages by showing the buyers and sellers at each level. Traders looking to buy YDN draw seven conclusions from figure 24.5:

- there are consistently large orders at every level below $1.62 down to $1.51

- some of these buyers are certain to become fearful and move their bid prices up towards the last-traded price. This will swell the buying orders at higher levels

- only two price slots—$1.57 and $1.53—do not have buy orders. An order placed in either of these gaps would be first in line and first filled if prices fell to this level

- placing a new order at $1.61, or $1.59, puts us second in line. This is only useful should prices fall to this level

- to get to the front of every line we need to meet the ask at $1.63

- if we want more than 3097 shares then we may have to bid to $1.64 to get our entire order filled

- the selling activity at $1.71 comes from many small orders. This suggests small traders rather than institutions. The larger order size on the buying side suggests large traders and experienced market participants. This conclusion is based on the assumption that size tends to equal experience.

Let's take a closer look at how this works to give traders an advantage. Assume the first buyer in line at $1.62 desperately wants 250 000 shares, for whatever reason. It may be that 250 000 rounds out his existing portfolio, or it may represent a dollar value he is prepared to commit to the market. If this is the case then the size of his order, 250 000 shares, will decrease as the price increases.

To fill his order in this market on current figures he must pay at least $1.64. A more likely outcome is that he will take out the existing sell orders between $1.63 and $1.68 and some orders at $1.71 to ensure he gets the number of shares he wants. His alternative is to wait until more sellers come into the market at $1.63, which is unlikely when prices are rising.

What will this buyer do? In a market where there are many other buyers he is going to have to bid up or run the risk of missing out entirely. During the day he is likely to move his bid price up. When we compare today's depth of market information with yesterday's it is quite common to see the same orders move up the bidding scale over several days.

Sellers and potential sellers watch this action and use it to fine-tune their tactics.

Traders chasing this stock and looking to enter a new buy order will meet the ask at $1.63, knowing three things:

- the large buying orders at $1.62 provide a floor for prices, making our purchase safer

- by meeting the ask we go straight to the head of the line and get a position in the stock

- prices have already risen by $0.04, and the large orders, if they are to be filled, will push the bidding higher.

Using this information confirms the shift of the balance of probability in the trader's favour on this day. Even if every other analytical tool screams 'buy at $1.61', this depth of market information tells us it is unlikely we will get stock at this price. If our financial analysis allows us to chase price to $1.65 then we shift the day's balance of probability in our favour by meeting the ask.

Traders looking to sell existing YDN stock have the opportunity to get a better exit. As prices move up many sellers back away, lifting their asking prices a few ticks above the current trade. With plenty of buyers chasing them they can afford to be coy. The large order flow blocks further price rises at $1.71, but any sell order placed at $1.66, $1.69 or $1.70 is first in line. These points represent better selling opportunities—but only if they also lock in profits based on previous financial calculations.

Had these calculations indicated $1.71 as the best sell point then it is now too late to place the order. With over 170 000 on offer at this level even an enthusiastic market is going to have a little trouble swallowing the volume. A better exit is at $1.70 in front of the selling pressure. This is selling into strength and guarantees order execution.

Going down

Essentially the same types of trading conclusions are drawn from figure 24.6 but in reverse. The selling order overhang of 64 143 tells buyers they can get their desired number of shares any time, just by bidding a cent or two higher. There is no pressure on the buyers to bid up. Prices have dropped $0.05 since yesterday's close and the volume on offer is nearly the same—64 143 compared to 70 000 sold yesterday.

Figure 24.6: depth of market, selling pressure

		Qty	BUY	SELL	Qty		
		30,000	0.25	0.27	15,000	16,000	10,000
		15,000	0.23		19,143	4,000	
		48,626	0.20	0.28	4,000	19,885	144
15,000	19,885	10,000	0.17		3,000	6,970	1,620
	10,000	30,000		0.29	10,000	4,000	1,080
					19,000	16,000	3,000

GDC Last sale 0.027

By waiting, there is a good chance the sellers will lower their price. With so many shares on offer the supply obviously outstrips the demand. Buyers don't need to jump ahead in the line because there is so much scrip on offer that nobody is in a hurry.

The seller looks pessimistically at figure 24.6. Unless she is very close to the front of the order line at $0.27 there is a low probability of getting out. With at least 15 traders behind her stretching back to $0.29 it is certain one of them will act decisively to cut their losses by meeting the bid at $0.25. Then the entire sell order structure is likely to cascade towards $0.25.

With such heavy selling in place it is difficult to ask $0.26 and have it filled, even though this new order goes to the front of a new line. When prices are falling it is difficult to entice buyers to bid up by lowering the ask to the mid-point between the current bid and ask. Better not to quibble when the depth of market looks like this. Meet the bid and get out at, or just beyond, your stop loss points.

The buyer sees figure 24.6 in an entirely different light. For the trader placing a new order the danger is the buyer at $0.25 will see the market depth, pull his order out, and re-insert it somewhere between $0.23 and $0.17. When markets fall, buyers retreat in front of the selling pressure, realising they do not have to pay as much as they originally estimated. An initial buy order, first in line, could be comfortably placed at $0.18, and monitored closely.

This bid increases only if more buyers flood in at higher levels, or if sellers refuse to lower their ask. This is a waiting game where the buyer holds the upper hand. Depth of market information allows the trader to see how best to implement his trading decision on the day.

Surfing the line

Accomplished surfers ride just ahead of the crest of a wave. We apply the same techniques to help manage an exit in a fast-moving stock. The objective is to stay just ahead of the surging buy orders so we achieve the best possible exit on the day. In this sense, we shed our skin, abandoning old sell orders so we can achieve our trade withdrawal under the most favourable conditions. This is a strategy of 'The golden cicada sheds its skin'.

The following shows the tactics we apply to manage the exit in the case study China trade in Shanghai-listed 600688. The application of these tactics calls for skill and judgement. The structure of the order lines changes, and it is not always possible to judge exactly how the buying and selling pressure may develop. When order lines are limited to five levels this can become a significant problem.

Here is the exit strategy with 600688:

- 600688 shows an RSI divergence. This suggests trend weakness. This may be temporary—just a dip and a rebound—or serious—a collapse of the trend

- the price spike to $4.58 was followed by a retreat and another attempt to reach $4.58. This creates a tweezers pattern. This is often a top of the trend pattern

- we aim for a defensive exit at $4.60.

Here are the exit tactics in figure 24.7 designed to shed our skin so we make a better trade escape:

- place a sell order at $4.60

- watch the activity of buyers

- if there is strong buying at $4.58 and there are many sellers joining us at $4.60, then we sell at $4.60

Figure 24.7: resistance at 4.60

	4.63	100
	4.62	300
	4.61	200
Resistance level	**4.60**	**60,000** includes our 5,400 to sell
	4.59	100
last sale	4.58	30,000 strong buying
	4.57	10,000
	4.56	3,000
	4.55	100
	4.54	300
	4.53	200

⊞ if there is strong buying at $4.58, but most sellers are clustered higher at $4.63, then we withdraw our sell order at $4.60 and place it again just below the main group of buyers at $4.63. We put a sell order at $4.62. The objective is to stay just ahead of the main 'resistance' created by sellers so that buyers will continue to lift their buy orders to chase the price. We surf the crest of buying pressure, as shown in figure 24.8.

Figure 24.8: resistance at 4.63

Resistance level	4.63	90,000	
	4.62	▲ 60	
	4.61	60	
	4.60	5,400	shift our order to 4.62
	4.59	50	
last sale	4.58	30,000	strong buying
	4.57	10,000	
	4.56	3,000	
	4.55	100	
	4.54	300	
	4.53	200	

It is important to avoid placing our sell order at the very end of the long order line at the resistance point. The resistance point may develop at a higher price than $4.63. We cannot always tell when we are limited to a depth of market five order lines above or below the last-traded price. The resistance level may be higher so we may need to keep moving the sell order upwards to keep ahead of buying pressure. This is not always easy to achieve. We recognise the resistance level, wherever it occurs, by the larger number of sellers clustered at this level. To get the best exit we must be one tick below the resistance level so we are the first sell order executed.

The ebb and flow of orders is the normal activity of the market. We use this ebb and flow to hide our order activity. Each withdrawn order sheds a skin, allowing our trade objective to grow larger and more successful.

In modern markets the old skills of tape reading, once used with the ticker-tape machine sitting on the trader's desk, have been transferred to the flow of order information across the screen. The velocity of trading, gauged by the blinking of amended orders on the screen, provides a guide to the thinking of our opponents, be they buyers or sellers. This is the lifeblood of the market, and taking its pulse improves our trade execution. In the next chapter we show how to also use these tape reading skills to further enhance our tactical trade execution.

Chapter 25

Testing shorts

In falling markets the market makers are reputed to 'run the stops' so they can 'shake out the weak hands'. This is a modern implementation of the Chinese strategy of 'Beating the grass to startle the snake'. Traders want to know where support is located and if it is solid. Traders want to know if a chart pattern will develop as anticipated or if the pattern is losing development momentum.

Traders have a choice. They can wait for the market to develop, or they can give it a nudge to see how it reacts. This is gaming the market and it used to be the exclusive preserve of market makers and large professional traders. Modern markets make it possible for everyone to participate in this activity, and this has contributed to higher intraday volatility. On a professional level it's called 'flash trading'; an algorithmic trading system embeds very short term trades in the broad flow of trading activity. There remains a suspicion that this may also involve 'front running', where trades are placed in advance of large market-moving orders.

Algorithm formulas search for the buy or sell intentions of larger funds and jump ahead of them. It's called gaming because it doesn't involve prior knowledge of the institutional orders. These market gamers use ultra-fast trading to unleash a torrent of small buy and sell orders designed to uncover hidden order instructions. These are contingent buy or sell orders that do not become active and appear in the order line until a trade takes place at a specified price. High-frequency trading does not mean trades are executed. It often means that orders constantly ping the market, looking for weakness created when stop loss triggers are hit.

When the market mechanism hits the grass—tests the order lines—it often does so with force and violence and speed. This strategy is designed to shake out the weak hands by placing small and progressively lower sell orders. These bring out the stop loss sell points, startling the snake and exposing weakness. There are many of these types of tactics used by market makers and now by the high-frequency traders. *The Market Maker's Edge* by Josh Lukeman is a very useful guide.

Running the stops and other techniques described by Lukeman are not strategies we approve of, but we must recognise they happen and use the effects of this as part of our trading arsenal. Others are vigorously 'beating the grass', chasing away the snakes so the new uptrend can resume with greater strength.

Short selling

Short selling in nervous or weak markets is an implementation of this strategy. It is a legitimate activity, but is often unfairly criticised. Market, or company, weakness is only found if the weakness already exists. If the danger is concealed then beating the grass using short selling will flush it out. This is an essential part of price and value discovery.

Rotten company management, dishonest accounting practices, greedy margin borrowing secured against substantial company shareholdings and misleading descriptions of debt ratings cause markets to fall, and to continue to fall in 2008. Short selling did not cause this destruction of asset values. Shorting did not cause the market to go down. The market goes down because long-side traders sell. They can sell to other long-side traders, or to short-side traders. However, short-side traders hold an open position. They must become buyers again at some time in the future so they can close their positions. Long-side sellers simply sell, close their positions, take their losses and walk away from the market. They drain liquidity from the market. In this sense short-side traders create upward pressure because they must re-enter the market at some stage as buyers to close their positions.

Banning short selling leaves people with no alternative but to lose money in this market. The result is predictable and shown in the chart extracts in figure 25.1 captured in October 2008. They will sell, and be forced to sell at even lower prices because there are no buyers. Market liquidity will dry up. The Shanghai Index chart shows what happens when short selling is not possible. Markets fall substantially.

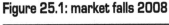

Figure 25.1: market falls 2008

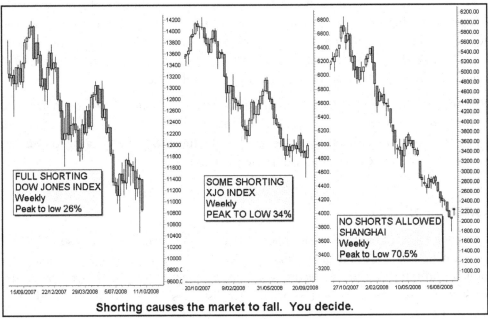

This market decline is a serious market problem that cannot be glibly put down to the impact of short traders, let alone some contagion of irrationality. The market knows these are not the reasons, and this is reflected in the 40% to 50% or more fall in Australian banks and financial institutions. Banning short sales in selected stocks is confirmation of the problems already shown in the charts.

Survival depends on a better understanding of the strategic situation so we can develop better trading tactics. When regulations force traders to trade from the long side—or not trade at all—then the vast majority of people will choose not to trade at all and this drains liquidity from a market already suffering a liquidity crisis.

Testing the market

Traders use small test buy or sell orders to assess the market intention. These orders are not designed to make a false impression. They are designed to establish the strength or weakness of the market, and once this is confirmed a trading tactic is initiated. Retail traders are generally the last group to learn to use these tactics. The 'flash traders' and the 'algo traders' regularly use these methods to test for market strength, and they are ready to instantly exploit any weakness, as the May 2010 'flash crash' in US markets proved. Traders need to be alert for this situation so they can manage the price cascade as automated stop loss orders are hit.

Every trend, every support level, every resistance level is a suspicious clump of grass potentially concealing a snake. If a snake is concealed in these situations, it is revealed when the market violates the trend line, or breaks the support level. When prices move back and test and retest these levels it tells us if a snake is in hiding. This test and retest behaviour is the equivalent of beating the grass. We do not beat the grass ourselves. The price activity forces other traders to do this for us and we observe the results.

The situation is most clearly revealed in a falling market. In this example in figure 25.2 we have used a head and shoulder pattern to identify a falling market. We set downside targets using the chart pattern, and these have been confirmed by a long-term support level at $6.75. Our strategy is to buy the stock at this support level in anticipation of a rebound back to the previous neckline. This is a simple trade with a potential 20% or better return. The danger is the unknown strength of the support level. When this level is tested the price rebounds, proving the support level.

The test and retest behaviour of price at this support level beats the grass. If a snake is hidden, we see the result as prices fall below the support level. Although it is tempting to buy when price first hits the support level, it is a more effective strategy to buy after the level has been tested and retested. Once we are confident the level will hold—that there is no hidden snake—we buy in anticipation of a solid rebound leading to a new uptrend. The trade is entered with more confidence near $7.00 after the support rebound. The application of this strategy is discussed in more detail in our DVD *Catching the Bounce*.

There are situations where we turn beater ourselves, ready to leap back if a snake is revealed. This is usually applied in conjunction with pattern-style trading opportunities, or when a market is confined by a strong resistance level. This includes patterns such as upwards-sloping triangles and flag patterns. We expect a price breakout to develop rapidly and carry prices to our target levels. A successful flag pattern breakout often hits targets within three to five days. A breakout from an up-sloping triangle may take longer.

Figure 25.2: head and shoulder pattern

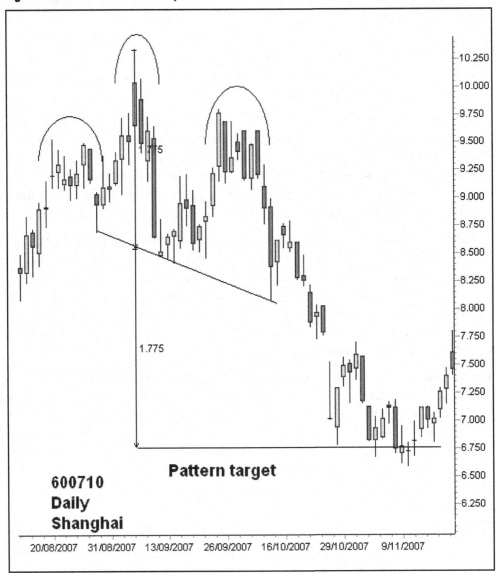

A flag pattern consists of a fast price rise over one to four days. This is a flagpole. This is followed by a price retreat lasting four to ten days. The upper edge of this down-sloping flag is defined by a straight edge trend line. When prices move above the trend line there is a high probability they will accelerate rapidly, reaching a price target equal to the degree of rise on the original flagpole.

We calculate the price value of the upper edge of the flag. We intend to buy the stock just below the upper trend line that defines the flag. We build the position in anticipation of the breakout. Is this trend strong, or does it conceal weakness? Usually we wait for prices to move above this value before we buy—others beating the grass for us. When we decide to beat the grass we employ a two-part strategy.

First we buy stock just below the value of the upper edge of the flag pattern. Then we beat the grass, buying a small order just above the value of the trend line defining the upper edge of the flag. This is a signal to other potential traders who have also been following the activity of this stock. If there is no trend weakness, other traders act on this signal, also buying the stock. Our small buy order is a catalyst, bringing other traders into the market. If the flag pattern is genuine, then this activity starts the momentum that carries the price rapidly higher to its projected targets. We benefit from this action because we have already established a position at a price lower than the breakout point.

And if there is a snake lurking in this grass we flush it from hiding by observing the trend weakness. If the market does not react to the trade above the upper edge of the flag—if the breakout fails—then we abandon this flag trade. The snake is revealed —the pattern is weak. This does not lead to a price fall, and we generally exit our original positions at about the same level as we entered, or even slightly better.

This example shows both the process and an unwelcome result where the snake is startled, revealing a pattern weakness.

The Arafura Resources chart extract in figure 25.3 shows the developing flag pattern on the day prior to entry and the subsequent development. The trading challenge is to decide how to manage the trade development. In this example we beat the grass. First we buy our planned order size at $0.35. This is our main trade. Second, we buy a very small order just above the value of the trend line defining the upper edge of the flag. The purchase price is at $0.36. The stop loss for both trades is set on a financial basis at $0.33. A fall to this level is evidence of pattern breakout failure.

Figure 25.3: developing flag pattern

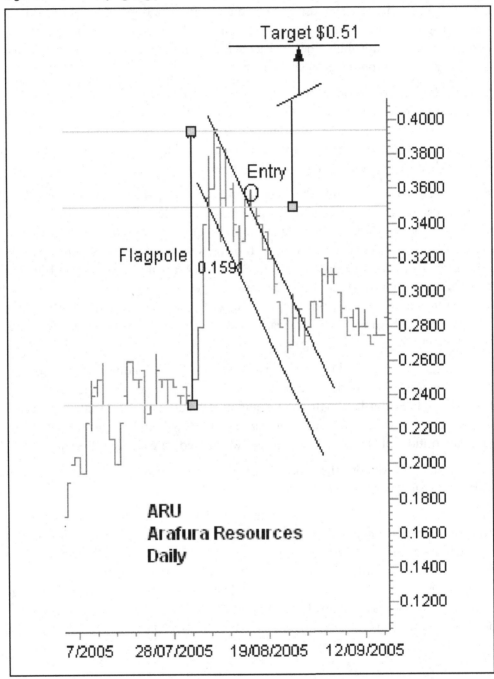

Other traders did not follow the lead set by our trade at $0.36. Our second buy order flushed the snake from hiding by confirming the trend weakness. The market did not react to the trade above the upper edge of the flag—the breakout failed—so we abandoned this flag trade, selling both open positions at $0.34.

When we enter a trade we expect it to develop as we anticipate. Generally, successful trades show their success very rapidly. Price moves quickly to make the trade profitable. We did not like the way this trade failed to develop when price moved above the upper edge of the flag so the trade is abandoned.

The Australian Securities Exchange chart extract in figure 25.4 shows the same processes, but in this case the test order confirms the breakout development. In this example we beat the grass and discover there is no snake—no weakness. First we buy our planned order size at $32.25. This is our main trade. Second, we buy a very small order just above the value of the trend line defining the upper edge of the flag. The purchase price is at $32.75. This order is a catalyst, and other traders watching for the breakout quickly join the trade, propelling prices higher and confirming the validity of the pattern.

The market is full of people who know a lot more than we do. They have information we do not possess and this informs their trading decisions. Their behaviour—their buying and selling activity—provides an early warning of the impact of the information they hold. Survival in modern markets means learning how to read the tape and how to analyse and use order line information. It also requires recognition of the informed messages delivered with buying and selling activity, and we discuss these methods in the next chapter.

Figure 25.4: confirmation of breakout development

Chapter 26

Patterns of informed trading

Information is not distributed democratically in the market. Information flow is delayed by circumstance, by deliberate decisions, through cover-ups or by accident. The more informed people in a company audit process more quickly recognise the warning signs of problems and they, or their friends, may decide to take action. So-called 'continuous disclosure' regimes are an attempt to deal with this aspect of the market, but they are not outstandingly successful. Informed trading has distinctive patterns of behaviour and they bring together tape analysis and pattern analysis.

The so-called 'speeding tickets', where a company is asked to explain why there has been a large change in its share price, are also not particularly effective. Often they are speeding tickets issued for the wrong type of event. In any case they are often evaded with the formulaic answer, 'We are not aware of any development which may be responsible for the price increase'—a reply that is all too often followed by an announcement a few days or weeks later confirming the 'development' so recently denied.

Research by the Australian Securities Exchange has confirmed that many company directors routinely ignore the 'blackout period' prior to release of market-significant results and reports. They trade their own company shares during this period. Compliance with the blackout code is voluntary. There is no reason to believe these behaviours do not apply in other market jurisdictions.

What to do? One response is to develop increasing layers of regulation in an attempt to really apply a continuous disclosure regime and enforce compliance with trading which inevitably makes use of information not known to the general public. The cat and mouse game between regulators and those who prefer less regulation will continue, and as individual traders we have no influence over these developments.

The second response is to learn to recognise the situations where informed trading may be taking place. Some of this informed trading may be insider trading, but that is a distinction for lawyers and regulators. Our concern as traders is to use the pattern of price behaviour to identify the potential clues provided by those who are trading with more informed decision-making than that available to the general public. We are not concerned with price manipulation. This is a different problem and has different trading solutions.

The collapse of markets in 2008 provided many opportunities for informed trading. The recovery of markets in 2009 continued to provide informed trading opportunities as some companies emerged from the rubble of the 2008 market collapse. The increase in the behaviour patterns associated with informed trading has not abated and it continues as a blight on market activity.

Identifying informed trading rests on some important assumptions.

- The first is that the market impact of information is most quickly revealed in price behaviour. The fact of price behaviour speaks more loudly than the denials or the claims of 'we are not aware' issued by company management.

- The second assumption is that people do not willingly lose money in the market when there is an easy opportunity to reduce the loss or cut the cost of entry. This is a foundation assumption when assessing the potential for informed trading.

- The third assumption is that while informed trading is commonplace, it is most easily observed in stocks with lower liquidity. It is easier to conceal informed trading in stocks with high volume and consistent liquidity. However, some patterns of informed trading behaviour are also visible in these stocks.

⊞ The fourth assumption, or component, is the interpretation of price activity. I want to try to understand the reasoning behind the price behaviour. Why has this trader acted in a way that seems contrary to her own best interest given the current market conditions? People do not voluntarily take a larger loss than necessary. They do not voluntarily pay a much higher entry price than necessary. When these situations occur there must be an extraordinary reason. Speculating on this reason is the heart of working with patterns of behaviour that hint at informed trading.

⊞ The fifth assumption is that although a fool and his money are easily separated, there are very few fools in the market. People may do foolish things, but generally they sincerely believe in their analysis and they are prepared to back it with money. The market is dominated by smart people and smart money.

Our purpose in identifying these patterns of potential informed trading is to make a profit. We don't know the nature of the information known by the informed trader, but we use this buying and selling activity as a guide to a high-probability outcome. We are not 'inside' trading because the price information and price behaviour is available at the same time to all market participants. Our task is to apply a better level of analysis and to profit from this. We call this the EWS (Early Warning System) strategy.

Patterns of informed trading provide advance warning of information that is not generally known in the market. There are four patterns of particular interest in the EWS strategy. They are:

⊞ Island in the Sun

⊞ Oil Rig Gusher

⊞ Denial

⊞ Pile Driver low.

The discussion below uses constructed charts to illustrate each generic pattern. Study of these generic patterns makes it easier to recognise them when they appear on charts in real time.

Island in the Sun

This is a bullish pattern. It appears in stocks with a steady level of trading volume. I call it the 'geologist's mother' effect because it is commonly seen in junior mining exploration companies. I like to speculate it is caused by the geologist ringing his mother, telling her of fantastic drill results and asking her to buy shares in the company immediately. Of course, she has little experience, so she simply places an order with instructions to spend a predetermined amount. When she rings the broker she does not specify a price. The order is simply 'buy the stock up to the value of $30 000'.

The broker fills the order, irrespective of price, and so creates a single price well above the surrounding price. This is the first part of the pattern. Often this price island will be 20% to 30% or higher above the previous traded price. The key recognition features, shown in figure 26.1, are:

⊞   a price island

⊞   consistent volume of trading activity in the period before and after the price island

⊞   low volume — this is usually just a single order from a single informed but unskilled buyer

⊞   a significantly higher price than the high of the previous day

⊞   disbelief in the market; on the next trading day the price returns to the previous lower trading range.

Why is this trader prepared to pay 20% to 30% more than the prevailing price? Simply by waiting he could fill his order at the lower price. This activity shows desperation. The buyer is worried he will miss out if he doesn't act quickly. He is happy to pay a higher price to get an entry right now because he believes the information he has will propel the price much higher than the price he has paid.

There is one important warning with this pattern. It does not apply to stocks that show consistent 'spotty' behaviour. These are stocks with erratically low volume, and many days where trading takes place at a single price.

Tactics

Buy the market's disbelief. The price island is created because the market does not believe the new higher price. The market is not aware of the information known by the informed trader so the price continues to trade in its previous range. This is the entry signal, with a sell target placed at the level set by the price island, $0.21 in this example. The sell order is placed at this level as soon as the trade is entered. The formal release of the market-moving information usually occurs within two to six weeks. If the trade does not develop in this period then it is closed.

Figure 26.1: key recognition features—Island in the Sun

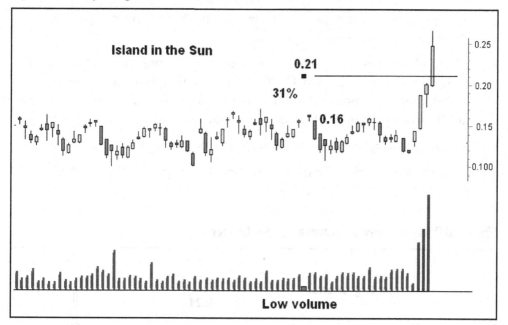

Oil Rig Gusher

This is a bullish pattern similar to the Island in the Sun pattern. The difference is that the price island is attached to the previous lows of the trading range. The large range days stand out like an oil rig gusher. And just like an oil rig gusher, it is quickly capped. The key to the pattern is the desperate desire to get a position in an otherwise sleepy stock. We could infer this is a conspiracy between the entire drilling crew. They all know the results and they are all desperate to buy the stock. They are a bit more skilled than the geologist's mother, so they place a 'buy at market' order, but with separate brokers. They tell the broker to 'do what it takes' to fill their order. As a result they end up competing with each other. The price starts at the same level as the previous day but rapidly accelerates under the buying pressure. The result is a price spike in excess of 15% and as high as 30% or more.

These are the key recognition features, shown in figure 26.2:

- a single up spike day showing a single long candle
- a consistent level of trading activity before and after the Oil Rig Gusher

- a close near to the high of the day gives a stronger pattern signal

- a marginal increase in volume. Volume is not the key behavioural pattern. It is the price spike that is most significant

- a handful of trades. This information comes from the order line but you must be watching to see it develop. Unfilled orders leapfrog each other to buy at a higher price. This shows desperation to have the orders filled. Leapfrog orders are discussed in chapter 24, Modern tape reading

- a significantly higher price and closing price than the high of the previous day

- disbelief in the market. On the next trading day the price returns to the previous lower trading range.

Figure 26.2: key recognition features—Oil Rig Gusher

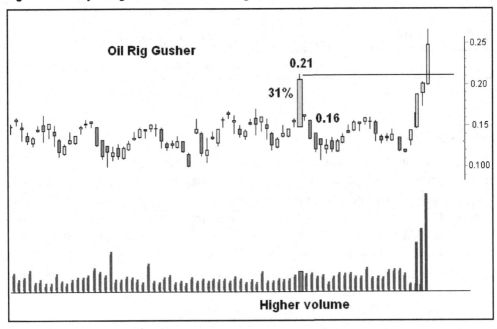

This behaviour is created by a small group of informed traders who are anxious to get a position in the stock. This leapfrogging cannot be observed unless you use a live screen. In our *EWS Trading* DVD we use an animated order screen example to explain this process. However, leapfrogging is inferred when a large price rise appears which is not accompanied by large volume.

Tactics

Buy the market's disbelief. The Oil Rig Gusher is created because the market does not believe the new higher price. The market effectively caps the gusher. They are not aware of the information known by the informed traders so the price retreats and continues to trade in its previous range. This is the entry signal around $0.16. The sell order is immediately placed at the level set by the high of the Oil Rig Gusher pattern. The sell order is placed at this level, $0.21 in this example, as soon as the trade is entered. The public release of this market-moving information usually occurs within two to six weeks. If the trade does not develop in this period then it is closed.

In both the Island in the Sun and the Oil Rig Gusher patterns the trader may continue to lift her sell price as the buying momentum continues. This is surfing the order line, trying to keep ahead of building price momentum. The $0.21 target in these two examples is the minimum anticipated return from these strategies.

Denial pattern

The Denial pattern is the most common type of informed trading pattern. I suspect it is created by a leakage of information. This leakage rapidly becomes widespread, and is usually described as a rumour. The result is a surge in volume and price. The price rise is large enough to warrant a 'speeding ticket' from the regulator. It's the market's response and the company response that create the denial pattern.

After the initial price surge many traders are reluctant to fully believe the story. However, they are intrigued enough to halt the price decline. The days following the sharp rise do not see a return to the previous trading range. Speculators and other hopefuls buy into the stock as it develops a small pullback. Volume is higher than before the rise. This pause and volume behaviour is created by traders riding the coattails of the original rumour, which may be endorsed by the financial media.

The second essential part of the pattern is the company response to the regulator's 'speeding ticket'. A denial — 'We are not aware of any development which may be responsible for the price increase' — is the first step. The market reaction to the denial is the second step. When the market refuses to believe the denial and the price rebounds from the retreat lows, then the denial pattern is confirmed. There is a high probability of a sudden announcement and confirmation of the rumour that started the first price and volume rise. This usually occurs within the next 10 to 20 trading days.

Figure 26.3: key recognition features—Denial pattern

The 'speeding ticket' is a very blunt instrument for identifying informed trading. It is blunted even further by the comfortable acceptance of the denial—'We are not aware of any development which may be responsible for the price increase'—and the failure to take action when the denial pattern is completed with release of news that confirms the original market rumour.

The key recognition features for this pattern, shown in figure 26.3, are:

- a surge in price and volume
- a retreat in price to around 50% of the first-day surge. This is usually accompanied by a reduction in traded volume

- a denial response to the regulator's enquiry. This is the 'we are not aware of any development which may be responsible for the price increase' reply

- day three or four of the pattern sees a resumption of upwards momentum and another surge in volume

- the pattern is confirmed on day 10 to 20 when the company acknowledges that it had been in significant takeover talks, made a large new discovery, been granted an important new patent or some other market-moving event. These denial relationship patterns occur far too frequently in almost every market to be a coincidence. The occurrence is so frequent that it provides a reliable trading opportunity.

Tactics

Buy after the company denial has been released. Buy when the denial announcement is followed by a price rebound. This is usually on day three or four of the pattern. There is no upside target as this is a type of momentum trade. The trade is closed if positive news is not released within the next 10 to 20 trading days.

Pile Driver low

This pattern is most common at the beginning of a bear market. The 2008 charts are full of this behaviour but it was more convenient to blame nasty short sellers than to identify the patterns of informed trading which might have shaken market confidence further.

The pattern occurs as part of an established uptrend, or as an extension of the normal pattern of rally and retreat behaviour in a generally uptrending stock. It signals in advance the minimum future downside target. It is created when a single shareholder or a small number of shareholders are aware of bad news. They are so terrified of the news that they dump the stock at any price in their desperation to get out. This is the first part of the pattern.

The pattern is confirmed when the price rapidly returns to the previous higher levels. The market, not aware of this information, does not believe the new lower price. In 2008 these price dips were derided as 'irrational behaviour'. The previously prevailing trend continues. A few days later the bad news becomes generally known and the stock quickly falls to the low established by the Pile Driver pattern. In a bear market this is the minimum price fall, and it is usually exceeded with lower lows.

Generally this pattern is created with a single down day rather than a price island. There are no significant volume relationships. The price rebound often occurs on good volume as other traders rush in to take advantage of buying the stock at unexpectedly low prices, as shown in figure 26.4.

Figure 26.4: key recognition features—Pile Driver low

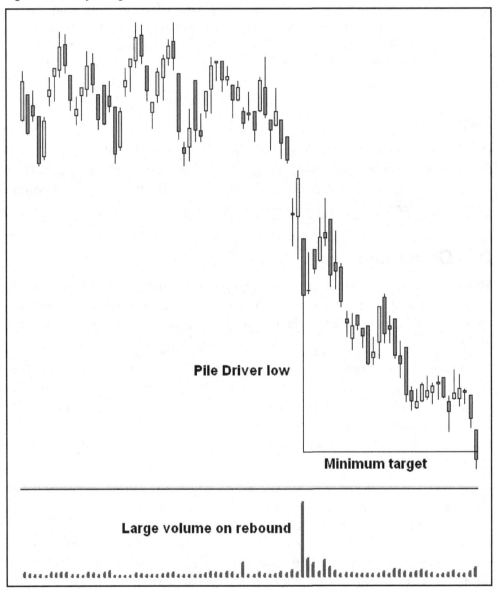

The pattern may also occur in a stock that is moving sideways and which has not yet developed a downtrend.

The key recognition features for this pattern are shown in figure 26.4 and figure 26.5:

- a large drop in price. This appears in a consolidation pattern, or in the early stages of a normal retreat in the previous uptrend

- note that a sudden price drop at the end of an established downtrend is a desperation drop where the market reaches for a capitulation bottom. It is not a Pile Driver low

- a recovery in price of more than 80% of the first-day drop. This is usually accompanied by a reduction in traded volume

- often there is no significant change in the volume of trading activity in the period before and after the Pile Driver low

- disbelief in the market. On the next trading day the price returns to the previous trading range and may even develop a reaction rally.

Figure 26.5: key recognition features—Pile Driver low

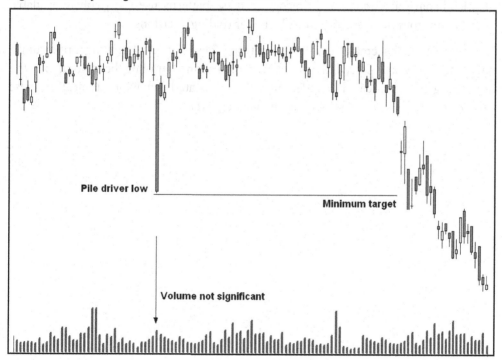

345

Tactics

When the market bounces back to the previous price level, sell any holdings you have. For short-side traders, the rebound is a signal to open short positions. The low is the minimum target price level for future price declines.

Insider trading

The patterns we have discussed point the way to the suspicion of informed trading. Insider trading does not always show these patterns. The chart extract in figure 26.6 shows the day when an inside trader spent around $39 000 to buy 50 000 shares in advance of a takeover offer. This exact information was released as part of his guilty plea. In this instance there is no volume or price clue to this insider trader activity.

The democratisation of market information has been greatly enhanced by the internet. However, information does not flow evenly to all market participants. There are, and always will be, people who know significant news before the rest of the market. They will make more informed trades based on more information than that available to other traders. In some cases this informed trading shows up in well-defined patterns of price behaviour. Traders who recognise these patterns use the publicly available information from price activity to make better trading decisions.

Takeover situations create a different but specialised type of trading opportunity. Sometimes they are preceded by patterns of informed trading behaviour, but the developing takeover can be traded using the repeated behaviour typical of these situations, and these are discussed in the next chapter.

Figure 26.6: insider trading activity

Chapter 27

Takeover arbitrage

Takeover strategies have not changed in modern market conditions. It's the same old game, sometimes played out more quickly, but always with the same steps. The first offer is inevitably refused and the market pushes up the price of the target company in expectation of a higher offer from the predator company. This offer and counter-offer delivers a set-piece trading strategy that provides no unique advantages as a result of the Global Financial Crisis. In time, as markets evolve, there will be a period of increased merger and acquisition activity. These tactics and calculations are ready to swing into action as the slow motion dance of a company death begins.

Our interest is in deciding which is the better way to participate and profit. Should we buy the target company or the predator company? If we already own shares, should we keep them, or sell them? The answers to these questions form the basis of a different strategy reaction to company takeovers. This is an implementation of the Chinese strategy of 'Observing the fire from the other side of the river'.

When companies are under attack we have the opportunity to both observe the action and to use the opportunity to grow profits. This provides an arbitrage-style opportunity where we match current prices with a known future price.

The fire—the conflict between predator and target—takes place externally to our own involvement in the market. The factors at play are in addition to any reasons we may have had for buying the predator or target stock in the first place.

There are two types of situations in this takeover environment. The first is where we already own the target stock. We have a simple question to answer: is it more effective to hold on to the stock we own or is it better to accept the offer from the predator? This arbitrage opportunity offers secure profits in an uncertain climate.

The second situation is where we deliberately enter the fray, buying either predator or target stock in the hope of benefiting from the fire on the other side of the river. In one sense, both these situations are combined as they are traded using a calculated arbitrage strategy.

We examine this strategy from a trader's perspective, so our intention is to collect the quickest gain possible from these situations. We look for shorter term benefits because we understand this is merely a skirmish in the ongoing battle to grow our portfolio profits.

Takeover arbitrage trading

We wait for the squabbling between takeover predator and target to develop, and then strike when we can gain the maximum return for the least effort. We wait on the sidelines of the market, observing the fire of the takeover on the other side of the river while carefully calculating the most advantageous attack conditions.

The market is sometimes an imperfect way of matching prices. The price differences are surprisingly large and arbitrage gives the trader a way to profit from this. Arbitrage trades arise in takeover plays, in rights trading and in some capital reconstruction situations. The trade is based on comparing today's price with a known price in the future. Takeover arbitrage is a very useful way of collecting largely risk-free or low-risk profits.

Some takeover arbitrage trades are complicated offers where the takeover predator offers, for example, five of their own shares for every seven of the target company shares, and sometimes adds a sweetener cash bonus. Traders should not let the apparent complexity of these arrangements deter them from exploring the arbitrage

349

possibilities. Hidden in this complexity are sometimes profits of anywhere between 5% and 30% on the trade. To explain how arbitrage works we take you step by step through the calculation process in a takeover situation. We use an arbitrage Excel spreadsheet template. This file is available free by emailing <support@guppytraders. com>. Head your email request 'free arbitrage spreadsheet'.

Most times takeover offers provide only a small arbitrage advantage. Sometimes when markets have fallen for other reasons the valuation relationship of the takeover offer changes, increasing the return from any arbitrage trade.

To make this discussion easy to follow, we use the term 'predator' to refer to the company mounting the takeover. The term 'target' refers to the company being taken over. The predator in this case is a company called SGW and the target is PML. The first step in calculating the arbitrage opportunity is to decide the number of target shares to purchase.

We start the calculations in figure 27.1 with a proposed purchase of 19 000 shares in PML when it was trading at the low of $1.05. This commits $19 950. These figures are added in the shaded cells.

Figure 27.1: proposed purchase of 19 000 shares in PML

COST OF TARGET SHARES			
Company	Current price	number	cost
pml	1.050	19,000	$ 19,950.00

The second calculation step adds the first of the conditions of the takeover. In this case the predator is bidding for target shares in blocks of 28, offering five predator shares for every 28 target shares. If the trader buys 19 000 PML shares then the predator counts these as a block of 679. This is calculated by adding 28 in the shaded cell in figure 27.2. These initial calculations establish the value of our buy-in price.

The next set of calculations establishes what our new target shares are now worth to the predator. This needs two figures, added in figure 27.3. The first is the number of predator shares swapped for target shares—in this case five—which is entered in the third shaded cell. From the predator's perspective, they offer us 3393 SGW shares. We receive five new SGW shares for every block of 28 PML shares we own.

Figure 27.2: target number of shares

CONDITION OF TAKEOVER OFFER (1)	
Size of target block	
Number of target shares in each block	28
Adjusted number of shares in block	679

Figure 27.3: value of shares to the predator

CONDITION OF TAKEOVER (2)				
Number of predator shares exchanged for each block				
Company	current price	Number exchanged	Total offered	Value
sgw	7.180	5	3,393	$ 24,360.71

Once we collect 3393 SGW shares, we could sell these immediately. The key question in the calculation is the price we expect for SGW once the takeover is completed. For the calculations in this example we use the price on the day after the offer closed, so $7.18 is entered in the second shaded cell. The total value is $24360.

The final calculations are shown in the summary 'assessment of arbitrage trade' box in figure 27.4. The PML shares cost $19950. When converted to SGW shares under the conditions of the takeover, and at the market price when the takeover offer closed, the value of the shares was $24360. This is a 22.11% return. The level of return varies depending upon the relative prices of the predator and target shares, so the developing fortunes and vicissitudes of the takeover offer are worth following regularly.

There is one major problem with this arbitrage trade. It assumes the conversion of target shares to predator shares is instantaneous. This is not always the case so speed is important.

As soon as the PML shares are purchased they must be converted into the equivalent number of predator shares quickly. The new parcel of predator shares is then sold at market. In this example the arbitrage calculations are based on the predator market value of $7.18. Any change in this price impacts on the profitability of the trade. Where the predator prices are relatively stable, the risk is reduced. Where the predator shares are in a well-established uptrend, the risk is reduced even further.

Figure 27.4: assessment of arbitrage trade

```
ASSESSMENT OF ARBITRAGE TRADE

          Cost to buy shares in target company   $  19,950.00
Value of predator share entitlement if sold on market  $  24,360.71
                              Return      4,410.71
                            %% return        22.11
            Cash sweetener if included  $         -
                        Total return      4,410.71
                          %% Return         22.11
```

This type of arbitrage trade is not as risk-less as straight cash takeover offers. Traders need to be very aware of the added risk of time, and be very careful not to trade share entitlements that they do not yet actually own. Explain to your broker what you are doing, and she will take care to make sure you have entitlement to the shares you are holding.

There is one way to make the arbitrage work before the closing date of the takeover offer. The trader buys an equivalent number of predator shares, in this case 3393, before he buys the target shares. This costs around $6.90 in this example. With entitlement firmly established, this first parcel can be sold at any time after the target PML shares are purchased, locking in risk-free profits.

Figure 27.5: assessment of arbitrage trade—buy predator shares before target shares

```
ASSESSMENT OF ARBITRAGE TRADE

          Cost to buy shares in target company   $  19,950.00
Value of predator share entitlement if sold on market  $  23,410.71
                              Return      3,460.71
                            %% return        17.35
            Cash sweetener if included  $         -
                        Total return      3,460.71
                          %% Return         17.35
```

You might expect low returns from this strategy as the market should efficiently reduce the price differential between the SGW and PML shares. However, the market is often inefficient. This strategy returns a 17.35% profit, shown in figure 27.5. When the takeover transfer entitlements to the second parcel of predator shares are fully cleared and processed, they are sold. In uptrending stocks, this results in additional profit. This approach adds another layer of risk, but in most cases this is quite small when compared to the arbitrage profits.

Some takeover offers provide additional incentives by way of a cash bonus or sweetener. For instance, this offer might include a $0.25 cash payment for every five target shares. In the SGW example in figure 27.6, this adds an additional $95 bonus to the profit equation. This boosts the return to 22.59% for this arbitrage trade.

Figure 27.6: value of cash sweetener

```
CONDITION OF TAKEOVER (3)
Value of cash sweetener
Cash       Size of
payment    target block
           applied to                                          Value
   0.025      3,800                                        $      95.00


ASSESSMENT OF ARBITRAGE TRADE

                 Cost to buy shares in target company  $   19,950.00
     Value of predator share entitlement if sold on market  $   24,360.71
                                         Return          4,410.71
                                      %% return             22.11
                    Cash sweetener if included  $           95.00
                                   Total return          4,505.71
                                      %% Return             22.59
```

Arbitrage trades are found by watching the exchange notices section in the newspapers. This section lists current takeovers. These are fires we watch from the other side of the river, ready to open a trade to collect the maximum benefit for the least effort.

There are no fancy twists or twirls required to bring this trading method into modern markets. The strategy remains a reliable standby and generates consistent low-risk profits. The strategy follows the developing news, but at a distance. There is no need to act quickly in the developing events because the trader has already positioned himself to take advantage of the expected news. This is very different from actively trading breaking news with the power of derivatives, as shown in the next chapter.

Chapter 28

Indexing the news

I work with CNBC Asia SquawkBox as a regular guest host and am known as the Chart man. Part of my task is to look at the charts of stocks making the headlines for the day. The objective is to identify the potential impact of news and breaking events. It's a challenging task calling for instant assessment and analysis. This immediacy of the connection between events and price is part of modern markets and not isolated to the demands of live television. The rapid connection between news and events contributes to market volatility. The clock cannot be wound back and the convergence of the relationship between news and price movements will continue to intensify.

In this chapter we look in detail at how two significant market-moving events were evaluated and traded in real time. We highlight both the success and the failure of these approaches. Rapidly identifying the warning signs of failure is essential in this style of trading. These are specific examples that apply generic principles of news-based trading with derivatives.

You may decide this style of trading does not appeal to you. You may conclude this style of trading is not possible because you have a full-time job. It would be unwise to conclude that this discussion has no relevance to you because there is an increasing number of market participants who apply these trading approaches. They provide a new background noise underpinning daily market activity. Our exposure is brief and limited to specific situations, but at the further extreme this is the flash and algorithmic trading increasingly practised by some fund managers and proprietary trading desks.

News trading is momentum trading based on the impact of a news event. Success depends on the trader's ability to correctly understand the impact of the news. Some news looks bullish, but ends up having a negative impact because the market is expecting better news. Some bad news has a bullish impact because the market expected worse news. Trading the news requires skill and discipline.

As these are primarily momentum trades, they are closed as soon as the momentum falters. If the trade does not take off it suggests the trader's news analysis was incorrect. These trades aim to collect the immediate impact of the news event. This is sometimes the start of a new trend, but the news-based trader does not pursue this as a trend trade. Weakening momentum triggers a sell signal.

Most of these trades are one- to three-day trades and use leveraged derivative instruments to magnify the impact of the news event. We look at two news-based trades as examples of very specific trading methods. These notes, written at the time in our weekly newsletter, explain our thinking and reactions as the trades developed. The identification and management of these trades includes the baseline tactics for this type of trading situation.

Dumping the Prime Minister

The dramatic dumping of the Australian Prime Minister Kevin Rudd in 2010 provided a short-term, news-based trading opportunity. We detail the analysis and trading steps we personally applied.

The news feeds from CNBC Asia SquawkBox showed there was a high probability Prime Minister Rudd would be defeated. The announcement was expected before the market opened for trading. This was seen as a positive for the newly announced Resources Super Profits Tax (RSPT). If not abolished, the tax would at least be subject to a greater level of genuine consultation. We believed this positive effect would feed through to the miners. There were three possible ways to trade the impact of this news event.

Trades were available in the two largest mining companies, BHP and RIO. This was the first type of trade opportunity. Prices would gap up on the open, so although the headline price increase was good, the actual price increase during the day would be much slower. Even trading with a CFD derivative instrument using leverage, the opportunities would be limited.

The second potential way to trade this opportunity was to trade the materials index. The problem is that this is a diluted index. It does include miners, but it also includes a range of other industries. It does not give pure exposure to the mining industry. Additionally, trading in this sub-index does not start until the market opens. It's the same problem as the miners. A gap up makes for a high entry and a reduced profit.

The third option was a broad trade in the S&P/ASX 200 XJO index.

The trading option we used for trading this breaking news was the XJO index. The change in political leadership was expected to have an immediate impact across the market. The key advantage of the XJO index is that CFD trading is possible in the pre-open period before the market opens. This allows the trader to take advantage of the gap-up activity prior to the market open. We use IG Markets for this style of CFD trading.

Entry is taken at 4490 at 9.50 am, as shown in figure 28.1. The position size is 450 for a total cash cost of $10 102.50. Keeping the trade size to around $10 000 is one method of managing risk with derivative trades. The entry is made using the momentum minute method discussed in chapter 11, Trend Volatility Line analysis.

The pre-open momentum carries the XJO index to 4517. The market open is slightly lower at 4515. If our analysis is correct then we would expect to see the market move rapidly higher. It does not. The market develops a retreat in the first 10 minutes of trading. This is a warning of market weakness. The Australian market has a rotational opening, so we wait for the full opening to be completed. Waiting is possible because the trade is already in profit.

The key basis of this analysis is the expected benefit for the mining industry so we watch the RIO and BHP charts. The gap up is between 2.2% and 2.5%, and then the momentum declines to under 2%. This is not the expected effect. It is a warning the momentum is going out of the market rise. This loss of momentum is confirmed with the XJO index, with a failure to move above 4517. This is designed as a short-term trade so the trade is closed near 4514, as shown in figure 28.2.

Figure 28.1: entry at 4490

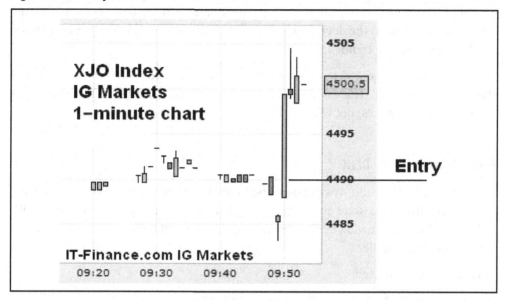

Figure 28.2: exit near 4514

The market continues the sideways movement. Later it develops a continuation of the uptrend but this is weak trending activity. The objective in the trade is to capture the initial market jump on the developing news, and if the momentum continues, to trade the developing strong trend.

The trade is closed near 4514. This is a $10 800 profit for a 106% return on the capital allocated to the trade. The essential lesson in news-linked trading is that the trader must trade what he sees, not what he believes.

Adjusting the tax

A few days after Mr Rudd was deposed the Resources Super Profits Tax was adjusted. Again announcements were made prior to the market open and carried on CNBC SquawkBox. It was hailed as a breakthrough, and this set up the conditions for a repeat of the news-based trade.

This is what we expected:

- RIO and BHP to gap up and to continue moving up quickly
- the XJO index to gap up and continue moving upwards quickly.

The strategy, based on this for RIO and BHP, was to wait for the first gap to develop and then enter the trade using a CFD as momentum continued. The strategy for the XJO index was to enter in the pre-market trading period and then ride the rise in momentum as the market started trading. This is a CFD derivative trade.

News-based trading rests on a strategic assessment of how the trader expects the market to respond to the news. Successful news-based trading does not depend on getting the strategic assessment correct. It depends on the trader's ability to quickly recognise and respond when the market moves contrary to her expectations. Modern market volatility metes out swift punishment to those who hesitate.

This is what happened:

- the market moved up for the first 20 minutes or so, and then declined. The pre-open up momentum was the entry signal, but the trade was closed as the XJO index turned down. The trade was managed with a simple trend line
- BHP gapped up on the open and then immediately fell, as shown in figure 28.3. No trade was entered

 RIO gapped up on the open, retreated, and then developed a rally rebound. A trade was entered on the rebound rally, but it was managed as a short-term trade.

Figure 28.3: BHP gap up and fall

The RIO price activity was different. The retreat was smaller and the price quickly moved above the opening high. The entry was taken at $66.10. The rising trend was defined with a trend line. The movement of the market was also tracked with the XJO index. It rapidly became clear the momentum was unsustainable, so when the price moved below the trend line an exit signal was triggered and taken, as shown in Figure 28.4. The trade was closed near $66.60.

The position size was 3050. The cash cost was $20160.50. A larger size is possible in this trade because the level of leverage is lower. The exit at $66.60 delivered a small 7.56% profit of $1525. In retrospect this trade was not worth the risk, however the trade was based on a set of strategic assumptions. If those assumptions had been correct then the trade could have returned a substantial profit.

Figure 28.4: RIO gap up and rally

The XJO index trade, taken at the same time and applying the same strategy, was more successful because entry was made during the pre-open period. This provided access to the initial gap up in the market.

The entry was made at 4265, as shown in figure 28.5. The exit was taken near 4278, prior to the open of the market because the strong uptrend failed. The uptrend was defined with the trend line. This behaviour was counter to our strategic expectations. The period prior to the open of trading should have seen a continuation of momentum. This warning was also transferred to conditions in the RIO and BHP assessments.

The position size cash value was $10 022.75. This smaller size is used with index trades as a means of managing risk in CFD trading. The close at 4278 locked in a profit of $6110. This is a 60.69% return on the capital used. Again, this trade had the potential to be very successful. It was closed quickly because it failed to act as expected. In news-based trading this is an essential stop loss feature.

Figure 28.5: XJO uptrend failure

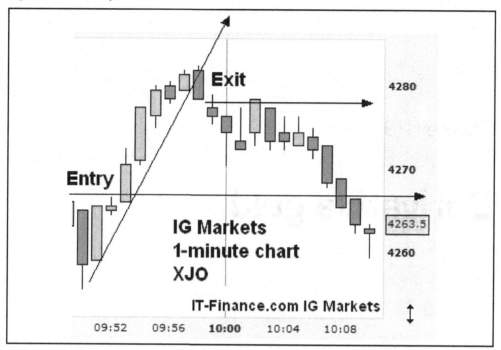

News for you

It took several days for the news of the defeat of Napoleon at Waterloo to reach England. Today it takes seconds for news to reach 360 million households, and that's just the CNBC footprint. News moves markets instantly, but just as quickly the impact of news can be discounted.

News-based trading is a direct engagement with modern volatility. In many ways it is the ultimate extension of the trading methods discussed in previous chapters. It brings together the analysis, the execution, the tape reading, the trade discipline and adds speed to the equation.

News-driven volatility provides specific trading opportunities which are often best secured using a derivative in a short-term trade. The opportunities offered by derivatives cannot be ignored, but derivative trading calls on a different set of skills from those applied with trading equities.

Chapter 29

Derivative gold

Derivatives cannot be ignored in modern markets. Forget the stupidity that bedevilled banks and financial institutions in the lead-up to the Global Financial Crisis. We are not in the business of designing suspect products and then selling them to others. The risk we have with derivatives is in the way we use the instrument. Derivatives, ranging from warrants and options, to CFDs (contracts for difference), to ETFs (exchange-traded funds) and ETNs (exchange-traded notes) are an essential part of the trader's strategy and the investor's portfolio. These are the instruments that reduce the risk of time spent in the market and allow retail traders to develop advanced hedging strategies to protect the value of their portfolios.

Derivatives have moved into the living room and out of the dark. They provide global exposure and global risk management. Some regulators have taken to alarmist tactics, describing some of these instruments available to retail traders as 'more risky than a bet on the horses'. The same regulators are largely silent on the massive failure of derivatives created by institutional financial engineers. Such ignorance should have no place among informed regulators. Different regulatory regimes make decisions about particular products based on their own market history and the level of vested interest. CFDs are not licensed for trading in the US. This leads to the false conclusion that if the US won't allow them then obviously they must be risky. One look at the extensive over-the-counter market trade in pink sheets in the US would have the same regulators refusing listing of these instruments in their own jurisdictions. A regulatory regime that allowed the development of the derivatives underpinning the sub-prime crisis is not a natural model of financial rectitude.

Unless specifically regulated, derivatives carry the counterparty risk that the issuer or the person on the other side of the trade will not be able to settle or deliver on the trade. This was one of the driving failures that created the Global Financial Crisis. For traders this may be a reason for keeping derivative trades short term and a low proportion of portfolio capital.

Derivatives are complex instruments and they require a good level of risk management and trading discipline. These features were examined in practical detail in chapter 28, Indexing the news. The same criticisms were levelled at warrants when they were first introduced, but they have since become part of the mainstream of retail investing. CFDs in particular provide a method to apply the Chinese strategy of 'Killing with a borrowed knife' and also to hedge portfolios. Our focus is on the way CFDs are used to reduce risk and magnify returns.

Use price leverage to accelerate returns from ordinary analysis

The aim of the strategy of 'Killing with a borrowed knife' is to use a third party to carry out our objectives. To achieve this strategic objective effectively the trader uses derivative products, such as warrants, options and CFDs. These instruments combine several features that allow us not just to make a 'killing' but to make a substantial killing. The borrowed knife is the derivative product. In the financial market, a killing is achieved by extracting a profit from our trading activity, as shown with these approaches. In this chapter we show how markets are interlinked and how the impacts of these linkages are traded using a derivative to magnify the returns from small differences. Following is a trade in gold, taken from our weekly newsletter, and it highlights the essential analysis and execution steps of using a derivative to 'kill with a borrowed knife'.

Derivative gold

In May 2010 smart investors entered the gold market as the rebound developed from the support features in the gold price chart. The first upside target was the previous chart pattern target level near $1250.

The movements in the exchange rate, best tracked through the dollar index, provide the volatility foundation for activity in the gold market. The weekly dollar index chart in figure 29.1 in May 2010 shows a parabolic trend.

Figure 29.1: parabolic trend in US dollar index chart

Volatility provides opportunity. Several factors came together in the combination of currency and commodity markets to develop several types of trading opportunities with the gold price at this time. We show how these are related in analysis designed to identify the best trade. We discuss a number of these trading methods more fully in our *Gold: Mining the Markets* DVD.

The key feature of parabolic trends is the way they collapse suddenly. The weekly chart suggested there is a limited time before the dollar index candle will inevitably cross to the right of the parabolic trend line. The development of this trend pattern is shown in chapter 23, Getting ahead of the curves. When this collapse happens there is a high probability of a sudden currency correction and a retreat to below $0.083. This collapse and retreat subsequently developed, and as anticipated it had an impact on the gold price. The eventual retreat moved to $0.77.

The imminent collapse of the US dollar signalled by the parabolic trend provides an opportunity to go long in gold in anticipation of a rise in the gold price. To maximise returns traders use a derivative. In this example, also used as a live case study in our weekly newsletter, we use the IG Markets Spot Gold CFD. The primary entry signal comes from changes in the dollar index. The exit is based on the price target projection derived from analysis of the gold chart. The first upside target for the trade is the previous chart pattern target level near $1250 and this is the planned exit.

The trade entry is made near $1206, shown in figure 29.2, in anticipation of an uptrend following the dollar index movements.

Position size is 166 contacts with a cash value of $20 019.60. The maximum stop loss is set at $1194. An exit at this level delivers a loss of $1992, which is 2% of total trading capital. This stop is managed with a guaranteed stop loss.

After the fast rise the stop loss is tightened to just below developing support near $1236, as shown in figure 29.3. Consistent with the trade planning, the trade is closed near $1250 as the target price is achieved. This delivers a 36% return and adds $7304 profit.

This is short-term derivative trading based on strategic analysis. Although the trade is initiated by gold price and dollar index movements, the trade is managed as a short-term trade because of the volatility in the market. The leverage of the CFD makes these small moves relatively profitable. By reducing the time necessary for the trade to return a good profit the risk of the trade is also reduced. In modern volatile markets time in the market becomes a significant risk factor. The volatility of gold and the related volatility of the dollar index make this market less suited to longer term trend trades.

Figure 29.2: trade entry

Derivatives are an essential trading method in modern markets. They deserve a place in every trader's toolkit because they can be used to reduce risk and reduce the risk of time spent in the market. In this chapter we considered the interlinking of gold and dollar markets and how the impact of these linkages are traded using a derivative to magnify the returns from small differences. In the next chapter we examine the impact of globalisation and the new trading opportunities it delivers.

Figure 29.3: trade exit

Exit

Spot Gold
IG Markets
15-minute chart

IT-Finance.com IG Markets

Part V

Beating the world

Chapter 30

International investor protection

In 2008 the world suddenly became a lot larger and, as a result, much closer to our home markets. And it's not going to change. The collapse of the US market and banking system battered markets and our sense of smugness. Many people retreated to the cocoon of their own domestic markets, battened down the hatches, and cautiously emerged several years later determined to remain local. This section is not for them.

Others indentified the significant changes that had developed and which continued to develop as globalisation pushed previously independent financial systems closer together. These changes cannot be ignored because they affect the foundations of the market mechanisms, regulations, structures and opportunity. This section is written for those who accept and welcome the inevitability of moving into the global financial world.

The seeds of the next financial crisis have already been sown in the recovery from the 2008 Global Financial Crisis. They have been sown because human behaviour, particularly crowd behaviour, does not change. There is an almost instinctive drive towards financial immolation—a financial system death wish. Regulations, despite the best intentions of regulators, are challenges to be avoided and evaded, subverted and bypassed. That's not meant to be a depressing picture, just a statement of reality. Private traders and investors work within this dark sea and we swim with the sharks that eventually bring down these systems. It's an evolutionary process, and just as the small mammals survived the fall of the dinosaurs, our objective is to survive the fall of financial systems.

The Global Financial Crisis opened the floodgates and let more of these international sharks into our pool. Some foreign sharks look friendly, hiding behind CFDs and ETFs, others are obviously predatory, hatched in the laboratory of financial engineering, and include the now extinct CDOs.

One of the most significant changes to evolve from the 2008 disaster was the increase in global interdependence. There is no escape from global markets. Just as money flows around obstacles to find friendlier investment environments, so too do market and fund operators. They gravitate to more friendly regulatory environments where older practices remain legal. It's why you still get phone calls from India-based boiler room operators. The result is a set of impacts starting somewhere remote, such as Thailand in 1996 and the currency crisis, or Greece in 2010 and the debt crisis. These reverberate through financial markets. These reverberations travel more quickly and inflict more damage thanks to the essential inter-connectedness of the world. There is a world of opportunity and a world of risk.

It's too early to identify the exact seeds of destruction in the next financial crisis, but traders will need to be alert for the weeds that pop up in the coming decades. Poisonous financial weeds have a habit of looking particularly attractive, so how can investors develop protection for local and international markets? Protection starts with the way we think about the market.

Endowment protection

Successful traders are different from unsuccessful traders because their beliefs are different. They look for protection in different areas. The core of this difference is the common belief that our own actions in making a choice *before* we play influences the outcome. This is the exact opposite of the thinking used by professional traders. These traders believe our own actions, *after* we have made the choice and selected a trade, can influence the personal outcome of the trade. In trading terms, our actions after the play has started are the management of the trade using stop loss and protect-profit measures.

The market is a continuous auction. Unlike a horse race, a hand of cards, the roll of a dice or the spin of the wheel, the market has no start to the event or end to the event. The Australian XJO monthly index chart in figure 30.1 provides multiple profitable entry points in a continuous trend. You have absolute control over the time you decide to enter. If things are not going your way, you can decide to get out at any time. You can withdraw all or some of your money. If things are going your way, you can add to your original trade commitment.

Figure 30.1: XJO monthly chart

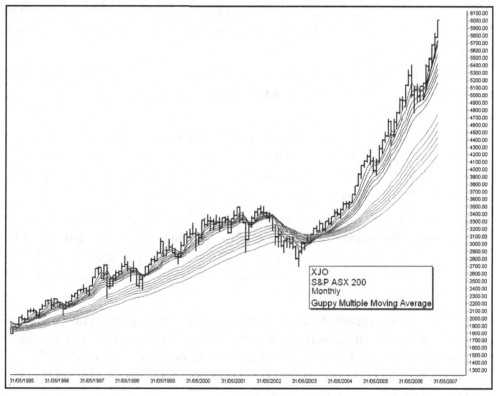

This is a more accurate understanding of the idea that time in the market is more important than timing the market. We have the ability to control the length of our time in the market, and this is our most significant trading advantage when it comes to outperforming the market through trading activity. This is the freedom of choice that really counts towards success.

This freedom to choose the action we will take is the 'edge' successful traders use. This freedom of choice is the foundation of risk management. We do not have to rely on a fortunate turn of events—luck—to win in the market. We create out own fortune by selecting the entry and exit conditions in a continuous activity. This is the thinking of professional traders, so how does the novice confuse this with the thinking that is more appropriate to gambling?

The core error for the novice is thinking that our own actions in making a choice *before* we play influences the outcome. It is not the act of choice that makes the difference. It is what we do with the choice that determines success or failure. Consider this example taken from a research project which used two different methods of allocating lottery tickets. The conditions of the lottery were the same in both cases and tickets cost $10.00 each.

In the first office people who purchased a ticket were given the next ticket out of the ticket book. They had no choice about the number or number sequence they were given.

In the second office people who purchased a ticket could choose their own tickets and number sequences. They were given a choice. As an additional outcome of the study, it was found when people were given a choice they purchased more tickets than the office where there was no choice.

The essential point is that the act of choice of ticket, or no choice, has no impact on the outcome of the lottery. The selection of the winning ticket is not influenced by whether you selected your own ticket or not. However, many people believe that by selecting the ticket they can have some influence over the outcome of the lottery. This conclusion is inferred from the next stage of the research project.

Two weeks later the researchers returned to each office. They explained the lottery had been very popular and the tickets had sold out. They wanted to buy some of the tickets back so they could sell them again to others who wanted to participate in the lottery. The results are of direct relevance to the way we approach the relationship between analysis, trade selection and trade management.

Office A had no choice in ticket selection. Many people agreed to sell their tickets back. Of course, realising there was high remand they asked, on average, for $2.00 above the face value of the ticket. They sold back for an average price of $12.00.

Office B was very different. People had been able to select their own tickets and numbers. Only a few people were willing to resell their tickets. Those that were willing to resell asked, on average, $20.00 per ticket. This was double the original purchase cost. The researchers concluded these people believed their choice had added more value to the ticket and that by selling it they were surrendering an opportunity they had personally identified. This conclusion was backed by further research into what is sometimes called the 'endowment effect'.

The idea that our choice of a ticket in a randomly drawn event can influence the outcome is very powerful. I was at a dinner one evening and raffle tickets were distributed. A woman at the table only had $50 notes with her and there was not enough change available. She was embarrassed at not being able to participate in the raffle, so I gave her several of my raffle tickets. One of those was the winning ticket. She was most reluctant to accept the prize because she felt the win was a result of my choice of ticket rather than just luck. In reality the act of choice has little relationship with the outcome other than the choice to participate in the event.

When we consider protection in the market these conclusions are relevant in these ways:

- many people believe the more time they take for personal research and analysis in a stock the better the probability the stock will perform as they expect. This is the endowment effect. They believe their act of choice affects the outcome

- the endowment effect facilitates our marriage to a stock. Because we have selected the stock it is more difficult to accept we have made a mistake. When the price goes down we go hunting for reasons *not* to sell. It rapidly becomes us against the market

- the act of personal choice before we select a stock to trade — not acting on a brokerage recommendation — creates an endowment effect. We believe our personal choice has an influence on the outcome. We believe our choices will go up.

In a bull market where almost everything goes up it is very difficult for new traders to recognise this endowment effect, and even after a market collapse it is difficult for investors to forget the endowment effect. With successful choice after successful choice they feel they have mastered the market. They believe that all these older traders talking about risk, risk management, trade discipline and the like are simply out of touch. Their personal experience during the bull market shows that their selection methods and lack of risk management, including averaging down in losing trades, have led to success time after time. Making money is easy, but they are fortunate — lucky — to have had their first experience of trading in a bull market.

Figure 30.2: different entry options

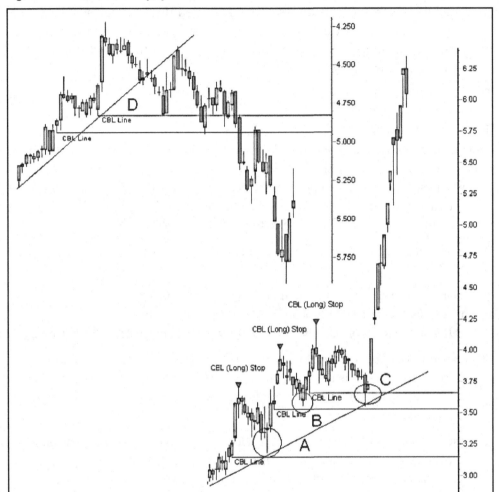

The professional trader is not immune to the endowment effect, but it generally plays a much smaller role. He is on guard against this effect, so the methods he uses help to mitigate the impact of the endowment effect. The professional trader knows this:

⊞ His act of choice in selecting a stock makes no difference to the eventual way the trade develops. His stock choice has no relationship with the way events unfold for the company, its products, its activity or the market the company is involved in. Consider the entry points A, B and C shown in the chart in figure 30.2. Each is technically similar with an entry near the count back line.

The result of entry C is far different from the previous entries. The size of this profit depends on what the trader does after he has made his entry choice.

- The time spent in analysis has no direct relationship with the eventual outcome. Some trades are identified in a few moments and are very successful. Others are identified after hours of analysis and they fail.

- His final choices are the best of the possible choices he has considered, but they are not the best of all the possible choices offered by the market. The professional has a group of preferred types of trading strategies and he searches mainly for those types of opportunities. He ignores other types of trades that may be equally as profitable because he does not have the skill to trade those types of opportunities.

- His personal choice tips the balance in his favour, but he still expects to get about a third of trades wrong. There is no automatic endowment because of his involvement, but the profit opportunity unfolds as a result of the action he takes in managing the trade development. The same count back line and trend line method applied to entry D in figure 30.2 results in failure. The outcome of the choice depends on how the entry is managed after the choice has been made. It does not depend on the choice itself.

This thinking leads the professional trader to a single inescapable conclusion. The way he manages the risk in the trade, to protect capital and later to protect profit, is the only guarantee of success. He makes his fortune year after year from a systematic approach to managing risk in an environment over which he has no control and no ability to influence unfolding events. These traders believe their own actions *after* they have made the choice and selected a trade influence the personal outcome and profit they take from the trade. No other person can take responsibility for your actions.

Between the flags?

The acknowledgement of personal responsibility stands in contrast to some of the efforts from regulators. The proposal from one regulator to identify 'between the flags' investment fails the most basic of tests. It simply begs the question by suggesting that between the flag investments include blue chips. Are we to assume that blue chips do not include General Motors, General Electric or Bear Stearns? Or that blue chips exclude Centro and Great Southern on the grounds that their 2008 failure shows they were really not blue chips after all? Or does blue chip include stocks like the Australian banks with an average peak to low loss from 2007 to 2009 of around 60%?

Investing, so we are told, is a long-term business with a 20-year time span. This means we should be selecting blue-chip stocks in 1988 with an eye to seeing strong performance all the way through to 2009. This, of course, is largely garbage. In 1988 I owned a top of the range PC with far less computing power than my current mobile phone. The 4.5 inch floppy disk was a dream, let alone a CD or DVD. In 1988 we were told our biggest future challenge would be what we would do with all our spare leisure time because the working week in 20 years' time would be 25 hours or less! In 1988 China was still a closed state and economy. Even if you had accurately forecast these developments there were simply not the investment vehicles available to allow you to capitalise on your predictions.

Table 30.1 shows the top 20 listed Australian companies in 1988, 1998 and 2010. They are stocks that meet the criteria to fall 'between the flags'. The survival rate is exceptionally low. The shaded stocks no longer exist or have been deleted from the top 20 index. Only four stocks in the 1988 list remain in the 2010 list. Around 15% of 1988 stocks either no longer exist or have been taken over by companies no longer in the top 20. Any investment holdings in these companies have been diluted in takeovers and restructurings. On a 20-year time frame you have an 80% chance of making a wrong choice.

Twenty years is a long time. Perhaps a 10-year blue-chip time frame is better. Now there are 45% of companies that survive 10 years in this list. You only have a 55% chance of making the wrong choice. That's pretty close to the odds on using a coin toss to make stock selections.

The suggestion of picking companies just because they are 'between the flags' shows an appalling ignorance of market reality and structure. The market index always rises, but the composition of the index changes. The index rises because it only includes winners: 15% from the 1988 list survive until 2009, 45% from the 1998 list survive until 2010.

Protection does not come from a third-party definition of a good company, no matter how well intentioned. Protection comes from vigilance. Investors know when a good company goes bad through watching price activity, which includes the behaviour of investors who really do know when a company is going bad.

The GTP chart in figure 30.3 shows how this works, with multiple warnings of the downtrend that dropped prices from $3.00 to a few cents. This was not a sudden surprise or an unexpected collapse. The charts from Centro, GM, GE, Bear Stearns and Satyam Computers all have the same characteristics. Look back in history and observe the charts of the now-defunct Enron—once called one of America's most successful companies—and WorldCom. Their 'sudden' collapses were preceded by the same long-term signals that had chart traders taking an exit, or going short. Others told investors these companies were fabulous bargains at these lower prices, almost right up until the time they stopped trading.

Table 30.1: top 20 listed Australian companies

BETWEEN THE FLAGS FAILURE

1988 20 years	1998 10 years	2010
BHP	News Corp	BHP
ANZ	AMP	ANZ
Boral	ANZ	NAB
Brambles	BHP	Westpac
BTR Nylex	Brambles	
Coles Myer	Cable & Wireless	
Comalco	CBA	
CRA	Coca-Cola Amatil	
CSR	Coles Myer	
Elders IXL	Colonial	
Goodman Fielder	Foster's	
ICI Australia	Lend Lease	
MIM	NAB	
NAB	National Mutual	
News Corp	Rio Tinto	
North Broken Hill Peko	Telstra	
Pacific Dunlop	Westpac	
TNT	WMC	
Western Mining	Woodside	
Westpac	Woolworths	

There are multiple warning signs of failure in the price activity. This is a fire alarm. You run first, and later forensically reconstruct the reasons why the company went bad.

Independent advice is preferable, but not always possible. Fund managers have a business to run, and you are part of the food chain that delivers fees. Brokers are in a business that requires them to develop good customer relations, but this is still a fee in fancy dress. All through the market collapse of 2008 the number of hold or buy recommendations vastly outnumbered the sell recommendations from the finance industry professionals. Independence is always potentially compromised when a fee is involved. Expect to pay for good analysis and quality advice, but you should always establish if there is a potential for a conflict of interest.

Figure 30.3: multiple warnings of downtrend

If you are aware of the potential conflict of interest you can make a better judgement about the quality and intent of the educational material provided. Investor protection comes from independent education backed up by regulation. Investor survival comes from trading the changes in trend rather than from blind buy and hold—flags or no flags.

Local global

Portfolio protection comes from diversity, and increasingly that also means global diversity. An awareness of the endowment effect and a rejection of silly notions of safety in the market are essential for protection in our domestic markets. They are critical for survival and success in international markets.

Markets move in displaced synchronicity. China and India are up while the US is down. Australia is up while Europe is collapsing. Bank stocks are galloping while transportation stocks have hit a traffic jam. Resources have unlimited profits while telcos find their margins are shaved even closer to their bottom line. Diversity in volatility, in sectors, in trend behaviour and in types of opportunity creates a better performing portfolio.

The techniques and methods of good trading in the local environment are transferred to trading in a global environment. The same objective rules apply, but when you move into an international environment the local protection available from regulation does not apply. Understanding the behaviour of the market becomes much more important, and later we look at how this applies in a real-time test environment that challenges preconceptions of the basis of market pricing. But first we look at the exchange-traded fund, which provides a method of reaching out for international diversification while staying under the protection of local regulation.

Chapter 31

Capturing the world

Every morning CNBC SquawkBox provides a rolling coverage of the overnight activity in European and US markets, and a preview commentary on the expected impact on China, Japan, Korea, Hong Kong, Singapore and Australian markets. As the SquawkBox 'Chart man', I am asked to provide on-the-spot chart analysis across multiple markets in reply to viewers' questions. In the past it has been very difficult for Australian traders to trade these international opportunities. This has changed with exchange-traded funds (ETFs).

The world is closing in on local markets, and if the world is inevitably coming to us then we have a choice. We can embrace the world, or find smaller and smaller corners to hide away from the world. Opportunities will always exist within a local context but it will become increasingly difficult to ignore the influence of global events. A knowledge of global drivers will help improve the identification of local opportunities. Traders and investors looking for a counterbalance to the global influence have an increasingly wide range of global solutions to help diversify local portfolios. The direct derivative involvement comes from the world of CFDs, discussed in previous chapters, where traders can follow opportunities in individual stocks or with the leveraged trading of indices.

CFD trading provides an easy way to trade these foreign opportunities without the need for multiple offshore brokerage accounts and their inherent currency risk. The range of available international markets is weighted towards Europe and the US. This reflects the historical development of CFD markets in the UK. The coverage of Asian exchanges is more limited, but it is growing. The balance of international exposure remains weighted towards individual European and US stocks.

The indirect involvement comes from the world of exchange-traded funds. They are a derivative, even though they are usually traded like ordinary stocks on the stock exchange. They provide international exposure with local regulation. Before 2008 they were a sleepy product offering the opportunity to match market performance and they did not have much appeal in a raging bull market. The years following the 2008 market collapse saw the ETF surge into popularity as a stable component of portfolios. We look at these classical understandings of the ETF and global diversification in the first part of this chapter.

The ETF also offers trading opportunities. These are tactical methods used to capture the cream from global markets and deliver better than market returns. We look at a handful of methods we use to enhance the ETF global performance.

Surprisingly rapidly the ETF became a victim of its own success and this has significantly changed the way ETFs are incorporated into a trading or investment strategy. They still provide global exposure and diversity, but they do not provide the rock of stability and low volatility that many people prefer in their portfolios. These changes have been rapid, and retail investors are listening to the echo of a speeding train that has already passed them by and changed direction. We close with some cautionary notes for the future of these derivatives.

ETF portfolio fit

Traders are very often not investors. The skills required for trading are not the skills required for investing so the challenge is to turn trading income into longer term wealth. ETFs offer this opportunity because of their exposure to the broader market. And then they offer the opportunity to seamlessly extend this skill to international markets. Generally the market movement is slower than the movement of its component stocks. The same trading skills are applied to the broad market, but at a slower speed. Building broad market exposure using an ETF provides a method to apply trading skills to an investment environment. It allows for the creation of a hybrid portfolio, shown schematically in figure 31.1. The trader uses her skills to add beta to the alpha of the ETF. Beta is a measure of the degree to which an investment outperforms or underperforms the broad market. A beta of 1 means if the market increases by 25% then the ETF will also increase by 25%.

Figure 31.1: hybrid portfolio

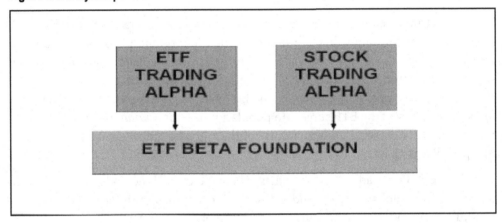

A hybrid portfolio uses a diversity of volatility exposure and skills to build a portfolio. Classic portfolio management theory urges diversity. In a simplified version, holding all the stocks in the DOW Industrials gives you diversified exposure to various segments of the market so you collect the broad market performance. It's a passive approach to the market designed to create the situation where the losing stocks in the index are broadly counterbalanced by the returns from winning stocks. It is theoretically attractive but devilishly difficult to implement, as the consistent underperformance of 90% of managed funds shows.

The hybrid portfolio is not a passive approach. It recognises the differences in risk profiles in various sections of the market and structures the portfolio to take advantage of areas of superior returns. It takes advantage of our ability to trade. An early variation of the hybrid portfolio structure was discussed in *Share Trading* in the chapter 'Six to twenty-one'. The ETF allows for further development of this concept for modern markets and includes a convenient exposure to internal market performance.

The ETF provides a beta foundation. Returns will be broadly the same as the returns from the underlying market. Alpha returns are generated by applying the ETF trading strategies discussed later in this chapter. Additional beta for portfolio growth and performance is added from funds accumulated through stock and other trading activity. This component of additional funding is generated using the trading methods discussed in earlier chapters. The ability to use the ETF as a foundation of a hybrid portfolio coupled with the ETF's ease of global exposure makes this is a powerful combination for the creation of wealth from trading income.

There is one important warning with this approach. The method is only applied when the market is rising. Outperforming a falling market by making a smaller loss than the market is not a winning strategy. Traders may choose to close the portfolio and reopen it when the market recovers. If the hybrid portfolio continues to be cash flow positive in the falling market then the portfolio remains open. Portfolios remain positive because the flow of funds from the stock trading alpha aspect of the hybrid portfolio approach keeps the returns in positive territory.

Traders who use this hybrid portfolio approach as an investment tool can also apply the zero cost averaging methods to build longer term no-cost or low-cost positions in the ETF and the portfolio. These methods are discussed in *Better Trading* in the chapter 'Securing capital'. They remain a foundation of portfolio construction in modern markets.

ETFs making global local

ETFs provide global diversity, and this classic feature creates rock-solid portfolio foundations. The trader is no longer at the mercy of her home market. Adverse moves in your home market can be offset against more positive moves in US or Asian markets. The ETF opens the door to effective diversification of risk and risk management.

ETFs have become a $1 trillion global industry. The range of ETFs grows rapidly, with ETFs that cover well-known indices, sector indices and specialist ETFs that bring together particular performance groupings. This diversity of ETFs, including reverse ETFs that short the market, is not yet available in all markets but they point the way to a more sophisticated approach to investing, trading and managing risk.

An ETF 'shadows' or replicates the performance of a particular market, index or sector. They are baskets of stocks that enable you to buy or sell a portfolio of securities in a single purchase. Unlike mutual and unit trust funds you can trade ETFs just as you would an individual stock. You can buy and sell them at intraday prices in a liquid market. They have four classic core advantages which show how to shift from capturing diversification in our local market to capturing diversification in a global market.

Index tracking

This is the core of the ETF concept. It provides the trader and investor with a simple way to buy or sell the index and benefit from the market rise.

The chart in figure 31.2 shows a simple ETF strategy using STW, which is an ETF on the Australian XJO index. An entry in September 2006 near $50.61 followed by an exit near $61 in June 2007 delivered a capital gain of 20.53%. It also delivered all of the dividend payments made by all XJO index companies during the period.

There are ways to improve on the very simple moving average crossover approach shown here. The objective in this example is to show how the broad trends in the market can be effectively traded without the need to select individual stocks.

Figure 31.2: ETF strategy

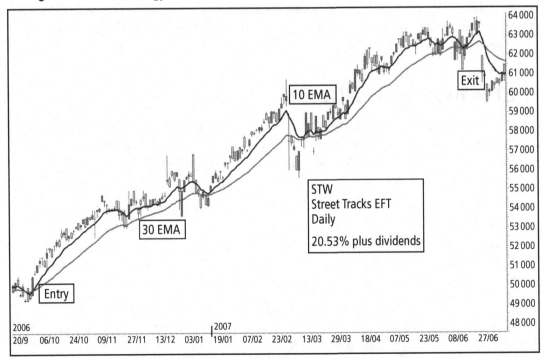

Capture 'unavailable' profits

I follow many markets as a result of my work with CNBC Asia and CNBC Europe. Often I come across opportunities in individual stocks like Taiwan company Han Hai Precision Industry. It manufactures all three of the hot video-game consoles that dominate the $10 billion worldwide video-gaming market and the Apple iPhone. It sounds like a great investment, but Han Hai cannot be traded easily from outside Taiwan. I would have to open a trading account in Taiwan, and the problems are not worth the trouble for a single company trade.

The MSCI Taiwan index ETF has Han Hai as its largest holding. Buying the ETF provided a way to capture profits that were essentially unavailable to us by any other means. As a bonus, it also provides exposure to the performance of the entire Taiwan market.

Diversification

The ETF is actually a diversified fund so if you pick the hot sector or hot market, then you pick up the profits that go with it. You never get burnt just because one stock failed. The ETF reduces specific stock risk.

The structure of the ETF means as stocks are dropped from the index they are also dropped from the ETF. As stocks are added to the index, they are added to the ETF. The ETF simply always trades with the leading stocks in the market that make up the index. The index survivor bias works in your favour. Survivor bias happens when the components of an index are regularly reviewed and changed. This gives a positive bullish bias because only the survivors—the best performing stocks—remain in the index. This is why the index always rises over long periods of time.

Global diversification

The objective in this strategy is to move from one strongly performing market to another. The cost of movement is limited to simple brokerage fees. There are no serious financial disadvantages imposed by a 'redemption' of funds, nor is there any waiting time. Trades are settled with the same speed as a trade with an ordinary stock.

This is diversification on a global scale made possible by trading a single series of instruments. It's a way to capture the world.

Market and index behaviour

There is an important and dangerous myth that confuses our understanding of both our local market and world markets. One of the most dangerous market myths is that the market always rises over time. The believers in this myth trot out historical charts reconstructed from the middle of the 18th century. And sure enough, the long-term trend marches inexorably upwards. Even crashes like those of 1929, 1987 and the Tech Wreck become just little blips in this overall magical rising trend. The message is clear: just buy and hold and the magic carpet of the market will carry you to undreamt-of riches.

This is so untrue that it should be labelled as false advertising.

The truth is that the market *index* always rises, but not the market. The market index rises because the index only includes winners. This is called survivor bias. The components of the index change on a regular basis. The Australian S&P/ASX XJO 200 index is rebalanced every quarter by Standard & Poor's, who compiles the index. In the quarter ending March 2010 three stocks were dropped from the index calculation because they were the worst performers. Three stocks were added because they were better performers.

When you drop the losers and add the winners it's no wonder the market (index) always rises. Blue-chip stocks that fail are obviously not suitable for the index, so they are dropped. Too bad if you happen to own them as an investment for the long term.

Despite these changes in the membership of the index, the index is still treated by many analysts and commentators as if it is a single unchanged entity. While it is true the concept of the index is unchanging it is important to remember the membership of the index is always changing to select retrospective winners.

This is survivor bias. It explains why Caterpillar Corp is a member of the unchanging DOW Jones index, which has a continuous history starting long before Caterpillar Corp started business. It explains why the index always rises.

You could track this index performance if you buy every stock within the index. However, you need to buy and sell regularly to keep your portfolio components exactly the same as the index. Apart from cost, time and effort, there is a significant taxation and brokerage impact. The ETF does all this work, and presents a single instrument with a single buy or sell price set by the market.

Matching market performance is a better result than that achieved by around 90% of fund and investment managers. In a bull market around 90% of managers deliver lower returns than those delivered by the market. In a bear market, around 95% of fund managers lose more than the market falls. When their management fees are added, the performance results are even worse.

The ETF allows the trader to trade the market index without the risk of specific stocks contained in, or deleted from, the index. It's a good solution for local portfolios and an excellent foundation for global market trading. ETF analysis leads to 16 analysis and trading strategies. They are:

- dividend hop: three strategies
- Swiss roll: three strategies
- yield trading: three strategies
- beta beaters: two strategies
- international: three strategies
- arbitrage: two strategies.

We use five trade management strategies for profit lock in ETF trading. They are:

- accumulation
- capital profit
- currency boost
- cost averaging
- currency lock.

In this chapter we discuss dividend hop and the Swiss roll or diversification strategies. The remaining strategies are discussed in our e-book *Profit Without Pain*.

Dividend hop

Dividend hop is designed as a trading method to skim the dividends payable on all the stocks that make up the underlying index. In a rising market it delivers a capital return and a dividend return. In a falling market the risk is greater because the strategy may incur a capital loss. We start with the application to our local market and then show how it's applied on a global basis.

ETF index dividends have three interesting features:

- the ETF gathers all the dividends paid at different times during the year by each of the underlying companies in the index. These dividends are consolidated into a single payment made twice a year. In some instances, with international ETFs, the payments are made every quarter

- the second feature impacts on trend behaviour when the ETF goes ex-dividend. Unlike trading in the underlying company—for instance, a large bank—there is no significant price reaction when the stock goes ex-dividend. If we trade a dividend in an individual stock then the risk is a substantial price drop—and a capital loss—when the stock goes ex-dividend. When the ETF goes ex-dividend there is usually a very small impact in price

- the performance of the index, and hence the ETF, is not dependent upon the performance of an individual company. This means the existing trend behaviour of the market is more powerful than the individual behaviour of any stock as it goes ex-dividend. As the ETF ex-dividend dates do not coincide with any particular individual event, there is a reduced impact on trend behaviour due to the ETF going ex-dividend. The market simply does not care and takes no notice. With an individual stock, the market does care, and it reacts accordingly.

Dividend hopping is the strategy of buying a stock a few days prior to the dividend date, then selling it as soon as it goes ex-dividend. The objective is to simply take the dividend. In many countries this method is subjected to an additional level of taxation. The implementation of dividend hopping–style strategies must always take this taxation impact into account.

The index ETF strategy is designed to reduce risk and collect the dividend. It is an income stream model. The risk is reduced by the trending behaviour of the ETF and the underlying index. We start with the application to local markets and then show how this is transferred to a global collection process.

This is more effective than trading dividends in individual shares. The consolidation of dividend payments into two dividends by the ETF reduces the complexity of trading. Dividend payment dates for Australian listed ETFs are around 24 June and 21 December each year.

In this example we use a 40-trading-day holding period. Trades completed inside the 40-day period incur a penalty tax because the 40-day period includes the ex-dividend date. Depending on the jurisdiction, the minimum holding period may be larger or smaller.

There are three potential entry points. They are shown on the chart extract in figure 31.3. The first enters around 40 days prior to the ex-dividend date and exits on the ex-dividend day. This is a very defensive strategy. If the index begins to trend downwards the trade can be abandoned with minimum capital loss. The dividend payment is lost, but capital is preserved.

Figure 31.3: dividend hop possible entry points

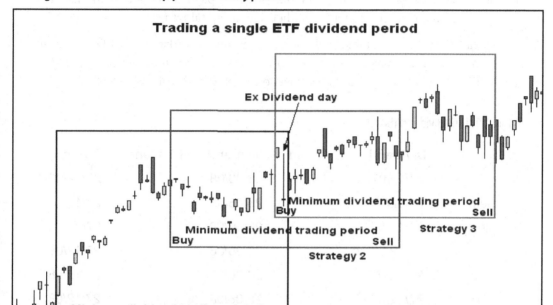

The second entry point is balanced either side of the ex-dividend day. The purpose is to ride an existing trend. This strategy has moderate risk because trending behaviour before the ex-dividend date is captured and this behaviour does not have to continue for an extended period after the ex-dividend date.

The third entry point is just prior to the ex-dividend day and holds the ETF for the required minimum period. The advantage of this entry is that the pre-existing trend is well established and there is a high probability it will continue. This is the strategy with the highest risk because it relies entirely on future trend continuation.

This type of dividend collection adds alpha to the ETF. Alpha is a measure of outperformance of the market and this is achieved by harvesting the dividends. This trading tactic is the basis of a global strategy to bring home international profits.

Global index ETF

The global multi-index ETF strategy uses the methods applied to trading a single ETF, but it creates a calendar spread using the trading of international listed ETFs. This is dividend hopping, moving from one dividend payment period to another. The objective is to reap an income return, rather than a capital return.

The spreadsheet extract in table 31.1 shows the ex-dividend dates for 14 ETFs. In this particular market the majority of dividend dates are 27 December and 26 June. The last four ETFs are US-based, and they have four dividend distributions a year.

Table 31.1: ex-dividend dates

	Dividend	Dividend	Dividend	Dividend	Dividend
ijp	27/12/07		26/06/08		27/12/08
iem	27/12/07		26/06/08		27/12/08
ioo	27/12/07		26/06/08		27/12/08
ive	27/12/07		26/06/08		27/12/08
izz	27/12/07		26/06/08		27/12/08
ihk	27/12/07		26/06/08		27/12/08
iko	27/12/07		26/06/08		27/12/08
isg	27/12/07		26/06/08		27/12/08
itw	27/12/07		26/06/08		27/12/08
stw	27/12/07		24/06/08		27/12/08
ivv	27/12/07	26/03/08	26/06/08	26/09/08	27/12/08
ijh	27/12/07	26/03/08	26/06/08	26/09/08	27/12/08
ijr	27/12/07	26/03/08	26/06/08	26/09/08	27/12/08
iru	27/12/07	26/03/08	26/06/08	26/09/08	27/12/08

Implementation of the strategy starts with an assessment of the dividend yield that applies to each of the ETFs. This is most difficult in period one, period three and period five, as there are 14 ETFs that go ex-dividend on the same date. The objective is to identify the ETF with the highest dividend yield. This type of information is aggregated on the iShares website, or by independent providers such as <www.XTF.com>.

In the example shown in table 31.2 we assume that the Hang Seng index ETF, trading as IHK, has the highest dividend yield for period one. It also has the best trend behaviour and meets the conditions for entry that we would apply if we were trading a single ETF. The trade captures capital gain and a dividend bonus.

Moving out of December we go to the next ETF dividend period in March. This applies to the ETFs covering the US market. Of these, in this example, the IRU ETF, which covers the Russell 2000 index, has the best dividend yield and trading characteristics. This dividend trading strategy 'hops' to the next most profitable ETF from a dividend yield perspective.

Table 31.2: dividend hopping

Period 1	Period 2	Period 3	Period 4	Period 5
27/12/2007	26/03/2008	26/06/2008	26/09/2008	27/12/2008
IHK	IRU	STW	IVV	IJP
Hong Kong	US	Australia	US	Japan

In the third period the trade hops to the StreetTracks ETF, STW, which covers the Australian market. The fourth period sees a hop to IVV, which captures the dividend return from the S&P 500. The fifth period hops to the dividend yield from Japan. A chart summary of this strategy is shown in figure 31.4.

Figure 31.4: capturing capital gains and dividends

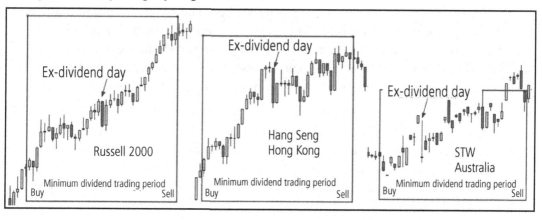

Each trade captures the ETF price activity and capital gain, and the dividend yield from the most successful individual ETF. These five trades capture capital gain and dividend yield generated by the underlying markets.

Delivering global diversification profits

The ETF index, multi-country strategy is based on the observation that markets move in displaced synchronisation. On a global basis the behaviour of markets is similar, but the market is characterised by leader and laggard behaviour. Some markets are rising while other markets are falling.

A classic approach to ETF trading suggests that buying a single ETF provides greater protection because the ETF automatically includes a level of diversification that is not easily available using other methods. Classic thinking believes this spread of stocks provides diversity, and hence a reduced level of risk.

This thinking is extended further, and it is suggested that when the trader increases the number of ETFs held, then the risk is further diversified. A trader with ETFs covering the Japanese, Hong Kong, S&P and Australian indices has a greater diversity than a trader who holds just an S&P 500 ETF.

This may be correct if we assume a diversity of directional behaviour, but unless actively managed the net result may deliver unexpectedly low returns. Indiscriminate holding of a diversified country index ETF may mean the gains in one market are offset by the losses in another. This type of hedging approach is suitable for passive funds management, but it does not deliver alpha returns.

The diagram in figure 31.5 shows three rising markets. The superior return in ETF C is 15%, but the portfolio return is 9.3% because the superior return is diminished by the underperforming ETF with a 3% return. Diversity can provide an average return, but when traded with a Swiss roll approach, diversity provides an enhanced return. The objective is to delete the losers, or low performers, and capture a slice of the winners' performance.

The foundation of this ETF strategy is to capture the capital appreciation between the entry and exit points in the trade. In this sense it is no different from a trade in an ordinary stock and similar analysis methods can be applied. The difference in trading the ETF is the relative stability of the ETF and the diversification of risk when compared to exposure to a single stock.

Figure 31.5: diversification

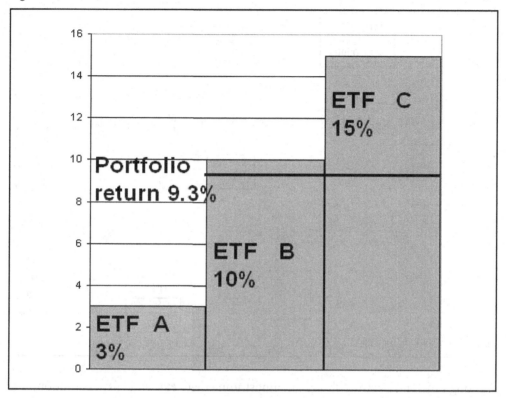

The chart in figure 31.6 illustrates the trading principle. First, markets do not move together. Second, markets move at different speeds. Third, traders improve returns by switching ETFs to the index that is outperforming other country indices in the selected period. Identifying this potential outperformance rests on a number of technical indicator analysis methods. They are no different from the methods discussed in previous chapters because the ETF trades in a manner similar to a stock. The boxes on the chart display show the period of each trade. The figures show the comparative returns from each market for the same period.

Entry and exit points may be based on momentum indicators. Index analysis can be simpler, or more complex, but the objective is to identify the preferred entry conditions for trade execution using an ETF. The objective is to identify increasing momentum and use this as an entry signal. When momentum begins to decline, the trade is closed and the search begins for a momentum entry signal being generated in another ETF.

Figure 31.6: Swiss roll strategy

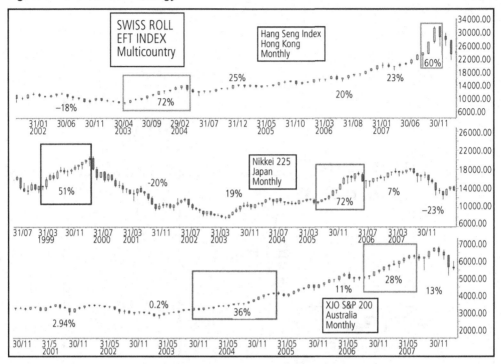

Although the chart extract shows an almost immediate exit and entry condition, it is more common for several weeks to elapse between closing one position and opening another. Momentum entry and exit signals must also be combined with an assessment of the velocity of the rise. A fast rise in a mature market may deliver a 2% return. A fast rise in an emerging market may deliver a 13% gain. The strategy trades the fast gain. The objective is to capture the behaviour—momentum—of the ETF and the velocity—percentage change.

This strategy is designed to diversify reward by capturing the best behaviour across multiple markets and time frames. It is a capital growth model. The risk is reduced by the diverse timing of the trending behaviour of the ETFs and the underlying indices. The risk is not reduced by diversity of markets.

Global success caution

Success always brings caution, and the rapid growth of ETFs has made them victims of their success. The size of the ETF market increased dramatically and this created difficulties in the process of market making. When volumes were lower it was easier to ensure ETF values remained within agreed or acceptable spreads. The tracking error remained small. As volumes increased the tracking error has grown, and this introduces a set of new problems in ETF trading. Tracking error is the degree to which the price of the ETF accurately reflects the price of the underlying index.

There are five cautions developing in ETF trading. They are cautions currently without tested solutions. We highlight them because they affect the way traders use ETFs and these inefficiencies may offer trading opportunities. The cautions are:

- tracking error expansion

- price spiking

- holiday arbitrage

- time zone arbitrage

- kissing cousins.

Off track

The ETF theory suggests the ETF will closely track the performance and behaviour of the underlying index. The degree to which this does not happen is called a tracking error. As ETF volumes increase, the degree of tracking error is also increasing. This reflects the difficulty of the issuer in being able to supply ETF units at a price that reflects the index behaviour. Powerful buying or selling creates some periods of temporary tracking distortion.

In the longer term there are two main tracking errors. The first is trend direction divergence and the second is trend behaviour divergence. Trend direction divergence appears when the trend of the underlying index moves in the opposite direction to the trend in the ETF. The chart in figure 31.7 shows three examples of this trend direction divergence, labelled TDD. Although it can be identified in short-term time frames lasting a few days, it is also at play in longer term time frames lasting several months. This is a more serious concern for using ETFs as a portfolio foundation.

In this example, based on the entry point shown at the left of the chart display, the difference in overall trend behaviour and return is substantial. The underlying Shanghai index increased by 3.34% from the entry point. The ETF fell by 6.15% over the same period. This is a substantial trend tracking error.

Figure 31.7: trend direction divergence and trend behaviour divergence

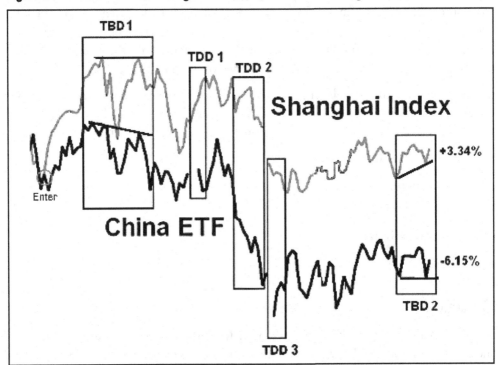

The second type of tracking error is the trend behaviour divergence. This is where the behaviour of the trend in the underlying index is not the same as the behaviour in the ETF. The first example of this, shown as TBD 1 in figure 31.7, shows the market making a double top. This behaviour is not reflected in the ETF where the market develops a downtrend over the same period with the second rally peak much lower than the first rally peak. This indicates the behaviour of the ETF is diverging from the behaviour of the underlying index.

The second example of the trend behaviour divergence at the right of the chart shows the ETF making a small double bottom—TBD 2—while the index is showing a series of rising bottoms in an upwards trend. The trend behaviour messages from the Shanghai index are different from those delivered by the ETF.

These two behaviours indicate an expansion of the tracking error in the ETF. It's a cautionary signal. Traders develop arbitrage opportunities from this divergence, but investor positions are damaged if the ETF is held in the expectation it will closely track the underlying index.

Nasty ETF behaviour

ETFs often appear to be an illiquid market although the market maker, or issuer, has a statutory responsibility to make a liquid market and to keep the traded spread within a defined limit based on the value of the underlying index, or combination of indices. In theory this means there is always a buyer or seller available for the volume you need to trade. In theory it means the intraday price movements should have relatively low volatility because the intraday volatility of the index is also low.

The chart extract in figure 31.8 shows the divergence between theory and practice. This ETF is dominated by massive intraday spikes that are clearly not related to the performance of the underlying index, or baskets of indices. It's another cautionary tale in the developing story of ETF trading. There are three aspects of this behaviour.

First is the issue of responsibility. The issuer, as the market maker, usually has a statutory obligation to keep pricing within a defined spread. Extreme and repeated movements beyond the limits of this spread are an issue that needs to be addressed by regulators and ETF issuers.

Second is the way the ETF is responding to trader and investor behaviour. These sharp rally and retreats on an intraday basis show a market that can be bullied by extreme buy or sell orders, or by extreme order size. It changes the nature of the market behaviour and this should be factored into any decision to use ETFs as a component of the portfolio. Although the market does quickly snap back there is no guarantee this will continue. There is the possibility these extremes of intraday behaviour may lead to a sustained divergence in trend behaviour between the ETF and the underlying index.

Third, there are fast intraday returns where price moves to an extreme and then returns to the mean, or average, of previous pricing. Even without leverage, the size of this volatility offers a short-term trading opportunity.

This is nasty pricing behaviour because it does not correctly reflect the stability and lower volatility of the underlying indices. Some ETFs are more susceptible to this behaviour, and exposure to these ETFs requires more caution.

ETF on holiday

The ETF in figure 31.9 does not have the volatility characteristics of the previous chart but it contains another interesting problem. The area between the two thick vertical lines looks like normal trading activity and it is in terms of the ETF.

Figure 31.8: price spiking

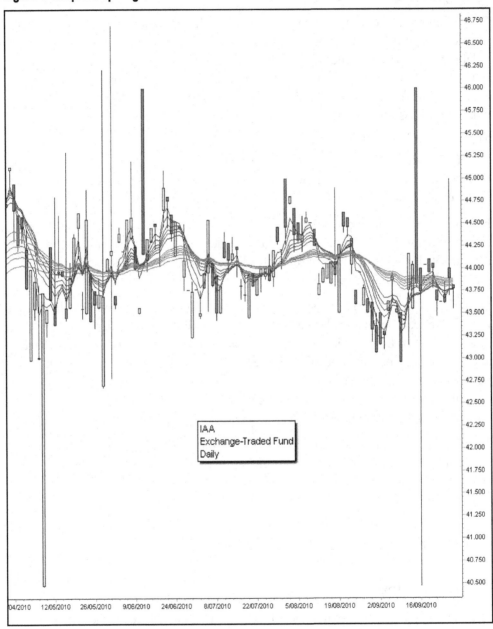

Unfortunately during this five-day period the market for the underlying index was closed for the Spring Festival holidays. When the underlying index is not trading we need to ask how the ETF issuer determines an appropriate price for the ETF. On what basis are the price points for each of these days decided when the underlying index is closed?

Figure 31.9: index holiday

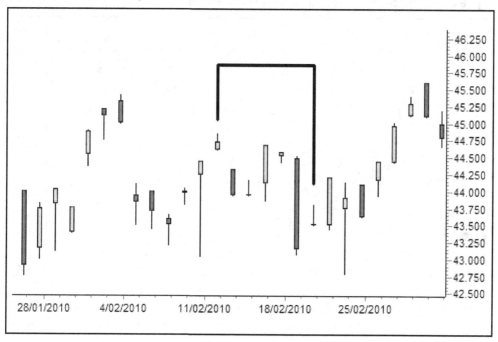

This is guesswork. If price is set by independent traders then they are making judgements about the potential for the opening level of the index in two to five days' time. There is nothing inherently wrong with this approach. Traders do this all the time when they take a trade prior to a holiday break. However, the ETF is supposed to be directly linked to the performance of the underlying index.

This continued trading activity during the holiday period suggests a change in the behaviour of the ETF market and a change in the way it is used. There is a gradual shift away from replicating market performance with the ETF to using the ETF to trade the expected market performance. The development of a more sustained trading component in ETF activity will change the risk profile of the ETF. This is also seen in the final caution notes.

Time zone arbitrage

Personally I do not trade markets that are open and active while I am sleeping. Some ETFs offer the reverse of this opportunity, allowing us to trade while others are sleeping. The chart in figure 31.10 is an ETF covering the US Standard & Poor's 500 index but it's traded in Australia. This offers several unique trading opportunities.

Figure 31.10 ETF covering US Standard & Poor's 500 index

Trading during market hours in Australia in this ETF is by necessity based on the anticipated pricing of the S&P index when the market next opens. The US market is closed during the entire period the Australian market is open. The ETF reflects in part the overnight trading in the S&P 500 index but, more importantly, it reflects future expectations of the S&P index when US trading resumes. In this sense the pricing of the ETF is speculative rather than linked to the S&P index. This increases the possibility of tracking error.

The Australian market closes before the US market opens, so traders can apply an opening price arbitrage. Traders take a position on the close of trade in the Australian-based ETF and arbitrage this against a higher opening price of the S&P index in the US several hours later. For small-scale traders the arbitrage opportunity is too small to be worthwhile, but for institutional traders this offers an interesting opportunity.

In all cases, an ETF that trades today over an index that is closed to trading either because of a time zone difference or because of holidays is an ETF that cannot accurately reflect or track the behaviour of the underlying index. It becomes, by nature or circumstance, a trading instrument rather than a portfolio foundation instrument. This offers a different range of trading and investment opportunities which must be managed independently of analysis of the underlying index.

Kissing cousins

At the height of the internet boom at the turn of the century many small mining companies turned away from gold and rebadged themselves as internet companies. They started to mine shareholder gold in a different way. When the internet boom collapsed and years later gold began to rise, they rebadged themselves again as new gold companies, and kept mining shareholder wealth. It's part of the financial market food cycle, so it's no surprise ETFs have spawned many competitors, including some zombie survivors from the Global Financial Crisis now claiming to be ETFs in disguise. ETFs have become so popular that many old-fashioned funds are claiming to be ETFs. Some mutual funds or managed funds, and some old index funds, are suddenly dressing themselves up with new clothes and images. These are kissing cousins, and although they look friendly they hide a range of significant differences from the ETF in its original structure.

A mutual fund is a type of collective investment managed by a third party, often a bank or insurance company. It gathers capital from investors and invests in a variety of instruments. Sometimes they are called a balanced fund, or a fund of funds or a managed fund. They usually invest in a mixture of stocks, bonds, short-term money market instruments and sometimes commodities and other derivatives. The fund manager trades the underlying securities in accordance with the fund's investment objectives or mandate. The fund investors have a direct interest—via the fund manager—in the assets of the fund. The profits or losses are distributed to the individual investors. The value of a share of the mutual fund is calculated daily based on the total value of the fund divided by the number of shares currently issued and outstanding. This is the net asset value (NAV) per share. The traded price of the fund may be very different from the NAV as traders anticipate future performance. Redemption, or trading, in funds may be suspended for extended periods, as many investors discovered in 2008.

A pure ETF has the following characteristics.

- The ETF is a derivative actively traded during the trading day. The ETF uses a variety of derivative instruments and trading strategies to achieve the sole purpose of the fund. ETFs do not sell their individual shares at their net asset value. Instead, financial institutions purchase and redeem ETF shares directly from the ETF in large blocks, usually between 25 000 and 200 000 shares. These are called creation units.

  Only authorised participants, usually large institutional investors, trade shares of an ETF directly with the fund manager. Authorised participants usually act as market makers on the open market and their trading activity provides liquidity of the ETF shares. Private traders trade ETF shares on this secondary market.

- The ETF mandate is to duplicate the performance of the index, or the performance of the aggregate basket of stocks if the ETF is tracking a particular market segment. This active management keeps the traded price of the ETF within a defined range of tracking error. This is not the hit and miss affair used with mutual or managed funds. This index tracking is a deliberately achieved outcome.

- Using a variety of methods and trading relationships the ETF buys and sells in a made market to keep the traded price within a defined spread when measured against the underlying index. The price is arbitraged back to the index performance. The activity in the trading of creation units by the authorised participants creates a public marketplace where the current publicly traded price is within a defined spread—in theory at least. The ETF does not aim to outperform. The ETF uses active management to duplicate the performance of a selected benchmark index. The ETF has much greater flexibility than the methods mandated in managed and mutual funds.

It sounds complicated, and it is. The bottom line is that when we trade ETFs we are playing in somebody else's backyard and in their sandpit. They use particular rules, and if we do not like them then our only choice is to stop playing.

In general, all of these cautions are aspects of the increase in tracking error between the ETF and the underlying index. This offers a range of new trading opportunities.

It also changes the way the ETF is analysed and incorporated into a hybrid portfolio structure. Traders must be alert for behavioural distortion in the ETF. The ETF tracking errors may dilute ETF portfolio advantages.

The ETF cannot be traded as a substitute for the index. Analysis of the index cannot be smoothly transferred to the analysis of the ETF. The most important conclusion is that traders must remember they are trading the ETF and not the index. With this in mind, the ETF can deliver the alpha returns discussed in the first part of this chapter.

The world is a difficult and diverse market universe. ETFs give us the protection of local regulation in a global environment but this does not deliver global understanding. Understanding the behaviour of the market as a primary foundation for trading the market becomes much more important. In the next chapter we look at how this applies in a real-time test environment that challenges preconceptions of the basis of market pricing and provides a method for trading global markets with confidence.

Chapter 32

Global trading and analysis

With contributing author Chen Jing, Chief Representative, Guppytraders, China

Does technical analysis and charting work? It may seem a little late to pose this question in the penultimate chapter but the internationalisation of markets makes the question more relevant. When we trade our home market we always apply a mixture of technical and charting analysis and fundamental analysis. In our home market there is no escaping the influence of local knowledge, news and experience. It provides a background to our selection of stocks from the stock pool and the way we manage the trade, so we always trade at least one remove from the application of pure technical analysis of markets. The internationalisation of markets demands we understand international trading and universal methods of analysis suitable for diverse markets.

When German manufacturer Daimler-Benz took over the US car maker Chrysler in 1998 it believed it was getting a profitable company. And it was, according to one set of accounting methods. Unfortunately it was not a profitable company according to the other set of accounting methods. Beyond the basics of broad fundamentals the analysis models quickly broke down. The same breakdown appears when we trade today's international markets, so we need solid methods to protect us against differences in regulatory and reporting standards.

When we trade international markets, and particularly Chinese markets, we are forced to apply pure technical analysis because we cannot understand the background noise of the market. We have no access to immediate news we can quickly read or understand. Our trading analysis and decisions are based on pure price behaviour, which is a reflection of crowd psychology and behaviour. If we try to force the market into our accustomed paradigms then we make critical errors because we stop listening to the behaviour of market participants.

Paradoxically, trading international markets with pure technical and charting analysis improves the trading of our home markets because it sharpens our ability to observe, evaluate and listen to what price action is revealing about human behaviour and motivation. Trading international markets adds additional confirmation of the effectiveness, validity and profitability of the methods we have covered in previous chapters.

The growth of China demands we understand the differences between China markets and market analysis and the methods with which we are accustomed. Starting in 2004 I have provided weekly China market analysis for the Chinese publications *Shanghai Security News* and *Hong Zhou Kan* weekly magazine. We have developed an understanding of the China market and the way technical analysis is applied to overcome the difficulties posed by language and cultural differences. We look at specific solutions and methods for China later in the chapter but we start with an overview of the issues involved in trading international markets.

Layers of risk

Trading international markets carries several layers of risk not found when we trade our home market. These risks are not barriers to trading international markets. They are factors we need to consider so we can develop trading approaches that hand the advantage back to us.

The risks include:

- language risk
- home ground advantage
- regulation risk
- time risk
- currency risk
- solutions.

Language risk

When we choose to trade in foreign markets we are nervous about our foreign exposure, in part because we cannot get the daily newspaper, or find out more about a company, its activity and prospects. The problems persist even if we decide to trade an index rather than a stock—a country rather than a company. How much do we really know about the US, France or Singapore? How much of our opinion is ill-informed, gathered second hand and based on untested assumptions? When we use technical analysis methods these questions are not relevant because the action of price and market behaviour provides the necessary answers.

Home ground advantage

Just because we use Microsoft products does not mean we understand Microsoft as a company in the same way as US traders. They have access to a wider range of information as part of their regular news background. US traders have a home ground advantage with a finer appreciation of the impact of news, the importance of events and the likely behaviour of their home markets.

As much as we may be attracted to top-performing overseas companies, the reality is that we are unlikely to know as much about them as traders who live in the same country. Most of our usual trading decisions are influenced by what we hear, what we know and what we think about a company. Charting and technical analysis provides a valid solution because it uses the objectivity of price as the basis for analysis.

Regulation risk

What looks and sounds the same as a situation in Australia may have quite different consequences in a foreign market. The difference between company bankruptcy in Singapore or Hong Kong and Chapter 11 protection in the US is an example.

Regulatory risk comes in two forms. The first is found in the mechanics of the market. Many markets trade in a single trading session without a lunch break in the middle. In other markets, such as China and Singapore, the trading day is divided into a morning and afternoon session. In the US, some markets have extended after-hours trading. Although we see a single price candle summarising price activity for the day, there can be significant differences between the morning and afternoon trading sessions.

Markets apply a variety of measures to control volatility. These include limit-up or limit-down restrictions similar to those applied in US futures exchanges. Trading in stocks may be halted temporarily after exceptional intraday volatility, as in the US. Some markets do not apply volatility limits, and stocks will regularly climb or fall by 30% or more in a day of trading.

The second layer of regulatory risk is found in the structure of market regulations. Disclosure and reporting standards vary dramatically. European accounting standards are different from US accounting standards, and both are different from Chinese standards. Types of trading disclosure acceptable in one country are unacceptable in another. Many countries restrict trading to 'lots' or 'parcels' rather than a user-selected number of shares, and this alters the interpretation of the volume display and the ability to manage risk. Some markets, such as the UK, use a mixture of order-driven and quote-driven markets.

In Australia we work with an order-driven market in shares. The range of buy and sell — of bid and ask — figures is set by the orders delivered to the brokers and the central order book foundation of the market. The market of many individual buyers and sellers — you and me — decides what prices are being offered and the spread between the bid and the ask.

In a quote-driven market, the range of buy and sell — of bid and ask — figures is set by a third party. This is a registered market maker — called a registered trader in the options market. The market maker decides the prices at which *he* is prepared to buy and sell, and as a professional trader he expects to make money out of this. The spread between the bid and ask is sometimes very large. In a busy market the spreads are narrower, but rarely so narrow that the professional market maker fails to make a profit.

Market theory suggests the market always efficiently matches the buy and sell orders and that any mismatches — any inefficiencies — will be quickly spotted by traders and ironed out. This is very true in a quote-driven market where the professional traders play full time. It is less true with an order-driven market which more accurately reflects the opinion of all market participants from the professionals to the mums and dads. There is good room for market inefficiencies to exist between the parent stock and the warrant because these are both order-driven markets.

Time risk

This is the deep sinking feeling in the pit of your stomach when you wake up in the morning, switch on the computer and realise your open position in Boeing Airplane Company has gapped down after bad news was released at noon, New York time.

This risk is more than just the risk associated with different time zones. Unless we want to remain awake every night watching open positions in the US or the UK, we need a way to protect our open trades.

Figure 32.1: chart patterns in Spanish index

Traders who want to participate in nearby time zones, such as Korea, Japan, Hong Kong or Singapore, reduce the time risk because they plan to be awake when these markets are open.

The key advantage of international trading comes with the ability to transfer our existing trading skills into a field of wider opportunity. The specific risks created by international trading are most effectively overcome with the application of technical and chart analysis. These analysis methods are applied to any chart, as shown in figure 32.1 with the Spanish IBEX index. The same trend line and support and resistance analysis we apply to stocks in our home market are applied to a chart of any stock or index in the world. Head and shoulder chart patterns appear and retain their validity, operating in the same way in all markets.

Currency risk

Following the Global Financial Crisis the market has been dominated by currency volatility. This has an impact on all currencies as they become cheaper or more expensive in relation to the US dollar. If you are trading very large amounts of capital this currency risk is hedged using currency market trading. Smaller traders find this more difficult to achieve. An effective solution is to use contract for difference currency trading to compensate for changes in the currency relationship.

If the currency moves against you then the return from overseas investments will diminish. A 10% return on paper may be reduced to 3% if there is an adverse currency movement. Protection against this comes from better selection of overseas opportunities and this requires better understanding of the trend. Currency risk is also reduced by limiting the length of each international trade to a few days or weeks.

Solutions

I trade many international markets. I find the effective solution for trading foreign markets is delivered to those who use the technical and charting analysis methods discussed in previous chapters. These differences focus on the nature of price activity and the characteristics of the trend. Rather than understanding the fundamental dynamics of a company, these traders want to understand the price dynamics.

Additionally, for those of us who do not speak Swedish, French, Spanish, Italian or Chinese the chart display overcomes these language barriers. A price trend, or chart pattern, is the same on any chart or in any country. The foundation of this style of international trading is the recognition of common types of technical opportunity. This may be as simple as locating a 10- and 30-day moving average crossover in the Swedish market. Few traders are comfortable with this entirely technical approach, but in trading markets where we do not have a home ground advantage the technical approach plays a much larger role in trade selection and management.

Figure 32.2: strong uptrend

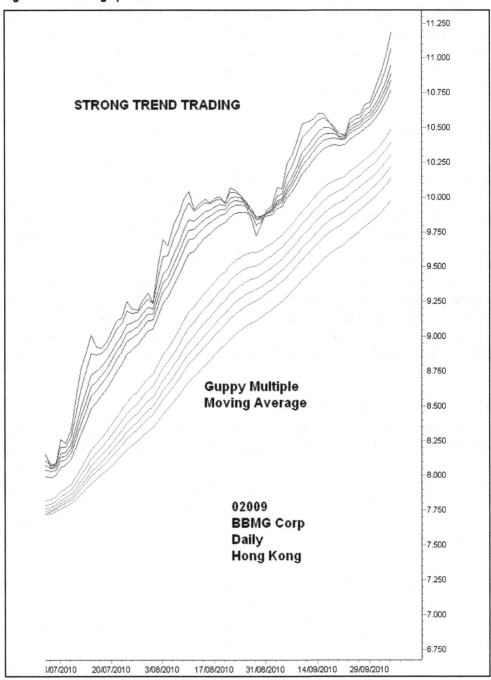

If we need to sleep and trade then there are two primary technical approaches available. The first is to locate and analyse a strong established trend with a low probability of sudden collapse, as shown in figure 32.2. The key selection feature is the nature and character of the trend. My preference is to apply Guppy Multiple Moving Average analysis, because this gives confidence in the nature of the trend strength. The geographical location of the market which includes a stock with this type of stable trend is less important than the opportunity offered by this type of trend. If you can find it and see it, then you can trade it.

Other methods include a simple trend line, Darvas-style trend trading and an established history of moving average reliability.

This is very different from having an open trend trade position in our home market. During the day we can easily choose to monitor the trade. We can react to new information or a news report and verify the impact on the trade. At night we sleep soundly because there is no trading in the stock. In contrast, a UK or US stock trades while we sleep, so we need to have much more confidence in the stability and continuity of the trend.

The second technical method is chart pattern trading, shown in figure 32.3. This method does not sit comfortably with all traders. Pattern recognition is a visual skill, and it provides an advantage in international trading if you have this skill. Chart pattern trading provides an excellent way of trading where we do not have home ground or time zone advantage. We search for high-probability patterns, such as bullish flags and triangles. These are precision patterns, because they are accurately defined according to tight rules and come with a high probability of success once the pattern develops. Their key advantage in international trading is the way the patterns provide exact stop loss prices and exact price projection targets.

The point where price drops below the lower edge of a chart pattern has an exact value. This is incorporated into a guaranteed stop loss order. The projected price target has an exact value, and the sell order is placed in advance. The guaranteed stop loss provides insurance and the chart pattern establishes an automatic profit target. It is easy to sleep well while the market trades.

These types of strategies treat the menu of foreign market listings as an extension of the trading search based on technical criteria. We use end-of-day price data collected by NextView and JustData from Singapore, Malaysia, Hong Kong, Korea and Thailand. It is subjected to the same technical analysis searches we apply to our home market data. We select the best opportunity irrespective of geographical location. When traders learn to use technical analysis methods we speak a common language that applies to all markets—even when it's in Chinese.

Figure 32.3: chart pattern trading

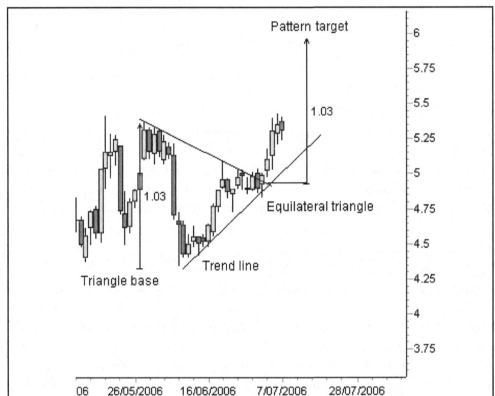

China trading and psychology

A common photograph in the Western financial media shows Chinese traders in front of a price screen where the prices are shown in red. The story with the picture describes this as disappointed Chinese investors watching the market fall. This is always an amusing picture because it shows many Western analysts do not understand the basic fundamentals of this foreign market. In Western markets red means a falling price. In China markets red shows a rising price. It's a simple mistake, but it is a good example of the unexpected difficulty in trading international markets and of what happens when we force our analysis paradigms into areas where they are not relevant.

When we trade international markets from China we must be aware of these differences and many others. The most significant danger comes when we apply Western analysis techniques to Chinese stocks. The difference is seen when we examine the trading characteristics of co-listed stocks in Hong Kong and Shanghai. This examination also confirms the central foundation of the trading and analysis approaches in this book — prices are set by market behaviour and not by fundamentals or concepts of fair value. Technical analysis provides a profitable solution to global trading and managing the risk of global trading.

These analysis notes were written with my colleague Chen Jing. She is the Guppytraders Chief Representative Officer in China, chief editor of *Global Technical Analysis* monthly and executive editor of *Red-K-Line* weekly. Together we researched these market relationships.

A study of the China and Hong Kong markets with a parallel listing of China-based companies confirms psychological trading behaviour has a much greater role to play in correct market pricing. It confirms the market price is the rational and valid price and acknowledges an emotional component in pricing. This confirms the role technical analysis has in understanding market behaviour and making sound trading and investment decisions.

The variety and differences in trend behaviour in these parallel listed stocks challenge many foundation assumptions about the relationship between price, value, fair pricing and the extent of the role of emotional behaviour in setting enduring price relationships.

Many traders believe financial markets are a mental fabrication where the price of a traded stock is driven primarily by the emotions and behaviour of participants. These traders make profits by understanding the psychology of the market and using charting and technical analysis methods to identify points of trend change or trend continuation. These are the methods we explored in previous chapters.

Many investors believe the market is about fundamental value based on the real business and performance of the company. When the traded price moves above or below this 'true' value they often lament the distortions introduced by market emotions and overreactions. They view the market as rational or irrational, forgetting that even the most excited person believes she is making a rational decision to buy. Their investment technique often rests on locating companies trading below their true value on the assumption the market price will eventually lift to match and reflect the true value.

Each of these belief systems has developed successful trading and investing strategies, and mythology. Traders who use technical analysis and charting methods have become accustomed to sustained criticism from the fundamentalists. It is difficult to respond to some of these criticisms because it is difficult to isolate the psychological component in price discovery, or to isolate and show how pricing is largely driven by behavioural and emotional factors.

Our involvement with China markets has provided a unique opportunity to explore these differences in a practical way rather than within the confines of economic or theoretical modelling.

Psychology plays a greater role in pricing than fundamental analysis suggests and this unique parallel market provides strong evidence of the impact. Rather than suggesting that emotion somehow distorts the 'truth' of market fundamentals, our experience confirms market pricing is dominated by emotional reactions. Trading success rests upon recognising the patterns of emotional behaviour and trend behaviour. Except in a very broad sense, market pricing does not rest on fundamentals.

The essential assumption in this comparative analysis is that these parallel listed stocks are essentially the same on a fundamental basis. The differences in trend behaviour are a result of different perceptions of risk. In simplistic terms, the risk profile adopted by Chinese investors and traders in relation to China Merchant Bank is different from the risk profile perspective adopted by traders and investors outside of China when they trade China Merchant Bank. In the parallel listed market, we have two quite distinct market groups so we more clearly see the impact of market psychology and market behaviour. We have a greater opportunity to separate the impact of the fundamentals from the impact of psychological behaviour and its relationship with price discovery.

The differences in trend and price behaviour are not the result of differences in fundamentals. They cannot be explained away by glib references to currency differences between the Chinese yuan and the Hong Kong dollar. They are, to a significant extent, the result of different perceptions of risk. These differences are the most significant component of pricing, price behaviour and trend behaviour in traded stocks. The market is not primarily a mechanism for matching fundamentals with price. It is a mechanism that reflects the level of emotional behaviour in response to different perceptions of risk.

The financial market rarely provides a real-time laboratory where competing approaches can be compared. Trading in several China-based stocks is the exception. The mainland China market is a closed market. It is essentially unavailable for trading by foreigners. We call this the China market. There are a small group of Chinese companies which are parallel listed and traded both in mainland China and outside of China. This is an international market. The companies traded across these parallel markets are unique.

The companies in both markets are Chinese companies, sometimes with international operations. Trading and investing is always in the mother company, irrespective of whether the trade takes place in the China or the international market.

The Chinese company Jiangxi Copper is our starting example and it illustrates all the conditions of this real-time laboratory investigation. Jiangxi Copper is listed in Shanghai and also parallel listed in Hong Kong. The fundamentals of the company are the same inside China as they are outside of China. The company remains the same, but it is listed in two separate locations. As a copper miner both listings react to the same movements in copper price.

Jiangxi Copper shares are not fungible. Jiangxi Copper shares purchased in Hong Kong cannot be swapped or exchanged for Jiangxi Copper shares purchased in Shanghai. This means there is no arbitrage mechanism available to bring Jiangxi Copper prices in Shanghai into agreement with Jiangxi Copper prices in Hong Kong.

In effect these are two completely separate, parallel and closed markets. Foreigners are unable to trade Jiangxi Copper shares in Shanghai. Mainland Chinese are unable to trade Jiangxi Copper shares in Hong Kong. There is a China market and an international market.

If market behaviour and pricing are closely related to fundamental analysis then we would expect to see a similarity in trend behaviour in the price activity of 600362 Jiangxi Copper in Shanghai and 0358 Jiangxi Copper in Hong Kong. This similarity is irrespective of any currency differences because the single company is reacting in separate locations to a single external movement in the price of copper.

When we compare Jiangxi Copper China with Jiangxi Copper Hong Kong we see a substantial difference in the behaviour of price. There are substantial differences in the behavioural characteristics of trends and entirely different trading opportunities. We use the same period of time, and compare the two charts independently from a technical perspective. We use the same analysis methods and examine the chart from three perspectives:

- the first perspective is Guppy Multiple Moving Average (GMMA) trend analysis
- the second perspective is trend line analysis. We assess the compatibility of price behaviour with trend line analysis
- the third perspective is chart pattern analysis.

If fundamental analysis approaches are correct then we would expect to see close similarities and high correlation in trending behaviour between the China-listed stock and the internationally listed stock.

GMMA trend analysis: Jiangxi Copper

The key feature is the strength and stability of the trend, and this is shown by GMMA analysis applied to Jiangxi Copper in figure 32.4. The long-term group of GMMA averages is well separated from 2007 February through to 2007 June. The Chinese market sell-off which developed at the end of February 2007 is a small dip in the short-term trend and has essentially no impact on the long-term trend. The long-term group does not compress. This suggests investors are coming into the market as buyers when the price drops. They see this as temporary price weakness rather than trend weakness.

The trend develops weakness in July. The long-term group compresses and turns downwards. The short-term group of averages confirms trend weakness with a significant separation from the long-term group.

The rebound that developed from the end of July through September is strong and a well-supported trend. The long-term group of GMMA averages separates quickly and confirms trend strength.

The key characteristics of this trend are its solidarity and strength, and the relatively low level of trading activity. The short-term group of averages shows a limited degree of compression and expansion. Traders buy and hold onto the stock for extended periods. The exception is the primary sell-off in June. This reaches its lowest on 19 July.

In this comparative analysis we are not concerned with the potential reasons for the June sell-off and the July rebound. However, we would expect to see this pattern of trend behaviour repeated in the Hong Kong–listed Jiangxi Copper chart. Instead we see a very different behaviour.

The sell-off in Hong Kong–listed Jiangxi Copper in figure 32.5 is sharper and more pronounced. The short-term group dips well below the long-term group before developing a rebound rally. The China listing shows trend weakness while the Hong Kong listing indicates a potential trend change.

Most importantly the period of maximum weakness in Hong Kong occurs on 17 August. This is nearly a month after the maximum weakness in Shanghai. Clearly the Jiangxi Copper Hong Kong listing is reacting to different emotional events from the Shanghai listing. This is the same company, exposed to the same movements in commodity prices, but traded in two distinct parallel markets. Each market is reacting to its own psychological, rather than fundamental, imperatives.

Figure 32.4: GMMA trend analysis—Jiangxi Copper China listing

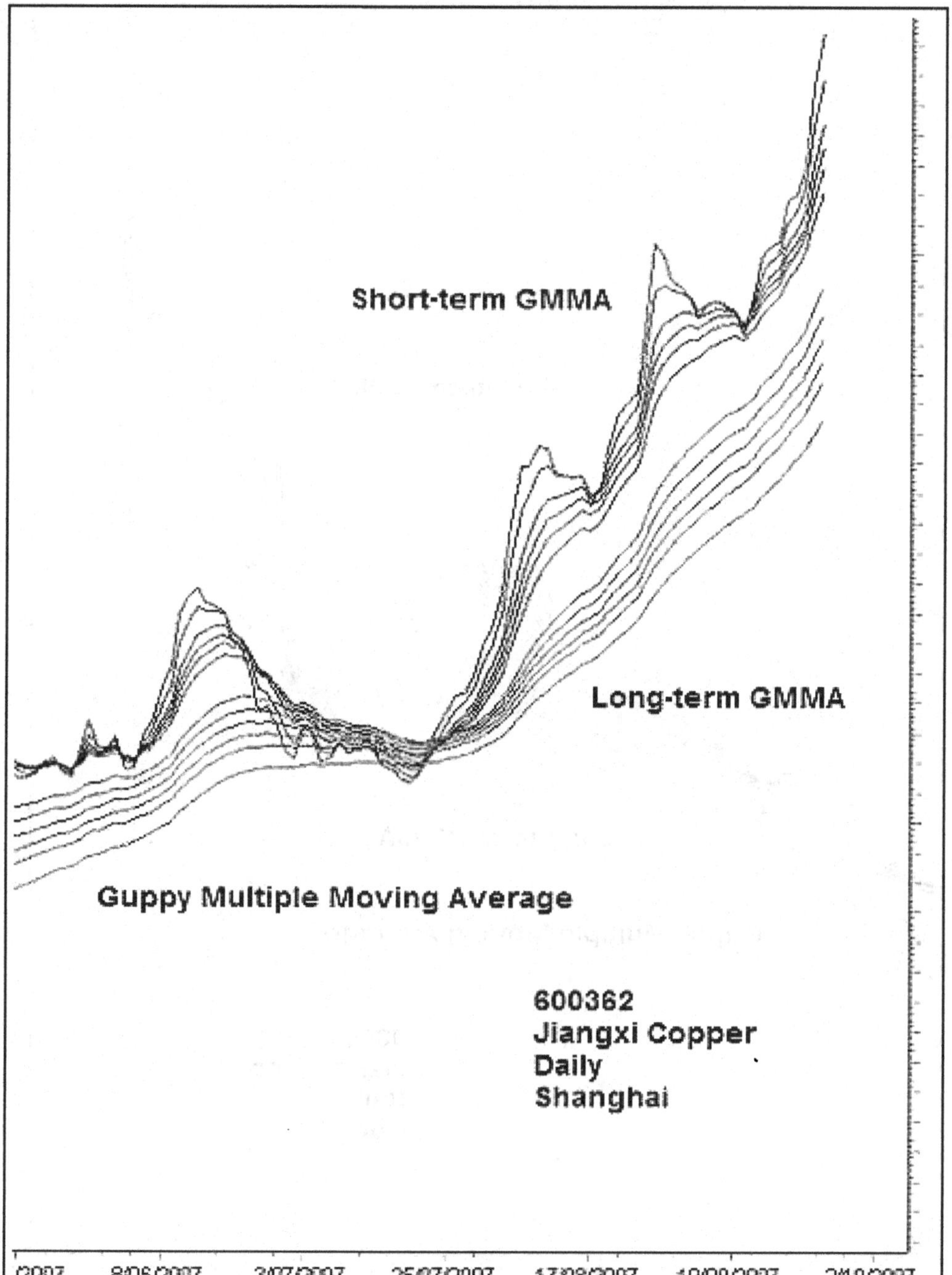

Short-term GMMA

Long-term GMMA

Guppy Multiple Moving Average

600362
Jiangxi Copper
Daily
Shanghai

/2007   8/06/2007   3/07/2007   25/07/2007   17/08/2007   10/09/2007   2/10/2007

Figure 32.5: GMMA trend analysis—Jiangxi Copper Hong Kong listing

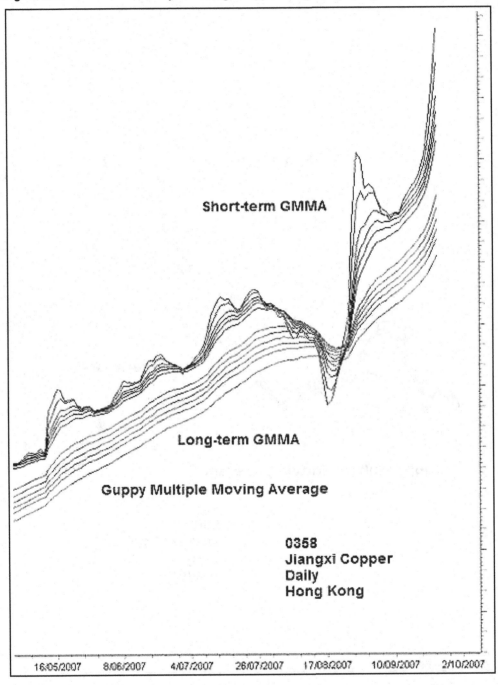

The Hong Kong Jiangxi Copper listing shows a strong and stable trend but with a slightly higher level of trading activity. The short-term group of averages shows a greater degree of compression and expansion.

When we compare the period from late 2006 and into February 2007 we observe two important differences. The first is the general downtrend and recovery towards the end of 2006 in the Hong Kong listing. The Shanghai listing shows a steady rise starting in November 2006. The difference in the nature and character of the trends is highlighted at the end of February. This is the China market sell-off after the end of Chinese New Year. It was widely credited with causing the sell-off in the DOW in February 2007.

The Hong Kong charts show a sudden and substantial dip at the end of February. The short-term group of averages dips into the long-term group. The Shanghai chart shows a small dip. The short-term GMMA does not touch the long-term group. The trend is not threatened.

What is more important is to note that the behaviour and character of the trend is significantly different even though the stock being traded is the same company. The difference in trending behaviour reflects differences in crowd psychology rather than differences in the fundamentals.

Pattern trading: Jiangxi Copper

Chart patterns are a reflection of trading psychology and provide a range of high-probability outcomes. The patterns develop in response to traders' perceptions of opportunity. Although the link with fundamental developments may be more tenuous, we would still expect to see a similar type of pattern development in this parallel listed stock. A range of different patterns confirms the importance of psychology in determining market pricing.

The Shanghai-listed Jiangxi Copper shows a complex level of trend behaviour and pattern development in figure 32.6. Trend line B defines the trend break starting in March 2007. This support line is broken in May 2007, and it provides a resistance point for the rally peak in June 2007.

Trend line A is a historical convenience. The two starting points in January and February 2007 are not confirmed until July 2007. This trend line is easy to plot retrospectively, but in real time it is more difficult.

Trend line C is a much more definite trend line. Projected from the start point in July 2007 it can be used to manage a trend entry in August and early September.

However, it is fair to conclude that trend line analysis is not the most effective way to define the trending behaviour of Shanghai-listed Jiangxi Copper. Shorter term trading opportunities are not well defined with this method for the China-listed stock.

Figure 32.6: pattern trading—Jiangxi Copper China listing

The China chart does contain two additional chart pattern features. The first is the flag pattern in August 2007. The flagpole measurement starts with the larger than usual range days starting 30 July. The six-day rise creates a flagpole. The subsequent bullish flag develops over eight days. This is a classic bullish flag and a classic high-probability breakout. Prices move quickly to the target at 45.00 before retreating.

The Shanghai chart also shows a second pattern. This is a distinctive China pattern we call a China cup. This is a reversal pattern. It occurs after a sharp sell-off after a fast-rising trend. The sell-off generally creates a rounding bottom over a 5- to 15-day period. The cup does not usually develop a handle. The usual target measurement methods are not applied. This is a trend continuation pattern.

The China-listed Jiangxi Copper shows a variety of chart patterns and it is, to a significant extent, incompatible with trend line analysis. The Hong Kong listing has quite different characteristics.

The pattern of trend behaviour in figure 32.7 is very different. The primary downtrend shown with trend line A was decisively broken in January 2007. The new uptrend line B was more strongly confirmed by the retreat and rally in March and then again in April. This was only possible to plot with certainty in April because the Chinese New Year dip carried price activity below the trend line. However, once plotted, trend line B provides a reliable rebound support level as the long-term rising trend developed. This is a clear trend during the period when the China-listed stock experienced trading activity that makes trend line definition unreliable.

The close below trend line B in August was a clear end-of-trend signal.

The flag pattern development in August on the China-listing chart is not reflected in the Hong Kong chart. The same August period in Hong Kong sees a dramatic and rapid retreat in prices followed by a rapid rebound. In this period the difference in the behaviour of these two markets is extreme.

In China, August includes a sharp flagpole rally, a flag pattern and a flag pattern breakout. In August in Hong Kong, we see the end of a long-term trend and a volatile price dip followed by a very sharp rise.

The sharp rise is followed by an apparently similar China cup pattern, but there are important differences. The late August rally carries prices to an unsustainable peak at 23.50. It is followed by a close at 20.35. This triggers a substantial fall and a sharp rise. The pattern of the price rise on the right side of this cup is exceptionally fast. This is a pure momentum trend. In contrast, the same period in the China listing shows less momentum, and some consolidation within the rise. The two patterns look similar, but they require different trading methods to protect profits.

Figure 32.7: pattern trading—Jiangxi Copper Hong Kong listing

Listen to the chart

China-listed Jiangxi Copper *could* be an entirely different company from the Hong Kong–listed Jiangxi Copper. Despite the common fundamental performance base, there is very little similarity in these two charts.

The nature and character of the trend is very different between the Shanghai-listed Jiangxi Copper and the Hong Kong–listed Jiangxi Copper. The underlying company, Jiangxi Copper, is unchanged and fundamental analysis would suggest the core trends should be essentially similar after discounting the impact of currency fluctuations.

The difference in GMMA analysis confirms a significant difference in the way the two groups of traders view the stock. As Jiangxi Copper is a single parallel-listed company we can reasonably expect this fundamental information will become available to all market participants at around the same time. We could also expect the market reaction to the same event—domestic or external moves in the copper price—would be similar in both the China and the international market. This would be true if the basics of fundamental analysis hold true.

Instead we find the patterns in Jiangxi Copper China and Jiangxi Copper Hong Kong are not correlated in time, diversity or duration. Jiangxi Copper China has different chart patterns from Jiangxi Copper Hong Kong. They appear at different dates, and persist for different lengths of time.

Figure 32.8: trend divergence in China Unicom

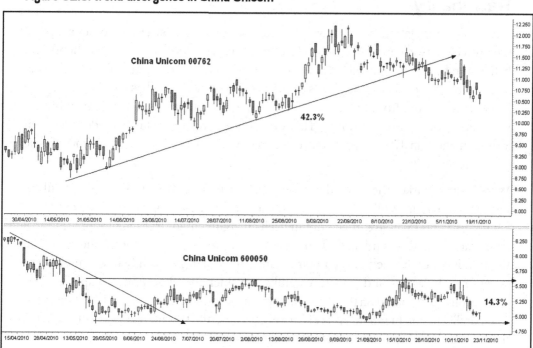

These differences confirm that the development of price behaviour is primarily a result of psychological factors rather than fundamental factors. The aggregated activity of China traders shows a different behavioural pattern to the aggregated activity of traders in the international market. Same company, different independent parallel markets and different results. Profitable success comes from using tools that identify the nature of trending behaviour rather than using analysis methods that are designed to establish a link between price behaviour and changes in company fundamentals.

We have used Jiangxi Copper as the primary example. A similar trend divergence developed in the telecom company China Unicom in 2010, shown in figure 32.8. The Shanghai listing spent six months moving sideways with a maximum return of 14.3%. The Hong Kong listing for the same company rose 42.3% over the same period in a strong and consistent trend. These trend divergences are frequent and continue for extended periods. The same divergence between the trending and trading behaviour of dual-listed China stocks in the China market and the international market is consistently observed and confirms the importance of technical analysis.

Rationality

This lack of correlation in these two markets also infers an answer to another aspect of the division between fundamental and technical analysis. Modern economic theory and behavioural financial modelling talk of the difference between rational and irrational behaviour. Rational behaviour leads to pricing that closely matches the theoretical fair value price derived from fundamental analysis. Pricing that is below or above this fair value is, by definition, irrational. The idea of 'irrational exuberance' is derived from a fundamental analytical approach to markets which in turn is derived from classic economic modelling.

Within each market the price discovered by the market mechanism is the result of rational behaviour. While we might want to argue the speed of increase in the mainland China market is excessive, this is not in itself an argument for irrationality, or 'irrational exuberance'. As the trend analysis has shown, the behaviour, character and nature of the trends for each stock in each market are quite different. Each behavioural pattern is rational. Investors and traders carefully consider the allocation of capital. Their evaluation of risk, based on the same fundamentals, is different within different markets. The parallel listing highlights this effectively because the two markets—China and the international market—are monetarily and regulatorily distinct and independent. They are united only by the common fundamentals of the company being traded.

This unique real-time laboratory provides an opportunity to test the idea of rational and irrational. While cynics might suggest the market for China stocks is irrational, it is more appropriate to regard both markets as potentially a rational response to the fundamental information available.

The differences in the trending and trading price behaviour in these parallel-listed stock cannot be adequately explained from a fundamental perspective. The wide variation in specific trend behaviours—to the extent where you may believe these are two different stocks—is not effectively accounted for by using fundamental analysis.

The market is founded on fundamentals, but price discovery and trending behaviour are primarily set by the emotions and behaviour of participants. This is emotional behaviour that is reflected in a rational decision-making process. People do not spend thousands of dollars in a fit of irrationality. Buying and selling is a rational decision filtered through a prism of emotion. The degree of emotion, aggregated in trading activity, defines the nature and character of the trend. This is the most significant and valid factor in price discovery. The differences in trending behaviour for the same company listed in two independent parallel markets confirms the importance of emotion and psychology in market price discovery. The differences confirm this is not a transient impact.

Trading China markets

How can traders and investors take direct advantage of this strategic market development in China when foreigners are unable to trade Shanghai and Shenzhen A-listed shares? There are three methods, and they start with the Hong Kong–listed iShares China ETF over the CSI 300 index. This gives the most direct exposure to the China market because the constituents of the ETF are only Shanghai A-share listings. As the Shanghai CSI goes so too does the ETF. It provides unleveraged and direct exposure to the China market for traders and investors.

The second method also uses China ETFs. Some China ETFs are a mixture of mainland shares and H shares, or red chips. These are Chinese companies listed outside of China, or Hong Kong–based companies with extensive business in China. These ETFs and funds do provide access to China market growth, but the access is diluted by the inclusion of Western-based and traded companies.

A third method is to trade a QFII (Qualified Foreign Institutional Investor) fund, such as Morgan Stanley China A which has direct access to mainland stocks and which has a good history of closely matching the index performance. QFII funds show a wide variety of performance as a result of the reliance on the selection of companies. One Australian QFII fund has lost 46% during the time the Shanghai Index retreated 18%. Traders protect themselves against this type of loss by learning to speak the common language of the markets.

Speak the market language

Markets have changed in many ways, but at their foundation they remain the same. Markets are driven by human emotion, and the trading methods we have discussed are designed to track these emotional behaviours. Traders' perceptions of the market create the current price and value. The differences between co-listed stocks in China and Hong Kong are an excellent example of the dominance of behavioural pricing in markets and the importance of technical analysis in developing trading solutions for domestic stocks and for stocks we trade internationally.

Improvements in internet speeds and the flow of information mean we get news more quickly and act more quickly. The trading and investment world is larger and closer than it ever has been, and it moves closer to our home markets every year. It cannot be ignored. Fortunately the language of technical analysis and charting is universal and it is a useful method for understanding the behaviour of price.

It is our responsibility to prise the opportunities from our home and global markets. The techniques and methods discussed in this book will continue to serve us well in developing market conditions.

Chapter 33

The A380 approach to Red Cliff

A giant, sophisticated A380 Airbus operated by Qantas Airlines suffered a catastrophic engine failure shortly after take-off from Singapore in late 2010. The commanding pilot and his crew successfully managed the crisis and landed the crippled aeroplane at Singapore's Changi airport. Singapore emergency services prevented a successful landing from turning into a disaster by smothering one of the remaining engines in foam — the only way to shut down the engine — and preventing leaking fuel from igniting on contact with red-hot brakes.

The A380 relies on complex computer systems and back-up systems to keep more than 550 tonnes of aircraft in the sky. When the engine exploded, the cockpit — according to captain Richard de Crespigny — was ablaze with 54 system failure alerts or warnings of impending failures. The manual tells pilots to fix the faults to restore stability. His decision was to ignore these failure signals because there were so many and concentrate on what was working. In dramatically changed circumstances his attention shifted, not to repair, but to working effectively with the surviving systems. Then de Crespigny called on the best support crews he could find, in this case on the ground with Changi's emergency services, and worked with them to develop a survivable solution.

The A380 continues to fly safely. Certain components in the engine systems have been modified. New operating guidelines were developed, and the design and operating specifications were adjusted.

The catastrophic failure of the economic system in 2008 narrowly avoided a crash landing but the post-crisis reviews are lengthy. Unlike the A380 incident reviews, the solutions to the Global Financial Crisis will inevitably bring with them new opportunities for failure and success. It's a new operating environment.

The management of the A380 crisis provides valuable insights into the way we can manage our portfolio of trades during and after an economic crisis. Most trades fly smoothly, but there are occasions when a trade suffers catastrophic failure. There are rare times when the economic system suffers catastrophic failure, and if it's in your lifetime you need to know how to focus on what is working, rather than trying to fix the old methods that are not working.

This approach reflects the essential principals in this book. The economic crisis caught most people unawares and, more disastrously, unprepared. Unlike Captain de Crespigny and his crew, most traders and investors do not practise preparations for emergencies. When the emergency develops they hold onto their seats, gripping portfolios tightly in fear, and keep on doing the same things in the hope it will all work out. A comparatively safe landing convinces them there is no need to change and so they learn little from the experience.

In the previous chapters I have tried to keep the focus on what works and what continues to work, rather than on what has failed. Much of what worked was already an essential part of pre-crisis planning. Understanding and applying risk control is as boring and as repetitive as the endless emergency landing drills practised by airline pilots and Changi emergency crews. The pay-off comes when a crisis does develop: the reactions are automatic and reflexive.

We cannot anticipate exactly what will happen. We cannot control what will happen. The markets, like the A380, are too big, too complex and too sophisticated to be managed by an individual, no matter how skilled. The only control we have is the control over our reactions to events as they develop. Some events we can reasonably anticipate, so the correct reactions are already codified and well known. Some events are so extraordinary, so unexpected, that survival requires the management of our own reactions so we can identify what continues to work—not what has failed. This is much more complex than the simple instruction 'don't panic' because it requires the suppression of an instinctive reaction and its replacement with careful analysis of changed circumstances.

Preparation is vital, and it's more than deciding which stock to buy. The 14th century Chinese classic *The Romance of the Three Kingdoms* covers a period of political and military turbulence in China's history. This complexity and chaos is emulated in market behaviour, and survival depends on preparation. One of the significant and decisive battles in this period was the battle of Red Cliff. This was popularised in the two-part film of the same name by John Woo. The attacking forces assembled by Generals Zhou Yu and Zhuge Liang are ready to engage Chancellor Cao Cao with fire ships sent across the river. The situation prior to the decisive battle was 'Waiting on the east wind'. The phrase is now used as shorthand for situations where all preparations are complete and the protagonists are just waiting on a final element before the attack is launched and a victory is achieved.

Traders always find themselves waiting on the east wind. Every trade requires planning, careful management and exacting risk calculations, but ultimately success depends on a single factor over which the trader has no control. The market may blow from the east—bringing success—or it may blow from another quarter and bring disaster, unless the trader understands when to act and when to stay his hand. Zhou Yu observes the turtles sunning on the river rocks and knows there is a high probability of an east wind developing. Captain de Crespigny watched the remaining working systems and used these to create a solution. Traders assess the balance of probabilities and align themselves with those with the highest chance of success.

The platform of success rests on four legs. The first is constant planning for failure no matter how successful the current situation. It's a repetitive drill of risk management. Preparing for failure lays the groundwork for success.

The second is informed flexibility. If we cannot understand what is happening we can at least understand what is working and use this to navigate to a successful landing. This ability and willingness to change your mind as necessary is the very essence of trading. The most dangerous thing you can do in the market is become wedded to a losing position. Most times it's a matter of fixing the faults, but like Captain de Crespigny, there are times when we need to recognise it is more important to ignore the faults and work with what remains. This is informed flexibility.

The third recognises we operate in an environment we do not control. Sitting in the cockpit of the A380 provides an illusion of control, but when catastrophic failure in a component occurs the illusion is shattered and we know we need all the help we can get. A bull market provides the same illusion because success comes effortlessly. When the market dives we soon find the difference between those who can fly and those who only know how to read the instrument reports.

The fourth leg comes from waiting for the east wind. Preparation is everything, but it cannot be blindly applied according to the steps in a manual or a 16-week trading course. Success, and survival, comes from knowing when the final component is in place so it becomes the perfect time to act.

The world of opportunity is also a world of turbulence. We may never be called upon to land a stricken A380 but every day we have the responsibility for the safe landing of our trades and our portfolios in constantly changing conditions, which sometimes change catastrophically. Red Cliff preparation and an A380 approach to problem-solving is a successful combination.

Acknowledgements

Chapter 5 contains extracts from an article by Daryl Guppy first published in the Nov./Dec. 2010 issue of *YourTradingEdge* magazine (www.YTEmagazine.com). All rights reserved Your Media Edge Pty Ltd © 2010.

Figures 12.3–12.6 by EzyCharts.

Figures 7.3, 12.3, 12.4, 22.1–22.2 and 22.4–22.9 by MetaStock.

Figures 11.5, 11.6, 11.8, 11.9, 11.12, 23.7–23.9, 28.1–28.5, 29.2 and 29.3 © IT-Finance.com IG Markets.

Figure 13.1 from Omnitrader by Nirvana Systems Inc.

Figures 11.13, 19.13, 22.4–22.9 and 31.3 by Guppytraders Essentials using data from JustData.

Figures 19.2–19.6, 19.10, 19.11, 19.15, 19.16 and 23.9 Microsoft Excel screenshots reproduced by permission from Microsoft.

Chapter 25 contains extracts from the Charting Asia column on CNBCAsia.com.

Chapter 32 contains extracts from 'True Price Value' by Daryl Guppy and Chen Jing, *Technical Analysis of Stocks & Commodities* magazine, Vol. 26, No. 4 (April 2008), Copyright 2008, Technical Analysis, Inc. Used with permission.

Publisher's note

Some of the material in this book has appeared in Daryl's earlier books and articles, as follows:

Chapter 1: Includes extracts from chapter 2, *Share Trading, 10th anniversary edition.*

Chapter 2: Includes extracts from chapter 8, *Share Trading, 10th anniversary edition.*

Chapter 3: Includes extracts from chapter 25, *The 36 Strategies of the Chinese for Financial Traders.*

Chapter 4: Includes extracts from an article originally published in *YourTradingEdge.*

Chapter 5: Includes extracts from chapter 17, *Bear Trading, second edition.*

Chapter 7: Includes extracts from chapter 9, *Trading Tactics.*

Chapter 8: Includes extracts from chapter 10, *The 36 Strategies of the Chinese for Financial Traders.*

Chapter 9: Includes extracts from chapter 12, *Trend Trading.*

Chapter 10: Includes extracts from chapters 13 and 14, *Trend Trading.*

Chapter 12: Includes extracts from chapter 4, *Snapshot Trading.*

Chapter 13: Includes extracts from chapter 30, *Trend Trading.*

Chapter 14: Includes extracts from chapter 31, *Trend Trading.*

Chapter 15: Includes extracts from chapter 6, *Chart Trading.*

Chapter 16: Includes extracts from chapter 7, *Chart Trading.*

Chapter 17: Includes extracts from chapter 1, *Better Trading.*

Chapter 18: Includes extracts from chapter 18, *Trading Tactics.*

Chapter 19: Includes extracts from chapter 6, *Better Trading.*

Chapter 20: Includes extracts from chapter 7, *Better Trading.* An outline of this concept was published in the US magazine *Active Trader* in April 2001.

Chapter 21: Includes extracts from chapter 10, *Share Trading, 10th anniversary edition.*

Chapter 23: Includes extracts from chapter 7, *The 36 Strategies of the Chinese for Financial Traders.*

Chapter 24: Includes extracts from chapter 15, *Trading Tactics* and chapter 21, *The 36 Strategies of the Chinese for Financial Traders*.

Chapter 25: Includes extracts from chapter 13, *The 36 Strategies of the Chinese for Financial Traders*. Short trading notes were originally published in the *Charting Asia* column on CNBCAsia.com.

Chapter 27: Includes extracts from chapter 9, *The 36 Strategies of the Chinese for Financial Traders*.

Chapter 29: Includes extracts from chapter 3, *The 36 Strategies of the Chinese for Financial Traders*.

Chapter 30: Includes extracts from an article first published in *YourTradingEdge*.

Chapter 31: Includes extracts from *The Wiley Trading Guide* and from an article published in *YourTradingEdge*.

Chapter 32: Includes extracts from an article first published in *Technical Analysis of Stocks & Commodities* magazine. An outline of some other concepts in this chapter was published in *YourTradingEdge*.

Index

2% rule 6–7, 32, 121, 130, 221–228, 232–236, 239–240
12-month highs 157, 161
36 strategies of the Chinese 29, 84, 293, 314, 326, 348

aggressive traders 153, 169, 287, 307, 308
Alchemy of Finance, The 12
algorithmic trading 42, 68–69, 117, 137, 326–327, 355
alpha returns 384, 385, 391, 394
anger 45
ask prices 44, 139, 311–325, 409
asymmetric volatility 106
automated trade execution 69
average traders 220–228, 258–263
Average True Range (ATR) x, 117, 235, 278–292
    see also traders Average True Range (ATR)

Bank of America 31, 48, 220
bears 108, 156–157, 164, 241
Bear Stearns xiv, 11, 22, 31, 45, 377, 379

'beating the grass to startle the snake' 326
behavioural finance 17–28
Berkshire Hathaway 9
beta returns 384–385
betting against analysis 33–37
'between the flags' investment 377–380
bid prices 44, 139, 311–325
blue-chip companies 48, 220, 377–380, 388
breakeven line 122–124, 130–134
breakouts 80, 97, 99, 111–112, 147, 150, 155–158, 304, 329, 331, 333–334
    — count back line and 269–275
    — false 96, 102–103, 300
    — support and resistance and 192–196
    — triangles and 206, 208, 211
brokerage 11, 44, 130, 253, 387, 388
brokerage houses 18, 84
    — market education and 40
buffer orders 314–317
Buffettology 9
Buffett, Warren 9–10
Bulletin, The 149–150
bulls 108, 156–157, 164, 241

capital gains 18, 393–394
charting 4, 57–67, 176, 406, 424–426
— eyeballing charts 58–67, 88
— pattern recognition x, 197–215, 298–305, 421–424
China markets 407
— accessing 427
— trading 414–427
Chrysler 406
CNBC SquawkBox ix, 241, 297, 354, 358, 382
company takeovers 346
— taking advantage of 348–353
computer programming xi
conditional entry orders 69
consolidation levels 186–188
contingent orders 241, 245, 327
continuous disclosure 139, 144, 335
contracts for difference (CFDs) xv, 43–44, 126–128, 307–310, 356, 362–363
— overseas markets and 383
count back line (CBL) x, 116, 123–135, 154, 267–277
— advantages of 273–274
— confirmation signal 269
— pivot point low 269–270
— significant price days 268–277
— traders Average True Range and 288–291
'creating something out of nothing' 293
crowd behaviour 17–28, 197–201, 204, 207–208, 212, 214, 371–372
— predicting 22–24
— recognising 21–22, 178–179
— support/resistance levels and 190–191
— taking advantage of 21–22, 24–27, 197–198
cup pattern 302–305, 423
currency markets 59
currency risk 411
cutting losses 43, 47, 225–228

'dagger sheathed in a smile' 83–91
Daimler-Benz 406

dark pool trading 42, 84, 136–152
— examples of 137
— impacts of 138–142
Darvas boxes x, 58, 117, 153–174
— automatic calculation of 164–166
— constructing 161–170
— equal highs and 164–165
— failure of 169–170
— ghost boxes 172–173
— stop loss and 170–171
Darvas trading 153–174
— adaptations to 157–159
— MetaStock and 174
— modern markets and 166–173
— significant price moves and 158
data manipulation 71–74
denial pattern 341–343
derivatives 6, 9, 198, 231, 255, 292, 354, 362–367, 383–405
disbelief in the market 338, 340–341, 345
displaced synchronicity 381
divergence 81, 83–91, 397–398
diversification 380–381
— global 383–387, 394–396
dividend hop strategy 389–394
dividends 9, 18, 389–394
— exchange-traded funds and 386
double bottoms and tops 201–202
Douglas, Mark 51
Dow Jones Index ix, 18, 388
— falls in ix
— Global Financial Crisis and 24–25
— Great Depression and 18
downside targets 83, 88, 90, 185, 206, 210, 329, 343

early warning systems x, 85, 88, 96
endowment effect 372–381
Enron 22, 379
entry signals 35, 58, 169, 287, 288, 365, 395
— discipline and 44
exchange-traded funds (ETFs) 382–405
— capturing 'unavailable' profits 387

—characteristics of 404
—make-up of 387
—market holidays and 399–401
—multi-country strategy 392–396
—strategies for trading 389–394
—time zone arbitrage and 402–403
—tracking errors 397–399
exit signals 47, 123, 125, 133, 278
—discipline and 44
—false 57, 109, 115, 117, 119, 126, 133, 288, 290–291
exponential moving average (EMA) 71–74, 98, 109

fear 12, 17, 19, 27, 30, 59, 199, 229–236, 255–264
—measuring 257–264
financial advisers 18
financial food chain 9
financial institutions xiii, 9, 10–15, 219, 362, 404
financial media 29, 58, 84, 179–184
—share prices and 148–152
flag pattern 331–334
flash trading xi, 42, 68–69, 117, 137, 326
front running 140, 326
frustration 45
fundamental analysis 31, 142, 406, 415–427
fund managers xi, 18, 220, 264, 379
—fees and 22

gaming the market 326–327
General Electric 377
General Motors 31, 377
Global Financial Crisis ix, 24–25, 42, 45, 88, 118, 153, 219, 229–230, 255, 264, 328, 348, 371–372, 383, 403, 411
—lessons from x, 3, 84, 116, 138, 157, 251
—rebound from 83, 115, 194, 371
global interdependence x, 372
gold 362–367
Goldman Sachs 48

Great Depression 18
greed xi, 17, 27, 33, 51, 199, 229
Guppy Multiple Moving Average (GMMA) viii, 22, 92–107, 154, 418–421
—features of 98
—probability and 102–104
—relationships between averages 112–115, 119, 121
—trade selection and 60–67
—trading with 108–115
Guppytraders 60
Guppytraders Essentials 93, 161, 164, 168, 169, 286, 294, 299, 300, 305

head and shoulder pattern 24, 59, 83, 84, 199, 329–330
—divergence in 88–91
—inverted 193–195
heteroskedasticity 105–107
Hong Kong market 415–428
hope 19–20, 215
hope, confidence, certainty 123–124, 130–132, 276–277
How I Made $2 000 000 in the Stock Market 172
hybrid portfolio 384–385, 405

independent traders 220, 401
—advantages for xi, 6–7, 15–16
—compared to institutional traders 10–15
index trading 356–358, 388–394
indicators 105, 121, 153, 208, 275
—complexity of 74, 79
—construction of 69–74, 92
—oscillators 69, 76–82, 85–88
—selecting 81
—testing 82
—trend following 69–82
—types of 69–82
informed trading 4, 136, 143, 335–347
—assumptions about 336–337
—techniques for trading 337–346

insider trading x, 4, 136, 142–148, 336, 346–347
— effectiveness of 143–148
institutional trading 139
— compared to independent trading 10–15
internet
— impact on trading x, 3, 16, 346, 428
— peer support and 14
— rumours and 143
intraday trading 57, 95, 108, 115, 126–130, 132–133
investment advice 39, 45, 175, 251
— market education and 40
investors 93–107, 108, 382, 426
— compared to traders 18–19, 95, 383
— support for 18
Island in the Sun 337–339

Jiangxi Copper 417–426

'kill with a borrowed knife' 363

language risk 408
leading indicators 4, 88
leapfrog orders 313–314, 340
Lehman Brothers 11, 22
leverage 6–7, 11, 106, 307, 362–367
— accelerating returns with 355, 363
Lewis, Michael 10–11, 13
Liar's Poker 10
liquidity 9, 66, 305, 328, 336
— dark pools and 42, 84, 139
losing trades 6, 12, 17, 44, 222, 233
— emotions and 45
— holding on to 31, 231
low-volume exits 314–317

market depth 311–325
— buying pressure 318–321
— mining 318
— selling pressure 321–322

market education 43, 222
— conflicts of interest in 38–41, 380
market makers 198, 326, 327, 399
market participants 197–201
— attitude of xi
— being humble 50
— emotional behaviour of ix, 17–28, 44–45, 229–236, 372–377
— personal trading techniques 6
— psychology of 415–428
— trading size and x, xi, 3–4, 6–7
market regulators 45, 138, 336, 341, 362–363
— derivatives and 362–363
— education and 39
— Global Financial Crisis and 42, 84
— insider trading and 4, 136
— modern markets and xii
markets
— drivers of ix
— efficiency of 138
— inferred activity 93–97
— interdependence of x
— manipulation of 42, 140
— opinion of 48–49
— secrecy and 138–140
— testing 326–334
maximum adverse drawdown 233
maximum position loss 244
MetaStock 71–73, 75, 93, 174
mid-trend entry 112, 115
mining companies 307–310, 337–341, 354–361
— internet boom and 403
misleading information 84, 327
modern markets ix, xii, 3–16, 38–41, 42–54, 57, 109, 158, 160, 166–173, 198, 219, 326, 348, 362
— time in the market and 59
— volatility and 237, 267–268, 295, 358
Modern Portfolio Theory xii
modern tape reading x, 311–325

momentum days 59–60
— trade selection and 65
momentum minute 128–130, 132
momentum trading 59, 294–296, 355
money management 6, 33, 220–228,
232–254
— importance of 48
money you can 'afford to lose' 30–31, 231
moving average convergence divergence
(MACD) 74–76
moving averages 71–76, 109–110
— combinations of 97
— construction of 71
— crossovers in 95–97
— relationships between 74
see also Guppy Multiple Moving
Average (GMMA)
mutual funds 9, 10, 15, 403–405

net asset value (NAV) 403–404
news event trading x, 12–13, 59, 293,
307–310, 354–361
— assessing the news 358
— volatility and 361
'no risk' boss 11–12
novice traders 6, 9, 28, 44–45, 221, 228,
238, 263, 374

'observing the fire from the other side of the
river' 348
Oil Rig Gusher 339–341
opportunity cost 31
order book 138–139, 409
order lines x, 245, 340, 341
— analysing 311–325, 327
— resistance points and 324
overseas markets xv–xvi, 371–381
— analysis of 406–428
— exchange-traded funds and 382–405
— home ground advantage 408
— regulations and 408–409
— risk and 407–414
— time risk and 409–411

paper profits 33
Parabolic SAR 309–310
parabolic trend lines x, 293–310, 365
— advantages and disadvantages of 296
— definition of 300
— plotting 298–305
— trade selection and 63–64
— use of 297–298
Paul, Jim 11–12, 14
performance searches 69–82
Pile Driver low 343–346
portfolio management theory 384
position size 10, 48, 232, 235, 239–254,
360, 365
— effect on trading performance 221–228
— theoretical maximum 243
— total planned spend 243
pre-open period 356, 358, 360
price dips 35, 117, 343, 423
price gaps 272, 307–310, 356–361
— dark pools and 142
— overnight 294, 305–307
price spikes 117, 389–400
price volatility 57, 115–117, 153
professional traders xi, 6, 9, 10–15, 28, 238,
376–377, 409
profitable trades 33, 44, 233
profit margins 10–11
protect-profit stop 271, 282
pyramiding into a trade 130–132, 276–277

raffle ticket research project 374–375
readers' dumps and bumps 148–152
regulation risk 408–409
relative strength index (RSI) 78–81
— divergence in 84–88
'replacing superior beams with inferior ones'
29–37
research 31
— access to 10, 15
resistance/support breakout 192–193
Resources Super Profits Tax 307–310
— effect on share prices 355–361

riding winners 46, 47
risk 30, 50–54, 256, 349, 362
—2% rule 6–7, 32, 121, 130, 221–228, 232–236, 239–240
—airbags 237–254
—defining 238
—effect of changes in 224–228
—management of x, xiii–xiv, 219–228, 238–240, 374
—overseas markets and 407–414
—reward and 238, 251–254
—time in the market and 59
—trade size and 48
risk of ruin 233
risk–reward ratio 15, 238, 252–254
Rogers, Jim 10
rogue traders 11
rounding bottom pattern 302–303
Rudd, Kevin 355
rumours 12, 143, 148
'rumourtrage' 143

Salomon Brothers 10
S&P/ASX 200 index 59
—construction of 388
—trading 356–361
saucer pattern 302–303
scaling into a trade 130–132, 276–277
share prices
—dark pools and 142
—dips in 35, 117, 343, 423
—gaps in 272, 307–310, 356–361
—highs and lows in 19–21
—overnight 294, 305–307
—spikes in 117
—volatility in 57, 115, 116–117, 153
—watching 43
short trades 90, 133, 268, 274, 307–310, 326–334, 385
—criticism of 327–328
significant rally highs 176
simple moving average (SMA) 71–74
Soros, George 10, 12

'speeding tickets' 335, 341
spotty price behaviour 66
Standard & Poor's 388
standard deviation 69, 73, 105, 188
stationarity 105
stochastic indicators 77–81
stock pools xii, 57
—building 68–82
stock selection 31, 238, 251, 256, 372–381
—endowment effect and 372–377
—sources for 58
stop losses 32, 123, 220, 230–236, 237–254, 256–264, 282–292, 309
—ability to act on 256–264
—automatic 69, 225
—execution price for 245–248
—intraday 250–251
—probability of success 245–247
—setting 240–251
—theoretical 241–243
—trailing 270–271
—trigger price for 243–245
strategic thinking 29
successful traders 6, 221, 224, 226, 228, 260, 372
support/resistance levels 60, 184–196, 268
—breakouts from 191–196
—change in polarity 185
—crowd behaviour and 190–191
—placement of 185–186, 189–190
—rules for 189–190
—trade selection and 60–65
survivor bias 387, 388

takeover arbitrage 348–353
—calculations for 350–353
technical analysis xiv, xvi, 4, 15, 69, 176, 184, 198, 222, 406
—objectives of 84
technology x, 3, 16, 346, 428
Tech Wreck 42, 143
theoretical maximum price move 20

time in the market 22, 373
— risk and 59, 365
time risk 409–411
time zone arbitrage 402–403
timing the market 22, 373
top 20 listed Australian companies 378–379
trade management 115, 122–135
traders 93–107, 108
— compared to investors 18–19, 95, 383
— responsibility for actions 45–46
— self-inflicted injuries 29–37
— top mistakes of 30–37
traders Average True Range (ATR) x, 117, 278–292
— advantages of 292
— applying 291–292
— calculating 279–285
— combined entry 287–288
— count back line and 288–291
— sliding entry condition 286–287
— uses of 279
trades
— analysing 50
— entering 13, 35–37, 44, 58, 121–122, 169, 287, 288, 311–325, 365, 395
— exiting 13, 44, 47, 123, 125, 133, 278, 311–325
— faster execution of 42, 267, 428
— managing 49–50
— micro-management of 49
trade selection 57–67, 68–82
trading
— developing a strategy 31
— discipline and 6, 33, 43–45, 255–264
— environment for 13–14
— expectations and 51–54
— flexibility in 51–54
— fundamentals of x
— identifying opportunities 58–67
— improving returns 221–228
— office and equipment for 14–15
— patience and 61
— planning for 46, 54
— 'quick solutions' 31–32
— reasons for 46–47
— rules for 42–54
— software for 4, 30, 31–32, 93, 294
— time frame for 21–22, 31
trading capital 224
— protecting 237–254, 256
— size of 233–236, 242
trading edge 374
— developing 4–8
transaction size see position size
trend lines x, 85, 175–196
— constructing 176–184
— incorrect placement of 179–184
— straight edge 34–35, 175–196
— trade selection and 60
  see also parabolic trend lines
trends 4, 19–21, 33–37, 92–107, 417, 426
— break outs from 111–113, 191–196, 269–277, 329–334
— changes in 4, 84
— identifying nature of 57–67, 92–93, 99–102, 108–115, 116–135, 153–159, 278, 298–305
— leaving 'insurance' 27–28
— taking advantage of 26–27
— types of 93–94
trend volatility 57, 115, 116–135
Trend Volatility Line x, 57, 116–135, 154
— intraday trading and 126–128
triangles 205–215
— construction of 205–207, 210–212, 214
— down-sloping 209–212
— equilateral or symmetrical triangles 212–215, 242
— up-sloping 205–209
— using 208–209
triple bottoms and tops 203

undervalued companies 4, 142, 204
unprofitable trades 230–236
— holding on to 257–264
— size of loss 231–233, 257–264
unsuccessful traders 19, 372

upside targets 210, 343, 364, 365
US dollar index 199–200, 297–298
— gold market and 364

volatility 57, 109, 115, 172, 235, 237, 267–277, 278, 361
— cluster behaviour 105–107
volatility wipe 117–118
volume 67, 143, 150, 152, 158, 306, 314–317, 341, 344, 397
V-shaped recovery 202–204

walking 'a mile' with the crowd 24, 26–27
Wall Street 13
weighted moving average (WMA) 71–74
What I Learned Losing a Million Dollars 11–12
Wilder, Welles 279
win/loss ratio 224–228
W-shaped bottom 201–202

Printed in the United States
By Bookmasters